INVESTING IN YOUR FUTURE

2002 EDITION

A complete guide to financial planning ...

... for every stage of life

THE AYCO COMPANY, L.P.

Published by
The Ayco Company, L.P. • P.O. Box 15073 • Albany, NY 12212-5073

ISBN 0-9708285-2-7

Table of Contents

Page 1

Introduction to Financial Planning

Page 13

Managing Your Cash Flow and Debt

Page 41

Retirement Planning

Page 79

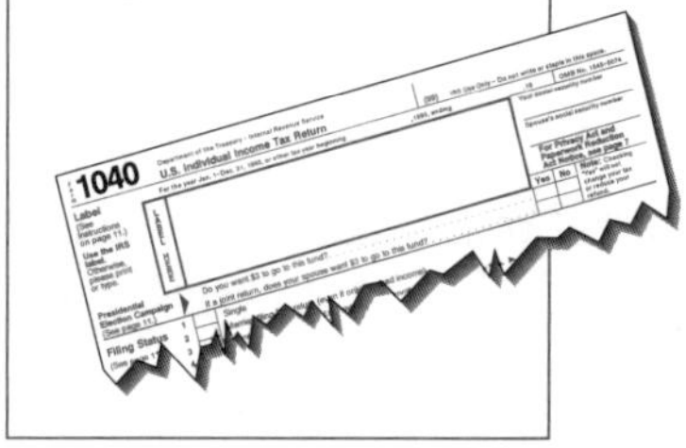

Income Taxes

Page 107

Investment Planning

Page 145

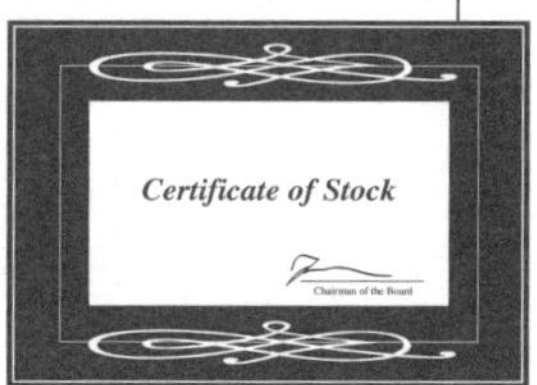

Company Stock Options

Page 157

Risk Protection

Page 179

Estate Planning

Page 217

Education Funding

Page 239

Social Security

Page 253

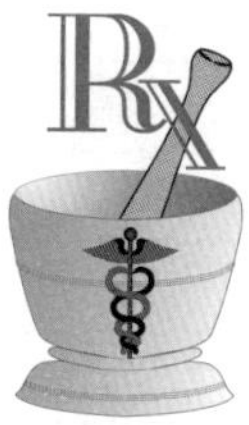

Health Care Coverage

Page 269

Life Management

Page 293

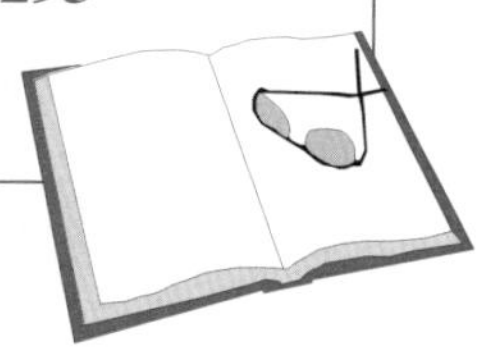

Glossary

Page 299

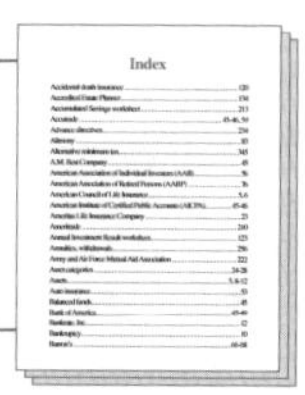

Index

Introduction to Financial Planning

There's more than a little confusion as to what financial planning is all about. Some people think it's about getting rich, and others think it's only for people who are rich to begin with. Actually, financial planning is about *improving your financial security*, no matter what your income level. Financial planning is the ongoing process of identifying goals and objectives, assessing alternatives, taking action and monitoring results. It all boils down to finding answers to simple, yet important questions you may have about your finances, present and future. For instance:

- ❖ How can I lower my income taxes?
- ❖ Will I have enough to retire at 55? At 60?
- ❖ How can I pay for some, if not all, of my child's education?

> "A good plan now is better than a perfect plan executed next week."
>
> *~ General George S. Patton*

In our experience, people usually don't fail to achieve their financial objectives due to one particular reason. Instead, a combination of things causes them to fall short. Here are some common financial-planning mistakes. Regardless of how old you are, or whether you are single or married, try to avoid these pitfalls:

- ❖ Procrastination
- ❖ Living day-to-day (that is, not having any defined goals)
- ❖ Too little knowledge
- ❖ Too much debt
- ❖ Overspending
- ❖ Having "all your eggs in one basket"
- ❖ Too little insurance or wrong kind of insurance
- ❖ Not having an emergency fund
- ❖ Not enough long-term investments for retirement purposes
- ❖ Not paying yourself first
- ❖ Not investing in yourself
- ❖ Giving up or depending on someone else
- ❖ Not having a will
- ❖ Doing things in an "all-or-nothing" way

Each chapter of this guidebook is designed to help you answer your financial-planning questions and help you avoid these common pitfalls. For example, you might be wondering whether you have enough life-insurance coverage. To help you with this question, turn to the **Risk Protection** chapter. There you will find a worksheet to determine your life-insurance needs, as well as a description of various life-insurance products that may be appropriate for you.

The more you know about financial planning, the more you'll see how worthwhile it is. You may have some work ahead of you, but once you understand the fundamentals and have goals to reach for, you'll be on the road to gaining control of your financial future.

Find Out Where You Stand: The *1-2-3-4 Test*

The key to financial planning is knowledge. This includes self-knowledge — an understanding of your likes and dislikes, habits and goals. And it includes knowledge about the financial system and the methods used by experienced financial planners.

Like many people, you may find it difficult to talk about your personal finances, so it might be hard to figure out if you're doing a good job of managing them. That's why we've created the *1-2-3-4 Test*. Just take a few minutes to use it, and you'll get a better understanding of the challenges ahead — and how financial planning can help. Revisit this "test" periodically to see if you've made progress toward increasing your financial security.

The *1-2-3-4 Test* contains four levels of skill in the eight key areas of financial planning. Start at the left for each category and circle the phrases that best describe your situation. When these circled descriptions no longer apply to you, cross them out and proceed to the next level. Your ultimate goal is to reach Level 4 in all categories. When these Level 4 descriptions apply to you, you'll have mastered the fundamentals of financial planning.

The *1-2-3-4 Test* — Find your financial-planning level

Start at the left for each category and circle each phrase that applies to you. If none of the phrases apply, move on to the next column to the right. As the phrases no longer apply to you, cross them out and move again toward Level 4.

ACTIVITY

	Level 1	Level 2	Level 3	Level 4
Spending	• Worrying constantly about money • Living "paycheck to paycheck" • Impulse buying • Spending patterns not understood	• Spending almost all of income on living expenses • No emergency fund • No prefunding of expenses (*e.g.,* car)	• Living within means • Established emergency fund of 3-6 months' living expenses • Prefunding of future expenses (*e.g.,* car) • Long-term savings plan in place	• Saving >10% of income • Nature and amount of monthly expenses are understood • Budget allows for comfortable living on an amount lower than paycheck(s) • Spending level consistent with other goals (*e.g.,* retirement, college funding)
Insurance	• Life insurance inadequate to support dependents, or no life insurance coverage at all • "Junk" insurance coverage such as mortgage, credit life, credit card • No insurance on your primary residence (*e.g.,* renters, home owners, condo) • No disability insurance • No health insurance • Low auto deductible ($100)	• Life insurance coverage in effect but still below needed amount • Short-term disability insurance coverage, but no long-term disability coverage • Little or no underinsured/ uninsured motorist coverage • Low auto deductible ($250) • If a homeowner, HO2 policy • Health insurance coverage • Personal Accidental Death and Disability insurance (AD&D)	• Life insurance need determined and adequate coverage in place • Proper type of insurance in place (term *vs.* cash-value insurance) • Auto liability of at least $100,000/ $300,000 and a deductible of $500 in place • Health insurance coverage • Property damage of $50,000 (auto) • Short-term and adequate long-term disability insurance • Full replacement coverage on home/possessions • If a homeowner, HO3 policy	• HO3 homeowner's policy with HO15 and any other appropriate optional coverages • Auto liability of $500,000 and a deductible of $500 or $1,000 • "Umbrella" excess liability of at least 1 million • Appropriate, up-to-date personal articles floater • Adequate underinsured/ uninsured motorist coverage • Health-insurance coverage in place and coordinated with spousal plan if applicable
Debt	• Carrying a credit-card balance • Pay bills late or juggle bills • High-interest-rate personal loan(s) • Feeling overwhelmed • Negative cash flow (spending more than you make	• Some credit-card debt • Pay most bills on time • Car loan(s)	• No credit-card debt • Always pay bills on time • Low-interest loans (*e.g.,* car loan) • Able to prepay mortgage • Car loan(s)	• No credit-card debt, cards are used to collect cash back, or some other reward • No car loan • No mortgage (or funds on hand to pay it off) • Only have tax-deductible debt • Prefunded major expense items

The *1-2-3-4 Test* (continued)

ACTIVITY

	Level 1	Level 2	Level 3	Level 4
Retirement	• No savings • Attitude that retirement is too far off in the future • No goals or time frame in mind • Assumption that pension and Social Security will be enough	• Saving approximately 6% pre-tax or at least enough to get a company match if applicable • Review of Social Security benefit estimate • No rhyme or reason to long-term investment plan of retirement assets	• Saving approximately 10% of income • Maximizing pre-tax savings plan • Rough idea of goal, time frame and future needs • Utilizing either deductible or Roth IRAs, if eligible, for yourself and spouse	• Saving > 10% of income • Maximizing all retirement savings vehicles: 401(k), 403(b), deferred comp, IRAs, SEP, Keogh, *etc.* • Using worksheets or computer programs to project realistic retirement needs and goals • Projecting retirement living expenses and the effect of inflation on these
Investments	• No investments • Unsure about how to invest • Savings and checking account	• Some, investments, but no rhyme or reason • Primarily fixed investments (CDs and money markets) used for long-term money • Heavily invested in one stock • Trying to time the market	• Investment portfolio has no more than your age – as a percentage – in fixed-income or bond investments • Established savings pattern • Using a discount broker • Well-versed in the investment products available • Using no-load mutual funds	• Mix of stocks and bonds per annual review, specified to your risk level • Maximum-return, minimal-risk portfolio in place (an optimal portfolio) • International and small-company investments included in the overall investment mix • Well-established savings and investment plan
Education	• No funds earmarked • "Seems impossible" • Too far in the future	• No regular savings • Small amount saved • Worried about cost	• Regular monthly savings • Thought-out investment plan • Set goal(s) • Analysis complete on the best type or account to use (QSTP, ESA*, Trust or UGMA) and familiarity with gifting and taxes	• Savings are/will be enough to pay ≥ 50% of the cost • Detailed projections of cost, needs, and returns on assets • Appropriate investment vehicles selected for these assets • Incorporation of education tax incentives in planning process
Taxes	• Inadequate record keeping • No IRAs or SEPs • No before-tax savings • Not using flexible spending accounts • Unsure of tax bracket; don't understand tax returns • Penalties for late filing, *etc.* • Haven't thought about itemizing	• No annual review of withholding • Some records, but no system • Substantial refund, or amount owed • Before-tax savings of < 6% • Using flexible spending accounts if available, and if needed • Some charitable-contribution deductions if you itemize • Carrying 'bad' debt (not deductible) if you itemize	• Records well-organized and systematic • Review of withholding annually • Maximize pre-tax savings • Minimal refund or amount owed • Use of appreciated assets to fund charitable contributions (not cash) • IRAs or other tax-sheltered vehicles used in conjunction with employer-sponsored plans • Analysis of tax-free investments completed, and results of this used in investment mix • Knowledge of tax rules on short- and long-term gains	• Bunching of miscellaneous deductions • Optimal long-term portfolio, using fixed investments in tax shelters and stock investments for taxable accounts • Using tax-efficient mutual funds • Annual analysis of tax liability, and required withholding incorporating deductions, stock options, tax-deferred accounts, *etc.* • Investment losses netted against gains
Estate Planning	• No will • No living will or health-care power of attorney • No planning • No durable power of attorney • No guardian named for minor children, if applicable	• Simple will, may be outdated • Living will, but no linked health-care power of attorney • Beneficiary designations not coordinated with will/trust • Durable power of attorney • Guardian named for minor children	• Current will reviewed within the past five years • Living will with health-care power of attorney • Will has an executor named • Knowledge of probate, and the pros and cons of this process	• Letter to spouse and/or children • If appropriate, an established trust that fits your specific needs • Estate-tax planning analysis complete • Coordination of disposition of all assets, including beneficiary designations • Effects of custodianship included in the estate-planning analysis

* The Coverdell ESA was formerly known as the education IRA.

Now that you've identified your weak points, you can start building your financial security. But you won't be alone. Through this guidebook, we'll be acting as your objective financial adviser — informing you and, at times, prodding you to think about the issues, make decisions and then act on them.

Focusing on your weaknesses will help you make gradual changes that will improve your financial well-being. Some of these changes will be major and some will be minor, but as they accumulate you'll begin to feel more secure. As you put elements of your foundation in place — a spending plan, a debt plan, an investment plan, an insurance plan, a plan for funding a child's education and a plan for maximizing your estate — your sense of confidence and accomplishment will grow.

Understand the Fundamentals

❖ Get Organized

Getting organized is the first step in taking control of your finances. You should set up a filing system that provides easy access to living-expense information, tax returns, investment-account statements, insurance policies, copies of wills, employee-benefit statements, Social Security estimates and anything else that may be important in your financial life.

❖ Identify Your Goals and Tie Them to Your Values

Goals should be specific and measurable. Determine how much you need, what for and when. You cannot hit a target you have not set.

❖ Get the Facts

Analyze your situation. Use the worksheets throughout this book to understand your personal financial needs. Shop before you make any investment, whether you are buying a car, life insurance, stocks or bonds. Understand the expected risks and rewards.

❖ Play "What If?"

What if you were to become disabled or die tomorrow? What if you lost your job? Could you retire at age 55? Or at age 60? Understand the effects of these and other scenarios on your finances.

❖ Write It Down

Writing things down helps crystallize your thoughts. Many people have found that writing out their goals, plans and dreams gives them strength. Putting things down in black and white makes them seem possible.

❖ Focus on What Is Important

Focus on *life events* (births, deaths, career changes, marriage, divorce, retirement) and how they will affect your finances. Also, take a "big-picture" view of your net worth, spending patterns and choices. Don't try to be too precise.

❖ Use Your Resources

Take advantage of your employee benefits — your savings plan, flexible spending accounts, charitable matching-gift programs and training. Also use your library, community resources, friends, colleagues, business contacts and, of course, the resources listed at the end of each chapter of this book.

- **Diversify Every Way You Can**

  There are three primary ways to diversify your investments: *among asset categories* (stocks, bonds, cash); *within asset categories* (small-company, large-company and foreign stocks); and *over time* (through dollar-cost averaging).

  You can also diversify styles of investing, ranging from conservative to aggressive. This approach means having several balls in the air, some at their peak, some on their way down and some moving back up again. *Don't be disappointed if all your investments aren't increasing at the same time.*

- **Take Control of Your Personal Finances**

  There are some tasks you cannot delegate. For most people, financial planning is one of those tasks. After you have done all you can do, you may want to go to a professional planner if you feel you need additional help or want a second opinion.

- **Do It Now!**

  Don't procrastinate. Accomplish something at least once each week. Even if you move only a few inches at a time, make it a habit and you will eventually attain your goals. The Chinese have a saying: "The longest journey begins with a single step."

Establish a Starting Point

When starting out in this process called financial planning, it's important to assess your current financial situation — that is, to summarize your assets (everything you own) and your liabilities (everything you owe). In other words, establish a statement of net worth: the amount of money you would have if you were to sell everything you own and pay off all your debts. By establishing your net worth as a starting point and updating it regularly, you can chart your progress.

Start today by preparing a statement of net worth. Use the worksheet on the following page to help you compile this statement, and don't forget to update it at least annually so that you can measure the success of the plan you'll develop for your financial future.

Your Net Worth

Write down the value of everything you own (these are your assets) and everything you owe (these are your debts or liabilities). Then subtract your total liabilities from your total assets. This is your net worth.

Assets	You	Your Spouse	Jointly Owned	Community Property	Total
Checking accounts	$ ______	$ ______	$ ______	$ ______	$ ______
Money market accounts	______	______	______	______	______
Savings accounts	______	______	______	______	______
Certificates of deposit	______	______	______	______	______
Stocks	______	______	______	______	______
Bonds	______	______	______	______	______
Mutual funds	______	______	______	______	______
401(k) plan	______	______	______	______	______
Pension plan	______	______	______	______	______
IRAs, SEPs, Keoghs	______	______	______	______	______
Your home	______	______	______	______	______
Other real estate	______	______	______	______	______
Art, collectibles, jewelry	______	______	______	______	______
Life insurance cash value	______	______	______	______	______
Car	______	______	______	______	______
______	______	______	______	______	______
______	______	______	______	______	______
Total assets	$ ______ +	$ ______ +	$ ______ +	$ ______ =	$ ______ (A)
Liabilities					
Mortgage	$ ______	$ ______	$ ______	$ ______	$ ______
Credit-card debt	______	______	______	______	______
Student loan(s)	______	______	______	______	______
Home-equity loan(s)	______	______	______	______	______
Auto loan(s)	______	______	______	______	______
Margin loan(s)	______	______	______	______	______
Personal loan(s)	______	______	______	______	______
______	______	______	______	______	______
______	______	______	______	______	______
Total liabilities	$ ______ +	$ ______ +	$ ______ +	$ ______ =	$ ______ (B)
					$ ______ (A)
					– $ ______ (B)
				(A – B) = Net Worth	$ ______

Identify Your Goals

One of the fundamentals of financial planning is to identify your goals and link them with specific steps to help you meet them. Below is a series of goals and actions to show you how this process works in a number of areas of your life.

I. Cash Flow and Debt

Goal: ***I want a lifestyle equal to $________ a year (in today's dollars). I want to enjoy life today, but I want to enjoy it tomorrow, too.***

Action: I will complete the *Cash Flow* worksheets in the **Cash Flow Planning** chapter to gain a better understanding of how I spend my money and, if necessary, modify my spending to conform to this lifestyle.

Goal: ***I want a sufficient cash flow so I will not feel squeezed each month, and so I will have more flexibility if I want to change my job/career.***

Action: I will avoid all nonhousing debt and set aside money each month for out-of-pattern expenses I anticipate in the next three to five years, such as my next car, house painting, or a new roof.

Out-of-pattern expenses anticipated in the next three to five years:

Item	Amount	When
____________	$____________	____________
____________	$____________	____________
____________	$____________	____________
____________	$____________	____________
____________	$____________	____________

Goal: ***I want to make being free of debt a high priority.***

Action: I will stop using charge/credit cards unless I can pay off the balance every month. I'll redirect my spending, do without and postpone purchases to live within my means. I'll pay off higher-rate credit cards first and, when possible, transfer debt to a lower-interest-rate card. The last debt I'll repay is my home mortgage.

Goal: ***I want my lifestyle secure in case I lose my job or have an emergency.***

Action: I will have three to six months of after-tax income (or expenses) in a money-market mutual fund (possibly a tax-exempt fund if I'm in the 27% tax bracket or above).

II. Income Taxes

Goal: ***I want to decrease my taxes.***

Action: I will accumulate *tax-deferred* savings, use company-sponsored flexible spending accounts, use a tax-exempt money market fund or other tax-exempt investment, take advantage of any tax-shifting opportunities and keep good tax records. I'll also consider itemizing deductions.

Goal: ***I want to avoid a big refund next year.***

Action: I will project my income, deductions and associated tax bill for the year. I will then adjust my *Form W-4* to match my withholding to my tax bill.

III. Retirement

Goal: ***I want to retire at age_______ on $_________ per year. I expect to live to age 85 (maybe longer), so I'll plan accordingly. I anticipate an annual inflation rate of ______% (4% is common) for my retirement.***

Action: I will complete the *Will You Have Enough to Retire?* worksheet in the **Retirement Planning** chapter. If I do not have enough to meet my retirement goal, I will retire later, save more and/or invest more aggressively. My time frame is (choose *long* or *short*). My overall investment need is (choose *growth* or *stability*). I should invest *at least* 10% of my income each year.

IV. Protecting Income and Property

Goal: ***I want to have enough assets at the time of my death to provide my family with $_________ a year in today's dollars. I want college-education funds of $_________ available for my children.***

Action: I will complete the *Determine Your Life Insurance Needs* worksheet in the **Risk Protection** chapter to calculate whether my assets and current life insurance are enough to generate the income needed. If not, I will explore sources for additional life insurance. I will also complete the worksheet for my spouse, if applicable.

Goal: ***I want to protect my lifestyle in case I am disabled.***

Action: If available, I will buy disability insurance through my employer and will look into any other group policies. I will keep debts and financial obligations at a minimum and maintain a cash reserve.

Goal: ***By carrying larger deductibles of up to $_________ on my home and $_________ on my automobiles, I am willing to be self-insured against these losses so I can lower my premiums.***

Action: I will contact my insurance agent and arrange for a $_________ deductible on my homeowner's and a $_________ deductible on my automobile policies.

Goal: ***I want to protect my assets against a potential loss from a major liability lawsuit and legal expenses, even if I ultimately prevail in such a suit.***

Action: I will purchase at least a $1 million excess-liability policy. I will verify with my insurance agent that the policy is coordinated with the underlying limits of my homeowner's and other policies.

V. Education

Goal: *I want to pay _________ % of my child's college education.*

Action: I will complete the Monthly Education Calculator in the **Education** chapter. As a result I need to set aside $_________ a month for college expenses. If I cannot set aside that amount each month, I will set aside at least $_________ a month and try to supplement it with larger sums from bonuses, overtime, tax refunds, etc. I will invest the money in a (choose *growth* or *stable*) investment.

VI. Estate Planning

Goal: ***I want my spouse to receive most of my property at my death.***

Action: I will make out a will, since in most states my spouse receives only half of my estate if I have children and die without a will.

Goal: ***I want to make sure my children are taken care of when my spouse and I die.***

Action: I will name a guardian in my will and leave instructions for the care of my children.

Goal: ***I want to protect my estate from needless expenses or taxes.***

Action: I will review my will. I will make sure it names a family member as executor.
I will read the **Estate Planning** chapter to find out what type of will I need.
I will call an estate-planning attorney to write my will.

Goal: ***I do not want to be kept alive by heroic methods if my illness is terminal.***
I want my spouse to have powers to manage our finances if I'm incapacitated.

Action: I will get a durable power of attorney, a health-care power of attorney and a living will.

VII. Other Goals and Actions

Goal: ______________________________

____

Action: ______________________________

____

Goal: ______________________________

____

Action: ______________________________

____

Goal: ______________________________

____

Action: ______________________________

____

Goal: ______________________________

____

Action: ______________________________

____

A financial plan is much like a strength-training program. It takes discipline and patience to succeed. You may not notice the results right away, but over time they can be substantial. And if you're like many people, once you get started, you'll find that the process itself is satisfying. There's nothing like the confidence you feel when you know that you've done all you could to guarantee your own financial security and that of your loved ones.

Items for Action

Depending on your circumstances, you may decide to work on several goals at once. For instance, you may want to begin putting aside money for your child's education *and* start saving for a major purchase like a vacation. Or you may decide you will concentrate first on sending your children to college and after they graduate save money for purchases you have put off. There is no right or wrong choice. Your decision is based on your personal situation and your approach to life. You should fine-tune your goals from time to time — reviewing them each year and making adjustments as needed. As your lifestyle changes, your financial goals may change, too.

Use the Action Items below to help you track your progress. Remember, one of the fundamentals is "Write It Down." Each chapter in this workbook ends with an Action Items list, and you should complete each as you come to it. You may have as many as 10 when you are finished, but you will have identified your goals in the process as well as the steps you need to take to reach financial independence.

For each of the following items, assign a priority based on its importance to you: A (highest), B (medium) or C (lowest). Then check off each item as it is completed.

	Priority	Completed
Review the Fundamentals of Financial Planning		
❖ Take the *1-2-3-4 Test* to find out where you stand currently.	______	❑
❖ Get organized. Set up a filing system that provides easy access to your important financial information.	______	❑
❖ Compile a statement of net worth and update it at least annually.	______	❑
❖ Identify your goals and tie them to your values. Determine how much you need, what for and when. Write them down!	______	❑
❖ Review your progress and your goals every year to determine if they have changed.	______	❑

Resources

HOMEFILE Publishing, Inc.

10025 Gov. Warfield Parkway #108
Columbia, MD 21044

This organization offers a variety of home filing organizer kits and books, including *The Financial Planning Organizer Kit* (#204; $24.95). To order or obtain additional information, call **800/695-3453** or visit their Web site at **www.organizerkits.com**.

Internal Revenue Service

You can get free telephone assistance by calling **800/829-1040**. For Publication 552, *Recordkeeping for Individuals*, call the IRS at **800/829-3676** or visit the IRS's web site: **www.irs.gov**. IRS publications are available at no cost.

Magazines/Books

Money (www.money.com)
The December, January and February issues usually have articles on tax and investment planning.

Kiplinger's Personal Finance Magazine (www.kiplinger.com)
The January issue focuses on financial planning (including tax planning) for the coming year. Mutual funds are reviewed in the September issue.

Smart Money (www.smartmoney.com)
Called *The Wall Street Journal Magazine of Personal Business*, this magazine offers articles on investing and financial planning.

Business Week (www.businessweek.com)
A weekly magazine focusing on current business news, *Business Week* contains articles on personal business, investing and financial planning.

Making the Most of Your Money
Quinn, Jane Bryant; Simon & Schuster, New York, NY; 1997; 1,066 pages; $30
This classic book of solid and practical financial advice has been refocused to address new tax laws, new ways of paying for higher education, new forms of health insurance and the current investment climate. Topics include investing, paying for college, buying a home, life and health insurance, retirement planning and finding a financial adviser.

Newspapers

The Wall Street Journal (www.wsj.com) is the most widely read business newspaper. It also has daily articles about investing and money matters.

The New York Times (www.nytimes.com) and *USA Today* (www.usatoday.com) both have excellent business sections.

Investor's Business Daily (www.investor.com) is considered more of a research tool than a traditional newspaper. It includes reports on business and economic news, educational articles and extensive mutual-fund coverage.

Managing Your Cash Flow and Debt

Understanding Your Cash Flow

Most people can tell you how much money they *earn* on a weekly, monthly or yearly basis. How many, though, can tell you where the money was *spent*?

"Cash-flow planning" is a term used to describe the process of matching your monthly or yearly income against your expenses. You track the money coming in *and* the money going out. If there is "excess income," that is, if you spend *less* than you earn, you can apply the excess to your financial goals by saving and investing. You can plan for a vacation, save for the future or invest for your child's education. If there are "excess expenses" — in other words, if you spend *more* than you earn — you limit your options severely and decrease your chances of getting what you want out of life.

In order to understand your cash flow, you have to determine how you spend your money. Getting a grip on spending is something no one likes. Often it involves spending *less* now so you can spend *more* later. At the very least, it may involve changing your spending *patterns* if not the *amounts* you spend. Maybe you should be spending more money on "experiences" (vacations, continuing education) than on "things." Perhaps you would get more satisfaction from spending money in the future (in your retirement years) than from things you could buy today.

It's critical to take a hard look at the trade-offs. Don't buy into the idea that handling your money prudently is either "penny-pinching" or being "cheap." Major corporations try to manage their expenses carefully, so why shouldn't you?

When "Enough" is Never Enough

A study was conducted to determine how much income people felt they needed to attain a lifestyle they would enjoy. The study found that people earning $30,000 to $40,000 felt they needed approximately $45,000 per year to have "enough." Those earning $45,000 to $55,000 felt they needed $65,000 per year, and those earning $60,000 to $70,000 needed $90,000 to $100,000! At every income level, people needed more to have "enough." In other words, for most people "enough" is *never* enough!

Part of this feeling may stem from the belief that an individual's earnings or lifestyle represents a "scorecard" of how well he or she is doing in life. Others may feel they don't have "enough" simply because they have not set measurable financial goals. They have no sense of accomplishment and are running on a financial treadmill with no end in sight.

Tracking Your Spending

You need to understand your spending patterns to:

- gain control over your money
- ensure that your spending reflects your values
- ensure that you're living within your means
- determine whether you're getting the best value for your money
- attain financial independence

To reach your financial goals, you may have to change your spending habits. To do that, you must identify how you are spending money. You don't have to make up an elaborate budget, category by category; just keep track of your current spending patterns. A good way to do this is to use the *Monthly Expense Summary* in this chapter for the coming month. You can make the job easier on yourself by using the paper trail that most spending generates. If you go to the grocery store, write a check or keep the receipt. Use the statements created when you use debit and credit cards. As you go through the month, simply fill out the amount you spend under each heading (use the untitled columns to create special headings of your own), and write the totals at the bottom of the page.

The moment of truth will come at the end of the month. Does your income exceed your expenses? Or is more cash flowing out than is coming in? Are there any surprises? Are you spending more in any one category than you thought?

Special Consideration:

More Than One Projection

Before you begin filling in the *Monthly Expense Summary, Cash-Flow Projection* worksheet and projection summaries, photocopy the pages first. This way you will be able to use them again in the future or play "what if?" games. As an alternative to these worksheets, you may want to use any one of a number of software packages that track cash flow. (See *Resources* at the end of this chapter.)

Monthly Expense Summary

The *Monthly Expense Summary* is a good way of tracking your spending throughout the year. You can establish guidelines for each category and try to stick to them. Writing down your expenses is a great way to control them.

Housing

	Mortgage/ Rent	Real-Estate Taxes	Furnishings	Telephone/ Cable	Utilities	Improvements/ Repairs	Homeowner's Insurance
January	$	$	$	$	$	$	$
February	$	$	$	$	$	$	$
March	$	$	$	$	$	$	$
April	$	$	$	$	$	$	$
May	$	$	$	$	$	$	$
June	$	$	$	$	$	$	$
July	$	$	$	$	$	$	$
August	$	$	$	$	$	$	$
September	$	$	$	$	$	$	$
October	$	$	$	$	$	$	$
November	$	$	$	$	$	$	$
December	$	$	$	$	$	$	$
Annual Totals:	**$**	**$**	**$**	**$**	**$**	**$**	**$**

Food and Transportaton

	Groceries	Dining Out	Lease/ Car Payment	Auto Insurance	Gas	Maintenance and Repair	Parking/ Fares
January	$	$	$	$	$	$	$
February	$	$	$	$	$	$	$
March	$	$	$	$	$	$	$
April	$	$	$	$	$	$	$
May	$	$	$	$	$	$	$
June	$	$	$	$	$	$	$
July	$	$	$	$	$	$	$
August	$	$	$	$	$	$	$
September	$	$	$	$	$	$	$
October	$	$	$	$	$	$	$
November	$	$	$	$	$	$	$
December	$	$	$	$	$	$	$
Annual Totals:	**$**	**$**	**$**	**$**	**$**	**$**	**$**

Monthly Expense Summary

Health and Clothing

	Medical Expenses	Dental Expenses	Drugs/Med. Supplies	Health Insurance	Life/Disability Insurance	Clothing Purchases	Dry Cleaning/ Alterations
January	$	$	$	$	$	$	$
February	$	$	$	$	$	$	$
March	$	$	$	$	$	$	$
April	$	$	$	$	$	$	$
May	$	$	$	$	$	$	$
June	$	$	$	$	$	$	$
July	$	$	$	$	$	$	$
August	$	$	$	$	$	$	$
September	$	$	$	$	$	$	$
October	$	$	$	$	$	$	$
November	$	$	$	$	$	$	$
December	$	$	$	$	$	$	$
Annual Totals:	**$**	**$**	**$**	**$**	**$**	**$**	**$**

Child Care, Education, Investments

	Child/ Elder Care	Tuition	Books/ Supplies	News/Magazine Subscriptions	Savings Plan	IRA Contributions	Pension Contributions
January	$	$	$	$	$	$	$
February	$	$	$	$	$	$	$
March	$	$	$	$	$	$	$
April	$	$	$	$	$	$	$
May	$	$	$	$	$	$	$
June	$	$	$	$	$	$	$
July	$	$	$	$	$	$	$
August	$	$	$	$	$	$	$
September	$	$	$	$	$	$	$
October	$	$	$	$	$	$	$
November	$	$	$	$	$	$	$
December	$	$	$	$	$	$	$
Annual Totals:	**$**	**$**	**$**	**$**	**$**	**$**	**$**

Monthly Expense Summary

Gifts, Recreation, Contributions

	Gifts	Vacation	Enter-tainment	Hobbies	Pet-Care Supplies	Organization/ Club Dues	Charitable Contributions
January	$____	$____	$____	$____	$____	$____	$____
February	$____	$____	$____	$____	$____	$____	$____
March	$____	$____	$____	$____	$____	$____	$____
April	$____	$____	$____	$____	$____	$____	$____
May	$____	$____	$____	$____	$____	$____	$____
June	$____	$____	$____	$____	$____	$____	$____
July	$____	$____	$____	$____	$____	$____	$____
August	$____	$____	$____	$____	$____	$____	$____
September	$____	$____	$____	$____	$____	$____	$____
October	$____	$____	$____	$____	$____	$____	$____
November	$____	$____	$____	$____	$____	$____	$____
December	$____	$____	$____	$____	$____	$____	$____
Annual Totals:	**$**____	**$**____	**$**____	**$**____	**$**____	**$**____	**$**____

Other

	Business Expenses	Credit-Card Payments	Major Home Improvements	____	____	____	____
January	$____	$____	$____	$____	$____	$____	$____
February	$____	$____	$____	$____	$____	$____	$____
March	$____	$____	$____	$____	$____	$____	$____
April	$____	$____	$____	$____	$____	$____	$____
May	$____	$____	$____	$____	$____	$____	$____
June	$____	$____	$____	$____	$____	$____	$____
July	$____	$____	$____	$____	$____	$____	$____
August	$____	$____	$____	$____	$____	$____	$____
September	$____	$____	$____	$____	$____	$____	$____
October	$____	$____	$____	$____	$____	$____	$____
November	$____	$____	$____	$____	$____	$____	$____
December	$____	$____	$____	$____	$____	$____	$____
Annual Totals:	**$**____	**$**____	**$**____	**$**____	**$**____	**$**____	**$**____

Your Cash-Flow Projection

Once you have determined on a month-to-month basis how you spend your money, you can develop a cash-flow projection for the coming year. Just follow these simple steps:

Step 1: Gather Information. For some people, this is the most daunting part of the process. Gather all your income and spending records. Fortunately, much of this information already exists in the form of receipts, check stubs and credit-card statements. Your paystubs, bank and/or brokerage statements, tax returns, etc., will also help.

Step 2: Estimate Your Income. The next step is to add up all sources of income, including wages, interest and dividends, etc., using the *Cash-Flow Projection* worksheet.

Step 3: Estimate Your Taxes. The next items on your *Cash-Flow Projection* worksheet are taxes — federal, state, local and FICA (Social Security and Medicare). You must reduce your total income by the total taxes to reach the amount of "spendable income" available to your family. For the federal and state amounts, use your federal and state tax returns. Use your *Form W-2* from last year for the FICA amount.

Step 4: Reconstruct Your Expenses. The next step is to add your expenses using the *Monthly Expense Summary* worksheet. Take the summary you're creating for the coming month and adjust it for seasonal items. Remember, it doesn't matter whether you paid cash or used credit, categorize each and every expenditure. For instance, during the summer you may spend more on lawn and garden expenses, while during the Christmas or Hanukkah season you may spend more on gifts. Add up your totals for the year and place them on the *Cash-Flow Projection* worksheet. Remember to consider nonpattern expenses if they are due this year. Examples of these are major home improvements, special vacations or a new car.

Step 5: Summarize Your Cash Flow. Once you've completed the *Cash-Flow Projection*, the final step is to prepare the *Cash-Flow Projection Summary*.

The summary takes the major categories from the *Cash-Flow Projection*, such as total income, taxes, living expenses and other cash commitments, and determines if you'll have "excess income" or "excess expenses." If you find you have excess expenses, you'll have to trim them or add to the income side of the equation. The same strategy holds true if you want additional excess income to meet your goals. See *Reducing Your Expenses* later in this chapter for advice on controlling your spending.

After projecting your cash flow for last year or this year, project it under other circumstances — play "What If?" What will cash flow look like if you retire? What will your survivors' cash flow be if you die? Don't forget to factor in inflation, which is discussed later in this chapter.

Cash-Flow Projection

Annual Income:	Last Year	This Year	Retirement	Survivors'
Sources				
Salary	$	$	$	$
Bonus				
Pension Annuity				
Social Security				
Rental Income				
Investment Income				
Interest Income				
Dividends				
Savings Plan Distributions				
IRA Distributions				
Other				
	$	**$**	**$**	**$**
Annual Taxes:				
Federal Income Taxes	$	$	$	$
State Taxes				
Local Taxes				
FICA Taxes on Earnings				
	$	**$**	**$**	**$**
Annual Living Expenses:				
Housing				
Mortgage/Rent	$	$	$	$
Real-Estate Taxes				
Furnishings				
Telephone/Cable				
Utilities				
Improvements/Repairs				
Homeowner's Insurance				
Food				
Groceries				
Dining Out				

Cash-Flow Projection

Expenses (cont.)	**Last Year**	**This Year**	**Retirement**	**Survivors'**
Transportation				
Lease/Car Payments	$	$	$	$
Auto Insurance				
Gas				
Maintenance/Repairs				
Parking/Fares				
Health				
Medical Expenses*				
Dental Expenses*				
Drugs/Medical Supplies*				
Health Insurance				
Life Insurance				
Disability Insurance				
Clothing				
Purchases				
Dry Cleaning/Alterations				
Child Care/Elder Care				
Education				
Tuition				
Books/Supplies				
Newspaper/Mag. Sub.				
Investments				
Savings Plan Contributions				
IRA Contributions				
Pension Contributions				
Other Investments				
Gifts				
Recreation				
Vacation				
Entertainment				
Hobbies				
Pet-Care Supplies				
Organization/Club Dues				
Charitable Contributions				
Other				
Business Expenses				
Credit Card Payments				
Major Home Improvements				
	$	**$**	**$**	**$**

* Not covered by insurance.

Cash-Flow Projection Summary

1. Total income .... $ ________________

2. Total taxes .... – ________________

A. Spendable income .... = ________________

3. Total living expenses .... – ________________

B. Excess income/(excess expenses) .... = ________________

If your cash-flow analysis shows excess expenses, you're spending more than you make. This may be the road to financial ruin. You should concentrate on the next few pages, which discuss ways to reduce your spending and/or your debt.

Retirement or Survivors' Cash Flow

The *Cash-Flow Projection* worksheet also can be used for a variety of other purposes. For instance, you can use it to determine how much income you will need to retire or how much your survivors would need if you were to die suddenly. *Keep in mind that most expenses will stay the same.* Also, be sure to include other sources of income, such as income from life insurance, pension plans and Social Security.

Take the totals from the *Cash-Flow Projection* worksheet and place them in the *Retirement or Survivors' Income Cash-Flow Projection Summary*. This projection can tell you if you'll have adequate income during retirement or your survivors will have adequate income to lead the kind of life they are enjoying now.

Retirement or Survivors' Income Cash-Flow Projection Summary

1. Total income .... $ ________________

2. Total taxes .... – ________________

A. Spendable income .... = ________________

3. Total living expenses .... – ________________

B. Excess income/(excess expenses) .... = ________________

If your retirement cash-flow analysis shows excess expenses, you may not be able to retire with the lifestyle you wanted — unless you act now. If your survivors' cash-flow analysis shows excess expenses, your survivors will not be able to maintain their current standard of living.

Planning for Inflation

You have completed a cash-flow projection for the current year and determined the cash flow available to you if you were to retire or to your survivors if you were to die right now. Financial planning, however, requires you to look farther into the future. For instance, one of your goals may be to save for your child's college education. Or you may be trying to gather a nest egg for retirement. In order to determine your needs far into the future, you must take inflation into account.

Inflation is generally measured by the Consumer Price Index (CPI), which reflects changes over time. No one can tell what the future will hold, but we have provided some charts that show what the yearly CPI has been in the past.

To assist you in projecting your cash flow at various rates of inflation, we have included the *Planning for Inflation* worksheet. For example, to adjust your retirement cash flow from today's dollars to future dollars, take the numbers from the retirement column of the cash-flow projection and then plug them into the *Planning for Inflation* worksheet. You'll end up with a good idea of how well you'll be prepared to deal with the challenges of the future — once you have taken inflation into account.

Annual Changes in the CPI 1987 – 2001*

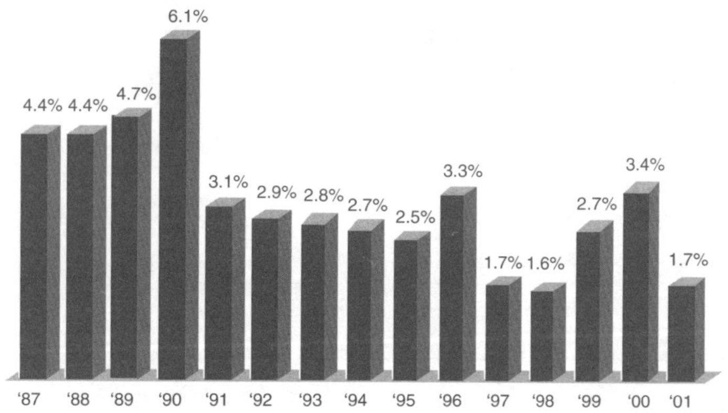

* As of December 31.

Historical Inflation Rates*

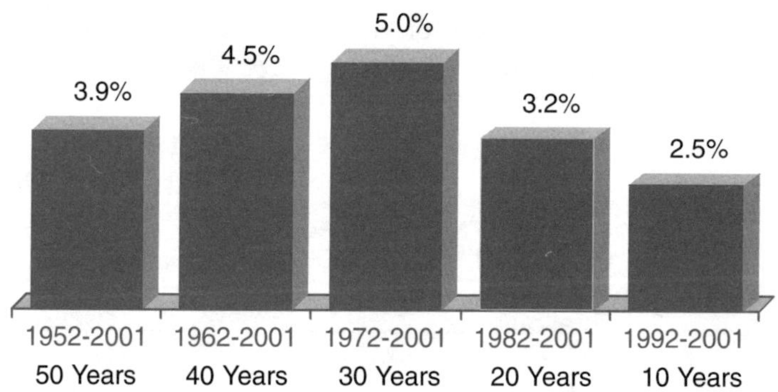

* As of December 31.

Planning for Inflation Worksheet

Example of a 10-year Projection

	Inflation Assumption*	Today's Dollars		Inflation Factor		Dollars in 10 Years
Spendable income	3%	$40,000	X	1.3439	=	$53,756
Less: Total expenses	4%	(36,000)	X	1.4802	=	(53,287)
Excess income/(expenses)		$ 4,000				$ 469

* Assumes income grows at 3% a year and expenses grow at a 4% rate.

Use the worksheet below to help you project *your* future cash flow. Use your best estimates of how much your income and expenses will grow.

Your Situation

	Inflation Assumption	Today's Dollars		Inflation Factor		Dollars in ____ Years
Spendable income	_____ %	$ _______	X	_______	=	$ _______
Less: Total expenses	_____ %	(_______)	X	_______	=	(_______)
Excess income/(expenses)		$ _______				$ _______

Inflation Factors

Year	3%	4%	5%	6%	7%	8%
1	1.0300	1.0400	1.0500	1.0600	1.0700	1.0800
2	1.0609	1.0816	1.1025	1.1236	1.1449	1.1664
3	1.0927	1.1249	1.1576	1.1910	1.2250	1.2597
4	1.1255	1.1699	1.2155	1.2625	1.3108	1.3605
5	1.1593	1.2167	1.2763	1.3382	1.4026	1.4693
6	1.1941	1.2653	1.3401	1.4185	1.5007	1.5869
7	1.2299	1.3159	1.4071	1.5036	1.6058	1.7138
8	1.2668	1.3686	1.4775	1.5938	1.7182	1.8509
9	1.3048	1.4233	1.5513	1.6895	1.8385	1.9990
10	1.3439	1.4802	1.6289	1.7908	1.9672	2.1589
11	1.3842	1.5395	1.7103	1.8983	2.1049	2.3316
12	1.4258	1.6010	1.7959	2.0122	2.2522	2.5182
13	1.4685	1.6651	1.8856	2.1329	2.4098	2.7196
14	1.5126	1.7317	1.9799	2.2609	2.5785	2.9372
15	1.5580	1.8009	2.0789	2.3966	2.7590	3.1722
16	1.6047	1.8730	2.1829	2.5404	2.9522	3.4259
17	1.6528	1.9479	2.2920	2.6928	3.1588	3.7000
18	1.7024	2.0258	2.4066	2.8543	3.3799	3.9960
19	1.7535	2.1068	2.5270	3.0256	3.6165	4.3157
20	1.8061	2.1911	2.6533	3.2071	3.8697	4.6610
21	1.8603	2.2788	2.7860	3.3996	4.1406	5.0338
22	1.9161	2.3699	2.9253	3.6035	4.4304	5.4365
23	1.9736	2.4647	3.0715	3.8197	4.7405	5.8715
24	2.0328	2.5633	3.2251	4.0489	5.0724	6.3412
25	2.0938	2.6658	3.3864	4.2919	5.4274	6.8485
26	2.1566	2.7725	3.5557	4.5494	5.8074	7.3964
27	2.2213	2.8834	3.7335	4.8223	6.2139	7.9881
28	2.2879	2.9987	3.9201	5.1117	6.6488	8.6271
29	2.3566	3.1187	4.1161	5.4184	7.1143	9.3173
30	2.4273	3.2434	4.3219	5.7435	7.6123	10.0627

The New Math: How to Create Large Sums Out of Small Sums

Here's an example of how you can look at your current spending patterns, change them and then link that change to an automatic savings vehicle.

One of our financial planners used to buy vending-machine soft drinks four times a day, at 60¢ a can ($2.40/day). As a good planner evaluating his spending habits, he asked himself how much he'd spend buying that soda over his entire career. As a first step he calculated that at $2.40/day, five days/week, 48 workweeks/year, he'd spend $576 in just a year.

Then he assumed that prices would increase at a rate of 5% a year. What if he invested that annual $576 (which would be 5% higher each year to adjust for the rising cost of soft drinks) at 8%? How much money would he have when he retired in 30 years? It turns out that $576, increasing by 5% annually and invested each year at 8%, would grow in 30 years to $110,000!

Of course, 30 years from now $110,000 would be worth quite a bit less than $110,000 today. But after a few more calculations, he discovered that $110,000 in tomorrow's (30 years from now) dollars is still the equivalent of $34,000 in today's dollars (assuming a 4% annual inflation rate)! He doesn't have that $34,000 now, but he'll save it over his career. He asked himself: "What's more important to me, adding to my retirement nest egg or buying soft drinks?

That was the day he decided to avoid the vending machine and start drinking water! Obviously an alternative would be to buy the soda at a discount store and keep it in the office refrigerator. He wouldn't save as much as he did by switching to water, but he could set aside a few dollars each month that would still grow to a substantial amount over time.

Here's the key: *Once he decided to forgo the vending machine, he had the extra $50 — the amount he used to spend on the soft drinks each month — automatically transferred from his checking account to a mutual fund (pay yourself first!). By linking his spending decision to an action, he really will save that $110,000 toward his retirement goal. And he's doing it painlessly.*

Now we have nothing against soft drinks or vending machines. But the previous example shows how the little things we do (or don't do) actually make a surprising difference.

We call this the accumulation of small advantages. Put enough small advantages together and you'll have a big advantage!

To some, this is "penny-pinching." But it also could be seen as a prudent, value-conscious approach. Regular evaluation assures us that our spending reflects our real priorities. Many people, however, want to take a short cut. They want to know what the average person in their income bracket spends on different items. But no one is just average; everyone has different values and priorities. That's why we advise you to take the time to evaluate your own spending.

Take a hard look at how your own spending could be redirected toward goals like retirement, travel, financial independence, education, even gifts to organizations or family members. Many of us already have the money we need; we just have to focus on what is truly important to us.

Reducing Your Expenses

If your spending exceeds your income — or if you would like to save more money — here are some practical tips to help you reduce expenses.

Transportation

- Buy a used car
- Use public transportation
- Sell second or third car
- Carpool
- Walk or ride your bicycle
- Do not renew vanity plates
- Slow down to 55, conserve gas
- Pump your own gas, and don't use premium if your car doesn't need it
- Change your own oil
- Drop collision coverage on older cars
- Take a defensive driving course to reduce insurance premiums
- Make your car last one more year
- Wash your own car
- Sell your boat

Shopping

- Use a grocery list
- Use coupons/double coupons
- Buy generic or store brands
- Use ammonia instead of expensive cleaners
- Don't use prepared foods
- Grow your own vegetables
- Buy at discount or warehouse stores
- Limit trips to the grocery store
- Use rebates
- Return bottles
- Buy clothing only on sale or at discount outlets
- Buy floor models/seconds
- Buy at garage sales, thrift and consignment stores
- Buy in bulk
- Be patient — everything goes on sale

Housing

- Move to a smaller house
- Move out of the city
- Move to an area with lower property taxes
- Challenge your property tax assessment
- Sell your second home

Housing (cont'd.)

- Refinance mortgage to a lower interest rate, if possible
- Get a roommate
- Mow your own lawn
- Have your local utility do an energy survey and make the improvements yourself
- Turn off lights/TV
- Use energy-efficient light bulbs or low-wattage bulbs
- Run only a full dishwasher
- Do not use the dishwasher heater
- Use water savers
- Lower temperature of water heater
- Lower toilet water level
- Turn down heat/air conditioner

General

- Use the phone book rather than driving
- Check out bargain rates on long-distance calls or phone cards
- Recycle
- Buy to last (cloth napkins, sponges, no disposables)
- Use rechargeable batteries
- Discontinue clubs with dues
- Discontinue health club; exercise at home
- Discontinue magazine subscriptions and recycle friends' magazines or use the library
- Borrow books from the library
- Reduce dry-cleaning bills
- Clean your own house
- Trade babysitting services
- Bring your lunch to work
- Give up smoking, drinking, gambling or playing the lottery
- Have preventative doctor/dentist visits
- Have film delivered by mail
- Fill prescriptions by mail, or use generic names
- Encourage your child to finish college in three years instead of four

Entertainment

- Eat in
- Eat out using coupons, 2-for-1 specials or at "all-you-can-eat" buffets
- Bring your own snacks to the movies
- Rent movies
- Discontinue or downgrade cable TV service
- Have potluck dinners or BYOB parties
- Use free community entertainment
- Eliminate or downsize vacation
- Travel during the "off season"

Financial

- Set up a budget and stick to it
- Donate time to charities, instead of money
- Donate appreciated securities, rather than cash, to charities
- Refinance installment loans
- Keep only one major credit card
- Raise deductibles on auto and homeowner's insurance
- Don't overinsure your life
- Don't insure your children's lives
- Use flexible spending accounts
- Review medical coverage for efficiency
- Use a credit card with no annual fees if you pay off your monthly balance
- Use a credit card with a low percentage rate if you carry monthly balances
- Purchase checks from mail-order suppliers
- Sell items you don't need or donate to charity for a write-off
- Use a discount broker to buy and sell investments

Consumer Debt

Perhaps you have been funding some of your spending through consumer debt — debt incurred through credit cards, car loans, lines of credit, personal loans and margin loans. Debt can be your worst enemy; yet it can also help you attain some of your goals.

To understand how widely debt is used, and how often it is used excessively, consider the following:

- By the end of 2000, the average cardholder had $8,123 in credit-card debt.
- As of September 2001, Americans owed a total of $1.5 trillion in consumer debt, of which nearly $700 billion was on credit cards.
- Four percent of credit-card payments were more than 30 days past due in the second quarter of 2001, while the delinquency rate of other types of consumer loans climbed to over 2.5%.
- 2001 U.S. bankruptcy filings were expected to equal or exceed the 1998 record of 1.4 million.
- At least 10% of people who file for bankruptcy will file a second time.

Measuring How Much is 'Too Much'

There are a number of ways to determine whether you have too much debt. One common measure is the debt-to-income ratio.

Banks have long used debt-to-income ratios to decide whether to lend money or extend credit. This ratio can be calculated on a monthly or annual basis.

The monthly debt-to-income ratio provides a good indication of how strong your financial situation is on a day-to-day basis. However, it overlooks long-term loans that may threaten your overall financial stability if the amounts of those loans are too great.

Take your total monthly debt payments (payments made to credit cards, car loans, etc.) and divide by your total monthly income (before taxes). This will give your monthly debt-to-income ratio. This number is expressed as a percentage.

Debt-to-Income Ratio

For example, ***you pay …***

	Total monthly payment
Mortgage	$500
Car loan	300
Visa	150
Mastercard	100
Department store	55
Dentist	35
Total	**$1,140**

and you earn …

Annual gross income	$25,000
Spouse's income	17,000
Alimony	0
Interest or dividends	0
Other	0
Total	**$42,000**
Divided by 12	÷ 12
Total Monthly Income	**$3,500**

Your monthly debt-to-income ratio is …

$1,140 ÷ $3,500 = .3257 or 32.57%

What Shape Are You In?	
If your monthly debt-to-income ratio is	
15% or less	You are in *excellent* financial shape if you have a mortgage. You are in *fair* shape if you don't have a mortgage.
16% to 20%	Some financial advisers consider 20% the top of the safety range for the debt you have, including your mortgage. However, you should try to reduce your nonhousing debt to no more than 10% and ultimately eliminate nonhousing debt altogether. That way, if you have a financial emergency or setback, you won't be burdened.
21% to 35%	At this level, your main goal should be to reduce debt. You can probably still get loans, but you may be finding a sizable portion of your income going to pay off your debt. Most Americans are in this category (and, consequently, don't have enough to reach their other goals).
36% to 50%	You definitely have too much debt! Your long-term and perhaps even short-term goals are being sacrificed. Start making smarter spending choices and stop charging on your credit cards. You're likely to have trouble getting approved for additional loans (which may be a blessing in disguise).
51% or more	You're in serious trouble. You should seek the assistance of a credit counselor. Bankruptcy may not be far away.

Most mortgage lenders follow the 28/36 percent rule when evaluating debt-to-income ratios. Here's how this rule works: To qualify for a mortgage, your monthly housing debt, including taxes and insurance, should not exceed 28% of your gross monthly income. Your total monthly debt payments — housing plus all other revolving and unsecured debt — should not exceed 36% of your gross monthly income.

Although you should concentrate on reducing *your debt-to-income ratio, your ultimate goal should be to have* no debt *at all!*

Credit Cards

Time to Cut Them Up?

Some of you probably have been looking through this book for "the big score" or "the hot tip" that can transform your life. Well, here it is: Buy up your own debt. If you pay it off and keep it off, *you'll make a killing*.

What are we talking about? How about failsafe returns in the 8% to 12% range? Not good enough? Then how about 20% per year — *guaranteed!* Have we pressed your hot button yet?

If you're like most Americans, you're carrying consumer debt. What you may not realize is that you can "invest" in that debt and get a great return — risk-free. Credit cards typically carry interest rates of 14% to 19% — some are even higher. Quite apart from investment potential, if you're paying that kind of interest on your debt, you need to mend your ways.

"OK," you may say, "I know I need to be careful about *adding* debt, but what do you mean when you say I can *invest* in the debt I already have?" We mean that you can invest not only in an *asset,* but you also can invest in a *liability*.

You can invest in a liability by paying it off. If you can do it all at once, fine. But most of us can't because we just don't have extra piles of money lying around. So chip away at it bit by bit — even as little as $10 or $20 per month. Assuming that you can pay off your consumer debt, including your credit cards, without incurring a prepayment penalty (and sometimes even if there *is* a penalty, providing it's not too steep), it almost always makes good sense to do that.

That's because the rate of return you'll earn on your money is the same as the annual percentage rate (APR) of the loan. So, if you're paying 19% on credit card debt, every dollar you pay toward the principal earns you 19% — and that's an after-tax return. It doesn't get much cleaner, neater or sweeter than that!

Four Easy Steps to a Lower-Rate Credit Card

1. Call your bank for a lower interest rate. Many banks have lower rates available to good customers, but they don't volunteer the information. You have to ask.
2. If your bank refuses to give you a lower rate, find one that will. (See the resources at the end of this chapter.)
3. Switch. Most banks will allow you to transfer your balance from your old card to the new, lower-interest-rate card. The new bank will often provide a blank "convenience check" to make the transfer. Ask the bank to waive any transfer fees. Many banks will electronically transfer your existing balance to a new bank card. Essentially, the new bank is paying off your old debt and re-establishing it with them — but with a lower interest rate.
4. Once you have your new card, cut up your old card, contact the bank that issued it, and ask them to close your account. About two weeks later, call to make certain the account has been closed. Following these steps could save you hundreds of dollars in interest charges in the first year alone.

Managing Mortgage Debt

There are many reasons why almost everyone wants to own a home. You don't have to contend with landlords; you can't lose your lease; you can decorate to suit your taste; you receive a tax deduction. Although a home may or may not be a great investment, owning a home is a way for you to reduce your living expenses during retirement. If your mortgage is paid off, you are, in essence, living for free. But rent continues forever.

Since almost everyone wants to own a home, and almost no one can afford to buy one with cash, a mortgage is a necessity. But make sure you shop for the best one!

Getting the Right Mortgage

Mortgages fall into two basic categories:

Adjustable-rate mortgages (ARMs) — With an ARM, the interest rate *and* monthly payments change periodically according to the general interest-rate environment. Initially, ARMs should cost less than fixed-rate mortgages. The rate begins lower than a fixed-rate mortgage and adjusts periodically. The periodic adjustments, as well as the lifetime adjustments, are usually capped.

ARMs are useful if you need a lower payment now, but expect to be able to make a higher payment in the future. *An ARM is attractive particularly if you plan to own your home for a short period of time.*

Conventional mortgages — These loans feature a fixed payment for the life of the mortgage. There is no fluctuation in the interest rate or the monthly payment. *Fixed-rate mortgages are attractive when interest rates, in general, are low.*

Note: Various combinations of adjustable-rate and fixed mortgages also are available; *e.g.,* a loan with an initial fixed rate for three years that converts to an ARM after three years. In addition, "balloon" loans are available offering an adjustable or fixed rate for a limited number of years with the balance due at the end of that time.

Should You Make Prepayments?

Prepaying your mortgage makes sense for many, but you *shouldn't even consider it* until all your nondeductible debts are paid off. *Prepayment is a wonderful, can't-miss proposition.*

How much can prepayments save? If you prepay $25 a month on a $100,000, 30-year fixed mortgage at 8%, you'll save over $23,000 in interest payments and cut 3½ years off your mortgage!

But is it the right investment? Or should you save/invest the $25 a month elsewhere?

In the example above, the mortgage rate was 8%. The $25 should be invested elsewhere only if you can earn more than 8% before-tax on that outside investment. That's a 5.8% rate of return on an after-tax basis, assuming you're in the 27% income tax bracket.

Before you prepay your mortgage, consider the following questions:

- Have you first paid off *all* nondeductible debt?
- Have you addressed your retirement-funding needs adequately?
- Are there any prepayment penalties?
- How much can you earn in another investment?

Should You Refinance Your Mortgage?

When you refinance, you take out a new mortgage at a lower interest rate and pay off your old mortgage. This can give you more cash to help you reach a variety of goals: fixing up your home, paying off other high-interest or nondeductible debt, saving for a car, for a college education or for retirement. Refinancing is not for everyone — but it may be right for you.

A new, lower interest rate means you'll pay less in interest on your new loan. If the term of your new loan is the same as your existing loan — say, 30 years — then your new monthly payment will be less than your existing payments.

However, when you refinance, you may choose a shorter-term loan — say, 15 years. In this case, even though you are paying a lower interest rate, your monthly payments may not be lower because you are paying off the principal at a much faster rate. In fact, your payments may even be *higher.* But trading your current mortgage for one that has a *lower* interest rate and a *shorter* term will take you that much closer to debt-free living and financial independence.

Refinancing usually involves closing costs for items such as title insurance, lender's fees and an appraisal of your home's current value. These can add up to significant up-front expenses. It's important to consider these costs, as well as the following factors, when deciding whether refinancing is right for you:

- Consider the interest-rate environment.
- Find out if there's a penalty for paying off your old mortgage.
- Find out your home's approximate market value to make sure your new lender will allow you to borrow enough to cover your existing mortgage.
- Compare your current monthly payment with your projected payment.

❖ Consider closing costs.

❖ Think about how long you plan to stay in your home.

Whether or not you decide to make prepayments or refinance, your goal should be to pay off your mortgage as soon as you can!

Should You Refinance Your Mortgage?

It can make sense to refinance your home if mortgage interest rates are lower than your current rate. A key factor in deciding whether to refinance is how long it will take to recover the costs. After all, if it takes three years to recover them but you expect to sell within that time, it's not worth refinancing. Here's an example and a worksheet to help you evaluate your situation.

Example:

- 30-year fixed mortgage for $150,000
- refinancing from current rate of 8% to new rate of 6.5%

	Example	Your mortgage
Step 1: Calculate closing costs (Call your lender for these costs)		
Total points*	2 points, $ 3,000	__ points, $ ______
Appraisal fee	300	______
Title insurance	500	______
Other fees, recording taxes**	+ 150	+ ______
Total closing costs	$ 3,950	$ ______
Step 2: Determine monthly savings (You can use the following chart to estimate)		
Current monthly payment (principal and interest)	$ 1,101	$ ______
New mortgage monthly payment (principal and interest)	– 948	– ______
Total monthly savings	$ 153	$ ______
Step 3: Divide the total in *Step 1* by the total in *Step 2* for number of months it would take to recoup financing costs.		
Total in *Step 1* (total cost of refinancing)	$ 3,950	$ ______
Divided by the total in *Step 2* (total monthly savings)***	÷ 153	÷ ______
Approximate total months to recoup closing costs	= 26	= ______

* No-point loans are often available: They're desirable if you believe you might refinance again or move before the expiration of the mortgage. Points on a refinancing are not deductible in the year paid. Instead, assuming you itemize deductions, you can deduct (amortize) a portion of the points over the life of the loan. Example: A borrower pays $2,000 in points on a $100,000, 30-year loan. Each year the borrower deducts $66.67 (= $2,000/30 years) as homeowner's interest.

** In some states, (*e.g.*, New York) you can avoid certain state taxes by getting a "loan modification" instead of refinancing your mortgage. The effect is the same: lower payments because of a lower interest rate.

*** If you desire greater precision, calculate the *after-tax* difference by multiplying this figure by 1 – your tax bracket %. For example, in a 33% combined federal and state marginal tax bracket, the monthly savings would be $103 ($153 x (1-33%)) and the time you'd need to live in your home to recoup closing costs would be 38 months (= $3,950/$103).

Monthly Principal and Interest Payments for a 30-Year Mortgage

Interest rate	Amount of mortgage $75,000	$100,000	$125,000	$150,000	$200,000	$250,000
6%	$449	$ 599	$ 749	$ 899	$1,199	$1,499
6-1/4%	461	615	769	923	1,231	1,539
6-1/2%	474	632	790	948	1,264	1,580
6-3/4%	486	649	811	973	1,297	1,621
7%	499	665	832	998	1,331	1,663
7-1/4%	512	682	853	1,023	1,364	1,705
7-1/2%	524	699	874	1,049	1,398	1,748
7-3/4%	537	716	896	1,075	1,433	1,791
8%	550	734	917	1,101	1,468	1,835
8-1/4%	563	751	939	1,127	1,502	1,878
8-1/2%	577	769	961	1,153	1,538	1,922
8-3/4%	590	787	983	1,180	1,574	1,967
9%	603	805	1,006	1,207	1,610	2,012
9-1/4%	617	823	1,028	1,234	1,646	2,057
9-1/2%	631	841	1,051	1,261	1,682	2,102
9-3/4%	644	859	1,074	1,289	1,718	2,148
10%	658	878	1,097	1,316	1,756	2,194
10-1/4%	672	896	1,120	1,344	1,792	2,240
10-1/2%	686	915	1,143	1,372	1,830	2,287
10-3/4%	700	933	1,167	1,400	1,866	2,334
11%	714	952	1,190	1,428	1,904	2,381
11-1/4%	728	971	1,214	1,457	1,944	2,428
11-1/2%	743	990	1,238	1,485	1,980	2,476
11-3/4%	757	1,009	1,262	1,514	2,018	2,524

What About a Home-Equity Loan or Line of Credit?

The home-equity loan or line-of-credit loan can be one of the most efficient and useful loans available, but it can also be one of the most dangerous. So before you sign, beware of the risks.

Why are home-equity loans and lines of credit so attractive? Many financial institutions and banks make them easy to get. You've probably seen advertisements that offer no closing costs, no application fee, no points and the like. More importantly, there are few alternatives for getting a tax deduction for the interest you pay. Interest on home-equity loans against your home is deductible as long as the debt doesn't exceed $100,000 — and the loan isn't for more than the original purchase price plus improvements.

Deductibility can reduce your interest expenses significantly. If you have $5,000 of credit-card debt at 19% interest and it takes you 10 years to pay it off, you will pay $6,200 in interest. If, instead, you took out a home-equity loan at 8% (5.8% after the tax deduction), paid off the $5,000 of credit-card debt and then took 10 years to pay off the home-equity loan, it would cost you only *$1,700* in interest. The deductible line of credit would be a much better deal, but it still would cost you $1,700!

A study by a market research firm specializing in financial services issues found that over a two-year period some 4 million households shifted $26 billion in credit-card debt to home-equity loans, and about 3 million of them paid off their credit-card debts entirely. This can save a lot of money, but the study also found that within a year about 70 percent of the people who had shifted their credit-card debt to home equity were again running up credit-card debt. Credit-card borrowers who go into bankruptcy see their credit damaged and may have trouble borrowing in the future. It's even worse for home-equity borrowers who default; they can also lose their homes. If you're a homeowner struggling with credit-card debt, you should be very cautious about loading more debt on your home. The real solution is to stop living beyond your means.

You've probably heard people say, "If I didn't pay mortgage interest, I wouldn't have any tax write-offs at all. I need that deduction!" Certainly, deductible interest is better *than nondeductible interest. But remember, it's best to eliminate interest payments. Deductible interest might cost you less — but it still costs.*

In addition to the deductibility of interest on a home-equity line of credit, there are other attractive features:

- You have the flexibility to draw down (borrow) as little or as much as you want, whenever you need it.
- Generally, you will pay a lower rate of interest than on other types of loans. The rate is variable and often tied to the prime rate.
- The repayment terms are both flexible and leisurely.

There are also some big risks that come along with your line of credit:

- *If you don't make your payments, you can lose your home.*
- It's very easy to borrow against — almost *too* easy. Most banks provide you with a checkbook. Whenever you want to borrow, you just write yourself a check. This can be a great temptation.
- It encourages you to live in a permanent state of debt. Since most lines of credit only require you to pay interest, you can make payments every month without reducing the principal of the loan.

Home-equity lines of credit are best used for expenses like tuition, recurring medical costs or a major home improvement. They *can* be used for buying cars and consolidating debts, but only if you're well-disciplined. Whatever you use them for, be sure to shop for your line of credit and *always read the fine print.*

Help When Things Are Out of Control

When you can't afford to pay all your bills, things have reached a critical stage and you must make a commitment to reduce your spending and debt and permanently change your habits. Of course, this is a long-term commitment — these behavioral changes won't happen overnight. In the meantime, you still have to pay your bills. Here's a way to prioritize what gets paid first when you can't pay everyone.

1. Pay those bills that provide basic needs and enable you to survive: rent, mortgage, property taxes, gas, electric, oil and water bills. Transportation to work and, of course, food are also necessities.
2. Pay bills that contribute to other family needs: telephone, insurance, clothing, home maintenance, basic and preventive medical care and transportation (other than to work). Pay any credit charges that contribute toward the first priorities.
3. Keep your goals alive by making contributions to savings and retirement plans.
4. Pay those bills that contribute to your quality of life: secondary insurance coverages, vacations, hobbies, gifts, contributions and tuition.

Contacting Your Creditors

If you're having trouble paying your bills, most creditors will negotiate repayment schedules. Don't ignore your creditors and skip payments, hoping your creditors won't notice. You shouldn't wait for collectors to contact you; that might do long-term damage to your credit rating.

Figure out how much you can afford to pay (perhaps with the help of a credit counselor), and call your creditors to discuss your situation. Make sure to write down any agreement you make with them and follow up with a letter confirming the arrangement.

If you make arrangements with your creditors to modify your payments, make sure to keep up your end of the bargain. A good-faith effort on your part will keep you in good graces with your creditor. If something happens and you can't make your payments (perhaps you've lost your job or you've become disabled), call again and make new arrangements.

Credit Counseling Services

There are hundreds of credit counseling services nationwide. Usually they are nonprofit corporations that are primarily funded through contributions from the major credit-card companies. Generally, they work this way: After signing up for their debt-management program (usually for a fee), you send them one payment per month. They, in turn, divide the money up and send it along to your creditors. By participating in their program, you *may* benefit from reduced payments, reduced interest and finance charges and fewer collection calls.

Should you use them? That depends. If your credit report reflects that you have paid creditors as agreed in the past, your participation in a payment plan could actually have a negative impact on your creditworthiness. Alternatively, if your credit report already reflects a poor payment history, your participation should help your credit rating. Also consider the fact that to qualify for these programs, debtors may be put on a budget — one that they might not be able to live with. This may explain the high dropout rate for some of these programs. Whether you join such a program or not, it could be a good source of information.

The National Foundation for Credit Counseling is a nationwide network of 1,450 credit counseling centers. Call their toll-free crisis hotline at 800/388-2227 or visit their Web site (www.nfcc.org) to receive counseling or to find a network agency near you. Alternatively, you may check your telephone directory or contact your local consumer-protection office for more information.

Debtors Anonymous

If you feel you've reached the end of your financial rope, you may want to consider getting help from Debtors Anonymous. Modeled after Alcoholics Anonymous, Debtors Anonymous helps compulsive debtors get their habits under control. Debtors Anonymous also publishes a number of brochures and a newsletter. For more information contact:

Debtors Anonymous
General Service Office
P.O. Box 920888
Needham, MA 02492-0009
781/453-2743
www.debtorsanonymous.org

Bankruptcy

Many people think that bankruptcy offers an easy way to start over. Actually, bankruptcy is a very serious financial step and should be considered a last resort. Bankruptcy has negative long-term effects on credit, reputation, etc. Here is a brief description of Chapter 7 and Chapter 13 of the bankruptcy code.

Chapter 7 — Sometimes called "straight bankruptcy," Chapter 7 may be used by businesses or individuals. A portion of the debtor's assets is liquidated (converted to cash) and distributed among creditors by a court-appointed trustee. You cannot file more than once in six years under this chapter.

Chapter 13 — Sometimes called the "wage-earner plan," it provides protection from creditors to individuals, including those who are sole proprietors of businesses, while they repay their debts from current assets and income, usually over a three- to five-year period. Chapter 13 can be filed at any time.

When this publication went to press, each chamber of the U.S. Congress had passed its own version of legislation requiring people to use Chapter 13 if they earn more than the median income in their state. However, a compromise version of the legislation that could pass in both Houses and be signed into law by the President had not yet been settled upon as this publication was being prepared.

Consumer Reporting Agencies

The federal Fair Credit Reporting Act allows you to obtain a copy of your credit report from any of the Consumer Reporting Agencies (CRAs) for a reasonable charge. Additionally, if you've been rejected for credit, you may be entitled to receive a free copy of your personal credit report.

The three major credit-reporting agencies are:

Equifax
PO Box 740241
Atlanta, GA 30374-0241
800/685-1111
www.equifax.com

Experian
PO Box 949
Allen, TX 75013-0949
888/397-3742
www.experian.com

Trans Union
PO Box 1000
Chester, PA 19022
800/916-8800
www.transunion.com

Your Credit Rating

Although creditors consider a number of factors in deciding whether to grant credit, most rely heavily on your credit history. That history will tell the potential new lender how you've handled your debts in the past. Credit bureaus gather this information and sell it to lenders and other institutions.

Your Credit History

Building a good credit history is important. If you have no credit history, it's difficult to establish credit — that is, get approved for a credit card or a loan. Your credit bureau report is based on information supplied over time by lenders and other creditors. It also provides information on where you live and work. It will make note of any judgments or bankruptcies. And, most importantly, it records payments that you've made on credit cards, installment loans and other credit accounts. These reports help the potential new lender decide whether or not you're a good credit risk.

Credit Scoring

In addition to your credit history, a lender may also make its decision to lend you money based on your personal credit score that it obtains from one of the credit bureaus. Credit scores are used by lenders to judge how credit worthy you are. A statistical model that evaluates the information in your credit file generates the score.

The most commonly known credit score, the FICO® score, is based upon the model developed by Fair, Isaac and Company, Inc. FICO® scores range from 300 to 850, with the higher scores being more favorable. Thirty-five percent of your FICO® score is based on your payment history (*i.e.*, whether you have paid past credit accounts on time). The amount you owe is the next most heavily weighted factor in your score (30%). While having credit accounts and owing money on them does not mean you are a high-risk borrower, owing a great deal of money on many accounts can indicate that you are overextended and at risk of defaulting. An additional 15% of your score is based on the length of your credit history — the longer the better. The remaining 20% of your score is based equally upon (1) whether you've recently obtained new credit and (2) the mix (or type) of credit you use.

Your FICO® score, like your credit report, is available for a small charge from Equifax. Credit scores are also available from the other credit reporting agencies listed earlier in this chapter. With your score you will receive explanations — reasons why your score was not higher. These explanations are more useful than the score itself in helping you determine whether your credit history might contain errors and how you might improve your score over time.

Improving Your Credit Rating

Creditors may deny you credit if there's negative information in your credit file. Negative information includes late payments, repossessions, accounts turned over to a collection agency, judgments, liens or bankruptcy. There is *nothing* you can do to remove negative information that is accurate. If this is your situation, don't consider paying someone to "clean up" your credit rating; work on making your credit report better.

If you have outstanding judgments, make sure you satisfy them first. Then work on paying off any delinquent or late debts. While you're reducing these debts, try to get approval for a credit card. Gasoline cards are the easiest to get. Or try a secured credit card. If you get approval, charge a little but only for something you *really* need. When the bill comes, pay off your entire balance in full. Improving your credit rating may take time, so you'll have to be patient.

How Can You Correct Errors in Your Credit Report?

You are entitled to have incomplete or inaccurate information in your credit report corrected without charge. If you dispute the information in your report, the credit bureau must reinvestigate it within a "reasonable period of time," unless the bureau believes the dispute is "frivolous or irrelevant."

If reinvestigation does not resolve your dispute, The Fair Credit Reporting Act permits you to file a statement of up to 100 words with the credit bureau explaining your side of the story. The credit bureau must include this statement in your report each time it sends it out.

Do's and Don'ts of Debt

- ❖ **DO** carry a credit card, unless you suffer from "compulsive charge syndrome," in which case do not carry any. Notice, we said to carry *a* credit card; one is usually enough. Two is OK; but eight, 10 or 12? *No way!* You do not need that many (especially department store cards, which tend to have sky-high interest rates). The more cards you have, the more you will be tempted to use them.

  Also, having extra credit cards can hurt your ability to obtain an important loan, such as a mortgage, because banks increasingly view your credit limit as *actual* debt rather than *potential* debt. In other words, they assume that if you have the credit, you will use it. And generally, they are right!

- ❖ **DON'T** use credit cards for day-to-day expenses such as food, gas, etc., unless you are disciplined enough to pay off the balance each month. Research has shown that using credit cards increases spending. In other words, *you will buy more when you charge* whether you need it or not.

- ❖ **DON'T** make interest-only payments on your home-equity line of credit even if your bank encourages this. Remember, each time you borrow against your line of credit, you are swapping your hard-earned equity for new debt.

- ❖ **DO** refinance credit-card debt or other high-interest debt with lower-cost credit, such as a home-equity line of credit, which may provide you with a tax deduction, too! After doing this, however, *make sure* you do not increase your credit card balance again. You will only make a bad situation worse. Unfortunately, one study found that 70% of households that used a home-equity line of credit to pay off credit-card debt had run up a credit-card balance within one year.

- ❖ **DON'T** pile debt on your house if you are a compulsive spender. In a worst-case scenario, you could lose your house.

- ❖ **DO** take money out of low-interest savings accounts to pay off high-interest debt. After paying down the debt, use the monthly payments you would have been sending to the lender to replenish your savings account.

- ❖ **DON'T** use credit cards for cash advances. This is one of the costliest ways to borrow, since it usually involves a transaction fee (which can be equivalent to an annual percentage rate of 24% or more) and no grace period on the interest due.

- ❖ **DO** consider sources of credit other than bankcards and home-equity loans — margin loans from your brokerage firm and loans from credit unions, life-insurance policies and your company savings plan. But do not borrow from Peter to pay Paul unless you are cutting your overall debt costs.

- ❖ **DO** go "cold turkey" on your credit cards for a month just to break the habit of using them. Don't drop them, but leave them in your wallet or at home and pay for everything with cash. Using cash will put you back in touch with your spending, a contact too many of us have lost. Then get rid of all your extra cards.

❖ **DON'T** take out a consolidation loan that carries a higher interest rate to pay off credit-card debt. This approach will stretch out the payments and may dig you deeper in debt.

❖ **DON'T** buy credit insurance if you can avoid it. It is usually unnecessary and always overpriced.

❖ **DO** pyramid payments to reduce your debt. Write down all of your debts and order them from highest interest rate to lowest rate, including the outstanding balance and the minimum monthly payment. For example, Megan has the following outstanding debt:

Outstanding Debt
(Highest to Lowest Interest Rate)

	Interest Rate	Outstanding Balance	Minimum Monthly Payment
1. Department store	21%	$ 1,200	$60
2. Visa	19%	3,000	100
3. Car loan	11%	6,500	200
4. Mortgage	8%	76,500	600

She adds an extra $50 a month to the monthly payment on her No. 1 debt, in this case the department store. So Megan will pay $110 each month until she pays the balance off (she will pay the minimum amount on all her other debts). Then, when the department store is paid off, she will apply the $110 each month she was paying to debt No. 1 toward her No. 2 debt, her Visa bill. That means Megan will send Visa $210 each month until it is paid off, then add $210 each month to her car loan payment. If you stack your monthly payments like this, you will be debt-free much faster, too!

❖ **DON'T** sign up for tax-refund anticipation loans. Once fees are calculated, these turn out to be a terrible deal (not to mention the fact that the loan, in most cases, will have a term of only three to six weeks). File for the refund yourself and forget about the loan. If your refund is large, you should review how you can eliminate your refund (by not overpaying your taxes) and use that money to help you reach your goals.

❖ **DO** realize you are signing up for an expensive loan every time you carry a balance on a credit card. Initially many people get a card "only for an emergency," but end up charging more and more as time goes by. This is a recipe for debt disaster.

❖ **DO** think about earning more money so you can reduce debt faster. If you think you need more education to advance at your job, look into your company's tuition-reimbursement program. Or get a second job. It may give you an opportunity to do something you really enjoy, and it can also enhance your skills.

Items for Action

Don't discount the importance of reviewing your cash flow. Cash flow is at the center of all of your decisions. Will you be able to retire at 55 or 60? Will you be able to send your child to his or her college of choice? Can you afford to buy that new TV or that cup of coffee? It all depends on your cash flow.

Debt, especially consumer debt, can become a major barrier to the achievement of your goals. Take steps now to eliminate debt, starting with high-interest-rate debt. With your debt and cash flow under control, you can then begin to see real progress toward those other goals you have established for yourself.

Use the following Action Items to create your cash-flow and debt goals. Update your cash-flow projection and net-worth statement once a year.

For each of the following items, assign a priority based on its importance to you: A (highest), B (medium) or C (lowest). Then check off each item as it is completed.

	Priority	Completed
Cash Flow		
❖ Begin to track your living expenses with the *Monthly Expense Summary.*	______	❑
❖ Complete the *Cash-Flow Projection* worksheet.	______	❑
❖ Review your retirement and survivor's cash flow.	______	❑
❖ Prepare the *Planning for Inflation* worksheet.	______	❑
Debt		
❖ Determine how much debt you are comfortable with.	______	❑
❖ Review your credit cards; switch and drop as necessary.	______	❑
❖ Reduce expenses; use extra cash to pay down debts.	______	❑
❖ Accelerate debt payments.	______	❑
❖ Get rid of your debt — all of it!	______	❑
❖ Review the Do's and Don'ts of Debt.	______	❑

Resources

Bankrate, Inc.

11811 U.S. Highway 1
North Palm Beach, FL 33408
561/630-2400

Bankrate, Inc. regularly surveys approximately 4,000 financial institutions in 50 states in order to provide the most current rates on banking products such as mortgages, new and used auto loans, credit cards and more. At their Web site (**www.bankrate.com**) you will be able to check for the best rates and terms in your area.

CardWeb.com, Inc.

P.O. Box 1700
Frederick, MD 21702
301/631-9100

Check out **www.cardweb.com** for information about all types of payment cards including credit cards, debit cards, smart cards, prepaid cards, ATM cards, loyalty cards and phone cards.

Federal Trade Commission

Consumer Response Center
600 Pennsylvania Avenue, NW
Washington, DC 20580

The commission makes available numerous free or low-cost publications about consumer debt, identity theft and the Fair Credit Reporting Act. Call the Consumer Response Center toll free at **877/382-4357** and ask for a free copy of *Best Sellers*, a list of FTC brochures. You can also download publications from the FTC Web site (**www.ftc.gov**).

Myvesta.org

Myvesta.org will work with individuals and families to solve their debt and spending problems. A fee is charged for each of their counseling or payment plans. Services generally are provided via phone conferences or the Internet. However, they also operate a walk-in office in Rockville, MD. Call **800/680-3328** for more information or visit their Web site at **www.myvesta.org**. Several free publications about debt and spending are available online.

Personal Finance Software

Computer software programs can help you manage your financial life without sacrificing too much personal time. *Quicken* and *Microsoft Money* are two of the more popular software packages available.

Retirement Planning

Poverty or Prosperity

No one intends to let the goals of security and financial freedom at retirement pass by — it just happens. Those who fail to prepare adequately make at least one of the same basic financial mistakes:

- They fail to plan.
- They fail to learn how savings and protection vehicles work.
- They depend on someone else to be responsible for their financial future (employers, bankers, brokers, insurance agents, accountants, etc.).
- They procrastinate.

Many factors contribute to poverty among our older population. But high among them is failure to plan for the financial future.

Poverty or prosperity: The choice is yours.

Have you set aside enough for retirement? Have you thought about retirement at all? Although it may seem far away, many of us will spend one-third of our lives in retirement. Saving enough money to cover living and health-care expenses for that amount of time is an enormous challenge. But you can make it easier if you use time to your advantage by starting to save today!

Eleven Retirement-Planning Myths

What's potentially worse than no plan? One that's based on false assumptions. That's because such a plan can lead to a false sense of security. That's why we've come up with a list of the 11 most dangerous myths to watch out for when developing your plans.

Myth 1: *Social Security should provide enough income to replace my salary during retirement.*

Social Security was never designed to replace all your earned income. In fact, the higher your pre-retirement income, the lower the percentage of your pay that will be replaced by Social Security benefits. As a general guideline, the following table shows what you can expect from Social Security.

Many people don't believe Social Security will still be in existence when they retire. All the more reason to save, save, save!

Projected Social Security Benefits

Average Earnings	Estimated Percentage of Pay Replaced by Social Security Benefits at Normal Retirement Age
$30,000	41%
$50,000	30%
$85,000 or more	25%*

* Of that portion of your pay subject to Social Security tax.

Myth 2: *My company-sponsored pension plan will provide me with almost as much income during retirement as my salary did while I was employed.*

Don't count on it. At best, the plan will replace some percentage of your pay provided you remain with the company for a considerable length of time (*i.e.,* 20 or 25 years). Should you leave prematurely, the payments may be reduced drastically.

Also, many companies are eliminating their formula-driven, "defined-benefit" plans altogether or replacing them with defined-benefit cash-balance plans or "defined-contribution" plans.

And even if you are entitled to collect a substantial pension benefit, chances are, it will not be increased annually for inflation. So what may *start out* as a pension that's sufficient to meet your expenses, may quickly become inadequate even with a modest inflation rate of 4% per year.

Myth 3: *My living expenses won't be nearly as high after I retire, so I won't need to replace that much of my current income to maintain the same standard of living.*

For most retirees, this simply is not true. Although you may eliminate some work-related expenses such as Social Security and Medicare taxes, commuting costs, lunches and dry cleaning, you will probably find that you replace them with other costs. For instance, you probably will spend more money on leisure activities, groceries, medical expenses and casual wear.

More important are the effects of inflation. Perhaps you've arranged to have your mortgage paid off by the time you retire. Great! But what about your real estate taxes, homeowner's insurance, utilities and maintenance expenses? These expenses are a larger portion of home ownership than you may realize. The truth is you're still going to be responsible for these costs, and they are heading in only one direction: up!

And what about medical expenses? As an active employee (or as a self-employed person), you probably are covered under your company health plan or group health plan. Even if you are required to contribute to the cost, your company probably subsidizes the majority of it. Companies that now offer post-retirement insurance may amend their plans in the future. They may require retirees to pay the full cost of coverage or they may terminate their plans altogether. Furthermore, you should assume that the cost of medical insurance will increase at a faster rate than inflation in general.

Myth 4: *I expect to live only 10 to 15 years after I retire, so the funds I have accumulated should be more than enough to live comfortably.*

While it may be true that some of us will live only 10 to 15 years beyond retirement, many of us will live a lot longer. The average life expectancy for men currently is 84 and for women, 88. This may mean you'll have 30 years of retirement — and a 30-year war against increasing living expenses. To be safe, your financial plans should assume that you'll live to age 85 or even 90.

Myth 5: *I plan to live off my interest and/or dividends only, without ever touching my retirement savings principal.*

Wishful thinking, *but it usually doesn't work out that way!* Let's look at an example:

Inflation Erodes Your Principal

Year	Principal Balance	Annual Earnings (7%)	Annual Expenses (4% Inflation)
1	$100,000	$7,000	$ 7,000
2	100,000	7,000	7,280
3	99,720	6,980	7,571
4	99,129	6,939	7,874
5	98,194	6,874	8,189
6	96,879	6,782	8,517
7	95,144	6,660	8,857
8	92,947	6,506	9,212
9	90,241	6,317	9,580
10	86,978	6,088	9,963
11	83,103	5,817	10,362
12	78,558	5,499	10,776
13	73,281	5,130	11,207
14	67,204	4,704	11,656
15	60,252	4,218	12,122
16	52,348	3,664	12,607
17	43,405	3,038	13,111
18	33,332	2,333	13,635
19	22,030	1,542	14,181
20	9,391	657	14,747

As you can see, with a 7% earnings rate and a 4% inflation rate, you will need to start drawing on your principal in the second year of retirement. And by year 20, you will have exhausted all the principal and interest. So your plan to live just on income is impossible to maintain unless you accumulate a *very large* nest egg.

Myth 6: *If worse comes to worst, I can always sell my house to increase my retirement savings.*

Yes, but this should be your last resort. The cost of renting *vs.* owning may not make a sale worthwhile, especially given the tax advantages associated with owning. And once you sell your home, especially if you haven't reached age 75, you've lost a valuable reserve in your retirement arsenal. The bottom line: Don't automatically assume that you will be better off by selling your home. Examine all options.

Myth 7: *I won't need to "save" any more after I retire.*

Absolutely untrue! You should always save some percentage of your annual income even during retirement. Most people should spend less than their full income until age 75. This is especially critical for those who won't receive a pension benefit.

To calculate the amount of your annual income that you can afford to spend, complete *Your Retirement Worksheet* found later in this chapter.

You can save money by cutting expenses. But you can also keep working. You may continue to earn money through part-time work or self-employment. The additional income, though less than your pre-retirement pay, will go a long way toward fighting inflation and building a cash cushion. The longer you can afford to leave your retirement funds intact — and growing — the better off you'll be.

Myth 8: *I'll be in a better position down the road to save for retirement. I'll make up for what I should be saving now.*

If only it were that easy. The truth is, *it's almost impossible to make up for lost time* because of the effect of compounding: The longer you save, the more your money grows. Look at the chart below. Five years of delay can reduce your retirement fund by more than $200,000!

The problem with delaying is that it puts off the day you begin saving in earnest. What happens if your cash flow never really improves? What if you become disabled or get a divorce or lose money in a bad investment? There is always something new to spend money on. Those of us in our 40s and 50s may earn more money, but we may have children to put through college. We may have to pay much higher insurance premiums as we get older. Or corporate downsizing may force us to retire early. Don't just assume that you will be able to play catch-up down the road. The odds are against you.

The High Cost of Waiting

$1,200 a year invested at 10%, compounded annually

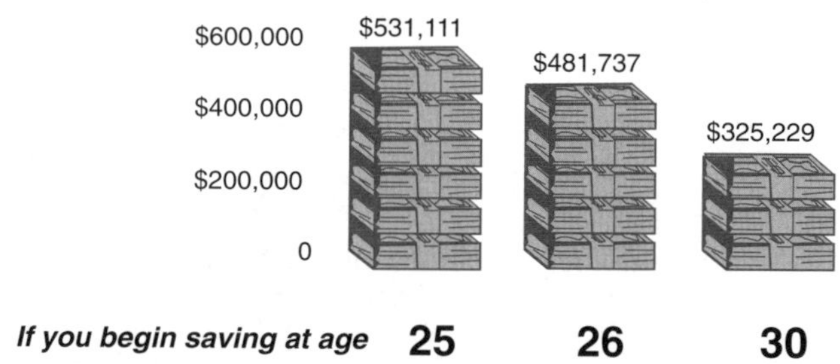

It costs more than $200,000 to wait five years!

This illustration is intended only to demonstrate compounding at a 10% annual earnings rate and is not intended to illustrate the performance of any actual program. Your actual earnings will depend on the investment vehicle you choose. This illustration does not account for taxes and assumes investment continues to age 65.

Myth 9: *During retirement I should invest only for safety because I can't afford to make up for any losses.*

As we pointed out earlier, for some people retirement may be a period of 20 to 30 years — certainly long enough to recover from any investment setbacks. Although your investment strategy should be more conservative during retirement, a portfolio invested solely in liquid interest-bearing instruments (*e.g.,* CDs, short-term bonds) can be every bit as dangerous to the retiree as one entirely invested in growth stocks. The risk, although of a different type, can be just as devastating. The reason? Inflation.

Inflation does not affect all investments equally, as you'll see. If we compare the annual performance (total return) of various investment options in the table on the next page from January 1, 1952, through December 31, 2001, with the inflation rate, the disadvantages of investing strictly for safety become more apparent.

Stocks, Bonds and Treasury Bills *vs.* Inflation

Total Annual Returns, 1/1/52 – 12/31/01	
Common stocks (S&P 500)	12.0%
Short/medium-term gov't. bonds	6.5%
One-month Treasury bills	5.3%
Inflation rate (CPI)	3.9%

If you had invested all of your retirement savings during that period in one-month Treasury bills — the "safest" investment there is — you barely would have kept ahead of inflation. And income taxes would have reduced your earnings below the level of inflation. Even long-term government or corporate bonds would have produced a negative return after accounting for inflation and income taxes. Only common stocks were able to outpace inflation and provide a positive after-tax return.

The bottom line: Don't invest all of your savings for growth *or* safety. You've got to diversify! *Don't be just a loaner, be an owner*. Even in retirement you need a *balance* of stocks, bonds and cash-equivalent securities. We'll talk more about this subject later in the chapter.

Myth 10: *Medicare will cover most of my medical expenses during retirement.*

Unfortunately not! First of all, Medicare coverage doesn't even *begin* until the first day of the month you reach age 65, *and* you must be entitled to receive a Social Security benefit. If not, you pay a monthly premium — currently $319 per month for part A only — to receive coverage.

Second, Medicare does not cover all expenses. Medicare is divided into two types of coverage: Part A helps pay when you are hospitalized or in a skilled-care nursing home, subject to meeting a deductible and depending upon the length of your stay. In limited circumstances, it also will cover the cost of home health care. Part B is designed to cover doctors' visits, lab tests, medical supplies and certain types of therapy. It covers about 80% of these costs (after the deductible), and you pay the remaining 20%. Unlike Medicare Part A, there is also a monthly premium. With health-care costs rising at a higher rate than inflation each year and with the gaps that exist in Medicare coverage, your medical expenses may represent a significant percentage of your post-retirement expenses. Plan accordingly!

Myth 11: *Things work out in the end.*

Sadly, they often don't. Many employees assume there's some master plan that guarantees that pensions plus Social Security plus outside income will be enough when they retire. But there is no such master plan unless you construct it. The bottom line: A secure retirement is *your* responsibility.

If you're an employee, your company is a facilitator of benefits. It's up to *you* to take advantage of those plans *combined* with your outside investments to have enough for retirement. Remember, company plans are subject to change. Pension plans may be discontinued, you may get laid off, the cost of medical coverage may continue to shift. You can't assume that what's available to your co-workers today will be available to you when you retire.

Building Your Nest Egg — Pre-Retirement Do's and Don'ts

- **Do** invest a minimum of 10% of your gross income each year toward retirement. Depending upon your age when you start saving, you may have to save more than 10%.

- **Do** take full advantage of your employer's 401(k) savings or thrift plan. We urge you to make the maximum before-tax contribution allowed. In 2002, the IRS will allow you to contribute $11,000 in before-tax dollars to a 401(k) plan. In 2003 and later years, the limit will increase in $1,000 annual increments until it reaches $15,000 in 2006. After 2006, this number is subject to change annually based on inflation. Be sure to check with your plan administrator to find out if any other plan limits apply to your contributions. But at a *minimum*, contribute enough to take full advantage of any company match. Of all companies offering 401(k) plans, approximately 70% provide a company match based on some percentage of the amount contributed by the employee.

  Depending upon your level of income, you may have additional incentive to contribute to your employer's 401(k) savings plan or to another qualified savings plan in 2002 through 2006 — the *Saver's Credit.* This tax credit is available on the first $2,000 you contribute and will offset up to 50% of your contribution. The credit rate depends on your filing status and AGI.

Adjusted Gross Income (AGI)

Credit Rate	Married Filing Joint	Head of Household	All Others
50%	Up to $30,000	Up to $22,500	Up to $15,000
20%	$30,001 – $32,500	$22,501 – $24,375	$15,001 – $16,250
10%	$32,501 – $50,000	$24,376 – $37,500	$16,251 – $25,000
0%	$50,001 and above	$37,501 and above	$25,001 and above

- **Do** make annual contributions to an Individual Retirement Account (IRA). If your employer offers a savings or thrift plan, it makes more sense to contribute *first* to that plan and then to an IRA, if your cash flow will allow it. That's because your company plan may match a percentage of your contributions. Since this is *free money*, you should take advantage of it. Second, you can defer taxes on your company savings plan contributions, but, depending on your adjusted gross income, your contributions to an IRA may or may not be deductible.

  Beginning in 2002, you and/or your spouse, may contribute up to $3,000 to an Individual Retirement Account per year (even if you have a nonworking spouse). The annual contribution limit is scheduled to increase to $5,000 by 2008, with annual adjustments for inflation thereafter. Follow the guidelines below to determine whether your contributions are deductible:

  - If neither you nor your spouse is an active participant in a company-sponsored retirement plan, regardless of your income, your contributions are entirely deductible.
  - If either you or your spouse is covered under a company-sponsored plan, but your adjusted gross income is less than $54,000 ($34,000 if you're single), your IRA contributions are completely deductible. The income limits increase in various increments through 2007 when the thresholds reach $50,000 for singles and $80,000 for joint filers.
  - If only one of you and your spouse is an active participant in company-sponsored retirement plans and your AGI is less than $150,000, you may deduct the IRA contributions for the non-participant spouse.
  - A nondeductible IRA known as a Roth IRA can be funded. The benefit of a Roth IRA is that, if you satisfy certain rules, distributions from it will be tax free. To satisfy the rules, and be

tax free, a “qualified distribution” must occur after you reach age 59½, after your death, or on account of your disability. (On a limited basis, distributions for a first-time home purchase also can be tax free.) However, to be a qualified distribution, you must wait at least 5 years from when you first fund the Roth IRA to draw money out.

One little-known advantage of a Roth IRA is that you can take withdrawals up to your cost basis (the amount you contributed) without taxes or penalties, even if you’re under 59½.

The opportunity to fund a Roth IRA is not available to you if your AGI exceeds $160,000 (married) or $110,000 (single).

If you are eligible to contribute to a Roth IRA, you should consider several factors in assessing the advisability of such contributions:

- Have you contributed enough to your 401(k) savings plan to obtain the maximum company match? If no, increase your savings plan contributions before funding a Roth IRA.
- Will you pay the income taxes due on your nondeductible Roth IRA contributions from other funds or by reducing the amount invested in the Roth IRA? If you pay the taxes from other funds, the Roth IRA can generate significantly more value over long periods of time.
- Do you think your income tax rate will be higher in retirement than it is today? If yes, a Roth IRA becomes more attractive.
- What types of investment will you make with funds available to you? Generally, the higher the rate of return you expect to earn, the more valuable the use of a Roth IRA becomes.
- How much time do you have before reaching age 59½ (or retiring)? If you expect the invested funds to be in the Roth IRA for at least five or six years, it is an attractive vehicle for your funds.

Even if you find that you’re *not* entitled to a deduction for your IRA contributions or to contribute to a Roth IRA — and assuming you’re making the maximum before-tax contribution to your 401(k) savings/thrift plan (or Keogh or SEP) — consider making *nondeductible* IRA contributions. (See the following illustration.)

IRA earnings compound tax-free

Even if you don’t qualify for a tax deduction, IRAs are still advantageous because earnings compound tax-free until you take the money out (without penalty as early as age 59½ or as late as age 70½).

Assumptions:

- $3,000 annual investment
- 10% compounded annually
- 27% tax bracket
- 40 years

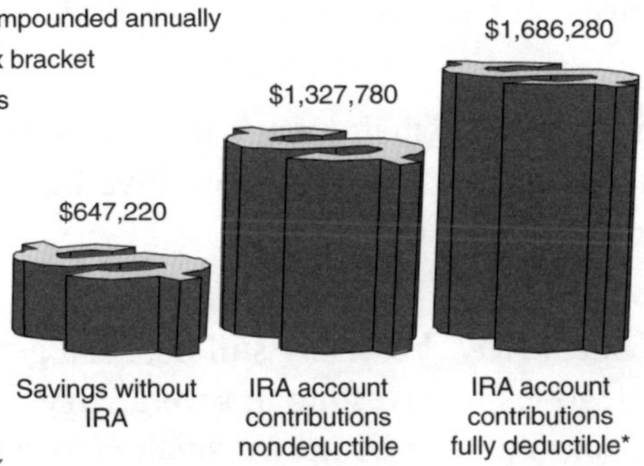

After-tax value:	**$647,220**	**$969,278**	**$1,230,983**

This illustration is hypothetical and demonstrates compounding at a 10% annual earnings rate and is not intended to illustrate the performance of any actual investment. The illustration is based on a constant rate of return, whereas actual investment performance will fluctuate. All investments involve risks, and there can be no assurance regarding performance results.

Although the tax-deferral advantages of IRAs are still available to everyone, tax law has reduced or eliminated deductions for contributions for active participants in employer-sponsored retirement plans. This illustration does not account for income taxes due at distribution.

* Includes the value of tax savings from contributions.

- **Do** consider setting up a Keogh or Simplified Employee Pension plan (SEP), if you are self-employed. Even employees who moonlight — for instance, a teacher who tutors in the evening — may fund a Keogh.

  There are several types of Keoghs you may choose from, each with advantages and disadvantages:

  Profit Sharing — This is the most flexible form of a Keogh plan and a good choice for those who cannot be certain of their annual self-employment income. You may contribute and deduct up to 20% of your net self-employment income to a maximum annual contribution of $40,000. The nice thing about it is that you are not committed to that amount. If there is no income, you don't have to make a contribution.

  Money Purchase — This plan is more appropriate for those who expect a steady stream of income each year. You may contribute (and deduct) up to 20% of income to a maximum contribution of $40,000. However, you are required to choose your contribution percentage in advance and continue with it.

  Defined-benefit — You choose the annual income you believe you'll need at retirement (the benefit cannot exceed 100% of your earnings), and an actuary will tell you how much you'll need to contribute each year to reach that goal. The advantage of this plan is that you are not limited by the 20%-or-$40,000-contribution threshold. The disadvantages are that you must retain an actuary, which increases your administrative costs considerably, and you must meet IRS-mandated minimum plan-funding requirements.

  You may set up a Keogh with a bank, credit union, insurance company, brokerage firm or mutual fund company, depending on the investment vehicles you prefer. Although you may contribute to several Keogh accounts (subject to the annual limits discussed above), fees and commissions make it preferable to have only one account.

- **Do** make "catch-up contributions" to your retirement accounts if you are age 50 or older. Recent legislation allows individuals who have attained age 50 by the end of the year to make additional catch-up contributions to their 401(k) savings plan, SEP plan or IRA. The amount of your catch-up contributions to a 401(k) or SEP is limited to $1,000 in 2002, $2,000 in 2003 and increases to $5,000 by 2006. The allowed catch-up contribution for IRAs is $500 in 2002 through 2005 and $1,000 thereafter. As with all other contributions to your retirement accounts, you must have compensation (or wage) income equal to or greater than your contributions. (In other words, you can't make contributions unless you have wage income.)

- **Do** invest a portion of your retirement savings in common stocks or stock mutual funds. Professional pension fund managers have known for years that the key to financial success lies in diversification of assets. In other words, invest in a mix of stocks, bonds and cash-equivalent investments.

  Unfortunately, many savings plan participants invest most of their money in fixed-income investments, such as money market and fixed-income funds. Although these investments generally are safe, they may not keep up with inflation over the long term.

- **Don't** invest too much of your retirement savings in any one stock or industry. You've heard the saying over and over: *Don't put all your eggs in one basket.* Yet many still do. As a general rule, we recommend that you diversify within asset categories by investing in several types of stocks or bonds. For instance, when investing in stocks, select a large-company, small-company and a foreign stock fund. When it comes to choosing a bond investment, select short-term holdings. (We don't currently recommend long-term bonds that mature in 12 or more years because the added risk you will undertake disproportionately outweighs the potential added gain.)

You also should diversify *over time*. If you need to make adjustments to your current allocation or if you will be investing a large sum of money all at once (*i.e.,* a lump sum from your retirement plan), you should consider spreading it out over time.

Employees often are asked to increase their ownership in their company, to "have a stake in the business." They are sometimes given financial incentives to do so. While the benefits of diversification are undisputed, each employee will need to decide for himself or herself whether the rewards of ownership outweigh the risks inherent in a less-diversified investment portfolio.

❖ **Do** consult with an adviser *before* you retire to make sure you'll have enough money to retire. If the outlook is not promising, take action immediately. There are a number of variables you can control to make your retirement situation work out:

- retire later
- develop an income during retirement
- reduce your retirement living expenses
- increase your retirement investments now
- change your investment mix to include more stock funds

Will You Have Enough to Retire?

You should think of retirement income as a three-legged stool. Your retirement income should come from the following:

- ❖ Pension/Retirement Plan
- ❖ Savings/Thrift Plan and other investments (including IRAs)
- ❖ Social Security

Just as the three-legged stool will not stand unless it has all three legs intact, your retirement income will not be as secure unless you have *all three* components.

Follow the next seven steps and use ***Your Retirement Worksheet*** to help determine how much income will be available from each of these sources to replace *your* salary at some given date in the future. Remember, retirement planning is not an exact science, and the ***Worksheet*** reflects many assumptions. Gather the following documents to help you through the ***Worksheet***:

- ❖ Your most recent company benefits statements
- ❖ Your most recent investment account statements

Follow Chris Down the Road to His Retirement

The *Worksheet* includes an example of one employee planning for his retirement.

- ❖ Chris is 40 years old and earns $40,000 per year.
- ❖ He wants to retire in 15 years at age 55.
- ❖ He has $50,000 in his company savings plan and contributes 6% of his salary (his company also matches his contributions).
- ❖ Chris also has $10,000 in a mutual fund, earmarked for retirement, to which he adds $1,000 each year.
- ❖ Chris is married, but his wife doesn't have any retirement benefits of her own.

Follow Chris through the process, and then do your own projection. You should plan on updating these worksheets once every year. This way, as your needs and ability to save change, you'll recognize these changes and be able to act upon them.

It's never too early. Get started now — *tomorrow may be too late!*

Step 6: Calculating Annual Surplus or Deficit

		Chris	You
	Expenses:		
Line 1:	Total from ***Step 1***	$30,000	$ ________
	Income:		
Line 2:	Pension/Retirement Plan from ***Step 2***	$ 8,600	$ ________
Line 3:	Income from Savings Plan from ***Step 3***	7,400	________
Line 4:	Social Security from ***Step 4***	10,000	________
Line 5:	Income from Outside Investments from ***Step 5***	+ 1,800	________
Line 6:	Total Income (Add ***Lines 2 – 5*** and round to the nearest $100)	$27,800	$ ________
	Annual Surplus/Deficit:		
Line 7:	Subtract ***Line 6*** from ***Line 1***, if positive, you have a deficit and should complete ***Step 7*** If negative, you have a surplus — congratulations!	$2,200	$ ________

Step 7: Calculating the Required Additional Savings

		Chris	You
Line 1:	Annual Deficit from ***Step 6***	$ 2,200	$ ________
Line 2:	Annuity Factor from ***Table F***	x 19.60	x ________
Line 3:	Multiply ***Line 1*** by ***Line 2***	$43,120	
Line 4:	Annual Savings Factor from ***Table G***	x 0.054	x ________
Line 5:	Required Annual Savings (multiply ***Line 3*** by ***Line 4***)	$ 2,328	$ ________
Line 6:	Current Salary	$40,000	$ ________
Line 7:	Divide ***Line 5*** by ***Line 6***	.058	________
Line 8:	Multiply ***Line 7*** by 100	x 100	x ________
Line 9:	Required Additional % of Annual Salary Savings (round to the nearest whole %)	5.8 %	________ %

Step 8: Calculating the Amount of Money You Should Start Retirement With

		Chris	You
	Expenses:		
Line 1:	Total from ***Step 1***	$30,000	$ ________
	Income:		
Line 2:	Pension/Retirement Plan from ***Step 2***	8,600	________
Line 3:	Social Security from ***Step 4***	+ 10,000	________
Line 4:	Total Fixed Income (add ***Line 2*** and ***Line 3***)	$18,600	________
	Annual Need from Savings Plan and Outside Investments		
Line 5:	Subtract ***Line 4*** from ***Line 1***	11,400	________
Line 6:	Annuity Factor from ***Table F*** (your number of years in retirement and growth rate)	19.60	________
Line 7:	Amount You Should Start Retirement With (multiply ***Line 5*** by ***Line 6***)	$223,440	$ ________

Your Retirement Worksheet

Step 1: Estimate Your Retirement Needs

		Chris	You
Line 1:	Current Annual Salary	$40,000	$ ________
Line 2:	Choose a percentage between 60 – 80%	x 75 %	x ________ %
Line 3:	Retirement Needs (multiply ***Line 1*** by ***Line 2*** and round to the nearest $100)	$30,000	$ ________

Step 2: Calculating Your Spendable Pension

		Chris	You
Line 1:	Annual Pension/Retirement Estimate	$12,000	$ ________
Line 2:	Inflation/Earnings Factor from ***Table A***	x 72 %	x ________ %
Line 3:	Annual Spendable Pension/Retirement (multiply ***Line 1*** by ***Line 2*** and round to the nearest $100	$8,600	$ ________

Step 3: Calculating Annual Income from Your Savings Plan

		Chris	You
Line 1:	Current Savings Plan Balance	$50,000	$ ________
Line 2:	Income Factor from ***Table B***	x 0.08	x ________
Line 3:	Income from Current Savings Plan Balance (multiply ***Line 1*** by ***Line 2***)	$4,000	$ ________
Line 4:	Future Savings Including Company Match	$3,600	$ ________
Line 5:	Income Factor from ***Table C***	x 0.95	x ________
Line 6:	Income from Future Savings (multiply ***Line 4*** by ***Line 5***)	$3,420	$ ________
Line 7:	Annual Savings Plan Income (add ***Line 3*** to ***Line 6*** and round to the nearest $100)	$7,400	$ ________

Step 4: Calculating Income from Your Social Security Benefit

		Chris	You
Line 1:	Annual Social Security Benefit (interpolated from ***Table D***)	$20,928	$ ________
Line 2:	Early Retirement Adjustment Factor from ***Table E***	x 48 %	________ %
Line 3:	Income from Social Security (multiply ***Line 1*** by ***Line 2*** and round to the nearest $100)	$10,000	$ ________

Step 5: Calculating Annual Income from Your Outside Investments

		Chris	You
Line 1:	Current Outside Investment Balance	$10,000	$ ________
Line 2:	Income Factor from ***Table B***	x .08	x ________
Line 3:	Income from Current Outside Investments Balance (multiply ***Line 1*** by ***Line 2***)	$ 800	$ ________
Line 4:	Future Annual Savings	$1,000	$ ________
Line 5:	Income Factor from ***Table C***	x 0.95	x ________
Line 6:	Income from Future Savings (multiply ***Line 4*** by ***Line 5***)	$ 950	$ ________
Line 7:	Annual Outside Investments Income (add ***Line 3*** to ***Line 6*** and round to the nearest $100)	$1,800	$ ________

Retirement Worksheet Instructions

Step 1: Estimate Your Retirement Living Expenses

You should assume that you must replace approximately 60% – 80% of your pre-retirement income during your retirement. Choose a percentage that seems right to you, bearing in mind that while some expenses (clothes, insurance, commuting) may go down after retirement, others may go up (medical, travel, leisure).

Step 2: Estimate Your Pension Plan Income

Check your most recent benefits statement or ask your benefits representative for an estimate of your pension plan benefit at some date of your choice in the future. To plan adequately for retirement, you *must* account for the effects of inflation. Use ***Table A*** (following the *Worksheet*) to reflect the effects of inflation on your pension.

Chris requested an estimate of his pension at age 55 — in 15 years. He can receive $1,000 per month for his lifetime beginning at age 55. Chris also has assumed he will live to age 85 and, therefore, be retired for 30 years. Chris assumed that inflation would average 4% per year and that he could earn 7% on his investments.

Step 3: Estimate the Income from Your Savings Plan

- Chris' current savings plan balance is $50,000.
- He also saves 6% of his $40,000 salary, or $2,400 per year.
- Chris has a 50% company match on his 6% contribution, or $1,200 per year.
- A total of $3,600 ($2,400 + $1,200) is added to his account each year.

We have assumed that Chris' salary will increase with inflation each year. Chris assumed he could earn a 3% "real" rate of return — that is, he expects to earn 3% more than inflation. Using ***Tables B*** and ***C,*** see how much your savings plan will contribute to your three-legged stool.

Step 4: Estimate Your Income from Social Security

If you've recently received a Social Security Statement, you can use the estimated retirement benefit that appears on it. Alternatively, you can either request a statement or estimate your own benefit online. To request a statement, you must submit *Form SSA-7004* by mail or submit an online request at www.ssa.gov. *Form SSA-7004* may be picked up at your local Social Security office, or it may be obtained by calling 800/772-1213 or downloading it from the Social Security Administration's Web site. You will receive your estimate three to four weeks after Social Security's receipt of your request.

Use ***Tables D*** and ***E*** while you wait for your estimate from the Social Security Administration. ***Table D*** provides approximate monthly benefits payable to you and your eligible dependents once you reach age 65. These figures are based on the assumption that you have worked steadily, received pay raises at a rate equal to the U.S. average throughout your working career and retired after working for 35 years or more. ***Table E*** will adjust the benefit if you are retiring before age 65.

The Road Less Traveled …

By completing this exercise, you're already far ahead of most people. Unfortunately, many of us believe we'll be able to retire whenever we want. As you now know, it takes a great deal of planning. Make a commitment to revisit this exercise once each year — perhaps when you receive your annual benefits statement.

A couple of final notes …

We've made a number of assumptions in these worksheets. For example, we assumed that you will live to age 85. That sounds conservative, but 15% of men live past age 90 and 16% of women live to age 94. Inflation, in Chris' example, was 4% — but it may be more or it may be less. Chris' pension could change. Social Security will likely be cut back in some way. Tax laws will change. Chris could lose his job, become disabled or suffer a pay cut.

You get the idea. *There are no guarantees!* We think you should invest *at least 10%* of your total gross pay for retirement. We think that represents a reasonable trade-off between a comfortable retirement tomorrow and a happy life today.

Table A: What Percentage of Your Pension Can You Afford to Spend?

Duration of Retirement in Years	Inflation Rate/Earnings Rate 3%/7%	3%/8%	4%/7%	4%/8%
5	96%	96%	95%	95%
10	92%	92%	89%	89%
15	88%	88%	84%	84%
20	85%	85%	80%	80%
25	81%	82%	76%	76%
30	79%	79%	72%	73%
35	76%	77%	69%	70%
40	74%	75%	66%	67%

Table B: How Much Income Will Your Current Balance Generate?

Years to Retirement	Real Rate of Return 2%	3%	4%	5%	6%	7%	8%
1	.05	.05	.06	.07	.08	.09	.10
3	.05	.06	.07	.08	.09	.10	.11
5	.05	.06	.07	.08	.10	.11	.13
10	.05	.07	.09	.11	.13	.16	.19
15	.06	.08	.10	.14	.17	.22	.28
20	.07	.09	.13	.17	.23	.31	.41
25	.07	.11	.15	.22	.31	.44	.61
30	.08	.12	.19	.28	.42	.61	.89
35	.09	.14	.23	.36	.56	.86	1.31
40	.10	.17	.28	.46	.75	1.21	1.93

The income above assumes interest and principal are distributed over a 30-year period.

Note: In ***Tables B*** and ***C***, "real" rates of return reflect your earnings after the effects of inflation.

Table C: How Much Income Will Your Future Contributions Generate?

Years to Retirement	Real Rate of Return 2%	3%	4%	5%	6%	7%	8%
1	.04	.05	.06	.07	.07	.08	.09
3	.14	.16	.18	.21	.23	.26	.29
5	.23	.27	.31	.36	.41	.46	.52
10	.49	.58	.69	.82	.96	1.11	1.29
15	.77	.95	1.16	1.40	1.69	2.03	2.41
20	1.08	1.37	1.72	2.15	2.67	3.30	4.06
25	1.43	1.86	2.41	3.10	3.99	5.10	6.49
30	1.81	2.43	3.24	4.32	5.74	7.61	10.06
35	2.23	3.08	4.26	5.88	8.10	11.14	15.31
40	2.70	3.85	5.50	7.86	11.24	16.09	23.01

Tables B and ***C*** assume payment of principal and interest are distributed over a 30-year period.

Table D: Monthly Social Security Benefits at Age 65

Your Age in 2002	Who Receives Benefits	Your Present Annual Earnings $20,000	$35,000	$50,000	$65,000	$84,900 and Up
65	You	$776	$1,119	$1,411	$1,531	$1,660
	Spouse	388	560	706	766	830
64*	You	787	1,136	1,434	1,560	1,698
	Spouse	392	567	715	778	847
63*	You	794	1,144	1,447	1,578	1,723
	Spouse	395	569	719	785	857
62*	You	805	1,160	1,471	1,609	1,761
	Spouse	399	575	729	797	873
61*	You	797	1,150	1,456	1,598	1,755
	Spouse	394	568	720	790	867
55*	You	788	1,139	1,435	1,597	1,797
	Spouse	387	559	704	784	882
50*	You	794	1,150	1,441	1,608	1,829
	Spouse	390	565	708	790	898
45*	You	771	1,120	1,398	1,560	1,779
	Spouse	375	544	679	758	865
40*	You	751	1,090	1,354	1,513	1,729
	Spouse	361	524	651	728	831
35*	You	756	1,101	1,361	1,522	1,739
	Spouse	363	529	654	732	836
30*	You	759	1,106	1,364	1,527	1,743
	Spouse	365	532	656	734	838

* These amounts are reduced for retirement at age 65 because the Normal Retirement Age (NRA) is higher for these persons; the reduction factors are different for the worker and the spouse.

Source: William M. Mercer Inc.

Table E: Adjustments to Social Security for Retirement Before Age 65

Age at Retirement	Factor
64	93%
63	87%
62	80%
61	75%
60	70%
59	65%
58	60%
57	56%
56	52%
55	48%

Cannot actually begin to collect benefits during these ages (61–55). Benefits can commence as early as age 62.

Factors do not account for increases in the Normal Retirement Age (NRA) for individuals born after 1937.

Table G: Annual Savings Factor

Years to Retirement	Real Rate of Return 2%	3%	4%	5%	6%	7%	8%
1	.495	.493	.490	.488	.486	.484	.482
3	.327	.324	.320	.317	.314	.311	.308
5	.192	.188	.185	.181	.177	.174	.170
10	.091	.087	.083	.080	.076	.072	.069
15	.058	.054	.050	.046	.043	.040	.037
20	.041	.037	.034	.030	.027	.024	.022
25	.031	.027	.024	.021	.018	.016	.014
30	.025	.021	.018	.015	.013	.011	.009
35	.020	.017	.014	.011	.009	.007	.006
40	.017	.013	.011	.008	.006	.005	.004

Table F: Annuity Factor

Years in Retirement	Real Rate of Return 2%	3%	4%	5%	6%	7%	8%
20	16.35	14.88	13.59	12.46	11.47	10.59	9.82
25	19.52	17.41	15.62	14.09	12.78	11.65	10.67
30	22.40	19.60	17.29	15.37	13.76	12.41	11.26
35	25.00	21.49	18.66	16.37	14.50	12.95	11.65
40	27.36	23.11	19.79	17.16	15.05	13.33	11.92

Over ➡

Chris, while waiting for his estimate, used ***Table D*** and found that if he worked until age 65, he and his wife would collect approximately $1,744 each month when they turn age 65. Because his salary is $40,000, he estimated his benefit between the figures in the $35,000 and $50,000 columns. Since Chris is planning to retire at age 55, he will not receive as much as the chart indicates. Also, Chris must remember that since he is retiring at age 55, he will not receive *any* Social Security payments for seven years until age 62.

Step 5: Estimate Income from Your Outside Investments

- Chris has $10,000 in a mutual fund earmarked for retirement.
- He adds $1,000 per year to this account.

Chris assumed he could earn a 3% "real" rate of return. Use ***Tables B*** and ***C*** to see how much your outside investments will contribute to that three-legged stool.

Step 6: Will Your Income Satisfy Your Retirement Needs?

Use this worksheet to put together all the pieces. If you have more income than expenses, then the future looks bright. If your income falls short, don't despair. You have the power to *change* the outcome!

Step 7: How to Satisfy Your Deficit?

If you found that you have a deficit in ***Step 6***, you won't be able to meet your retirement goals if you continue on your current path. You *can* change the outcome using these four alternatives:

- Save more.
- Work longer and retire later.
- Spend less during retirement.
- Invest differently — to earn a higher rate of return.

You may want to go through the ***Steps 1 – 6*** again to play "what if?" What if I worked longer? What if I spent less? What if my investments earned a higher rate of return? Some of these changes might allow you to meet your retirement goals. You may find that your only alternative — or at least the one that will make the greatest impact — is to save more. To determine how *much* more you will have to save to reach your goals, use ***Tables F*** and ***G***.

Step 8: How Much Do You Need to Start Retirement?

In ***Steps 2*** and ***4***, you calculated the value of your fixed sources of income. ***Step 8*** gives you an alternative view of retirement. This step helps you calculate how much you should start retirement with in your savings plan and other investments.

Planning Considerations for Distributions From Company Retirement Plans

Lump Sum *vs.* Annuity

Some pension plans offer more distribution options than others. All must offer a single life annuity or SLA (a monthly check for the employee's lifetime, no matter how long or short) and a 50% joint-and-survivor annuity (a reduced payment for the employee's life and half that payment for a spouse's lifetime following the employee's death). From there, pension plans can offer other options, higher or lower survivor annuities, term-certain options and lump sums. Older plans tend to express an employee's benefit as an annuity which, if the plan offers, can be taken as a lump sum. The newer plans — often called cash-balance or pension-equity plans — tend to express an employee's benefit as a lump sum that could be taken as an annuity.

When offered the choice, employees tend to gravitate toward the lump-sum option. But while that's the right choice for some, it's all wrong for others. No one should choose a lump sum without asking a few key questions:

- ❖ **Do I need income from the pension now or later?** An employee leaving a company with the intention of working a few or many more years may want a lump sum so that he/she can defer tax *via* a rollover and invest the money in hopes of producing more income later. But if immediate income is needed, a lump sum must be invested relatively conservatively. Otherwise, the retiree must be willing to take on the investment risk involved in turning the lump sum into a higher monthly check than an annuity would have provided.
- ❖ **How long will I live?** If only we knew the answer to this question, retirement planning would be a breeze. Just remember: You can outlive a lump sum, but annuities are for life.
- ❖ **How have I handled money in the past?** If you've always lived paycheck to paycheck, consider a lump sum your last paycheck. It takes discipline to refrain from spending it too rapidly, and if you've always been a spender, will retirement change your basic nature? What about your spouse? Would he or she be comfortable with investing large sums in the event of your death?
- ❖ **Do I have a plan?** Taking a lump sum means that you've taken on all of the investment risk of your retirement. What if the first 10 years of retirement coincide with a prolonged bear market? Do you have enough in retirement assets to allow you to invest a good bit of your money in bonds to produce income and to preserve capital in the event of a stock-market decline? Even if you plan to seek out professional management of your nest egg, you have to know enough about investing to make sure you're getting good advice.

We don't favor annuities in all cases; they have their downside, too, in that they don't increase over time, while inflation shrinks their buying power. Also, an early demise would seriously reduce the value of an annuity, whereas the value of a lump sum would be unaffected. *The decision to take a lump sum should be made after weighing the risks as well as the potential rewards.* And the risks tend to be higher with a lump sum than with an annuity.

The Discount Rate

A major variable to consider when assessing a lump sum from a traditional pension plan is the rate of return used to calculate the lump sum — the discount rate. This rate is supposed to reflect the rate of return you could earn on your money if you took the lump sum and invested it for your lifetime. The lower the discount rate, the higher the value of the lump sum.

For example, if you were 55 years old and were entitled to a monthly single-life annuity of $1,000 based upon your salary and service, you would be entitled to the following lump-sum amounts depending on the discount rate in effect at that time and assuming a life expectancy of 27.7 years:

5% Discount Rate	7% Discount Rate	9% Discount Rate
$179,350	$146,230	$121,810

No matter what the discount rate used by the pension plan, you would end up earning the same rate of return on your money over your expected lifetime. As you can see, though, the discount rate makes a big difference in the lump sum you receive.

If you're considering retirement, be sure to find out the discount rate your company uses. If you're confident you can earn a higher return on your investments over the long run, consider the lump-sum option.

Be careful: *If your investments fail to earn at least as much as the discount rate — or if you live beyond your life expectancy — you could run out of money.*

One last consideration is convenience. Your company retains the investment responsibility — and associated risks — of the pension fund that pays your monthly annuity. Also, the annuity offers professional management of your assets and the convenience of guaranteed monthly payments. You may even arrange to have the payments deposited directly into your checking or savings account.

If you opt for the lump sum, *you will have to be your own money manager* or hire one. The investment responsibility lies with you. Even if you hire a professional to take management responsibility for your assets, you still retain the investment risk. If your manager performs well, you reap the benefit. If your manager "underperforms," you bear the loss. You must also distribute the money to yourself; no one will just send you monthly checks unless you arrange this service through one or more of your accounts.

Types of Annuities

If your company doesn't offer a lump-sum option, it must by law offer a single-life annuity and a 50% joint-and-survivor option to married employees. What's the difference? When you elect a single-life annuity, you are guaranteed to receive a monthly payment for your lifetime. At your death, all payments stop — plain and simple. Under a joint-and-survivor option, you receive a *reduced* payment for your lifetime, but payments are made to your survivor after your death.

If you're married when you retire, the law dictates that your basic benefit is a 50% joint-and-survivor option (if you die first, your spouse gets 50% of the annuity you received). To elect either a lump sum or single-life annuity option, you must have your spouse's written and notarized consent.

So if you're married, which is better — the single-life or joint-and-survivor annuity? There is no easy answer, but you should carefully consider the following:

Your health and your spouse's health — Although you can't know whether you or your spouse will die first, you should look at your ages and your health. If your spouse is likely to die first, it may make sense to elect the single-life annuity, since he or she may never receive payments and since the single life annuity is reduced to "pay for" the assumed survivor benefit. On the other hand, if you're in poor health and/or your spouse is younger than you, you may favor the joint-and-survivor annuity.

Your need for income — When you elect a joint-and-survivor annuity, the payments you receive during your life are reduced. This reduction is intended to compensate for the fact that payments will be made over a longer period of time (your joint life expectancy). In most cases, the reduction is based on the difference in age between you and your spouse. The younger your spouse, the greater the reduction of your benefit.

You must weigh your need for current income against your spouse's need for income after your death. In some cases the reduction to your payment might be so great that you couldn't afford to retire. Or maybe your spouse is entitled to his or her own pension benefit, in which case the single-life annuity might be more appropriate.

Other available assets — If all of your assets (*i.e.,* IRAs, stocks, bonds, life insurance, etc.) combined would provide a sufficient income to your spouse after your death, you may choose to forgo the survivor option. If this is not the case — or if you have a considerable amount of debt — seriously consider the survivor option. Social Security alone just won't be enough.

Savings, Thrift and Profit-Sharing Plans

If you've participated in either a savings [401(k) or 401(a)], thrift or profit-sharing plan, you also will need to choose a payment option. However, you may be able to postpone your distribution and allow your funds to continue to grow tax-deferred. But before deferring, ask the following questions:

Are there any restrictions about when you may request your money?— Most companies allow you to defer your distribution to any date between retirement and age 70½. You may have to wait 30 to 60 days from the date of your request to receive the funds, but your money is not "locked up" until age 70½. *Make sure this is the case.* If you must irrevocably choose whether to take your money immediately or defer until a specified age, consider taking your money now.

Can you transfer your money among the various investment funds? — Although most companies allow retirees to transfer money among investment choices, this is not true of all. If you're forced to stick with your preretirement fund choices during the deferral period, consider taking your money immediately.

Does your plan allow partial withdrawals? — Some do, some don't. If you're electing deferral to a specified age, this important feature provides added flexibility. You'll be able to get at your money if you need to.

Are you age 55 or older when you retire, but younger than 59½? — If so, deferring the distribution — especially if your plan allows you to make partial withdrawals — spares you any difficulties with the 10% additional tax on early distributions from retirement plans. (See discussion on page 61 for more information on the 10% tax.)

Are you satisfied with the investment options? — If not, don't defer. As an active employee, you were limited to your company's investment options. That's not the case when you retire. If you take your money, you can invest it in one or more regular IRAs that will continue to grow tax-deferred. The investment options are up to you.

Your company plan's fees and expenses may be lower than those of an IRA, but shop around because fees vary considerably. When you're ready to receive your money, you typically may choose among a lump sum, installment and/or annuity option. They each have advantages and disadvantages.

Lump Sum

As we pointed out earlier, the advantage here is that you may roll all or any portion of a qualified lump sum into a regular IRA. By doing so, you continue to defer income taxes. You'll also avoid penalties and have complete financial flexibility. You may choose your own investments, "pay" yourself as much or as little as you would like and control how much of it will be taxed (more about this later). On the flip side, you'll bear the investment risk — the risk that you'll outlive your money — and the burden of arranging for payments.

Installments

Installment payments (monthly, quarterly, annual) offer a convenient way to supplement your other sources of income (*i.e.*, a pension) and to limit the amount of taxable income you'll receive each year. However, installments have their drawbacks.

First of all, your election may be irrevocable — meaning you can't cancel a payment option once you start receiving payments. Be sure to check with your plan regarding the rules for cancellation. What happens if you have an emergency and need to withdraw more than your scheduled installment? Many plans *do* allow you to cancel and receive the balance of your account (which would be eligible for an IRA rollover).

Another potential negative with leaving the money in your company's plan is that your investment options may be limited. Some plans may prohibit you from transferring among funds. Even if your company plan has no such restriction, you may desire the expanded investment selection available through IRAs.

Annuities

Under this option — if available in your company's plan — your account balance is used to purchase an annuity contract from an insurer. This annuity contract functions like an annuity payment from your company's pension plan and has the same features, benefits and potential drawbacks. You'll get regular periodic income (usually a monthly check) for the rest of your life while shifting the investment responsibility and risk from you to the insurer. Even if you outlive the life expectancy the insurer assumes for someone your age, you'll continue receiving an annuity check.

Unlike installments — where your plan account stays intact and you draw from it — you no longer have an account balance that you could outlive. The possible drawback is that if you were to die before your life expectancy, the insurer would keep the money it didn't have to pay you. If you elected installments and died before you exhausted your account balance, the remainder would go either to your designated beneficiaries or your estate.

If you're married and thinking of electing an annuity payout from your company plan, see if survivor options are offered. If they're available, review the same considerations you would before electing a specific *pension* annuity survivor option: your health and your spouse's health, your projection for your actual life expectancies and your current combined cash needs along with those for a survivor.

Remember that your company savings plan probably gives you the added flexibility of one more option than your pension plan does: installments. Finally, weigh the pros and cons of each option and consider your choices in light of your pension plan options.

Tax Considerations

Tax planning becomes even more important as you near retirement. Before deciding on how to receive your money, you should seriously consider the tax consequences of each option. *Also, we strongly encourage you to consult your own tax advisor or financial planner before making these decisions.*

Tax Considerations for Distributions From Company Retirement Plans

This section provides tax information on retirement-plan distributions. These types of plans include an employer-sponsored:

- pension plan;
- savings/thrift plan; or
- employee stock ownership plan (ESOP or PAYSOP).

A payment from any of these plans is considered a "qualified" payment, while a payment from a company's operating funds is classified as "nonqualified."

Nonqualified payments are taxed the same as salary and other wages. Therefore, regardless of what form of payment you elect (*e.g.,* lump-sum, installments or annuity), nonqualified payments are subject to regular federal income taxes in the year received. Such payments also may be subject to FICA (Social Security and Medicare) taxes.

RETIREMENT

Paying Taxes on a Qualified Plan Distribution

With **qualified-plan distributions**, you must decide whether you should pay taxes now or later. Many retirees choose to defer taxes through an IRA rollover. The rationale is that it may be wise to avoid paying taxes now because you may be in a lower marginal bracket later in life. Another way to "pay later" may be to leave your qualified plan right where it is. With many qualified plans, you have the option of deferring the distribution of your account. Check to see if deferral is available for your plan account.

You also may choose to defer your distribution to a later date to avoid the 10% early distribution tax. It's possible to avoid the 10% additional tax on a distribution before age 59½ by meeting one of the exceptions in the law (see discussion beginning at page 61).

Alternatively, some people find that paying now is more favorable. Not all distributions or all taxpayers are eligible for favorable tax treatment, so the "pay-now" strategy is not for everyone. And even those who are eligible for favorable tax treatment may decide an IRA rollover is a better alternative.

As you'll see, these tax issues are complicated. We strongly advise you to consult a professional tax advisor before making any distribution decisions. The following information on IRA rollovers, the 10% early distribution tax, forward averaging, etc., only applies to "qualified" plan distributions. These topics *do not* apply to nonqualified payments or Roth IRAs (except that the 10% additional tax can apply to distributions from a Roth IRA).

Federal Tax Withholding on Qualified-Plan Distributions

Income taxes are withheld at a flat 20% rate on most distributions from qualified retirement plans. The only exceptions are:

- after-tax contributions whether paid out directly to you or rolled over to an IRA since they were taxed when you made the original contributions;
- direct rollovers to an IRA or other employer's qualified plan;
- annuity payments (*e.g.,* a monthly pension);
- installment payments over 10 or more years;

- ❖ minimum distributions required after age 70½;
- ❖ distributions that consist entirely of employer stock where the only cash is for a fractional share; or
- ❖ cash distributions of $200 or less.

The 20% federal withholding applies only to distributions from an employer-qualified plan. There is no mandatory federal withholding on distributions from IRAs.

Any taxable distribution paid directly to you from a qualified plan and eligible for rollover to an IRA will be subject to mandatory withholding of 20%. The mandatory 20% withholding is *not* an extra tax. Just like withholding from a paycheck, the amount withheld is applied toward your income tax liability for the year. If you roll over an amount equal to the *entire* taxable distribution within 60 days, there are no taxes due currently. When you file your tax return, the IRS will refund any excess withholding.

Deferring Taxes With a Rollover to a Regular IRA

Most taxpayers are familiar with Individual Retirements Accounts (IRAs) as a vehicle that allows for annual additions to retirement savings. But there is another way you can fund an IRA — with a rollover from your employer-sponsored, qualified retirement plan.

Many taxable distributions from an employer's qualified retirement plan (*e.g.,* a pension plan, savings plan or ESOP) can be rolled over to an IRA. The only distributions that *cannot* be rolled over are:

- ❖ annuity payments or other payments based on life expectancy;
- ❖ any installment payments paid over a schedule lasting 10 or more years; and
- ❖ minimum distributions at age 70½.

The advantage of an IRA rollover is that you defer paying income taxes and the 10% additional tax on the amount rolled over. The ability to continue accumulating retirement savings on a tax-deferred basis can be very valuable, too. For example, a $25,000 distribution invested in an IRA earning 7% will be worth almost $50,000 in 10 years and almost $97,000 in 20 years.

An eligible distribution from a qualified plan can be distributed by the company in one of two ways:

- ❖ You can request that all or any portion of the distribution be paid in a "direct rollover" to an IRA; or
- ❖ All or any portion of the distribution can be paid directly to you.

Direct Rollover — Your company pays the amount of the distribution you designate (all or any portion of a lump sum) directly to the trustee of your IRA. There is no tax withholding or current income tax due on the amounts rolled to your IRA.

60-day Rollover — If you receive a distribution and want to postpone taxes, you will have 60 days from the date you receive the distribution to complete a "60-day rollover" of the taxable amount. However, the federal tax law requires that 20% withholding be deducted from the taxable portion of the distribution. Unless you have after-tax contributions or another source of funds to make up the difference, the 20% withholding will leave you short of making a rollover of the entire taxable amount. Since a 60-day rollover could result in some unexpected taxes, usually a direct rollover is the better option.

Special Consideration:

Transferring a Distribution to a New Employer's Plan

As an alternative to an IRA rollover, it may be possible to roll over your distribution, including after-tax contributions, directly to a new employer's qualified plan. If the new plan accepts rollovers of after-tax contributions, it must provide separate accounting for such contributions and the earnings on them. Ask your new employer for details.

If you're looking for a new job, you can establish a separate "conduit" IRA just for the rollover distribution. As long as you don't contribute to the conduit IRA, you'll have the option of rolling over the IRA balance, excluding any after-tax contributions, to a new employer's plan at a later date. After-tax contributions can't be rolled over from an IRA into a qualified plan.

Special Consideration:

Company Stock

When an entire distribution is paid in company stock, there is no 20% withholding requirement. This makes a 60-day rollover a more practical alternative, since not all IRAs accept a direct rollover of company stock. If you want to hold the shares, consider opening an IRA with a stock brokerage. If you don't use a brokerage, ask if the IRA custodian accepts shares of company stock as a rollover.

If you want to sell the shares, you can do it once the stock is in the IRA or you can sell during the 60-day rollover period. Selling during the 60 days could result in some unexpected taxes, unless you roll over the right amount. For example, assume you receive shares valued at $3,000 on your distribution statement. If you sell them for $3,100, you'll need to roll over the entire amount, unless you want to pay taxes on the $100 profit. In contrast, if there is a loss, you will need to roll over only an amount equal to your proceeds. So if you sell the shares for $2,900, you would have to roll over $2,900 to avoid any current tax consequences.

Establishing IRAs — You can establish an IRA at most financial institutions, including banks, brokerage firms, mutual fund companies, insurance companies and credit unions. Before opening an account, ask about:

- annual fees, commissions and transaction costs, including any charges for closing or transferring your account;
- the different types of investments available; and
- when and how often you can take withdrawals from your account.

To give yourself flexibility and some time to make investment decisions, consider putting the entire rollover distribution in a short-term cash account (*e.g.,* a money market fund within your IRA). You can then gradually invest the funds over time.

To meet your investment objectives, you may need to open additional IRAs following the initial rollover. You can move funds from one IRA to another in one of two ways:

- The IRA trustee can make a direct "trustee-to-trustee" transfer (there may be a charge for this); or

❖ You can request a distribution and roll it over to a new IRA within 60 days. If you choose this method, remember that the IRS limits you to one rollover in a 12-month period with respect to funds withdrawn from a particular IRA. There is no mandatory 20% withholding on an IRA distribution.

IRA Withdrawals —When you withdraw funds from your IRA, you will be subject to regular income taxes on the taxable amount withdrawn. In addition, if you take a withdrawal before age 59½, you may be subject to the 10% additional tax. So, if possible, the best strategy is to avoid taking withdrawals from your IRA until you are at least age 59½. If this is not practical, then refer to the discussion of "Avoiding the 10% Early Distribution Tax" later in this chapter. There may be a legitimate way around this tax penalty. Again, note that taxable IRA withdrawals are not subject to the mandatory 20% federal withholding that applies to certain qualified plan distributions.

IRA Rollovers: *Common Questions and Answers*

Q: Can I roll over my distribution to an IRA and then elect forward-averaging treatment at a later date?

A: No. Taxable distributions from your IRA are subject to regular income taxes upon receipt. Forward averaging, pre-1974 capital gains and net unrealized appreciation (NUA) tax treatment (discussed later in this section) are not available for IRA distributions.

Q: I am going to elect an installment distribution from my savings plan. Can I roll the installments to an IRA?

A: It depends on the number of years you spread your installments over. If you choose installments over nine years or less, all or a portion of each distribution is eligible for an IRA rollover. There also will be a 20% mandatory federal withholding on the taxable portion of each installment. Installments over 10 or more years are *not* eligible for an IRA rollover, and there is no mandatory 20% federal withholding. If, however, before receiving the final installment, you elect to accelerate the distribution of your account and take a lump-sum payment, the amount in excess of the regular installment can be rolled over to an IRA (and will be subject to the mandatory 20% withholding requirement).

Q: Should I name my spouse beneficiary of my IRA?

A: Generally, yes — because a surviving spouse can roll over your IRA to his or her own IRA. This allows the account to continue growing tax-deferred, and may postpone taxable distributions. A non-spouse beneficiary, *e.g.,* your children, cannot roll the funds over, so all the money in the account must be withdrawn within five years from the date of death, or taken over the beneficiary's life expectancy. (The rules are different if the decedent had already begun taking required minimum distributions at age 70½.) A beneficiary will not have to pay the 10% additional tax because death is an exception to this tax.

For example, George is 58 years old and has an IRA with a $100,000 balance. He names his wife, Lisa, as beneficiary. Upon his death, Lisa may roll the entire balance into her IRA and defer distributions until *she* reaches age 70½. However, if George names his daughter, Megan, as beneficiary, upon his death she must either:

- ❖ withdraw the entire balance within five years from December 31 of the year in which George dies; or
- ❖ take distributions over *her* life expectancy (the IRA must remain in George's name for Megan to do this). Distributions must begin by December 31 of the year following George's death.

10% Additional Tax on Early Distributions

If you withdraw taxable funds from a qualified plan or IRA, you will owe ordinary income taxes regardless of your age. If you are younger than 59½, you will owe the 10% early distribution tax in addition to regular income taxes. For example, if you receive a distribution of $5,000 and you are younger than 59½, you'll owe regular income taxes on the distribution plus an additional $500. There are, however, several exceptions to this tax.

Exceptions to the 10% Tax — If you are under age 59½, avoiding the 10% tax should be one of your priorities. This can be accomplished in a number of ways:

1. Defer the distribution until after you reach age 59½, either with an IRA rollover or by deferring distribution within your company plan. This will avoid the penalty but not provide you with cash flow.
2. If you are at least age 55 during the year you separate from service, then your company's qualified retirement plan distributions are exempt from the 10% tax. However, ***this exception does not apply to IRAs***. If you roll over this distribution to an IRA, you are subject to the 10% tax penalty on withdrawals from the IRA until age 59½. So when deciding how much to roll over, you may want to "carve out" enough to meet your cash-flow needs until you reach age 59½.
3. Elect an annuity or life-expectancy payment option from either your company's qualified retirement plan or from an IRA. For example, if you receive a monthly pension benefit over your lifetime, it is not subject to the 10% tax. Neither are savings plan or IRA withdrawals based on life expectancy.
4. Distributions used to pay for medical expenses allowed as an itemized deduction.
5. Distributions from an ESOP in the form of dividends.
6. Distributions from IRAs to cover the costs of qualified education expenses for yourself, your spouse, or your child. Education expenses include tuition, room and board, fees and books.
7. Distributions from IRAs for a "qualified first-time homebuyer acquisition."
8. Distributions from IRAs to cover the costs of medical insurance (if you have received unemployment compensation for at least 12 consecutive weeks or could have received unemployment except for being self-employed). The distribution from the IRA must be received in the same or subsequent year that the unemployment benefits are received.
9. Distributions from either a qualified plan or an IRA due to, or on account of, death or disability.
10. Distributions from either a qualified plan or IRA made as part of a child-custody, separation or divorce agreement (classified as a qualified domestic relations order (QDRO) when it affects a company-sponsored qualified plan).

To qualify for many of the exceptions, you'll need to complete IRS *Form 5329.* We strongly recommend you consult a tax advisor for more information. For your tax advisor's reference, information concerning the 10% additional tax can be found in Section 72(t) of the Internal Revenue Code (IRC).

10% Additional Tax: *Questions and Answers*

Q: Can I avoid the 10% additional tax if I roll over my distribution to an IRA or the qualified plan of another employer?

A: Yes. A rollover is one way to at least defer, if not avoid, the 10% additional tax. The taxable amount of a distribution that is rolled over is not included in your income. Therefore, it is not subject to the 10% additional tax.

Q: What if I separate from service at age 50, but defer my distribution until age 55? Will I be exempt from the 10% additional tax?

A: No. You must actually separate from service *during or after the year you reach age 55* to qualify for the exception.

Q: Will the distribution of any after-tax contributions be subject to the additional tax?

A: No. The 10% additional tax applies only to taxable distributions. Since after-tax contributions are nontaxable, there is no penalty tax. However, the *earnings* on after-tax contributions are subject to the 10% additional tax, so be sure to roll them to an IRA along with the rest of your plan balance.

Using Substantially Equal Periodic Payments

One way to avoid the 10% additional tax is to receive your distribution from an IRA — and, possibly, from a qualified plan — in "substantially equal periodic payments" (SEPPs) based on your life expectancy. To qualify for this exception, you must receive these payments at least annually over your life expectancy (or the joint life expectancies of you and a beneficiary).

Once you begin withdrawing SEPPs, you must continue this distribution method for the ***longer*** of five years or until you attain age 59½. If you change the payment schedule before meeting one of these requirements, the 10% additional tax will be imposed retroactively on all early (pre-age 59½) distributions. To illustrate, if you start taking SEPPs at age 57 and modify your payment schedule before age 62, the IRS imposes the 10% penalty on all taxable withdrawals before age 59½.

Calculating SEPPs — There are several ways to qualify a withdrawal as a SEPP. One is by purchasing a commercial annuity contract from an insurance company. An annuity payable for your life with a term-certain feature will also qualify under this exception. However, a form of payment consisting solely of a term certain — for example, 10 equal installments — does not qualify because it is not based on life expectancy.

You don't have to invest in an annuity to qualify under the SEPP exception. Those who have other investments in their company's qualified plan or IRA — like stocks, bonds and mutual funds — can take withdrawals (annually or more frequently) that will qualify as SEPPs. Many company savings plans offer a "life-expectancy" distribution option that qualifies as a SEPP. Or you can take SEPP withdrawals from your IRA or company's qualified plan, if there is a right to post-retirement withdrawals.

In IRS *Notice 89-25*, three methods for calculating SEPPs were approved. In subsequent private rulings, the IRS has indicated that these payment methods are intended to serve as examples and are not the only distribution methods that will satisfy its requirements. However, until the IRS issues definitive regulations, we recommend one of the three "safe-harbor" methods described on the following page.

Special Consideration:

Age for Determining Life Expectancy

When directed to find the life expectancy, look for the factors for your attained age for the year of the required distribution. This guideline applies both for SEPP calculations and Required Minimum Distributions (see page 72).

SEPP "Safe-Harbor" Methods

Life-Expectancy Method — Divide your account balance as of December 31 of each year by the appropriate life-expectancy factor for your age or the ages of you and your beneficiary.

Example: December 31 account balance $50,000
Age 50
Life expectancy 33.1 years (from page 64)
$50,000 ÷ 33.1 = $1,511 payment for following year

You must recalculate the payment amount each year, using the balance as of December 31 of the prior year and your current life expectancy. If you compare the life-expectancy method to the other two methods, it produces the lowest initial payment but provides larger amounts in later years.

Amortization Method — A second alternative is to amortize your account balance over a number of years equal to your life expectancy using a "reasonable" interest rate on the date payments begin. This payment can be calculated using a financial calculator or by using the *Calculating SEPPs Using the Amortization Method* worksheet. The amount is fixed for the life of the SEPP — you shouldn't recalculate each year.

Example: Account balance $50,000
Age 50
Life expectancy 33.1 years
Interest rate 7%
$3,920 annual payment

Calculating SEPPs Using the Amortization Method

Use the two tables on the next page to help you complete this worksheet.

		Example	You
Line 1:	Your current age	50	
Line 2:	Life expectancy (rounded)	33 years (IRS)	
Line 3:	Reasonable interest rate	7%	
Line 4:	Account balance	$50,000	
Line 5:	Factor from the following page (Look up the factor based on your interest rate and life expectancy)	12.7538	
Line 6:	Divide Line 4 by Line 5 to calculate the annual SEPP (50,000 ÷ 12.7538)	$3,920	

Note: This calculation assumes that both principal and interest are depleted gradually over your lifetime. The life expectancy in this example is based on the IRS Unisex Single Life Expectancy Table.

IRS Unisex Life-Expectancy Table
For Single Life from Regulation 1.72-9

Age	Life Expectancy in Years	Age	Life Expectancy in Years	Age	Life Expectancy in Years
25	57.0	50	33.1	75	12.5
26	56.0	51	32.2	76	11.9
27	55.1	52	31.3	77	11.2
28	54.1	53	30.4	78	10.6
29	53.1	54	29.5	79	10.0
30	52.2	55	28.6	80	9.5
31	51.2	56	27.7	81	8.9
32	50.2	57	26.8	82	8.4
33	49.3	58	25.9	83	7.9
34	48.3	59	25.0	84	7.4
35	47.3	60	24.2	85	6.9
36	46.4	61	23.3	86	6.5
37	45.4	62	22.5	87	6.1
38	44.4	63	21.6	88	5.7
39	43.5	64	20.8	89	5.3
40	42.5	65	20.0	90	5.0
41	41.5	66	19.2	91	4.7
42	40.6	67	18.4	92	4.4
43	39.6	68	17.6	93	4.1
44	38.7	69	16.8	94	3.9
45	37.7	70	16.0	95	3.7
46	36.8	71	15.3	96	3.4
47	35.9	72	14.6	97	3.2
48	34.9	73	13.9	98	3.0
49	34.0	74	13.2	99	2.8

Factors for Calculating SEPPs — Amortization Method

Remaining Life Expectancy	6%	7%	8%	9%	10%	11%	12%
10	7.3601	7.0236	6.7101	6.4177	6.1446	5.8892	5.6502
11	7.8869	7.4987	7.1390	6.8052	6.4951	6.2065	5.9377
12	8.3838	7.9427	7.5361	7.1607	6.8137	6.4924	6.1944
13	8.8527	8.3577	7.9038	7.4869	7.1034	6.7499	6.4235
14	9.2950	8.7455	8.2442	7.7862	7.3667	6.9819	6.6282
15	9.7122	9.1079	8.5595	8.0607	7.6061	7.1909	6.8109
16	10.1059	9.4466	8.8514	8.3126	7.8237	7.3792	6.9740
17	10.4773	9.7632	9.1216	8.5436	8.0216	7.5488	7.1196
18	10.8276	10.0591	9.3719	8.7556	8.2014	7.7016	7.2497
19	11.1581	10.3356	9.6036	8.9501	8.3649	7.8393	7.3658
20	11.4699	10.5940	9.8181	9.1285	8.5136	7.9633	7.4694
21	11.7641	10.8355	10.0168	9.2922	8.6487	8.0751	7.5620
22	12.0416	11.0612	10.2007	9.4424	8.7715	8.1757	7.6446
23	12.3034	11.2722	10.3711	9.5802	8.8832	8.2664	7.7184
24	12.5504	11.4693	10.5288	9.7066	8.9847	8.3481	7.7843
25	12.7834	11.6536	10.6748	9.8266	9.0770	8.4217	7.8431
26	13.0032	11.8258	10.8100	9.9290	9.1609	8.4881	7.8957
27	13.2105	11.9867	10.9352	10.0266	9.2372	8.5478	7.9426
28	13.4062	12.1371	11.0511	10.1161	9.3066	8.6016	7.9844
29	13.5907	12.2777	11.1584	10.1983	9.3696	8.6501	8.0218
30	13.7648	12.4090	11.2578	10.2737	9.4269	8.6938	8.0552
31	13.9291	12.5318	11.3498	10.3428	9.4790	8.7331	8.0850
32	14.0840	12.6466	11.4350	10.4062	9.5264	8.7686	8.1116
33	14.2302	12.7538	11.5139	10.4644	9.5694	8.8005	8.1354
34	14.3681	12.8540	11.5869	10.5178	9.6086	8.8293	8.1566
35	14.4982	12.9477	11.6546	10.5668	9.6442	8.8552	8.1755
36	14.6210	13.0352	11.7172	10.6118	9.6765	8.8786	8.1924
37	14.7368	13.1170	11.7752	10.6530	9.7059	8.8996	8.2075
38	14.8460	13.1935	11.8289	10.6908	9.7327	8.9186	8.2210
39	14.9491	13.2649	11.8786	10.7255	9.7570	8.9357	8.2330
40	15.0463	13.3317	11.9246	10.7574	9.7791	8.9511	8.2438
41	15.1380	13.3941	11.9672	10.7866	9.7991	8.9649	8.2534
42	15.2245	13.4524	12.0067	10.8134	9.8174	8.9774	8.2619
43	15.3062	13.5070	12.0432	10.8380	9.8340	8.9886	8.2696
44	15.3832	13.5579	12.0771	10.8605	9.8491	8.9988	8.2764
45	15.4558	13.6055	12.1084	10.8812	9.8628	9.0079	8.2825
46	15.5244	13.6500	12.1374	10.9002	9.8753	9.0161	8.2880
47	15.5890	13.6916	12.1643	10.9176	9.8866	9.0235	8.2928
48	15.6500	13.7305	12.1891	10.9336	9.8969	9.0302	8.2972
49	15.7076	13.7668	12.2122	10.9482	9.9063	9.0362	8.3010
50	15.7619	13.8007	12.2335	10.9617	9.9148	9.0417	8.3045

Annuity Plan Method — A third alternative is to divide your account balance by a monthly or annual annuity factor (the present value of an annuity of $1 per year beginning at your age when distributions begin and continuing for your life) based upon the UP-1984 mortality table, (which is derived from a "reasonable" interest rate on the date payments begin). To calculate the payment using this method, you can use the *Calculating SEPPs Using the Annuity Plan Method Worksheet*, or consult with a tax advisor or an actuary. Under this method, too, the SEPP amount remains fixed and is not recalculated.

Example: Account balance $50,000
Age 50
Interest rate 7%
$4,139 annual payment

Calculating SEPPs Using the Annuity-Plan Method

Use the table on the following page to help you complete this worksheet.

		Example	You
Line 1:	Your current age	50	
Line 2:	Reasonable interest rate	7%	
Line 3:	Account balance	$50,000	
Line 4:	Factor from the table below (look up the factor based on your age and interest rate)	12.0787	
Line 5:	Divide Line 3 by Line 4 to calculate the annual SEPP (50,000 ÷ 12.0787)	$4,139	

Note: This calculation assumes both principal and interest are depleted gradually over your lifetime.

Factors for Calculating SEPPs — Annuity Method*

Current Age	Interest Rate 6%	7%	8%	9%	10%	11%	12%
35	15.4583	13.8278	12.4966	11.3954	10.4731	9.6921	9.0239
36	15.3472	13.7449	12.4337	11.3468	10.4350	9.6617	8.9993
37	15.2311	13.6577	12.3672	11.2951	10.3942	9.6291	8.9728
38	15.1098	13.5661	12.2967	11.2401	10.3507	9.5940	8.9442
39	14.9832	13.4698	12.2224	11.1818	10.3042	9.5565	8.9135
40	14.8511	13.3688	12.1438	11.1198	10.2546	9.5163	8.8805
41	14.7135	13.2628	12.0610	11.0541	10.2017	9.4732	8.8449
42	14.5702	13.1518	11.9737	10.9845	10.1455	9.4272	8.8068
43	14.4213	13.0357	11.8820	10.9110	10.0858	9.3781	8.7660
44	14.2667	12.9146	11.7857	10.8335	10.0227	9.3260	8.7225
45	14.1064	12.7882	11.6848	10.7518	9.9558	9.2705	8.6761
46	13.9403	12.6565	11.5790	10.6659	9.8850	9.2117	8.6266
47	13.7686	12.5197	11.4686	10.5757	9.8105	9.1495	8.5741
48	13.5916	12.3778	11.3535	10.4813	9.7322	9.0839	8.5186
49	13.4092	12.2309	11.2339	10.3827	9.6502	9.0149	8.4601
50	13.2212	12.0787	11.1093	10.2796	9.5640	8.9422	8.3981
51	13.0277	11.9212	10.9797	10.1719	9.4736	8.8656	8.3327
52	12.8288	11.7585	10.8452	10.0597	9.3791	8.7853	8.2638
53	12.6251	11.5911	10.7062	9.9432	9.2806	8.7013	8.1916
54	12.4162	11.4186	10.5624	9.8222	9.1779	8.6134	8.1158
55	12.2022	11.2409	10.4136	9.6965	9.0708	8.5214	8.0362
56	11.9826	11.0577	10.2593	9.5656	8.9588	8.4249	7.9524
57	11.7577	10.8690	10.0998	9.4296	8.8420	8.3238	7.8644
58	11.5278	10.6753	9.9352	9.2887	8.7205	8.2183	7.7721
59	11.2934	10.4769	9.7659	9.1432	8.5945	8.1085	7.6759
60	11.0542	10.2733	9.5914	8.9925	8.4636	7.9940	7.5751
61	10.8106	10.0650	9.4120	8.8370	8.3279	7.8749	7.4699
62	10.5630	9.8523	9.2281	8.6769	8.1876	7.7513	7.3604
63	10.3122	9.6359	9.0401	8.5126	8.0432	7.6236	7.2469
64	10.0589	9.4164	8.8487	8.3447	7.8950	7.4922	7.1298

* Using the UP-1984 Mortality Table.

SEPPs: *Questions and Answers*

The IRS has not yet issued regulations outlining all of the details on SEPPs. The answers below are based on IRS *Notice 89-25* and a series of IRS private letter rulings. Private letter rulings (PLRs) can be relied on only by the taxpayer requesting the ruling. However, they are useful as a means to understand the IRS' approach to an issue. Please note, however, that future IRS communications could supplement or modify these answers. Therefore, we strongly recommend that you consult your tax advisor for more information.

Q: Is it necessary to aggregate all of my IRAs when calculating SEPPs?

A: The Internal Revenue Code does not require the aggregation of IRAs for this purpose. So if you have two regular IRAs (to which you are making $2,000 annual contributions), you can take SEPPs from one and not the other (PLR 8946045). Also, according to another private letter ruling (PLR 9525062), it's possible to divide a lump sum from a company-sponsored retirement plan into numerous IRAs, and take SEPPs from only one of the IRAs.

Q: Can the method for calculating SEPPs be modified?

A: Once you begin taking SEPPs, the distribution method (life expectancy, amortization or annuity plan) may not be modified (other than by reason of death or disability) before the later of (1) five years after the date of the first payment; or (2) attaining age 59½. Otherwise, the 10% additional tax may be retroactively imposed. Even though the SEPP distribution method *cannot* change, you can change your IRA investments. Further, your distribution method can account for changes in the payment amount to reflect inflation. However, the IRS has not provided clear guidance on just how to incorporate such an adjustment.

Q: What interest-rate assumptions are considered "reasonable" for computing SEPPs?

A: In *Notice 89-25*, the IRS permits the use of an interest rate that does not exceed a reasonable rate on the date payments begin for purposes of the amortization and annuity-distribution methods. What is reasonable will depend on the facts and circumstances at any particular time. In private letter rulings, the IRS has approved the use of the following interest rates:

- long-term applicable federal rate — monthly compounding;
- adjusted federal long-term rate under IRC § 382;
- 120% long-term applicable federal rate — annual payments;
- 120% Pension Benefit Guaranty Corporation (PBGC) rate;
- prime rate; and
- expected rate of return on investments.

Q: What life expectancy assumptions are considered "reasonable" for computing SEPPs?

A: According to *Notice 89-25*, IRS mortality tables (contained in Tables V and VI of Regulation 1.72-9) should be used under both the life expectancy and the amortization methods. (A single life expectancy table meeting this requirement is on page 64.) But under the annuity method, *Notice 89-25* explicitly permits the use of any reasonable mortality table (such as the UP-1984 Mortality Table).

Q: My calculated SEPP distribution is $12,000, but I won't take my first withdrawal until October. Do I have to withdraw the full $12,000 in the first year, or can I take a portion for the last three months, in this case $3,000?

A: If in the first year of SEPPs you withdraw the full annual amount, then in the last year of your SEPP distribution you'll also have to withdraw the full annual amount. However, if in the first year you withdraw a *pro-rata* portion, then in the last year of SEPPs, you must also withdraw at least a *pro-rata* portion — $9,000 in this case. In either case, it is important that you stay with your schedule of payments for a full five years from the beginning date and until after you reach age 59½.

Favorable Tax Treatment for Lump-Sum Distributions

Favorable tax treatment is available for lump-sum distributions from qualified retirement plans. To qualify, the distribution must meet specific IRS requirements:

- payment must be from an IRS-qualified plan (pension plan, savings plan or ESOP);
- the distribution must be on account of separation from service or death, or made after you have reached age 59½;
- a distribution representing your entire balance in the plan must be made within one tax year; and
- you must have at least five years of participation in the plan before the year in which your account is distributed.

If you receive a lump-sum distribution meeting all these requirements, you may be eligible for the following special tax treatment:

- 10-year forward averaging;
- pre-1974 capital gains; or
- net unrealized appreciation on employer securities.

10-Year Forward Averaging — Forward averaging provides an alternate way of calculating the federal income taxes on a qualifying lump-sum distribution. It is a separate calculation from your regular federal income taxes. So your other taxable income (i.e., salary, pension annuity, interest, dividends, etc.) is not part of the forward-averaging tax computation. The use of 10-year forward averaging depends upon your date of birth.

If you were born before January 1, 1936 …
then you are "grandfathered" under the Tax Reform Act of 1986. You can use 10-year forward averaging. In addition, if you participated in an employer's qualified plan before 1974, you are also eligible for special capital-gains tax treatment on the pre-1974 portion of your lump-sum distribution. Five-year forward averaging was repealed effective January 1, 2000.

If you were born after December 31, 1935 …
then you are not eligible for 10-year forward averaging.

Special Consideration:

Aggregation Rule

If you elect forward averaging, you must elect this tax treatment for all qualifying lump-sum distributions you receive in the same tax year. If you receive two qualifying lump-sum distributions in the same tax year — for example, one from a pension plan and one from a savings plan — then forward averaging must be elected for both distributions. You cannot elect averaging for one distribution and rollover for the other. If you want to treat the distributions from the plans differently, check to see if you can defer distribution of one of the plans to another tax year.

You can elect forward averaging only once in your lifetime. To estimate your forward-averaging tax, use either IRS *Form 4972* or the worksheet on the following page. The 10-year averaging tax is always calculated using the 1986 Single Taxpayer Rate Schedule. This rate schedule is used regardless of how you file for regular income tax purposes.

When compared to regular income taxes, forward averaging may result in a lower overall tax on your lump-sum distribution. But you do not pay the tax over 10 years — the entire tax liability is due the year the distribution is received. Before electing this tax treatment consider several factors, including:

- your cash-flow needs
- current and future tax rates
- state and local income taxes
- investment alternatives
- your age
- size of the distribution

Before making a distribution election, we recommend that you consult a tax or financial advisor for assistance.

10-Year Averaging: Common Questions and Answers

Q: I'm thinking of deferring my savings plan account balance. Will I be able to use forward averaging at a later date?

A: Yes, assuming you'll receive a "qualifying lump-sum distribution" and you didn't use forward averaging for another qualified plan (and you were born before 1936).

Q: Can I roll over a portion of my savings plan lump sum and forward-average the remaining balance?

A: No, you must forward-average the entire lump-sum distribution.

Q: I have taken a withdrawal from my company savings plan. Can I still use forward averaging?

A: The answer depends on when you took the withdrawal, when you retired, and when you take a distribution of the remaining value of your account. The tax rules are complicated, but the key to qualifying for the averaging tax treatment is that the lump-sum distribution must be the first money to come to you from the plan after the later of your retirement or reaching age 59½.

Q: My company has an ESOP and recently added a leveraged ESOP for the company match to the savings plan. Can I elect averaging for one plan but not the other?

A: This is a very confusing area of the tax law. We recommend that if you want to use averaging, you should take both your ESOP and the savings plan (including the leveraged ESOP) as lump sums in the same tax year and elect averaging for both.

Estimating Your 10-Year Forward Averaging Tax*

For Taxpayers Born Before 1/1/36

1. Total taxable distribution. ______
2. Subtract employee after-tax contributions. – ______
3. Preliminary taxable amount (Line 1 minus Line 2). ______

Minimum Distribution Allowance

If Line 3 is > $70,000, enter -0- on Line 4.

If Line 3 is $20,000 or less, enter ½ of Line 3 on Line 4 below.

If Line 3 is between $20,000 and $70,000, go through Lines (a) through (d).

(a) Subtract $20,000 from Line 3, but not less than -0-. ______

(b) Divide Line (a) by 5. ______

(c) Maximum MDA. 10,000

(d) Subtract (b) from (c), but not less than -0-; enter the result on Line 4. ______

4. Minimum distribution allowance. ______
5. Net taxable amount (Line 3 minus Line 4). ______
6. Divide Line 5 by 10. ______
7. Look up tax on the amount on Line 6 using the 10-Year Averaging Tax Rate Schedule. ______
8. Multiply Line 7 by 10. This is your estimated 10-year averaging tax. ______

* This worksheet does not take into consideration pre-1974 capital gains. Use IRS *Form 4972* to calculate the actual tax.

10-year Averaging Tax Rate Schedule*
1986 Single Individuals Tax Rates

Taxable Income			Tax Liability			
Over		But not over	Base Amount	Plus	Percent	On income over
$ 0	–	$ 1,190	$ 0.00	+	11%	$ 0
1,190	–	2,270	130.90	+	12	1,190
2,270	–	4,530	260.50	+	14	2,270
4,530	–	6,690	576.90	+	15	4,530
6,690	–	9,170	900.90	+	16	6,690
9,170	–	11,440	1,297.70	+	18	9,170
11,440	–	13,710	1,706.30	+	20	11,440
13,710	–	17,160	2,160.30	+	23	13,710
17,160	–	22,880	2,953.80	+	26	17,160
22,880	–	28,600	4,441.00	+	30	22,880
28,600	–	34,320	6,157.00	+	34	28,600
34,320	–	42,300	8,101.80	+	38	34,320
42,300	–	57,190	11,134.20	+	42	42,300
57,190	–	85,790	17,388.00	+	48	57,190
85,790	–		31,116.00	+	50	85,790

* Federal law requires the use of the 1986 single tax rates when calculating 10-year forward averaging regardless of your marital status.

Estimated Taxes on Lump-Sum Distributions

	Born After 12/31/35, and Younger Than 55 in Year of Separation	Born After 12/31/35, and 55 or Older in Year of Separation	Born Before 1/1/36
Taxable distribution	$50,000	$50,000	$50,000
Ordinary income tax*	(14,000)	(14,000)	N/A
10-yr. averaging tax	N/A	N/A	(5,874)
10% additional tax	(5,000)	N/A	N/A
Net distribution**	$31,000	$36,000	$44,126

* Based on a 28% marginal tax rate. Actual tax is computed on IRS *Form 1040*.
** Does not include state income tax.

10-Year Averaging

Taxable Distribution	10-year Averaging* (Based on 1986 Rates) Tax	Effective Rate
$ 10,000	$ 550	5.5%
25,000	1,801	7.2%
50,000	5,874	11.7%
100,000	14,471	14.5%
150,000	24,570	16.4%
200,000	36,922	18.5%
250,000	50,770	20.3%
300,000	66,330	22.1%
350,000	83,602	23.9%
400,000	102,602	25.7%
450,000	122,682	27.3%
500,000	143,682	28.7%

* Assumes no pre-1974 capital gain allocation.

Pre-1974 Capital Gains

If you participated in an employer's qualified plan before 1974, you may be able to tax a portion of your qualifying lump-sum distribution at a special 20% capital gains tax rate. As with forward averaging, eligibility for this tax treatment depends on your age.

If you were born before January 1, 1936 ...

then the portion of your distribution eligible for this tax treatment is based on the following ratio:

$$\frac{\text{Pre-1974 months of plan participation}}{\text{Total months of plan participation}} \times \text{Taxable Balance Distributed}$$

If you were born after December 31, 1935 ...

then pre-1974 capital gains treatment is no longer available.

Your pre-1974 allocation will be provided by the plan administrator on IRS *Form 1099-R*.

RETIREMENT

Net Unrealized Appreciation on Employer Securities

Generally, employer securities that are part of a qualifying lump-sum distribution are eligible for "net unrealized appreciation" (NUA) tax treatment. If the distribution is not a qualifying lump sum, then only appreciation on employer securities attributable to your after-tax contributions is eligible for this tax treatment.

NUA is the excess of the fair market value (FMV) of the shares distributed (valued at distribution), above the cost of the shares when purchased (this is referred to as the trustee's basis):

	FMV of Employer Shares at Distribution
Less:	Trustee's Basis
Equals:	NUA

The amount of NUA will be provided to you on IRS *Form 1099-R.*

As a general rule, the taxable income on a qualifying lump-sum distribution is based only on the trustee's basis of the shares distributed. This allows you to defer taxes on the appreciated value until you sell the shares. When the shares are sold, *the appreciation above the trustee's basis will be taxed as capital gain.* The capital-gains tax rate that will apply to the NUA upon sale is a maximum of 20%. Any increase in value from the date of distribution to the date of sale will be treated as long-term gain, as long as the shares have been held for at least 12 months following distribution from the plan.

Electing NUA tax treatment is optional. Depending on your situation, it may be more appropriate to include the full current value of the shares distributed in determining the taxable income on your distribution (*e.g.,* when electing forward averaging). Alternatively, it might be advantageous to roll over part of a lump-sum distribution but retain shares of company stock and use NUA treatment on those shares. Consult your tax advisor before making a decision.

Special Consideration:

Net Unrealized Appreciation (NUA)

If you meet all of the requirements of a qualifying lump-sum distribution except the five years of plan participation, your distribution is still eligible for NUA tax treatment. Further, NUA also applies to appreciation on after-tax contributions, regardless of whether the distribution was a "qualifying lump sum."

Minimum Distributions at Age 70½

The tax rules governing minimum distributions are complicated. However, on January 11, 2001, the IRS issued regulations that greatly simplified the distribution rules for tax years after 2001. The following discussion is intended to provide an overview of important issues but is not a comprehensive review of all the rules. Consult a professional advisor or an appropriate IRS publication to help you assess the tax rules, based on your individual circumstances.

The IRS requires you to begin taking at least minimum annual withdrawals from any regular or rollover IRA, and from any qualified plan, by April 1 following the year you reach age 70½. (This date is referred to as the "required beginning date," or RBD.) The penalty for not taking a required minimum distribution is 50% of the amount you should have withdrawn. (See IRS *Publication 590* for more information.) This minimum-distribution requirement does not apply to Roth IRAs while the account owner is alive.

Minimum distributions are calculated using the December 31 balance of all your IRAs or qualified plans. (If you have both IRAs and a qualified plan, you need to calculate the required distribution for each category and withdraw the appropriate amount from that category.) The account balance is divided by the distribution period (*i.e.*, the divisor) to determine the required minimum distribution for that year. For subsequent years, a new divisor is obtained and divided into the December 31 balance from the prior year.

Uniform Distribution Table

Age of IRA Owner	Distribution Period	Age of IRA Owner	Distribution Period
70	26.2	93	8.8
71	25.3	94	8.3
72	24.4	95	7.8
73	23.5	96	7.3
74	22.7	97	6.9
75	21.8	98	6.5
76	20.9	99	6.1
77	20.1	100	5.7
78	19.2	101	5.3
79	18.4	102	5.0
80	17.6	103	4.7
81	16.8	104	4.4
82	16.0	105	4.1
83	15.3	106	3.8
84	14.5	107	3.6
85	13.8	108	3.3
86	13.1	109	3.1
87	12.4	110	2.8
88	11.8	111	2.6
89	11.1	112	2.4
90	10.5	113	2.2
91	9.9	114	2.0
92	9.4	>115	1.8

Under the regulations, almost all taxpayers calculate their minimum distribution for the year based on the distribution period found in the Uniform Distribution Table. For example, a 70-year-old would use a divisor of 26.2 for the first required distribution, 25.3 for the second, 24.4 for the third, etc. (A separate table is used if you name a spouse who is younger than you by more than 10 years as your beneficiary.) The Uniform Distribution Table is based on the joint life expectancy for you and a beneficiary with the assumption that the beneficiary is 10 years younger than you are.

Not only are the rules for minimum distributions simpler now than before, they also produce a smaller required distribution than under the old rules. The small required distribution will allow for longer deferral of income taxes on more money, if desired, and can allow greater accumulations up to the owner's death.

Minimum Distributions at Death

Before the RBD

If the IRA owner (or qualified plan participant) dies before the RBD, the tax law dictates that distributions must be made to the beneficiary under either of two methods:

- The entire interest must be distributed by December 31 of the fifth year following the owner's death; or
- Distributions based on the beneficiary's life expectancy must begin by December 31 of the year following the year of death.

If the beneficiary is the owner's spouse, he or she has alternatives to the preceding rules:

- The surviving spouse can wait to begin receiving distributions until the owner would have been age 70½.
- The surviving spouse can roll over the owner's IRA to the spouse's own IRA.

After the RBD

If death occurs on or after the RBD, the beneficiary will have the opportunity to receive distributions from the decedent's IRA based on the beneficiary's life expectancy. For a non-spouse beneficiary, life expectancy is determined using the beneficiary's age as of his or her birthday in the year after the year of death, reduced by one for each subsequent year. If the spouse is the sole beneficiary, the spouse has the option to make the IRA his or her own or to take distributions based upon his or her own life expectancy, recalculated each year, until death. If a spouse is the beneficiary of an IRA but dies before distribution of the entire account, a subsequent (or successor) beneficiary can continue to take distributions over a period of years equal to the life expectancy of the spousal beneficiary in the year of his or her death. Clearly, the current rules allow for significant income-tax deferral even after the account owner's death.

Under current law, the IRA remains subject to estate tax, so planning to minimize or eliminate estate taxes, as well as income taxes, should be considered. Since the issues regarding required minimum distributions are complicated, we strongly recommended that you consult a personal tax advisor for assistance based on your circumstances.

Miscellaneous Tax Considerations

There are a few more tax considerations that may help you reduce your taxes or plan more wisely for them during the coming year.

Taxability of Retirement Income to Your Former State of Residency

If you relocate after retiring and receive retirement income (*e.g.,* annuity, lump-sum or installment) from a qualified plan (pension plan, savings plan or ESOP), IRA, Simplified Employee Pension Plan (SEP), §403(b) contract, §457 government plan, or a nonqualified plan that "mirrors" one of these plans, your former state of residency cannot tax the retirement income. Instead, these distributions will be taxed to your current state of residency based upon its tax laws.

If you have a supplemental executive retirement plan (SERP), elective deferred compensation plan or non-mirrored, non-qualified plan, you have to meet one of the following exemptions to avoid taxation by the former state of residency. The payment must be:

- ❖ part of a series of periodic payments (at least annual) spread over your life expectancy, or the life expectancy of you and your beneficiary; or
- ❖ paid over a schedule of 10 or more years.

For example, you worked in New York state and then retired to Florida. New York has a state income tax, Florida does not. New York can no longer tax a portion of your monthly pension check, because you are now subject to Florida's laws.

Surviving Spouses, Alternate Payees and Other Beneficiaries

In general, the same qualified-plan tax rules apply for payments to a surviving spouse and to a spouse or former spouse who is considered an "alternate payee." You are an alternate payee if your interest in the qualified plan results from a qualified domestic relations order (QDRO). A QDRO is an order issued by a court, usually in connection with a divorce or legal separation.

If you are a surviving spouse or alternate payee, you may roll over the distribution to an IRA. If you are planning to roll over a distribution, you should always roll to a new or separate IRA. This will ensure the rollover is not subject to the 10% additional tax on early distributions. However, future distributions may be subject to these taxes. In contrast, a non-spouse beneficiary, for example a child receiving a distribution following a parent's death, cannot roll over the distribution. The taxable portion of a distribution following death that is not rolled over is subject to taxes, but there is no 10% early distribution tax.

Favorable tax treatment (10-year forward averaging, pre-1974 capital gains or net unrealized appreciation) is available to anyone receiving a qualifying lump-sum payment because of the plan participant's death, provided the participant met the appropriate age requirements at the time of his or her death. (The five-years-of-participation requirement does not apply.)

Items for Action

If you're retiring or separating from service, you should understand all of the tax consequences of a retirement-plan distribution before you make a distribution election. If you're retiring, remember your retirement accumulations must last a lifetime. Your goals, with respect to your retirement accumulations should be:

- create cash flow to replace your paycheck;
- avoid the 10% additional tax; and
- preserve principal.

If you're separating from service and moving on to a new job, you should preserve your retirement accumulations for your eventual retirement. You can accomplish this with a rollover to a new employer's plan or an IRA.

For each of the following items, assign a priority based on its importance to you: A (highest), B (medium) or C (lowest). Then check off each item as it is completed.

Item	Priority	Completed
The Early Years		
❖ Start saving for your retirement today. Ideally, you should save each year a minimum of 10% of your gross income.	_______	❑
❖ Take full advantage of any matching program offered in your company savings plan.	_______	❑
❖ If eligible, take advantage of the Saver's Credit.	_______	❑
❖ Make deductible or nondeductible contributions to a regular IRA.	_______	❑
❖ Consider establishing a Roth IRA if you qualify.	_______	❑
❖ If self-employed, set up and fund a Keogh or SEP.	_______	❑
❖ Make "catch-up contributions" to your retirement accounts if you are age 50 or older — in 2002, $500 to IRAs and $1,000 to 401(k)s and SEPs.	_______	❑
❖ Diversify your retirement investments among and within investment classes.	_______	❑
Retirement Planning		
❖ Review your pension and savings plan distribution options.	_______	❑
❖ Review your Social Security statement.	_______	❑
❖ Start the Social Security application process two or three months before you want to begin receiving your benefit.	_______	❑
❖ Complete the worksheet in the *Will You Have Enough to Retire* foldout.	_______	❑

Items for Action (continued)

Tax Considerations for Retirement-Plan Distributions

	Priority	Completed
❖ Consider a direct rollover to an IRA to defer all income taxes and avoid the 20% mandatory federal withholding.	_______	❑
❖ Determine whether your distribution will be subject to the 10% additional tax on early distributions.	_______	❑
❖ Consider taking substantially equal periodic payments (SEPPs) as a way of avoiding the 10% additional tax.	_______	❑
❖ Determine if you are eligible for 10-year forward averaging.	_______	❑
❖ Use the worksheets to estimate your 10-year forward averaging tax.	_______	❑
❖ Consider using Net Unrealized Appreciation on a lump-sum distribution of employer securities.	_______	❑
❖ Compare IRA options before selecting an investment for your rollover contributions.	_______	❑
❖ At age $70\frac{1}{2}$ (or April 1 following the year you reach age $70\frac{1}{2}$), calculate and withdraw your minimum distributions from your IRA.	_______	❑

Resources

AARP

601 E Street, NW
Washington, DC 20049
202/434-2277

Anyone age 50 or over can join AARP for $10 per year. For membership information call **800/424-3410** or see **www.aarp.org**. Information and research on aging are available from the AARP in addition to its well-known member discounts and services.

Internal Revenue Service

You can get free telephone assistance by calling **800/829-1040**. Additionally, the following publications are available without charge by calling the IRS at **800/829-3676** or by downloading from the IRS's Web site (**www.irs.gov**):

- ❖ Publication 554, *Older Americans' Tax Guide*
- ❖ Publication 575, *Pension and Annuity Income*
- ❖ Publication 590, *Individual Retirement Arrangements (IRAs)* (including *Roth IRAs* and *Education IRAs*)
- ❖ Publication 915, *Social Security and Equivalent Railroad Retirement Benefits*

Pension and Welfare Benefits Administration

U.S. Department of Labor
200 Constitution Avenue, NW
Washington, DC 20210

The PWBA offers several free publications about saving for retirement, 401(k) plans, and pension and health-care benefits. Publications are available online at its Web site (**www.dol.gov/dol/pwba**) or by calling **800/998-7542**.

Social Security Administration

Office of Public Inquiries
6401 Security Boulevard
Room 4-C-5 Annex
Baltimore, MD 21235-6401

Social Security has a toll-free number that operates from 7 a.m. to 7 p.m., Monday to Friday: **800/772-1213**. If you have a touch-tone phone, recorded information and services are available 24 hours a day, including weekends and holidays. Additionally, you may obtain information, including several publications, access retirement planners and request a Social Security Statement online at the Social Security Administrations Web site: **www.ssa.gov**.

Free publications available from the Social Security Administration include:

- ❖ *Social Security — Retirement Benefits* (Pub. No. 05-10035)
- ❖ *Social Security — Understanding the Benefits* (Pub. No. 05-10024)

Income Taxes

Can you really plan around taxes? Yes! The amount of income taxes you pay each year is probably your biggest single financial commitment and, in one sense, your greatest obstacle to achieving financial success. One of the worst feelings in the world is to enter April with a lot of money in the bank and to leave the month with your savings account drained.

Yet there are ways to keep yourself from unpleasant surprises and minimize your federal income taxes. Almost all of the financial planning decisions you make — about investments, insurance, education, housing, retirement and estate planning — have tax ramifications. With a little planning and a basic understanding of federal income taxes, you will be able to make better decisions.

Please note: *This chapter focuses only on federal income taxes. You should consult a tax advisor for information on how state taxes may affect your finances.*

Tinkering with the federal tax code has long been popular in Washington. The information in this chapter reflects many of the changes brought about by the Economic Growth and Tax Relief Reconciliation Act of 2001 (2001 Act) which was signed into law by the President in June of 2001. In light of the fact that many of the law's provisions phase in slowly over the next several years or don't even begin for several years, we've focused here on the provisions that have an immediate impact. You also should note that the 2001 Act's provisions are scheduled to end after 2010; consequently, unless Congress takes further action, all of the tax provisions that were effective prior to these recent changes will be reinstated in 2011.

The broadest and most direct change brought about by the 2001 Act is the reduction in individual tax rates. A new 10% tax rate was carved out of what was previously the lowest tax bracket — 15%. Additionally, tax rates that previously were higher than 15% are scheduled to drop 3% to 4.6% over the period from 2001 to 2006. In 2006, the highest tax bracket will be 35%, instead of the 39.6% bracket that existed prior to the 2001 Act.

Another major change, which indirectly affects income tax, is an increase in the amounts that can be saved on a tax-favored basis for retirement. Familiarity with the new rules will help you coordinate your overall planning and maximize the benefits available to you both in terms of tax savings and the value of your retirement plans.

Projecting Your Federal Income Taxes

Smart tax planning starts with projecting your tax liability. Using the *Federal Income Tax Worksheet*, you can project your taxes in four easy steps:

Step 1: Review Last Year's Taxes — Using your latest tax return as a guide, fill in the first column of the *Federal Income Tax Worksheet*.

Step 2: Project This Year's Taxes — Estimate your income, adjustments, deductions and exemptions for this year and then go to the appropriate rate schedule to calculate your tax liability. (See Worksheet Notes later in this chapter for more information.)

Step 3: Estimate Your Withholding — Use your paystub year-to-date figure and then estimate withholding for the balance of the year. If you expect a bonus or other special payment between now and year end, multiply it by 27% to determine the appropriate withholding amount. If you make estimated tax payments, be sure to include them.

Step 4: Calculate Your Tax Refund or Balance Due — Compare the taxes you expect to owe from Step 2 with the amount you expect to pay in from Step 3. If there is a large discrepancy either way, you probably need to adjust your withholding or estimated tax payments. (See *Tax Withholding* later in this chapter for more information.)

Federal Income Tax Worksheet Based on IRS *Form 1040*

	Last Year		This Year	
Income				
Salary/bonus	$ _______		$ _______	
Special payments	_______		_______	
Before-tax contributions	(_______)		(_______)	
Imputed income	_______		_______	
Pension, savings plan and/or IRA distributions	_______		_______	
State tax refund	_______		_______	
Dividends/interest	_______		_______	
Capital gains/losses	_______		_______	
Rents, partnerships income/loss	_______		_______	
Miscellaneous income	_______		_______	
Total income		$ _______		$ _______
Adjustments				
Deductible IRA contribution	$ _______		$ _______	
SEP/Keogh plan contributions	_______		_______	
Alimony paid	_______		_______	
Moving expenses	_______		_______	
Student loan interest	_______		_______	
Higher education expenses	N/A		_______	
Half of self-employment tax paid	_______		_______	
Total adjustments		$(_______)		$(_______)
Adjusted Gross Income (AGI)		$ _______		$ _______
Itemized deductions				
State and local taxes	_______		_______	
Real-estate taxes	_______		_______	
Mortgage interest	_______		_______	
Investment interest	_______		_______	
Charitable contributions	_______		_______	
Medical/dental expenses (7.5%)	_______		_______	
Casualty/theft losses (10%)	_______		_______	
Miscellaneous items (2%)	_______		_______	
Total itemized deductions	$ _______		$ _______	
Allowed itemized deductions		$(_______)		$(_______)
Standard deduction (non-itemizers)		$(_______)		$(_______)
Allowed personal exemptions		$(_______)		$(_______)
Taxable income		$ _______		$ _______
Long-term capital gain		$(_______)		$(_______)
Net taxable income		$ _______		$ _______
Ordinary income tax from table		$ _______		$ _______
Tax on LTCG @ 10% or 20%		$ _______		$ _______
Self-employment tax		$ _______		$ _______
Total income tax		$ _______		$ _______
Total withholding/estimated payments		$(_______)		$(_______)
Child/education/savings/dependent care credits		$(_______)		$(_______)
Projected tax owed (refund due)		$ _______		$ _______

2001 Tax-Rate Schedules

Married Couples Filing Joint Returns and Qualifying Widow(er)s

TAXABLE INCOME:		TAX LIABILITY IS:			
Over –	But not over –	Base amount	Plus	Percent	On income over
$ 0	$ 45,200	$ —	+	15.0%	$ 0
45,200	109,250	6,780.00	+	27.5%	45,200
109,250	166,500	24,393.75	+	30.5%	109,250
166,500	297,350	41,855.00	+	35.5%	166,500
297,350	and above	88,306.75	+	39.1%	297,350

Single Taxpayers

TAXABLE INCOME:		TAX LIABILITY IS:			
Over –	But not over –	Base amount	Plus	Percent	On income over
$ 0	$ 27,050	$ —	+	15.0%	$ 0
27,050	65,550	4,057.50	+	27.5%	27,050
65,550	136,750	14,645.00	+	30.5%	65,550
136,750	297,350	36,361.00	+	35.5%	136,750
297,350	and above	93,374.00	+	39.1%	297,350

Heads of Household

TAXABLE INCOME:		TAX LIABILITY IS:			
Over –	But not over –	Base amount	Plus	Percent	On income over
$ 0	$ 36,250	$ —	+	15.0%	$ 0
36,250	93,650	5,437.50	+	27.5%	36,250
93,650	151,650	21,222.50	+	30.5%	93,650
151,650	297,350	38,912.50	+	35.5%	151,650
297,350	and above	90,636.00	+	39.1%	297,350

Married Individuals Filing Separate Returns

TAXABLE INCOME:		TAX LIABILITY IS:			
Over –	But not over –	Base amount	Plus	Percent	On income over
$ 0	$ 22,600	$ —	+	15.0%	$ 0
22,600	54,625	3,390.00	+	27.5%	22,600
54,625	83,250	12,196.88	+	30.5%	54,625
83,250	148,675	20,927.50	+	35.5%	83,250
148,675	and above	44,153.38	+	39.1%	148,675

2002 Tax-Rate Schedules

Married Couples Filing Joint Returns and Qualifying Widow(er)s

TAXABLE INCOME:		TAX LIABILITY IS:			
Over –	But not over –	Base amount	Plus	Percent	On income over
$ 0	$ 12,000	$ —	+	10.0%	$ 0
12,000	46,700	1,200.00	+	15.0%	12,000
46,700	112,850	6,405.00	+	27.0%	46,700
112,850	171,950	24,265.50	+	30.0%	112,850
171,950	307,050	41,995.50	+	35.0%	171,950
307,050	and above	89,280.50	+	38.6%	307,050

Single Taxpayers

TAXABLE INCOME:		TAX LIABILITY IS:			
Over –	But not over –	Base amount	Plus	Percent	On income over
$ 0	$ 6,000	$ —	+	10.0%	$ 0
6,000	27,950	600.00	+	15.0%	6,000
27,950	67,700	3,892.50	+	27.0%	27,950
67,700	141,250	14,625.00	+	30.0%	67,700
141,250	307,050	36,690.00	+	35.0%	141,250
307,050	and above	94,720.00	+	38.6%	307,050

Heads of Household

TAXABLE INCOME:		TAX LIABILITY IS:			
Over –	But not over –	Base amount	Plus	Percent	On income over
$ 0	$ 10,000	$ —	+	10.0%	$ 0
10,000	37,450	1,000.00	+	15.0%	10,000
37,450	96,700	5,117.50	+	27.0%	37,450
96,700	156,600	21,115.00	+	30.0%	96,700
156,600	307,050	39,085.00	+	35.0%	156,600
307,050	and above	91,742.50	+	38.6%	307,050

Married Individuals Filing Separate Returns

TAXABLE INCOME:		TAX LIABILITY IS:			
Over –	But not over –	Base amount	Plus	Percent	On income over
$ 0	$ 6,000	$ —	+	10.0%	$ 0
6,000	23,350	600.00	+	15.0%	6,000
23,350	56,425	3,202.50	+	27.0%	23,350
56,425	85,975	12,132.75	+	30.0%	56,425
85,975	153,525	20,997.75	+	35.0%	85,975
153,525	and above	44,640.25	+	38.6%	153,525

Worksheet Notes

To help you complete the *Federal Income Tax Worksheet*, here is an overview of some basic tax rules and some IRS resources for more information. To help you use the worksheet, we have organized this section to follow the *Federal Income Tax Worksheet.*

Items of Income

Salary, Bonus and Special Payments — Start by looking at your paystub(s). Include any income reported on a *W-2* by the end of the tax year. If you receive an incentive award or a "nonqualified" payment, include it here. Similarly, if you exercise a non-qualified stock option, include the income here.

Before-Tax Contributions — Make sure to subtract before-tax contributions to company-sponsored plans. This might include before-tax contributions to a savings/thrift plan, flexible spending account contributions or other before-tax contributions to a flexible benefits program. It also would include any deferrals of salary or bonus to a non-qualified deferred-compensation plan.

Imputed Income — The IRS considers the value of certain noncash benefits income. The amount reported on last year's *W-2*, if any, is probably a good estimate.

Pension, Savings Plan and/or IRA Distributions — Include the taxable amount of a pension or savings-plan distribution not rolled over, as well as any taxable withdrawals from your IRA. If you roll over any distributions to an IRA, have after-tax contributions or elect forward averaging, don't include the amounts on this line.

State Tax Refund — If you itemized deductions last year and received a state tax refund, it is considered income this year.

Dividends and Interest — Estimate income from savings accounts, stocks, bonds, mutual funds and other investments here. Again, your most recent IRS *Form 1099* from payors are probably the easiest sources for a reasonable estimate.

Capital Gains and Losses — This entry is for the net gain or loss from the sale of capital assets like stocks, bonds, mutual funds and investment real estate.

❖ **Gains** — Short-term capital gains are taxed at the same rate as all other income. Long-term capital gains (LTCG) are taxed at 10% (if you are in the 15% tax bracket) or at 20% (for all other brackets). Capital assets are classified as long-term if they are held for more than one year.

  A special LTCG rate applies to property held for at least five years before its sale. This special rate was available to a taxpayer in the 15% ordinary income tax bracket beginning in tax year 2001, and it results in a LTCG tax rate of 8% (to the extent that the gain otherwise would have been taxed at 10%). For all other taxpayers, the special rate will be 18% but will apply only to assets acquired and held for at least five years beginning January 1, 2001, or later.

  In our worksheet, you should include the full amount of capital gains (including long-term gains) in the "Income" section. You will back out the LTCG and account for the lower tax on that income in the bottom portion of the worksheet.

❖ **Losses** — All capital losses can be used to offset gains. However, if you have a large net capital loss, you can only take a loss up to $3,000 in one year. Any excess losses are carried forward to future years.

Rents and/or Partnership Income/Losses — Real-estate and limited-partnership investments are considered "passive investments." Except for a special rule for rental real estate, losses from these investments can only be used to offset income from other "passive investments." [See IRS *Publications 527, Residential Rental Property* and *925, Passive Activity and At-Risk Rules*, for more information.]

Miscellaneous Income — If you have income from annuities or the surrender of a life-insurance policy, include it here. In addition, if you convert a regular IRA to a Roth IRA, include the income here.

Special Consideration:

Rental Real Estate

By definition, real estate is considered a passive investment. However, there is an exception to the passive-loss rules for real estate investors who *actively* manage their property and have adjusted gross income (AGI) under $100,000. Up to $25,000 in losses from rental real estate can be deducted against salary and investment income. The allowable loss gradually phases out for taxpayers with AGI over $100,000 and is eliminated when AGI exceeds $150,000.

Adjustments to Income

Deductible IRA Contributions — Every working taxpayer can contribute up to $3,000 to an IRA beginning in 2002. (For 2001, the limit was $2,000.) The limit is scheduled to rise to $5,000 by 2008. However, if you earn less than the limit, the contribution cannot exceed your *W-2* earnings. If you are married and only one of you is working, you can contribute up to $3,000 in the non-working spouse's IRA also (as long as your earned income is at least $6,000). For this "regular IRA," earnings on your contributions are not subject to tax until you withdraw them.

Special Consideration:

Phase-Out of Deductible IRA Contribution

If you're an active participant in a company-sponsored retirement plan, the question of whether your IRA contribution is deductible depends on your AGI. These AGI limits are scheduled to increase each year, reaching $100,000 for a married couple (in 2007) and $60,000 for a single taxpayer (in 2005). The dollar limitations for 2002 are shown in the following table.

	Adjusted Gross Income (AGI)		
Filing status	**Deductible IRA**	**Phase-out Range**	**Nondeductible IRA**
Married	< $54,000	$54,000 – $64,000	≥ $64,000
Single	< $34,000	$34,000 – $44,000	≥ $44,000

For example, Jim is a married taxpayer who is an active participant in a company-sponsored plan and has an AGI in 2002 of $58,000. He contributes $3,000 to an IRA for himself and can deduct $1,800 from the couple's income taxes. The balance of the contribution is classified as "nondeductible." In this situation, it would be appropriate to limit Jim's deductible IRA contribution to $1,800 and place the remaining $1,200 in a Roth IRA or fund an IRA for his spouse. See "Roth IRAs" later in this chapter.

If you make nondeductible contributions, you should file and retain IRS *Form 8606* for the life of the IRA. You will need these records when you take withdrawals to determine the tax-free portion of each withdrawal. [See IRS *Publications 17, Your Federal Income Tax* and *590, Individual Retirement Arrangements (IRAs)*, for more information.]

For a spouse who doesn't have any employment income (or net earnings from self-employment), a different income test will apply. If the couple's AGI is less than $150,000, contributions (up to a maximum of $3,000) to the non-working spouse's IRA will be fully deductible even if the working spouse is an active participant in a company-sponsored retirement plan. In the example of the IRA phase-out in "Special Considerations" above, a fully deductible contribution of up to $3,000 could be made to an IRA for Jim's spouse if she doesn't have any employment income of her own.

SEP/Keogh Plan Contributions — Self-employed taxpayers can make tax-deductible contributions to a Simplified Employee Pension (SEP) or Keogh. [See IRS *Publication 560, Self-Employment Retirement Plans for Small Business (SEP, SIMPLE and Keogh Plans),* for more information.]

Alimony Paid — If you're making alimony payments to an ex-spouse, they are considered an adjustment to income. If you're on the receiving end, add the alimony payments to your income under the "Miscellaneous" category. Please note: *Child-support payments are not considered alimony.*

Moving Expenses — An employee or self-employed individual who moves because of a change in his principal place of work may deduct certain expenses if the mileage and work-requirement tests are met. The cost of moving your household goods, personal effects and traveling to your new home (including lodging) are deductible. There is no dollar limit on the amount that can be taken.

Student-Loan Interest — Interest paid on student loans for education expenses can be deducted subject to certain limits. First, prior to 2002, the deduction was allowed only for interest paid during the first 60 months that interest payments were required on the loan. (However, this limit on interest deductibility has been repealed beginning with the 2002 tax year.) Second, an individual claimed as a dependent on another person's tax return cannot claim the deduction. Third, the maximum amount of interest that can be deducted is $2,500 in 2002. Finally, the AGI limit is $50,000 – $65,000 for a single taxpayer and $100,000 – $130,000 for a married couple filing jointly. Prior to 2002, the limits were $40,000 – $55,000 for single taxpayers and $60,000 – $75,000 for married taxpayers filing jointly.

Higher Education Expenses — A new deduction for qualified education expenses is available to taxpayers beginning in 2002. The deduction is not available after 2005. Depending upon your AGI, you may be able to take a deduction for tuition, fees and the cost of books and supplies you paid on behalf of yourself, your spouse or your dependents for post-secondary education. The maximum deduction is $3,000 in 2002 and 2003 for taxpayers whose AGI doesn't exceed $65,000 ($130,000 for married taxpayers filing a joint return).

The deduction is not available in any year in which the Hope or lifetime learning credit is claimed for *any* of the students' expenses. Additionally, the deduction generally cannot be claimed for expenses that were paid with tax-free withdrawals from a Coverdell ESA or qualified state tuition programs. However, withdrawals from state tuition programs that represent contributions to the plan will not be counted as an offset in determining the amount of the deduction. Consequently, depending on your circumstances, it might be possible to benefit from a tax-free withdrawal and to claim the deduction for higher education expenses.

Deductions: Standard or Itemized

Standard Deduction — Taxpayers who don't itemize their deductions are entitled to a standard deduction. For 2002, the basic standard deduction amounts are:

- Married/joint $7,850
- Head of household $6,900
- Single $4,700
- Married/separate $3,925

Taxpayers who are at least age 65 or are blind receive an extra standard deduction: $900 for each spouse older than 65 or blind, if married filing jointly; $1,150 single or head of household.

Itemized Deductions — Compare the standard deduction amount to your itemized deductions and take whichever is higher. Itemized deductions include:

- State and local income taxes and real-estate taxes (*e.g.,* school and property taxes).
- Mortgage interest on a first or second home. This includes interest on debt used to purchase, construct or substantially improve your home (up to a maximum of $1,000,000 of debt). In addition, you may deduct interest on up to an additional $100,000 of home-equity debt. [See IRS *Publication 17, Your Federal Income Tax,* and IRS *Publication 936, Home Mortgage Interest Deduction,* for more information.]
- Investment interest up to the amount of your investment income.
- Charitable contributions.
- The following items are deductible to the extent they *exceed* certain AGI limits.

Itemized Deduction	AGI Limit
Medical and Dental	7.5%
Casualty/Theft	10.0%
Miscellaneous	2.0%

Some common miscellaneous deductions are:

- Union dues and expenses
- Job-search expenses
- Subscriptions to professional publications
- Depreciation on a home computer required by an employer
- Appraisal fees to figure a casualty loss
- Clerical help connected to collecting investment income
- Passport for business trip
- Protective work clothing
- Research expenses of a college professor
- Tools and supplies used in your work
- IRA trustee fees, if separately billed and paid
- Investment management and advice
- Safe deposit box rental (if holding securities)
- Service charges on dividend-reinvestment plans
- Tax advice and return preparation
- Medical exams required by an employer
- Business gifts (maximum $25 per person)

Special Consideration:

Phase-Out of Itemized Deductions

In 2002, if your AGI exceeds $137,300 ($68,650 if married filing separately), then a portion of your itemized deductions is disallowed. To estimate the amount disallowed, multiply the amount of your AGI in excess $137,300 by 3%. This phase-out does not apply to deductions for medical expenses, casualty losses or investment interest. Further, your deductions will never be reduced by more than 80% of the otherwise allowable amount. Under the 2001 Act, the limitation on itemized deductions will be repealed gradually, starting in 2006.

Personal and Dependency Exemptions

In 2002, you're entitled to a personal and dependency exemption worth $3,000 for yourself and each of your dependents. However, for high-income taxpayers the exemptions are phased out by reducing the exemption amount by 2% for each $2,500 of income over the applicable AGI threshold.

Filing Status	Full Exemptions	2002 Adjusted Gross Income (AGI) Phase-out Range	No Exemptions
Married/joint	< $206,000	$206,000 – $328,500	> $328,500
Single	< $137,300	$137,300 – $259,800	> $259,800
Head of household	< $171,650	$171,650 – $294,150	> $294,150
Married/separate	< $103,000	$103,000 – $164,250	> $164,250

The 2001 Act will reduce the personal exemption phase-out beginning in 2006 and repeal it after 2009.

Self-Employment Tax

Net earnings from self-employment are subject to income tax and to the self-employment (SE) tax. The SE tax is imposed in lieu of the Social Security and Medicare withholding that is taken from an employee's pay (and that is matched by the employee's company).

Any taxpayer with $400 or more of net earnings from self-employment must file Schedule SE. (If you're a farmer or in business for yourself, you're considered self-employed.) Special rules apply to ministers and members of religious orders.

The SE tax is composed of two parts: a tax of 12.4% for old age, survivor and disability insurance (OASDI), and a tax of 2.9% for health insurance (*i.e.,* Medicare). The amount of income subject to the OASDI tax is capped, and the maximum changes each year; for 2002, the maximum income subject to OASDI is $84,900. The income subject to the Medicare tax is not limited.

If you have both *W-2* income (from working for an employer) and self-employment income, you should reduce your net self-employment income by your *W-2* income to calculate your SE tax. In addition, you'll reduce your net self-employment income by half of the SE tax that you pay. The federal Schedule SE leads you to the proper result by calculating the OASDI portion of the SE tax only on 92.35% of your net self-employment income. Finally, you are entitled to deduct half of the SE tax on your *Form 1040* as an adjustment to income.

Child Tax Credits

A tax credit will be available for each child younger than age 17 who can be claimed as a dependent. The credit is $600 though 2004 and increases to $1,000 per child by 2010. The credit allowed per child is reduced by $50 for each $1,000 (or part of $1,000) that the taxpayer's income exceeds an AGI threshold. That threshold is $110,000 for a married couple ($55,000 for married filing separately) or $75,000 for a single taxpayer.

Education Tax Credits

Two credits are available for expenses of post-secondary education. Again, income tests apply to limit or eliminate the credit actually taken.

The Hope Credit — Equal to 100% of the first $1,000 of qualified tuition and fees (not room and board) and 50% of the next $1,000 of qualifying expense, the Hope credit is subject to a maximum possible credit of $1,500 and is available only for the first two years of post-secondary education for a given student.

The Lifetime Learning Credit — Equal to 20% of the first $5,000 of qualifying expense (increasing to $10,000 in 2003), the Lifetime Learning Credit carries no limit on the number of years you can claim it.

The Hope credit is based on an eligible student and his or her expenses, while the Lifetime Learning credit is based on expenses paid by the taxpayer. Additionally, you cannot claim both credits for the same student in one year. Finally, you cannot claim either credit in any year that you have withdrawn money from an educational IRA and excluded the appreciation on the contributions from taxation.

The credits are available for expenses paid on behalf of the taxpayer, spouse or a dependent. Both credits are phased out based on AGI limits of $82,100 – $102,000 for joint returns and $41,000 – $51,000 for other returns.

New Saver's Credit

For 2002 through 2006, taxpayers within certain income levels will have a new credit designed as an incentive to save for their retirement. For eligible taxpayers, the credit will be based on up to the first $2,000 they contribute to IRAs, 401(k) savings plans and other retirement plans. The credit rate — 50%, 20% or 10% — depends on your filing status and AGI. The maximum credit is $1,000. The availability of the credit is phased out for married taxpayers filing a joint return at AGIs above $50,000, for persons filing as head of household with income above $37,500 and for all other taxpayers with AGIs above $25,000. You must be at least age 18, not a full-time student, and not claimed as a dependent on another person's return in order to take advantage of this credit.

Dependent-Care Tax Credit

If you maintain a household that includes a dependent under age 13, a spouse or dependent incapable of self-care, or other qualifying person, a credit is available for up to 30% of eligible child-care and dependent-care expenses. To claim the credit you must have paid a caregiver to care for your child or qualifying person so that you (and your spouse if filing a joint return) could work or look for work during the year. In 2002, the amount of employment-related expenses is limited to $2,400 for one qualifying individual or $4,800 for two or more. However, for tax years after 2002, the limits rise to $3,000 and $6,000 and the maximum rate increases from 30% to 35%. Therefore, the maximum credit available after 2002 will increase to $1,050 if there is one qualifying person ($2,100, if two or more persons) from the current maximum of $720 ($1,440, if two or more).

The current 30% credit rate is reduced, but not below 20%, by one percent for each $2,000 (or fraction thereof) of AGI above $10,000. This phase-down of the credit is also liberalized after 2002. The table below reflects the current dependent-care tax credit rates, as well as the rates after 2002.

Dependent-Care Tax Credit Rates

2002 Total Family AGI*	2002 Tax Credit	2003 and Later Total Family AGI*	2003 and Later Tax Credit
Up to $10,000	30%	Up to $15,000	35%
$10,001 – 12,000	29%	$15,001 – 17,000	34%
$12,001 – 14,000	28%	$17,001 – 19,000	33%
$14,001 – 16,000	27%	$19,001 – 21,000	32%
$16,001 – 18,000	26%	$21,001 – 23,000	31%
$18,001 – 20,000	25%	$23,001 – 25,000	30%
$20,001 – 22,000	24%	$25,001 – 27,000	29%
$22,001 – 24,000	23%	$27,001 – 29,000	28%
$24,001 – 26,000	22%	$29,001 – 31,000	27%
$26,001 – 28,000	21%	$31,001 – 33,000	26%
$28,001 and up	20%	$33,001 – 35,000	25%
		$35,001 – 37,000	24%
		$37,001 – 39,000	23%
		$39,001 – 41,000	22%
		$41,001 – 43,000	21%
		$43,001 and up	20%

* AGI (adjusted gross income) excludes any tax-deductible IRA contributions, before-tax savings/thrift plan contributions or alimony paid.

An alternative to taking the dependent-care credit is to fund a dependent-care spending account if this vehicle is available through your employer. When you use a dependent-care spending account, you pay for dependent-care expenses on a tax-advantaged basis with dollars you've contributed to your account from your wages on a pre-tax basis. (Flexible spending accounts, including dependent-care accounts, are discussed later in this chapter.) Expenses reimbursed from your spending account cannot be used for determining the federal tax credit. The worksheet below will help you determine whether you'll get a better tax break from the dependent-care tax credit or from a dependent-care spending account.

Federal Dependent-Care Tax Credit *vs.* Dependent-Care Spending Account

1. $ ____________ (per week) x ____________ (weeks) = $ ____________ (A)

2. ____________ (federal tax rate) % + 7.65% (Social Security tax rate) = $ ____________ (B) %

3. $ ____________ (Line 1(A)) x ____________ (Line 2(B)) = $ ____________

4. $ ____________ (Line 1(A)) x ____________ (tax credit rate) = $ ____________

Which is larger — Line 3 or Line 4?

If *Line 3* is larger, you'll probably get a better tax break using a dependent-care spending account.

If *Line 4* is larger, the federal dependent-care tax credit probably will be better for you situation.

Line 1: Estimate your annual child-care expenses. Multiply your weekly dependent-care costs by the number of weeks you use the care. Don't count vacations and other times during the year when you don't have to pay for dependent care.

Line 2: Estimate your federal tax rate. Find your federal tax rate in the tax rate schedules earlier in this chapter. Then add the Social Security tax rate of 7.65% (In 2002, you'll pay Social Security tax on the first $84,900 you earn, and a 1.45% tax on the rest. This doesn't include the tax break you might receive from your state taxes.)

Line 3: Calculate your tax break using a dependent-care spending account. Multiply Line 1A (but not more than $5,000) by Line 2B.

Line 4: Calculate your tax break using the federal dependent-care tax credit. Multiply Line 1A (but not more than the IRS limits of $2,400 for one child or $4,800 for two or more children in 2002) by your tax-credit percentage from the table on page 88.

Tax Withholding

Smart tax planning involves matching, as closely as possible, the amount you owe the IRS with the amount you pay through tax withholding and estimated payments. If you pay in too much, you get a refund. That may feel good momentarily, but a tax refund is not a windfall — it's just money you never should have paid to Uncle Sam in the first place. Many people deliberately have excess money withheld from their earnings as a way to force themselves to save. The problem with this approach is that the government does not pay interest on your tax withholdings. A better way to save would be to have money automatically transferred from your checking account to your savings account each month.

If you owe the IRS a large amount on April 15th, it's usually the result of claiming too many withholding exemptions. Or, if you are in the 30% or higher tax bracket, you may be underwithheld because you received a bonus or other single-sum payment withheld at a flat 27% rate. The frustration resulting from a surprise tax bill can be compounded by a penalty for underwithholding.

Minimum Withholding Requirements

You may be required to pay an underwithholding penalty if your balance due is greater than $1,000. To satisfy the minimum withholding requirements and avoid this penalty, you must:

- complete an accurate IRS *Form W-4;* and
- meet certain minimum withholding requirements.

Most taxpayers can do so by paying the lesser of:

- 90% of your current year's tax liability (90% test); or
- 100% of last year's tax liability (100% test).

You should plan to withhold either 100% of last year's tax liability (unless last year's AGI was more than $150,000) or 95% (not 90%) of the liability you project for this year, whichever is less. That way you'll have a cushion in case your tax projection is off. Likewise, if you have to make estimated tax payments, pay 35% (not 25%) in the first quarter, 30% in the second quarter, 25% in the third quarter and 10% in the fourth quarter.

Special Consideration:

Qualified "100% Test" for Some Taxpayers

You might not be able to use the 100% test if your AGI on last year's return is over $150,000. For such taxpayers, the 100% test has been modified. The percentage of the prior year's tax that must be paid is 110% for 2001, 112% for 2002 and 110% for 2003 and beyond. To avoid an underwithholding penalty, these taxpayers must pay either 90% of their current year's tax liability or the necessary percentage of the prior year's tax liability.

Withholding Tips

Here are some tips on managing your withholding. For more information, including details on estimated tax payments, ask the IRS for *Publication 505, Tax Withholding and Estimated Tax.*

Wages — *Form W-4*

Lower allowances	=	Higher withholding
Higher allowances	=	Lower withholding

Form W-4 — To adjust your withholding, fill out a new IRS *Form W-4.* Decreasing the number of allowances increases the amount taken out of each paycheck, while increasing the number of allowances will decrease the amount taken out of each paycheck. Use the worksheet included with *Form W-4* to figure out how many allowances you should claim.

Two-Earner Families — When both spouses work, they're often underwithheld based on the "married" withholding rates. To compensate, you can have your withholding based on the higher "single" rates. Or you can specify that an additional amount be withheld from each paycheck.

27% Statutory Withholding — Federal law requires your employer to withhold a minimum of 27% on most bonus, incentive compensation or other single-sum payments.

20% Mandatory Withholding — Federal law requires your employer to withhold 20% of most non-annuity distributions from qualified retirement plans. But you can avoid the 20% withholding if you make a "direct rollover" to an IRA.

Tax-Saving Strategies: 11 Tax Tips

There is no magic to saving taxes — it's just a matter of understanding some basic strategies. These strategies focus on deferring, shifting and excluding income, and taking advantage of legitimate tax deductions. Read each Tax Tip and adjust your projection on the *Federal Income Tax Worksheet* when you find items that help you save taxes.

Tax Tip No. 1: *Defer Income* — Take Advantage of Tax-Deferred Retirement Plans

Company-Sponsored Savings/Thrift Plans — Reduce your taxable wages without taking a cut in pay by making before-tax contributions to your company's 401(k) savings plan (or deductible IRA contributions, if eligible). Before-tax contributions allow you to avoid current taxes while accumulating retirement savings on a tax-deferred basis. As the illustration below shows, saving on a before-tax basis rather than on an after-tax basis can actually *improve* your current cash flow.

Before-Tax *vs.* After-Tax Savings: Impact on Cash Flow

	Before-Tax	*vs.*	After-Tax
Annual Salary	$40,000		$40,000
Before-tax Contributions @ 8%	(3,200)		(0)
Gross Income	$36,800		$40,000
Federal Taxes*	(4,203)		(5,067)
After-tax Contributions @ 8%	(0)		(3,200)
Net Salary After Taxes	$32,597		$31,733
Tax Savings/Increased Cash Flow		**$864**	

* Based on 2002 rates for a single taxpayer using the standard deduction and one personal exemption.

INCOME TAXES

Special Consideration:

Access to Before-Tax Savings Plan Contributions

Distributions of before-tax contributions are restricted until the earliest of retirement, death, disability, termination of employment or age 59½. Unless your company's plan has a loan or withdrawal provision, the only way to access these funds is to qualify under the plan's "hardship withdrawal" rules. If you take a withdrawal or default on your loan payment, you'll pay regular income taxes on the amount withdrawn. If under age 59½, you also may owe additional tax of 10%. Saving on a before-tax basis offers a great opportunity to defer taxes, but if you'll need access to your funds in one to five years, saving your money on an after-tax basis may be better.

IRA or After-Tax Company Savings Plan Contributions — If you aren't eligible to deduct your IRA contributions, it may still make sense to make non-deductible contributions because the earnings compound tax-deferred (or, in a Roth IRA, tax-free). Similarly, if you cannot make further before-tax contributions to your company savings plan, it may be wise to make after-tax contributions, even if you qualify for a Roth IRA. Even if you don't qualify for a Roth IRA and future tax rates increase, a nondeductible IRA or after-tax contribution can be a more attractive investment than tax-exempt bonds. In fact, the longer the deferral period, the more attractive these options become.

Nondeductible IRA *vs.* Tax-Exempt Bonds

$3,000 invested each year

	Value in 10 Years	Value in 20 Years
Nondeductible IRA (8%)		
Value before taxes	$43,460	$137,286
Value after taxes at		
27% tax rate	39,826	116,419
30% tax rate	39,422	114,100
35% tax rate	38,749	110,236
40% tax rate	38,076	106,372
50% tax rate	36,730	98,643
Tax-Exempt Bonds (4.5%)	$36,865	$94,114

Note: If you contribute to a Roth IRA, the value after taxes for a qualifying distribution will equal the "Value Before Taxes" entry.

Tax Tip No. 2: *Shift Income* — Use Appreciated Investments for Charitable Giving

When you give appreciated assets you have held for more than one year to a charity, you avoid paying the capital gains tax and you can deduct the value of the property at the time of your donation. For example, suppose you want to give $500 to your favorite charity, and you have shares of stock worth $500 you originally purchased for $100. Here are three options:

Option No. 1: Give Cash			
Write a check for	$500	Your out-of-pocket cost	$500
Your tax deduction	$500	Charity receives	$500
Option No. 2: Sell Stock, Give Cash			
You sell stock worth	$500	Your tax deduction	$500
Your cost or basis	(100)	Your out-of-pocket cost *(cost plus taxes)*	$180
Capital Gain	$400		
Taxes @ 20%	$ 80	Charity receives	$500
Option No. 3: Give Stock			
Give charity stock worth	$500	Your out-of-pocket cost	$100
Your tax deduction	$500	Charity receives	$500

Option No. 3 makes the most financial sense. In each of the three options the charity receives the same amount, and the tax deduction is the same. But Option No. 3 has the lowest out-of-pocket cost. Although the example focuses on a gift of stock, the rules apply to gifts of other appreciated capital-gain property as well, such as mutual-fund shares.

If you believe your investment will continue to grow, use the cash you would have given the charity to repurchase the same investment. In effect, this strategy allows you to increase your basis in the investment. You'll probably have to pay transaction costs (commissions) to repurchase the investment, but they are likely to be less than the tax savings.

Special Consideration:

Charitable Gifts of Stock

To receive a charitable-contribution deduction for the current year, make sure the stock is registered in the charity's name by December 31. Ask either your stockbroker or the charity for details on how to complete the transfer. Your tax deduction is based on the average of the high and low price for the stock on the date of the transfer.

Tax Tip No. 3: ***Exclude Income*** **— Contribute to a Roth IRA**

Contributions — Taxpayers can contribute to a type of IRA known as a "Roth IRA" subject to AGI limitations. Contributions to Roth IRAs are not deductible and provide no immediate tax benefit.

The maximum annual contribution to a Roth IRA is $3,000 beginning in 2002, but any amount contributed to a regular IRA counts against the $3,000-per-year maximum. The opportunity to contribute to a Roth IRA is phased out for a single taxpayer with AGI between $95,000 and $110,000 and for a married couple with AGI between $150,000 and $160,000.

Earnings — All earnings in the Roth IRA are tax-deferred.

Withdrawals — "Qualified distributions" from Roth IRAs are not taxable. A qualified distribution is one made:

- after age 59½;
- after death or because of a disability; or
- on a limited basis for first-time homebuyers.

However, a qualified distribution cannot occur until at least five years following the year in which a contribution first is made to the Roth IRA. (For example, if you made a contribution to a Roth IRA in 1998, the earliest you can receive a qualified distribution is the year 2003.)

With respect to qualified distributions for first-time homebuyers, the following conditions must be met:

- the buyer can be you or your spouse, or an ancestor or descendant of either of you;
- the buyers cannot have owned a home in the two years preceding the acquisition;
- the maximum that can be withdrawn over the lifetime of the IRA owner is $10,000; and
- the IRA distribution must be used within 120 days to pay acquisition costs for the principal residence of the buyers.

Conversion — If you have an existing regular (or rollover) IRA, you may be able to convert it to a Roth IRA. Such a conversion requires you to recognize the taxable value of your IRA and pay tax on that amount now, thereby allowing any future growth in its value to be tax-free, if received in a qualified distribution. However, this conversion opportunity isn't available to you in any year that your AGI exceeds $100,000. (Note that the income from the conversion is not counted in determining your AGI for purposes of the $100,000 limitation.)

If you have an IRA and are eligible to convert it to a Roth IRA, you should review the financial implications of a conversion carefully. By converting, you are choosing to pay tax sooner than you have to, and in return you have the prospect of tax-free growth on your money going forward. Depending on current and future income-tax rates, whether your existing IRA includes nondeductible contributions, the rate of return on your investments and the length of time before you need/want to use the money, a conversion may or may not be attractive. Before making a decision to convert, you should consider all these issues and/or consult a tax or financial advisor.

If you qualify to contribute to a Roth IRA, here are some points to consider in weighing whether you should do so:

- You should first be sure to contribute enough to your company savings plan to get the maximum possible employer matching contribution.
- You generally should contribute as much as possible to your company savings plan on a pre-tax basis, because the immediate income-tax benefit can assist you in meeting other financial goals.

- Contributions to your company savings plan (either pre-tax or after-tax) are done through payroll deduction, which maximizes the convenience of your retirement savings strategy.
- The younger you are, the greater is the potential value of the tax-free growth in a Roth IRA.
- The higher the rate of return you expect to earn on your money, the greater is the potential value of a Roth IRA.

IRS *Form 8606* is used to report not only nondeductible IRA contributions, but also conversions from traditional to Roth IRAs, distributions from Roth IRAs and distributions from Coverdell ESAs.

Tax Tip No. 4: *Exclude Income* — Consider a Tax-Free Investment

Should you invest in taxable or tax-exempt securities or mutual funds? It depends on your combined federal and state "marginal" tax rate (the percentage at which your next $1 of income will be taxed). To see if it makes sense to invest in tax-exempt instruments, use the following worksheets:

I. Determine Your Effective Marginal Tax Rate	Example	You
A. Your Marginal Federal Tax Rate	27%	_____ %
B. Your Marginal State Rate	5%	_____ %
C. Impact of Federal Deduction for State Taxes [1 – A] (1 – .27)	x 73%	x _____ %
D. Effective Marginal State Tax Rate [B x C] (.05 x .73)	3.7%	_____ %
E. Combined Marginal Federal and State Tax Rate [A + D] (.27 + .037)	30.7%	_____ %

Suppose you could invest in a tax-exempt money-market fund (holding instruments only of your state of residence) paying 3.5%, or in a bank account or other taxable money market fund paying 5.25%. Which is better?

II. Compare Taxable and Tax-exempt Yields	Example	You
F. Tax-Exempt Yield Available to You	3.5%	_____ %
G. Subtract Line E from 1. [1 – E] (1 – .307)	69.3%	_____ %
H. Tax-Equivalent Yields [F ÷ G] (.035 ÷ .693)	5.1%	_____ %

In this example, a 3.5% tax-exempt rate is equal to a 5.1% taxable rate. Since the taxable money market fund is paying more than 5.1%, you're better off investing in it. If the taxable money market fund was paying less than 5.1%, you would be better off investing in the tax-exempt investment. For people in one of the higher tax brackets, a tax-exempt investment usually will yield a greater after-tax return. Below is a table showing the tax-equivalent yields at the various federal income tax rates (effectively disregarding the idea of using a single-state fund to avoid state income taxes on the "tax-exempt" fund).

Tax-Equivalent Yield Chart

Tax Rate	Tax-Exempt Yields 2.00%	2.50%	3.00%	3.50%	4.00%	4.50%	5.00%	5.50%
10.00%	2.22%	2.78%	3.33%	3.89%	4.44%	5.00%	5.56%	6.11%
15.00%	2.35%	2.94%	3.53%	4.12%	4.71%	5.29%	5.88%	6.47%
27.00%	2.74%	3.42%	4.11%	4.79%	5.48%	6.16%	6.85%	7.53%
30.00%	2.86%	3.57%	4.29%	5.00%	5.71%	6.43%	7.14%	7.86%
35.00%	3.08%	3.85%	4.62%	5.38%	6.15%	6.92%	7.69%	8.46%
38.60%	3.26%	4.07%	4.89%	5.70%	6.51%	7.33%	8.14%	8.96%

Tax Tip No. 5: *Exclude Income* — Take Advantage of Flexible Spending Accounts

If your employer offers reimbursement or "flexible spending" accounts for health care and/or dependent care, you can contribute before-tax dollars to pay for certain expenses. Funds in these accounts are subject to the "use-it-or-lose-it" rule. But remember, you're cushioned by the tax savings, and the tax savings is permanent!

Suppose you incur unreimbursed medical expenses of $500 this year. Paying the expenses out of pocket means the cost is $500.

Alternatively, you could set aside $500 in a health-care spending account. If you're in the 27% federal tax bracket, you'll save $135 in federal income taxes ($500 x 27%). You'll also save $38 or 7.65% in FICA taxes, bringing the total tax savings to $173. And depending on where you live, you may save state income taxes, too. Excluding the effect of state taxes, using the account costs only $327 to pay the expenses.

Now suppose you had only $400 of unreimbursed medical expenses during the year. The law requires you to forfeit the remaining $100 in the spending account. Was it smart to use the account? Absolutely! You saved $173 in federal taxes alone, so you're still $73 ahead.

You can enroll in or adjust your health-care or dependent-care flexible spending account only during your company's annual open enrollment period or when you experience a "qualifying life event," such as the birth of a child, marriage, divorce, death, etc.

Tax Tip No. 6: Restructure Your Debt and Pay Off Personal Interest Loans

Interest on home-equity debt under $100,000 generally is deductible. A home-equity loan or line of credit can be used in many states to refinance other debt, which can be financially advantageous because the interest on loans such as credit-card and automobile debt is nondeductible. Make certain the loan is secured by your home or secondary residence; it should also be properly recorded as a lien interest under local law. But be sure to shop for the best deal. A low-cost student or auto loan may be more cost-effective than a deductible (but higher-cost) home-equity loan.

From a tax viewpoint, home-equity debt offers a way to finance purchases without losing your tax deduction. Nevertheless, debt is still debt. If you take out a home-equity line of credit, you should be aware of the following:

- Many lines of credit are *interest-only* loans for some period of time: Your monthly payments are never applied to the principal.
- Most of these loans charge interest at a variable above the prime rate. Look for a home-equity line of credit that has a lifetime cap; you should know the maximum interest rate you can be charged over the life of the loan.
- A number of fees (points, recording fee, mortgage tax, etc.) may apply. Be sure to find out what costs are involved.
- Make sure you are disciplined enough to pay off the debt — your home is on the line!

Tax Tip No. 7: Deduct Mortgage Interest and Points

Financing your home often requires the payment of "points" to the lender. When you secure the initial mortgage to buy your home, any points you pay are deductible in the year paid. In contrast, for most refinancings, points can only be deducted over the life of the loan. For example, you can deduct 1/30 of the points per year when refinancing a 30-year mortgage. The only exception to this is when you're using the proceeds from the refinancing to make improvements. Any points not deducted by the time the home is sold or the mortgage is refinanced a second time may be deducted that year in a lump sum. [See IRS *Publication 936, Home Mortgage Interest Deduction*, for more information.]

Tax Tip No. 8: "Bunch" Two Years' Worth of Miscellaneous Deductions Into One

Because miscellaneous deductions are deductible only to the extent they exceed 2% of your adjusted gross income, time the payment of these expenses carefully. It is usually better to pay the rental fee on a safe-deposit box for two years at once in a year when your income is lower. Tax rules prohibit distortion of income and expenses, so you cannot deduct prepaid expenses more than one year in advance. See the itemized deduction section in the Worksheet Notes earlier in this chapter for a list of common miscellaneous deductions.

Tax Tip No. 9: Turn a Mutual Fund Sales Charge Into an Immediate Tax Loss

If you plan to invest in mutual fund "A" — which carries a 3% load and is one of a family of mutual funds — first consider investing the money instead in mutual fund "B" (also a 3% load fund and member of the same "family"). Be sure to apply for the telephone-switching option when you open the account. Then, after 90 days or more, switch from fund "B" to fund "A."

This might create a short-term capital loss when you sell fund "B." Most mutual fund families do not charge an additional 3% when you switch into fund "A," and any short-term capital loss will reduce your taxable income for the year. However, tax law requires you to wait at least 90 days to make the switch. If you do it sooner, the 3% load on fund "B" is included in the cost of the shares, and no "swap loss" is available.

If you plan on using this technique, the category of investment assets you use can increase or decrease your tax loss. For example, if fund A is a bond fund and fund B is an international stock fund, the fluctuation in fund B during the 90-day waiting period could increase or decrease the tax loss. There may even be a taxable gain in fund B. Due to the possibility of market fluctuations, try to get funds A and B in the same investment category.

Tax Tip No. 10: Make Charitable Contributions of Used Clothing and Household Goods

During the year, collect clothing and miscellaneous items you no longer use. Then make a list of the items, including a per-item estimate of market value, and give the items to a charity. You are entitled to a charitable deduction equal to the property's current value. If you donate more than $250 to a charity, federal law requires you to have a receipt in order to claim the deduction. In addition, if the total value of *all* noncash contributions exceeds $500 in one year, you must complete IRS *Form 8283* — Noncash Charitable Contributions. (See IRS *Publication 526, Charitable Contributions,* for more information.)

If you are in the 27% bracket, a donation valued at $400 saves you $108 in federal taxes. And, depending on the state law, you'll probably reduce your state taxes as well. Another approach is to have a garage or yard sale, then donate the proceeds to a favorite charity.

Tax Tip No. 11: Forgotten Requirements

Today, good tax planning requires compliance with IRS rules. Here is our checklist of most-overlooked requirements.

- **Social Security Numbers** — You need one for any dependent who is listed on your tax return. If you need a number, request it now by visiting your local Social Security office or calling 800/772-1213 and completing *Form SS5*. If your dependents have not been assigned a number before you file, attach to your return *Form CA-5028* (Receipt for Application for Number). If you pay alimony, you'll also need a Social Security number for the recipient of your payments.

- **IRS *Form 2119* Sale of Residence** — Keep forms from any sale before 1998 as long as you own your home. The form reports the deferral of any gain on the sale of your prior residence. Also, retain any supporting documents, such as closing statements, as well as receipts and records that relate to the capital improvements.

- **IRS *Form 8606* Nondeductible IRA** — File this form each year to document an after-tax contribution to an IRA. Keep a copy for the life of the IRA. Also, retain IRS *Form 5498,* which you'll receive from the IRA custodian. It's used to report both contributions made to an IRA and the fair-market value of any IRA balance as of December 31.

- **IRS *Form 4868* Filing Extension** — You can request an extension until August 15 by filing this form with the IRS by April 15. You must pay 100% of your tax liability by the time you file the extension, or you'll face an interest penalty on the underpayment for the entire period you were late. You can request a second extension and postpone your filing date until October 15 by filing IRS *Form 2688*. State extensions are also available.

- **Cost Basis for Sale of an Asset** — If you own 300 shares of XYZ Company stock and want to sell 100, the IRS allows you to stipulate which shares you are selling. But don't wait until tax time to figure it out—identify the stock being sold at the time of the sale. If you hold the securities through a brokerage firm, give your broker specific instructions about which shares to sell and ask your broker for a written confirmation. If you don't specify which shares you're selling, the IRS imposes a first-in, first-out rule (*i.e.,* the first shares acquired are the first shares sold).

- **Statute of Limitations** — Even though the IRS generally must assess any additional tax or penalty within three years of your filing date, there are exceptions. If your gross income has been understated by more than 25%, the IRS has six years to assess additional tax. And, if you file a false or fraudulent return or fail to file at all, the IRS can assess additional taxes at any time — no statute of limitation applies. So retain your income-tax returns for at least six years, if not indefinitely, and keep all records relating to the cost of an asset for at least six years after it is sold.

Tax Rules on Home Sales

Under the old deferral-of-gain rules, when you sold your home and bought a more expensive one, any capital gain from the sale of the old house usually was deferred. In fact, assuming you purchased a more expensive residence within 24 months, the tax law required you to defer the gain. Effective for sales on or after May 7, 1997, the old rules have been repealed.

Under the new rules, you can exclude up to $250,000 ($500,000 if married filing a joint return) of gain from the sale of your primary residence if you have owned and lived in the home for at least two of the five years before the sale. No age requirement applies to this treatment, and there is no limit on the number of times gain from the sale of a principal residence can be excluded.

Note that various transition rules apply to sales between May 7, 1997, and August 5, 1997, as well as to cases involving a rollover of gain from a prior home and sales that occur because of a change in employment. Check with the IRS or your own tax advisor if these provisions might affect you.

Calculating the Gain on Your Home

The capital gain on the sale of your home is the difference between the selling price (less expenses) and the tax basis. To calculate the tax basis, take the original cost of the property and reduce it by the following items:

- capital gains realized on prior residences but not taxed;
- any depreciation deductions taken or that should have been taken on past tax returns; and
- any uninsured portion of casualty losses deducted on prior income-tax returns.

Then increase the amount by improvements, replacements or alterations that prolong the property's life, add to its value or adapt it to a different use.

Use the *Sale of Home Worksheet* to estimate the gain on your home. Following the worksheet is a list of some items that may be included in the tax basis of your home. Do not include items in the property's tax basis unless they're included in the sale. You must document these additions and improvements.

Sale of Home Worksheet

		Example		Your Situation
1.	Selling price of home.[1]	$200,000	1	
2.	Expense of sale.[2]	12,000	2	
3.	Amount realized. Subtract Line 2 from Line 1.	188,000	3	
4.	Basis of home sold.[3]	50,000	4	
5.	Gain on sale. Subtract Line 4 from Line 3.	138,000	5	
6.	Excludable amount ($250,000 if single; $500,000 if married). Assume single.	250,000	6	
7.	Taxable gain. Subtract Line 6 from Line 5 (if a negative number, enter 0).	0	7	

[1] Don't include personal property that you sold with your home.

[2] Include sales commissions, advertising and legal expenses and also any loan charges, such as points charged to the seller. Don't include fixing-up expenses.

[3] If you filed *Form 2119* when you originally bought your old home, use the adjusted basis of the new home from the last line of *Form 2119* as the starting point to figure the basis of your old home. Then, using the list provided, add any capital improvements. If you didn't file *Form 2119* when you bought your old home, use the cost of the home as the starting point.

For more information on determining the cost basis of your home, see IRS *Publication 523, Selling Your Home,* and/or *Publication 551, Basis of Assets.*

Additions and Improvements

Additions and improvements that add to the basis of your home must be items permanently attached and must either increase the home's value or extend its useful life.

Exterior

Additional acreage or lots

Building Additions

- Worksheds or outbuildings
- Aluminum siding
- Breezeway
- Garage
- Porch

Garden and Land

- Lawn sprinkler system
- Water well and pump
- Shrubs, bushes and vines
- Trees
- Plants, bulbs and seeds
- Topsoil and fill
- Grading
- Grass seed
- Fertilizers and conditioners
- Telephone and electrical outlets
- Retaining walls
- Fences and gates
- Play yard
- Driveway — paving or gravel
- Walks
- Pathways
- Barbecue pit
- Survey of property
- Roofing additions and replacements
- Flashing
- Gutters, leaders, drain pipes and dry wells
- Waterproofing
- Termite proofing
- Storm windows and doors
- Mail box
- Terraces and patios
- Cement staircases
- Swimming pool
- Lampposts

Interior

- Carpeting and padding
- Linoleum
- Flooring — wood, tile, etc.
- Stairs, new or replaced
- Ceilings (acoustical)
- Cabinets
- Closet shelves
- Bookcases, built-in furniture
- Radiator covers
- Ventilators
- Window seats
- Fireplace mantels
- Closets
- Cupboards
- Conversion of attic or basement to recreation or bedroom

Windows

- Replacement
- Screens
- Storm sash
- Window shades
- Weather stripping
- Venetian blinds

Inside Walls

- Altering or plastering
- Wood paneling
- Wall tiles

Plumbing and Sanitation

- Floor drains
- Grease traps
- Hot water tank
- Pumps
- Septic system
- Hot water pipe
- Copper tubing
- Cold water pipe
- Water supply system
- Traps
- Sump pump
- Vent pipe

Heating and Air Conditioning

- Cooling equipment
- Air conditioning
- Attic fan
- Circulating system
- Furnace and appurtenances
- Boiler
- Hot water heater
- Fireplace heater
- Radiators and valves
- Warm air grills and registers
- Space heaters
- Automatic thermostats

Electricity and Lighting

- Circuit breakers
- Fuse boxes
- Lightning rods
- Wiring system
- TV antenna and wiring

Hardware, Fixtures and Locks

- Cabinets and closets, doors, windows, curtains and draperies
- Lighting fixtures
- Sinks
- Tubs
- Ventilator
- Hamper
- Linen chute
- Supply cabinets

Kitchen

- Counter tops
- Dishwasher
- Drain boards
- Food freezer
- Sinks
- Ventilator
- Range
- Range hood
- Garbage disposal

Bathrooms

- Tub
- Tub hanger
- Tub sliding doors
- Unit heater
- Towel racks
- Shower controls
- Shower cabinet
- Mirrors
- Medicine cabinet

Communication Equipment

- Call bells or chimes
- Intercommunication system
- Telephone raceways
- Fire or burglar alarm system

Other Equipment
(if permanently attached)

- Fireplace equipment
- Workshop equipment
- Mirrors
- Dumbwaiter
- Insulation

Alternative Minimum Tax

The alternative minimum tax (AMT) was designed to ensure that at least a minimum amount of income tax is paid by all taxpayers and corporations. In essence, the AMT functions as a recapture mechanism, reclaiming some of the tax breaks available under the law. The AMT is calculated separately from, but at the same time as, your regular income tax. You pay the larger of your regular income tax or the AMT.

A taxpayer's AMT is the excess of the tentative minimum tax over the regular tax calculated using IRS *Form 1040*. The AMT is computed on IRS *Form 6251*. The calculation starts with your income (after deductions *but before personal exemptions)* from your *Form 1040* (line 37 on the 2001 form):

	Taxable Income
+/–	Adjustments to Taxable Income
+	Tax Preferences
=	Alternative Minimum Taxable Income (AMTI)
–	Exemption Amount
x	26% up to $175,000; 28% on the amount over $175,000
–	Foreign Tax Credit
=	Tentative Minimum Tax
–	Regular Tax (not including any forward-averaging tax)
=	Alternative Minimum Tax (AMT)

AMT Adjustments

Certain increases or decreases are made to taxable income to arrive at AMT income. Some adjustments that apply to individuals are outlined below:

Adjustment	Description
Standard deduction	No deduction.
Itemized deductions	Itemized deductions for taxes, certain interest and most miscellaneous deductions are not allowed. The limitation on itemized deductions for certain levels of AGI will not apply for the AMT.
Refund of taxes	Refunds of state and local income taxes are subtracted from income for AMT.
Depreciation	Depreciation for AMT might differ from the depreciation for regular tax depending on the property and the date placed in service.
Certain installment sales	Installment method generally does not apply for AMT.
Passive-activity income or loss	The difference between AMT and regular tax income or loss.
Incentive stock options	"Spread" or bargain element at exercise is added to regular income.

AMT Tax Preference Items

Tax preference items are other income items that receive special treatment under the tax law. They must be added back to the taxable income in figuring alternative minimum taxable income. Some tax preference items for individuals are listed below:

Tax Preference	Description
Certain tax-exempt interest	Interest on specified private-activity bonds.
Depletion and intangible drilling costs	This may affect taxpayers with oil and gas tax shelters.
Accelerated depreciation	Excess depreciation on real-estate investments.

AMT Exemption Amount

The AMT exemption amount is based on your filing status and your alternative minimum taxable income. The exemption amount starts to phase out if your AMTI exceeds the levels stated below:

Filing Status	Exemption Amount	AMTI/Exemption Phase-out
Married/joint	$49,000	$150,000
Single or Head of Household	$35,750	$112,500
Married/separate	$24,500	$ 75,000

AMT Credit

If you pay the AMT, a credit is allowed to the extent the AMT is attributable to deferral preferences or adjustments (like the spread from the exercise of an incentive stock option). The credit is determined by recalculating the AMT using only exclusion items. If the recomputed AMT (using only exclusion items) is less than the regular tax, the credit is equal to AMT payable. In the following year, the credit can be used to the extent that the AMT in that year is less than the regular tax in that year. After you apply your AMT credit for a particular year, any unused portion can be "carried forward" to future years. IRS *Form 8801* is used to calculate the AMT credit and credit carry-forward.

Items for Action

Knowing your tax bracket can help you make other decisions, like whether to invest in a tax-free investment or restructure your debt or exercise your stock options. Making sure your withholding is appropriate for your personal situation can often free up money to help you reach your goals. Use the following Action Items to realize your tax-planning goals. Update your income-tax projection twice each year.

For each of the following items, assign a priority based on its importance to you: A (highest), B (medium) or C (lowest). Then check off each item as it is completed.

	Priority	Completed
Projecting Your Federal Income Taxes		
❖ Use last year's tax return as a guide, but don't just copy the numbers.	______	❑
❖ Read through the worksheet notes when completing the *Federal Income Tax Worksheet.*	______	❑
❖ Account for all tax withheld and estimated payments made.	______	❑
Tax-Saving Strategies: 11 Tips		
❖ Contribute at least 6% to your company's savings plan; more if possible.	______	❑
❖ Consider making nondeductible IRA contributions, or after-tax contributions to your savings/thrift plan.	______	❑
❖ Give appreciated assets (held more than one year) instead of cash to a charity.	______	❑
❖ Consider contributing to a Roth IRA.	______	❑
❖ Open a taxable or tax-free money-market fund for emergency money and other cash balances.	______	❑
❖ Take advantage of your employer's flexible spending accounts for medical and dependent care expenses.	______	❑
❖ Avoid credit-card debt and all personal nonhousing debt.	______	❑
❖ Keep good records relating to the cost of your assets.	______	❑
Tax Rules on Home Sales		
❖ Use the *Sale of Home* worksheet to project possible income taxes.	______	❑
❖ Check IRS *Publication 523, Selling Your Home,* for information on the treatment of gains from your residence.	______	❑
Alternative Minimum Tax		
❖ Each year prepare IRS *Form 6251* to see if you're subject to the AMT.	______	❑

Resources

Internal Revenue Service

You can get free telephone assistance by calling **800/829-1040**. Additionally, the following publications are available without charge by calling the IRS at **800/829-3676** or at the IRS's Web site (**www.irs.gov**):

- Publication 1, *Your Rights As a Taxpayer*
- Publication 17, *Your Federal Income Tax*
- Publication 334, *Tax Guide for Small Businesses*
- Publication 463, *Travel, Entertainment, Gift, and Car Expenses*
- Publication 501, *Exemptions, Standard Deductions and Filing Information*
- Publication 502, *Medical and Dental Expenses*
- Publication 503, *Child and Dependent Care Expenses*
- Publication 504, *Divorced or Separated Individuals*
- Publication 505, *Tax Withholding and Estimated Tax*
- Publication 513, *Tax Information for Visitors to the U.S.*
- Publication 514, *Foreign Tax Credit for Individuals*
- Publication 521, *Moving Expenses*
- Publication 523, *Selling Your Home*
- Publication 525, *Taxable and Nontaxable Income*
- Publication 526, *Charitable Contributions*
- Publication 527, *Residential Rental Property*
- Publication 529, *Miscellaneous Deductions*
- Publication 530, *Tax Information for First Time Homeowners*
- Publication 550, *Investment Income and Expenses*
- Publication 551, *Basis of Assets*
- Publication 552, *Recordkeeping for Individuals*
- Publication 554, *Older Americans' Tax Guide*
- Publication 564, *Mutual Fund Distributions*
- Publication 575, *Pension and Annuity Income*
- Publication 590, *Individual Retirement Arrangements (IRAs)*
- Publication 915, *Social Security and Equivalent Railroad Retirement Benefits*
- Publication 919, *How Do I Adjust My Tax Withholding?*
- Publication 926, *Household Employers Tax Guide*
- Publication 929, *Tax Rules for Children and Dependents*
- Publication 936, *Home Mortgage Interest Deduction*
- Publication 968, *Tax Benefits for Adoption*
- Publication 969, *Medical Savings Accounts*
- Publication 970, *Tax Benefits for Higher Education*
- Publication 972, *Child Tax Credit*

BBB Wise Giving Alliance

4200 Wilson Boulevard, Suite 800
Arlington, VA 22203

The BBB Wise Giving Alliance collects and distributes information on hundreds of nonprofit organizations that solicit nationally or provide national or international services. The information collected includes the nature of the organizations' programs, governance, fund-raising practices and finances. The Alliance does not recommend one charity over another, but helps donors make their own decisions regarding charitable giving. Charity reports are available online at **www.give.org**. Additionally, you may obtain a free copy of the *BBB Wise Giving Guide* by requesting one by regular mail at the above address, e-mail (**give@cbbb.bbb.org**) or phone (**800/575-4483**).

CCH INCORPORATED

4025 West Peterson Avenue
Chicago, IL 60646

Use the tax guide the professionals use — CCH's *2002 U.S. Master Tax Guide* ($52). This guide reflects the tax law changes as of November 2001 and provides reliable answers to questions affecting individual and business income tax. For more information or to place your order, call CCH at **800/248-3248** or visit their Web site at **www.cch.com**.

J.K. Lasser Institute

P.O. 56540
Boulder, CO 80322

J.K. Lasser offers a monthly newsletter, J.K. LASSER's *Monthly Tax Letter*, that provides useful tax-saving tips and information (12 issues for $29.95 plus $5 shipping and handling). For $16.95 they also offer *Your Income Tax 2002*, an 800-plus-page tax guide loaded with helpful tips for preparing your 2002 income tax return. For more information or to place your order, call J.K. Lasser at **800/678-0484** or visit their Web site at **www.jklasser.com**.

The Salvation Army

Do you find it difficult to value the clothing and other household items that you donate to charity? Visit The Salvation Army's Web site at **www.salvationarmy-usaeast.org/help/valuation_guide.htm** for a listing of commonly donated items and their estimated values.

Research Institute of America (RIA)

395 Hudson Street
New York, NY 10014

As an alternative to CCH's tax guide, consider RIA's *Federal Tax Handbook* ($51.50). It provides comprehensive answers to questions on individual and corporate taxation, pension plans, employee benefits, deductions, passive losses, estate and gift taxes and much more. For more information or to place your order, call RIA at **800/950-1216** or visit their Web site at **www.riahome.com**.

Tax-Preparation Software

Consider Turbo-Tax or other popular software packages.

Investment Planning

Investment planning is probably one of the most important components of your personal financial plan. By following some basic investment strategies, you'll be able to make your money work harder so you can reach your goals more easily. Investment planning is also an important component of your retirement. During retirement, your investments are likely to produce a source of income to supplement your pension and Social Security.

Step 1: Establish Financial Goals

Before investing your money, you need to know *why* you're investing. For instance, saving for a vacation and investing for retirement require two completely different strategies. After you *identify your goals* you'll be able to select the appropriate investment mix. Each person's financial goals will be different.

Special Consideration:

Time Horizon

No matter what your financial goal is, the longer you have to reach it, the more risk you can take.

Below is a list of possible financial goals. We placed a star (*) by the goals we think are most important.

- Contribute at least 10% (or enough to receive the full company match) to your company's savings or thrift plan*
- Eliminate high-interest personal debt*
- Save for your or your children's education*
- Increase your retirement savings*
- Save for a down payment on a house
- Pay cash for a new car
- Save for a vacation
- Buy new furniture

These are only a few financial goals. Adding yours to the list will help you begin *your* investment plan.

Your Goals

Don't feel discouraged if attaining your goals seems a long way off. You can reach them gradually. For example, in order to contribute at least 10% to your company's savings or thrift plan, increase your contribution percentage by 1% each January. Keep doing this each year until you reach 10% or higher.

Taking a pro-active approach will help you meet your goals. When you've paid off your car loan, continue to make the same monthly payment to a money market account. By saving your car-loan payment, you may be able to purchase your next car for cash, or, at least, reduce the amount of your next auto loan.

Special Consideration:

Savings-Plan Contributions

Your primary objective should be to contribute enough to receive your employer's full company match on savings-plan contributions.

You also should establish a rate-of-return objective. In other words, figure out what you must earn on the money once it's invested. There are two different ways to determine your required rate of return.

Periodic Saving: A savings or investment program where you're investing a constant amount periodically (monthly, quarterly, annually) with the goal of achieving a specific balance at some point in the future.

Lump-Sum Saving: The investment of a lump sum today with the goal of achieving a specific balance at some point in the future.

Use the following chart to calculate a savings goal. Assume that you want to buy a car in seven years. You know the price of the car today, but you must determine the future price.

	Example	Your Situation
Line 1: Amount of purchase today.	$20,000	________
Line 2: Assumed inflation rate.	4%	________
Line 3: Years to goal.	7	________
Line 4: Use the *Lump-Sum Future Value Chart* to find the factor (look down the column keyed to the inflation rate listed on Line 2 until you get to the year listed on Line 3).	1.3159	________
Line 5: Amount needed in the future to reach your goal (multiply Line 1 by Line 4).	$26,318	________

Lump-Sum Future Value

If you have $10,000, and you want it to grow to $25,000 in 10 years, what after-tax rate of return must you earn? The *Interest Rate for Lump-Sum Future Value* worksheet can help you answer this question.

Interest Rate for Lump-Sum Future Value

	Example	Your Situation
Line 1: How much money will you need in the future?	$25,000	________
Line 2: How many years do you have to reach this goal?	10	________
Line 3: What is the lump sum's current value?	$10,000	________
Line 4: Divide Line 1 by Line 3 ($25,000 ÷ $10,000).	2.5	________
Line 5: Go to the *Lump-Sum Future Value Chart* on the next page to find the interest rate (look for the year listed on Line 2, then read across to find the factor closest to the number on Line 4.)	10%	________

Using our example, you must earn an annual after-tax rate of return of almost 10% to have $25,000 at the end of 10 years.

The *Lump-Sum Future Value Chart* can also be used to find the future value of a single lump sum. Use the *Future Value of a Lump Sum* worksheet to help you with this calculation.

Future Value of a Lump Sum

	Example	Your Situation
Line 1: How much money is invested?	$5,000	________
Line 2: What is the assumed after-tax interest rate?	8%	________
Line 3: How many years will the money be invested?	15	________
Line 4: Find the factor from the *Lump-Sum Future Value Chart* (look down the column for the number of years listed on Line 2 until you get to the row listed on Line 3).	3.1722	________
Line 5: Multiply Line 1 by Line 4 to find the future value.	$15,861	________

Based on the assumption of $5,000 invested earning 8% after taxes, you will have $15,861 at the end of 15 years.

Lump-Sum Future Value Chart

Year	Rate 3%	4%	5%	6%	7%	8%	9%	10%	11%	12%	13%	14%
1	1.0300	1.0400	1.0500	1.0600	1.0700	1.0800	1.0900	1.1000	1.1100	1.1200	1.1300	1.1400
2	1.0609	1.0816	1.1025	1.1236	1.1449	1.1664	1.1881	1.2100	1.2321	1.2544	1.2769	1.2996
3	1.0927	1.1249	1.1576	1.1910	1.2250	1.2597	1.2950	1.3310	1.3676	1.4049	1.4429	1.4815
4	1.1255	1.1699	1.2155	1.2625	1.3108	1.3605	1.4116	1.4641	1.5181	1.5735	1.6305	1.6890
5	1.1593	1.2167	1.2763	1.3382	1.4026	1.4693	1.5386	1.6105	1.6851	1.7623	1.8424	1.9254
6	1.1941	1.2653	1.3401	1.4185	1.5007	1.5869	1.6771	1.7716	1.8704	1.9738	2.0820	2.1950
7	1.2299	1.3159	1.4071	1.5036	1.6058	1.7138	1.8280	1.9487	2.0762	2.2107	2.3526	2.5023
8	1.2668	1.3686	1.4775	1.5938	1.7182	1.8509	1.9926	2.1436	2.3045	2.4760	2.6584	2.8526
9	1.3048	1.4233	1.5513	1.6895	1.8385	1.9990	2.1719	2.3579	2.5580	2.7731	3.0040	3.2519
10	1.3439	1.4802	1.6289	1.7908	1.9672	2.1589	2.3674	2.5937	2.8394	3.1058	3.3946	3.7072
11	1.3842	1.5395	1.7103	1.8983	2.1049	2.3316	2.5804	2.8531	3.1518	3.4785	3.8359	4.2262
12	1.4258	1.6010	1.7959	2.0122	2.2522	2.5182	2.8127	3.1384	3.4985	3.8960	4.3345	4.8179
13	1.4685	1.6651	1.8856	2.1329	2.4098	2.7196	3.0658	3.4523	3.8833	4.3635	4.8980	5.4924
14	1.5126	1.7317	1.9799	2.2609	2.5785	2.9372	3.3417	3.7975	4.3104	4.8871	5.5348	6.2613
15	1.5580	1.8009	2.0789	2.3966	2.7590	3.1722	3.6425	4.1772	4.7846	5.4736	6.2543	7.1379
16	1.6047	1.8730	2.1829	2.5404	2.9522	3.4259	3.9703	4.5950	5.3109	6.1304	7.0673	8.1372
17	1.6528	1.9479	2.2920	2.6928	3.1588	3.7000	4.3276	5.0545	5.8951	6.8660	7.9861	9.2765
18	1.7024	2.0258	2.4066	2.8543	3.3799	3.9960	4.7171	5.5599	6.5436	7.6900	9.0243	10.5752
19	1.7535	2.1068	2.5270	3.0256	3.6165	4.3157	5.1417	6.1159	7.2633	8.6128	10.1974	12.0557
20	1.8061	2.1911	2.6533	3.2071	3.8697	4.6610	5.6044	6.7275	8.0623	9.6463	11.5231	13.7435
21	1.8603	2.2788	2.7860	3.3996	4.1406	5.0338	6.1088	7.4002	8.9492	10.8038	13.0211	15.6676
22	1.9161	2.3699	2.9253	3.6035	4.4304	5.4365	6.6586	8.1403	9.9336	12.1003	14.7138	17.8610
23	1.9736	2.4647	3.0715	3.8197	4.7405	5.8715	7.2579	8.9543	11.0263	13.5523	16.6266	20.3616
24	2.0328	2.5633	3.2251	4.0489	5.0724	6.3412	7.9111	9.8497	12.2392	15.1786	18.7881	23.2122
25	2.0938	2.6658	3.3864	4.2919	5.4274	6.8485	8.6231	10.8347	13.5855	17.0001	21.2305	26.4619
26	2.1566	2.7725	3.5557	4.5494	5.8074	7.3964	9.3992	11.9182	15.0799	19.0401	23.9905	30.1666
27	2.2213	2.8834	3.7335	4.8223	6.2139	7.9881	10.2451	13.1100	16.7386	21.3249	27.1093	34.3899
28	2.2879	2.9987	3.9201	5.1117	6.6488	8.6271	11.1671	14.4210	18.5799	23.8839	30.6335	39.2045
29	2.3566	3.1187	4.1161	5.4184	7.1143	9.3173	12.1722	15.8631	20.6237	26.7499	34.6158	44.6931
30	2.4273	3.2434	4.3219	5.7435	7.6123	10.0627	13.2677	17.4494	22.8923	29.9599	39.1159	50.9502

Periodic Saving

Assume you've set a goal of having $30,000 in 10 years. What after-tax rate of return must you earn if you save $2,000 each year for 10 years? Use the *Required Rate of Return for Periodic Saving* worksheet below to find the answer.

Required Rate of Return for Periodic Saving

	Example	Your Situation
Line 1: How much money is needed in the future?	$30,000	________
Line 2: How many years will it take to reach your goal?	10	________
Line 3: How much will be saved each year?	$2,000	________
Line 4: Divide Line 1 by Line 3 ($30,000 ÷ $2,000).	15	________
Line 5: Use the *Periodic Saving Chart* to find the interest rate (look down the left column of the table for the year listed on Line 2, then read across to find the factor closest to the number on Line 4).	8% – 9%	________

In our example, 15 falls between 8% and 9%. This is the after-tax rate of return you must earn to meet your goal. What type of investment will yield 8% to 9% after taxes? More on this later in this chapter.

The *Periodic Saving Chart* also can be used to find the future value of a series of equal payments. For example, if you invest $1,200 each year and earn a 7% after-tax rate of return, how much will you have in 20 years? Use the *Future Value of Periodic Saving* worksheet to find the answer.

Future Value of Periodic Saving

	Example	Your Situation
Line 1: How much will be saved or invested each year?	$1,200	________
Line 2: What is the assumed after-tax rate of return?	7%	________
Line 3: How many years will this amount be invested?	20	________
Line 4: Use the *Periodic Saving Chart* to find the factor (look down the column listed on Line 2 until you get to the row listed on Line 3).	40.9955	________
Line 5: Multiply Line 1 by Line 4 to find your future value.	$49,195	________

Our example shows that at the end of 20 years you'll have $49,195 if you invested $1,200 each year at a 7% rate of return.

Periodic Saving Chart

Year	Rate 3%	4%	5%	6%	7%	8%	9%	10%	11%	12%	13%	14%
1	1.0000	1.0000	1.0000	1.0000	1.0000	1.0000	1.0000	1.0000	1.0000	1.0000	1.0000	1.0000
2	2.0300	2.0400	2.0500	2.0600	2.0700	2.0800	2.0900	2.1000	2.1100	2.1200	2.1300	2.1400
3	3.0909	3.1216	3.1525	3.1836	3.2149	3.2464	3.2781	3.3100	3.3421	3.3744	3.4069	3.4396
4	4.1836	4.2465	4.3101	4.3746	4.4399	4.5061	4.5731	4.6410	4.7097	4.7793	4.8498	4.9211
5	5.3091	5.4163	5.5256	5.6371	5.7507	5.8666	5.9847	6.1051	6.2278	6.3528	6.4803	6.6101
6	6.4684	6.6330	6.8019	6.9753	7.1533	7.3359	7.5233	7.7156	7.9129	8.1152	8.3227	8.5355
7	7.6625	7.8983	8.1420	8.3938	8.6540	8.9228	9.2004	9.4872	9.7833	10.0890	10.4047	10.7305
8	8.8923	9.2142	9.5491	9.8975	10.2598	10.6366	11.0285	11.4359	11.8594	12.2997	12.7573	13.2328
9	10.1591	10.5828	11.0266	11.4913	11.9780	12.4876	13.0210	13.5795	14.1640	14.7757	15.4157	16.0853
10	11.4639	12.0061	12.5779	13.1808	13.8164	14.4866	15.1929	15.9374	16.7220	17.5487	18.4197	19.3373
11	12.8078	13.4864	14.2068	14.9716	15.7836	16.6455	17.5603	18.5312	19.5614	20.6546	21.8143	23.0445
12	14.1920	15.0258	15.9171	16.8699	17.8885	18.9771	20.1407	21.3843	22.7132	24.1331	25.6502	27.2707
13	15.6178	16.6268	17.7130	18.8821	20.1406	21.4953	22.9534	24.5227	26.2116	28.0291	29.9847	32.0887
14	17.0863	18.2919	19.5986	21.0151	22.5505	24.2149	26.0192	27.9750	30.0949	32.3926	34.8827	37.5811
15	18.5989	20.0236	21.5786	23.2760	25.1290	27.1521	29.3609	31.7725	34.4054	37.2797	40.4175	43.8424
16	20.1569	21.8245	23.6575	25.6725	27.8881	30.3243	33.0034	35.9497	39.1899	42.7533	46.6717	50.9804
17	21.7616	23.6975	25.8404	28.2129	30.8402	33.7502	36.9737	40.5447	44.5008	48.8837	53.7391	59.1176
18	23.4144	25.6454	28.1324	30.9057	33.9990	37.4502	41.3013	45.5992	50.3959	55.7497	61.7251	68.3941
19	25.1169	27.6712	30.5390	33.7600	37.3790	41.4463	46.0185	51.1591	56.9395	63.4397	70.7494	78.9692
20	26.8704	29.7781	33.0660	36.7856	40.9955	45.7620	51.1601	57.2750	64.2028	72.0524	80.9468	91.0249
21	28.6765	31.9692	35.7193	39.9927	44.8652	50.4229	56.7645	64.0025	72.2651	81.6987	92.4699	104.7684
22	30.5368	34.2480	38.5052	43.3923	49.0057	55.4568	62.8733	71.4027	81.2143	92.5026	105.4910	120.4360
23	32.4529	36.6179	41.4305	46.9958	53.4361	60.8933	69.5319	79.5430	91.1479	104.6029	120.2048	138.2970
24	34.4265	39.0826	44.5020	50.8156	58.1767	66.7648	76.7898	88.4973	102.1742	118.1552	136.8315	158.6586
25	36.4593	41.6459	47.7271	54.8645	63.2490	73.1059	84.7009	98.3471	114.4133	133.3339	155.6196	181.8708
26	38.5530	44.3117	51.1135	59.1564	68.6765	79.9544	93.3240	109.1818	127.9988	150.3339	176.8501	208.3327
27	40.7096	47.0842	54.6691	63.7058	74.4838	87.3508	102.7231	121.0999	143.0786	169.3740	200.8406	238.4993
28	42.9309	49.9676	58.4026	68.5281	80.6977	95.3388	112.9682	134.2099	159.8173	190.6989	227.9499	272.8892
29	45.2189	52.9663	62.3227	73.6398	87.3465	103.9659	124.1354	148.6309	178.3972	214.5828	258.5834	312.0937
30	47.5754	56.0849	66.4388	79.0582	94.4608	113.2832	136.3075	164.4940	199.0209	241.3327	293.1992	356.7868

Now that you have established your financial goal(s) and worked through the worksheets, identify the constraints that may keep you from reaching your financial goal(s).

Step 2: Identify Constraints

Personal limitations are very important when making your investment decisions. Since there are so many investment options to choose from, these limitations will help you weed out the ones you should *not* invest in.

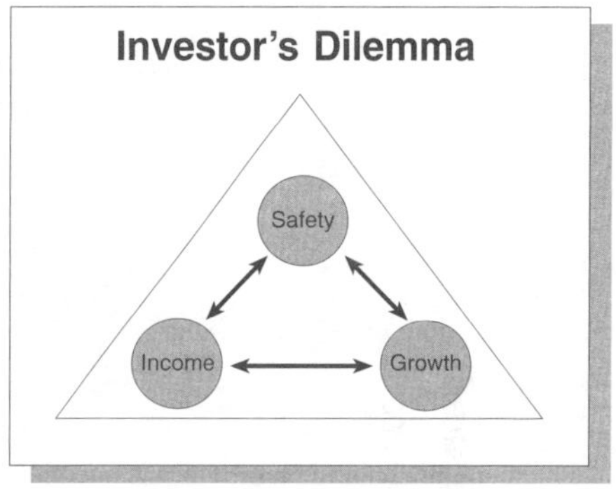

The Investor's Dilemma

All investors want a high-yielding, high-growth, very safe investment. Unfortunately, such an investment doesn't exist. As you seek safety, you move away from growth and income. Seeking income, you move away from growth and safety. Choosing growth, you lose potential for income and safety. Since you cannot have it all, you must decide which trade-offs are right for you.

Risk Tolerance

To compensate an investor for risk, any investment will provide some rate of return. The higher the level of risk, the greater the *expected* rate of return. For instance, owning stocks is riskier than owning Treasury securities. So the expected rate of return is greater on a stock investment than on a Treasury security investment.

As you determine your personal risk tolerance, you should keep the following items in mind:

Your Age — Younger investors are usually willing to take on more risk because they have a longer time horizon. They can live with the ups and downs of a risky investment expecting over time they will receive a higher rate of return. Retirees typically are more conservative because they cannot afford to lose their investment.

Personality — Some people are more aggressive than others. Some are risk-takers, while others are risk-avoiders. Ask yourself this question: "Can I sleep at night with my money in this investment?"

Future Financial Expectations — If you expect your annual income to continue to increase, you may be more comfortable with a higher level of risk than someone who expects his or her annual income to level off or decrease.

Degree of Concern About Market Fluctuations — How easily can you replace any investment loss? How calm are you about fluctuations in the market? What would you do if an investment lost money in the short term? In the long term?

In order to help you determine your risk tolerance, we have included a short quiz later in this chapter.

Time Horizon

As you review each of your investment goals, ask yourself this question: How long can I afford to keep this money invested? Your answer will guide you toward the right investment.

Short-Term — Your goal is one to five years away. Safety should be a primary concern. Possible investments include money market accounts, short-term bonds and CDs.

The Stock Market is a Roller Coaster — Be Prepared!

S&P 500 Performance from December 1949 to December 2001

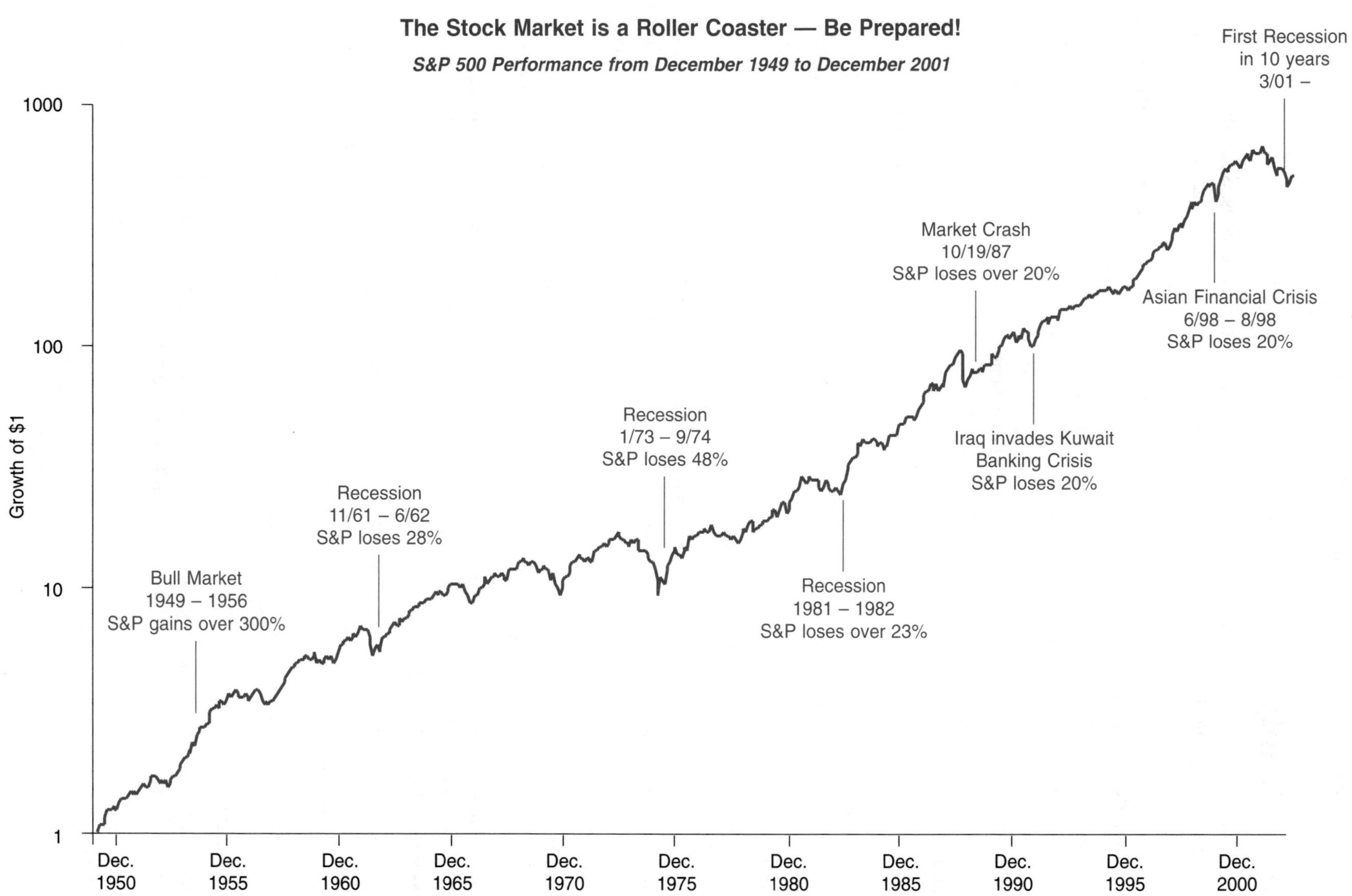

Medium-Term — Your goal is six to 10 years away. You may have enough time to invest for growth, but you don't want to take too many chances. In this case, consider income-producing investments. High-dividend stocks, as well as medium-term bonds, would be suitable.

Long-Term — Your goal is more than 10 years away. The main focus of your investments should be growth. A well-diversified stock portfolio should work best. As the *Historical Before-Tax Returns* chart shows, stocks have provided a greater return over a long period of time.

Historical Before-Tax Returns

1-year periods

	1991	1992	1993	1994	1995	1996	1997	1998	1999	2000	2001
Cash (1-Month Treasury Bills)	5.6%	3.5%	2.9%	3.9%	5.6%	5.2%	5.3%	4.9%	4.7%	5.9%	3.8%
Short-/Medium-Term Gov't Bonds*	15.4	7.2	11.2	– 5.1	16.8	2.1	8.3	10.2	– 1.8	12.6	7.6
Large Co. Stock (S&P 500)	30.6	7.7	9.9	1.3	37.6	23.1	33.4	28.6	21.0	– 9.1	– 11.9
Small Co. Stock	44.6	23.3	20.9	3.1	34.4	17.6	22.8	– 7.3	29.8	– 4.0	22.8
Foreign Stock (EAFE)	10.2	–13.9	32.9	8.0	9.4	4.4	1.8	20.3	27.3	– 14.0	– 21.2
Inflation Rate (CPI)	3.1	2.9	2.7	2.7	2.7	3.3	1.7	1.6	2.7	3.6	1.7

5-year periods ending December 31

	1982 – 1986	1987 – 1991	1992 – 1996	1997 – 2001
Cash (1-Month Treasury Bills)	8.6%	6.7%	4.2%	4.9%
Short-/Medium-Term Gov't Bonds*	17.0	9.4	6.2	7.3
Large Co. Stock (S&P 500)	19.9	15.4	15.2	10.7
Small Co. Stock	17.3	6.9	19.5	11.8
Foreign Stock (EAFE)	28.8	9.0	8.5	1.2
Inflation Rate (CPI)	3.3	4.5	2.8	2.2

10-year periods ending December 31

	1962 – 1971	1972 – 1981	1982 – 1991	1992 – 2001
Cash (1-Month Treasury Bills)	4.5%	7.8%	7.7%	4.6%
Short-/Medium-Term Gov't Bonds*	4.6	5.8	13.1	6.7
Large Co. Stock (S&P 500)	7.1	6.5	17.6	12.9
Small Co. Stock	12.3	17.3	12.0	15.6
Foreign Stock (EAFE)	N/A	10.6	18.5	4.8
Inflation Rate (CPI)	3.2	8.6	3.9	2.5

50-year period ending December 31, 2001

Cash (1-Month Treasury Bills)	5.3%
Short-/Medium-Term Gov't Bonds*	6.5
Large Co. Stock (S&P 500)	12.0
Small Co. Stock**	14.4
Foreign Stock (EAFE)***	11.0
Inflation Rate (CPI)	3.9

* Five-year average maturity.

** Based on the fifth quintile of stocks on the NYSE for the period 1952 to 1981 and on the Dimensional Small Company Stock Fund from 1982 to the present.

*** Returns available from 1970.

Time, Willingness and Ability (TWA)

Do you have the TWA — time, willingness and ability — to invest and manage your money? You may have one or two, but not all three. A good money manager has all three. If you don't like to manage money or don't understand the different markets, perhaps you should invest your money with a professional.

If you do have the TWA to choose your own investments, use the following guidelines:

- Plan your portfolio allocations first, then choose investments
- Match investments with objectives
- Construct a core portfolio
- Emphasize stocks for long-term growth
- Develop a stock-picking or fund-picking style
- Monitor results against proper benchmarks
- Focus on prospects, not past results
- Formulate a strategy for when to sell
- Diversify into global markets
- Review performance regularly

Step 3: Diversify, Diversify, Diversify

As the saying goes, never keep all of your eggs in one basket. Diversifying your investment portfolio allows you to balance the ups and downs of each investment.

Diversification *Among* Asset Categories

There are three basic financial asset categories: cash equivalents, equities (stocks) and fixed-income securities (bonds). Generally speaking, the stock and bond markets do not move in tandem, while cash investments have provided a safe and steady return. Since stocks and bonds tend to move differently and cash is stable, you need to strike a balance that will cushion your portfolio against the investment swings in any one asset category.

A Diversified Portfolio Can Give You a Greater Return With Less Risk

	Portfolio #1	Portfolio #2
Expected return	6.5%	6.9%
Standard deviation (risk)	5.4%	5.0%
Portfolio allocation:		
Cash-equivalents	—	5%
Short-term bonds	100%	88%
Large-company stocks	—	2%
Small-company stocks	—	2%
Foreign stocks	—	3%

Portfolio 2 provides a higher expected return with lower risk. How? Through diversification.

Diversification *Within* Asset Categories

It also pays to diversify within an asset category. For instance, if you want to enhance your diversification by adding stock to your investments, don't buy just one type of stock. Buy all three classes of stock:

Large-Company Stocks — Well-established U.S. companies with long corporate histories and leadership positions in their industries. Many pay dividends, providing a steady income stream. Listed in the S&P 500 Index, on the New York Stock Exchange (NYSE) or on the American Stock Exchange (AMEX). These companies have market capitalization of more than $2 billion. This portion of the portfolio should be diversified among several different stocks and should cover a broad range of industries, typically with no single industry or stock comprising more than 10% of the portfolio's total value.

Small-Company Stocks — Often young and rapidly growing businesses that tend to fluctuate more in value than large-company stocks. These stocks can provide a return on your investment when they grow in market value as opposed to the more regular dividend payments of large-company stocks. Listed Over the Counter (OTC) or through the National Association of Securities Dealers Automated Quotation (NASDAQ). These companies typically have market capitalization of less than $2 billion. This portion of the portfolio should be diversified among several different stocks and should cover a broad range of industries, again with no single industry or stock comprising more than 10% of the portfolio's total value.

Foreign Stocks — Issued by companies headquartered outside the United States. Like stocks in the U.S. market, foreign stocks are influenced by general business and economic conditions, but foreign market cycles are likely to differ from those in the United States. Currency fluctuations also have an impact on the price movement of international stocks. Listed on overseas stock exchanges or on the New York Stock Exchange, American Stock Exchange or NASDAQ as American Depositary Receipts (ADRs).

You can also diversify your fixed-income investments:

Cash-Equivalent Securities — Fixed-income instruments maturing in less than one year such as six-month CDs, 120-day Treasury bills, etc.

Short-Term Bonds — Fixed-income securities maturing in one to five years.

Medium-Term Bonds — Fixed-income securities maturing in six to 12 years.

The most efficient way to get this type of diversification for most investors is to invest in mutual funds. Mutual funds also may be a more practical alternative than purchasing individual stocks, especially small-company and international stocks.

Diversification Over Investment Styles

Many studies have compared the long-term performance records of growth and value stocks. History has proven that each style has unique characteristics that benefit overall portfolio performance during different economic and stock market cycles. Consequently, an investment strategy that includes both value and growth stocks can enhance diversification.

Growth stocks are the stocks of companies with potential for better-than-average earnings growth. These companies typically reinvest most of their earnings into their businesses rather than pay them as dividends to shareholders. Growth stocks typically perform their best late in an economic cycle when investors place a higher value on high-quality companies with above-average earnings. On the other hand, value stocks are those of companies that are currently undervalued but whose worth may be recognized by the market eventually. Value stocks tend to perform well as economic cycles begin. Certain stocks may exhibit both value and growth characteristics.

Value and Growth Stocks Converge Over the Long Term

	1/76 – 12/01 Average Annual Return	Number of Times Best Performing by Calendar Year	Number of Times Best Performing by Rolling 3-Year Period
Value Stocks (S&P 500 Barra Value Index)	14.7%	12	13
Growth Stocks (S&P 500 Barra Growth Index)	13.2%	14	11

As the table above indicates, value and growth stocks perform similarly over the long term. However, they may diverge over the short term. After studying 26 years of data, we believe that allocating your stock investments equally between growth and value styles can enhance your portfolio's diversification.

Diversification Over Time

It's also important to use time as a diversification strategy. As the *Range of Returns* graph shows, volatility is reduced the longer an asset is held. With stocks, the possibility of loss exists over any five-year period. However, no 10-year time period since 1952 has produced a negative return in the S&P 500 Index.

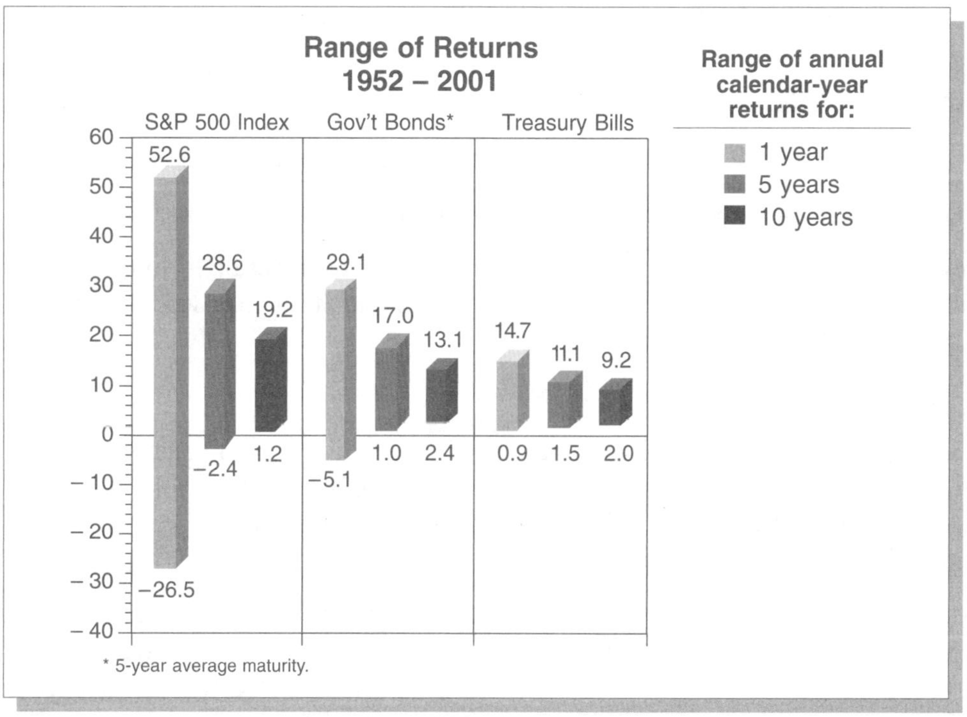

Diversifying over time can also help when *purchasing* securities. Some investors try to "time" the stock market by jumping in and out of it rather than using diversification over time as a strategy. Market timing only works if you're able to predict the stock market's direction. Few people can do this reliably because they have to be right twice: once on the "buy" side and again on the "sell" side.

The stock market's movements are often short and fast. A classic example is the upward surge in stock prices that occurs as a bear market ends and a new bull market begins. The shift from bear to bull comes with no warning, *and the first days of a bull market are often the most lucrative part of the entire market cycle*. Investors who are on the sidelines in an attempt to avoid losses from the bear trend almost never reinvest in time to participate in the big rally that comes at the onset of a bull market.

The graph below reflects this point. It shows the value of $1 invested for 50 years (since January 1, 1952) in the Standard & Poor's 500 Index. One dollar then would have grown to $288.95 by December 31, 2001 (before taxes and transaction costs such as brokerage fees). On the other hand, had the investor tried to time the market and missed the *35 best months during that period*, the investment would be worth only $12.91!

While it's unlikely that an investor would miss the best 35 months, what this illustration shows is that most of the market gains over the 50-year period — that's 600 months — occurred in just 35 months. By trying to time the market, you take the chance that you'll be out of the market during one of these surges. The moral of the story: It may be riskier to be *out* of the market than to stay in it.

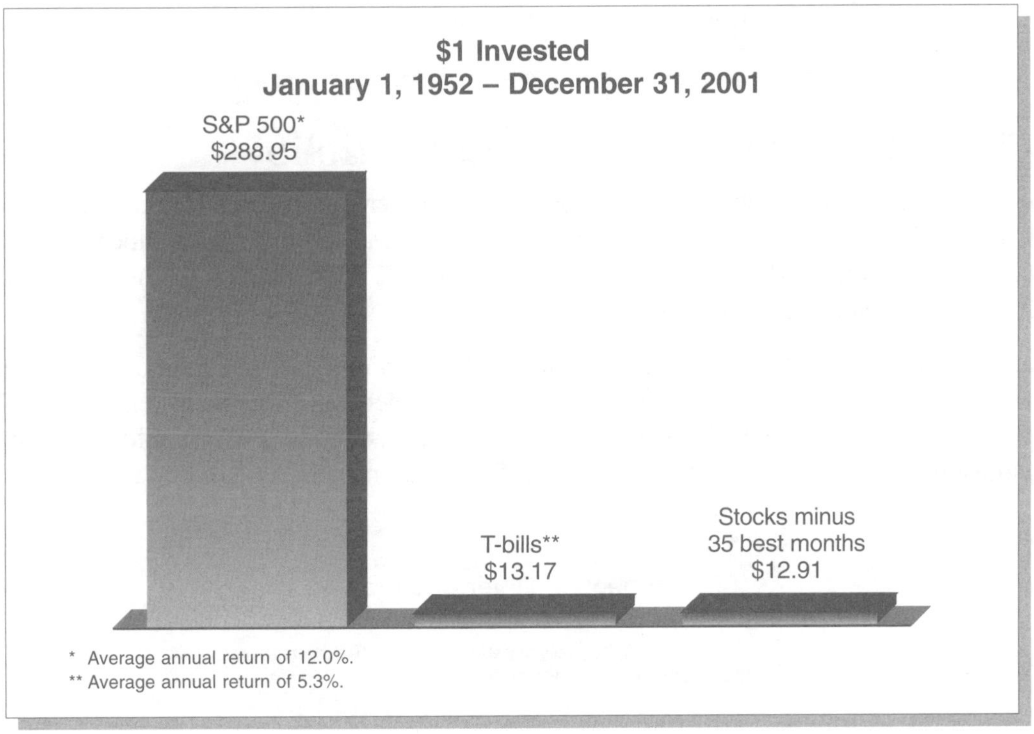

INVESTMENTS

Dollar-Cost Averaging — Rather than trying to time the market, try an investment strategy known as "dollar-cost averaging." Dollar-cost averaging is a systematic approach to investing that takes the guesswork out of deciding when to invest. Your contributions to a company savings plan are a good example of this strategy. By investing approximately the same amount of money at regular intervals over time, you significantly reduce the risk of poor market timing.

For example, suppose you invested $100 per month for a five-month period in a stock mutual fund. The fund sells for $25 in the first month, $22 in the second, $22.50 in the third, $23 in the fourth and $24 in the fifth month. Your total investment is $500 ($100 a month for five months.) You would own 21.5044 shares. When the fund's price went down to $22, your $100 monthly investment bought 4.5455 shares; when the price was $22.50, your $100 investment bought 4.4444 shares. If the shares are valued at $24, then your total account is now $516.10 (21.5044 shares x $24). This is approximately a 19% (annualized) return on your investment, even though the per-share value is less than it was at the beginning of the five-month period. Conversely, had you invested the entire $500 in the first month, you would own only 20 shares, and your return would be negative (approximately minus 4%).

Effect of Dollar-Cost Averaging on Your Investments

Investment	Share Price	No. of Shares
$100	$25.00	4.0000
100	22.00	4.5455
100	22.50	4.4444
100	23.00	4.3478
100	24.00	4.1667
$500		**21.5044**

Average cost per share: $23.25 ($500 ÷ 21.5044).

Step 4: Determine Your Optimal Portfolio

It's important to have a diversified investment portfolio, but there are many different ways to accomplish this end. You need to choose the mix that's right for you. Experts call this "asset allocation." For example, suppose you had $10,000 to invest and could earn 7% after taxes on that money. At the end of 25 years you would have $54,274.

But what would happen if you invested $2,000 in five different investments? Suppose one investment performed so poorly you actually lost the $2,000 while the other four investments earned 0%, 7%, 10% and 15% on an after-tax basis. At the end of 25 years, the diversified portfolio would be worth $100,362. This is almost double what you would have earned if you had invested all $10,000 at 7%.

Impact of Diversification

Investment	After-Tax Return	Amount in 25 Years
$10,000	7%	$ 54,274
	vs.	
$ 2,000	—	$ 0
2,000	0%	2,000
2,000	7%	10,855
2,000	10%	21,669
2,000	15%	65,838
$10,000		$100,362

In the previous example we assumed the $10,000 investment was equally divided among five different assets. To determine *your* optimal portfolio, we suggest that you consider a model developed by a Nobel Prize-winning economist. According to this "Modern Portfolio Theory," having the right mix of assets is crucial in determining how your investments will perform over time. By investing in several types of investments, which have different ups and downs, your portfolio will be cushioned from the down cycle of any one investment. Your risk will be lower, so your portfolio will be more efficient.

Using 50 years' worth of quarterly data (except for the foreign-stock category, which reflects approximately 32 years of data), the model uses certain market indices to determine how the assets track relative to each other. Then, for each expected investment return, the model will produce a mix of asset classes providing the least amount of risk or volatility. We traditionally have limited the allocations to cash and to foreign stock to a maximum of 5% and 20%, respectively, of all assets. However, the limitation on cash affects only the most conservative investor, while the limitation on foreign stock has no impact because the allocation in foreign stock never reaches 20%. The combination of all these optimal portfolios produces the *efficient frontier* of portfolios (the curved line on the graph). Portfolios lying on or near this line provide the greatest expected return for the least amount of risk. For example, when looking at the *Efficient Frontier of Portfolios* graph, portfolio B is clearly better than portfolio A for two reasons. Portfolio B has a lower expected risk, as well as a greater expected return. That is a win-win situation. As long as you could invest in portfolio B, you would not invest in portfolio A. It should be every investor's goal to move his or her portfolio toward the efficient frontier.

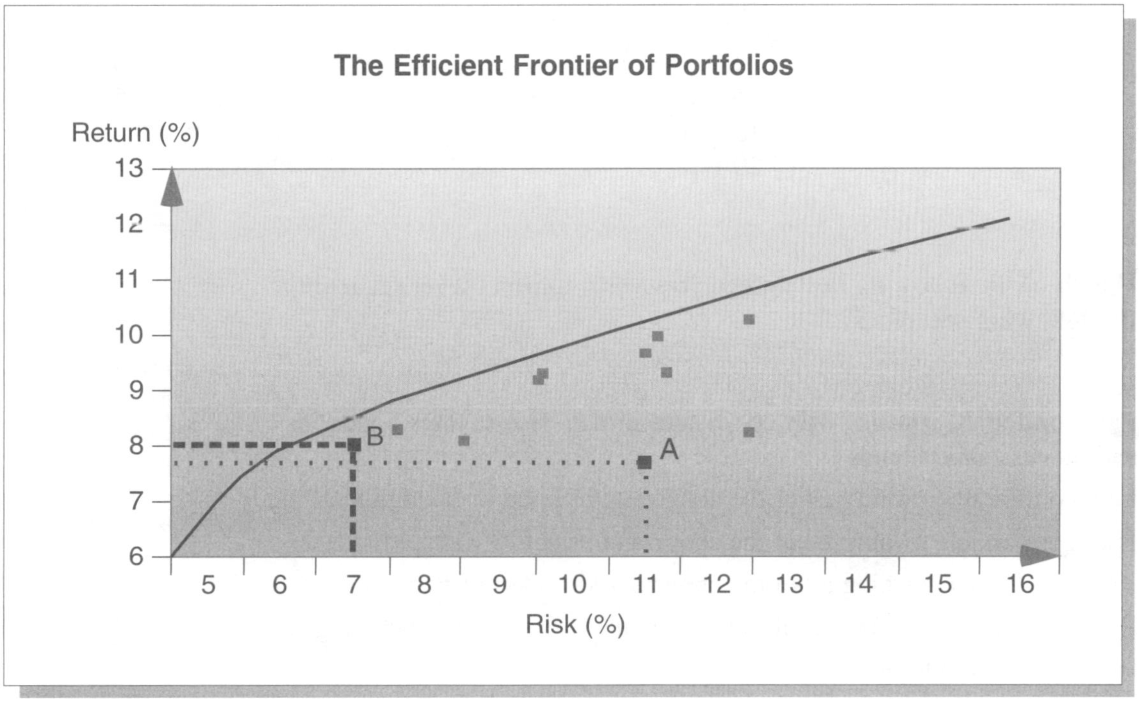

INVESTMENTS

Fixing Your Mix

In determining your optimal portfolio allocation, you have to consider *all* of your investments. In addition to mutual funds, stocks, bonds and CDs, include your company savings plan balance, IRA balances and investments in tax-deferred annuities.

The first part of the optimizing process is to find your risk tolerance. Here is a simple 3-step method:

Step 1: Understand Your Tolerance for Risk — Ask yourself the following six questions, and enter the number of points for each answer in the appropriate box.

1. What is your age?

Age	Points
60 +	10
50 – 59	6
40 – 49	4
30 – 39	2
under 30	1

☐ points

2. What is your investment time horizon? In other words, in how many years will you begin to use your invested assets?

Money Use	Points
1 – 4	10
5 – 12	5
13 – 20	3
20 +	1

☐ points

3. Which of the following best categorizes your comfort level regarding the following securities?

	Points
I am comfortable owning only certificates of deposits, savings bonds and money market funds	8
I am comfortable owning all of the above and/or bond or bond mutual funds	6
I am comfortable owning all of the above and/or equity mutual funds	3
I am comfortable owning all of the above and/or individual stocks	2
I am comfortable owning all of the above and/or derivatives including call and put options and warrants	1

☐ points

4. What are your expectations for the future value of your portfolio over your investment time horizon?

	Points
I want to preserve principal and keep pace with the current inflation rate	10
I expect my portfolio to earn a conservative rate of return that is higher than inflation but lower than the stock market	5
I expect my portfolio to increase at the same rate as the stock market	3
I expect my portfolio to outperform the stock market	1

☐ points

5. How long are you willing to sustain a loss in your investment portfolio?

	Points
I am not willing to sustain any loss	10
1 year or less	5
1 – 2 years	3
More than 2 years	1

☐ points

6. If the stock market were to experience a sharp selloff, what would your course of action be?

	Points
Sell immediately	8
Wait for a rebound and then sell	6
Do nothing	3
Buy more	1

☐ points

Step 2: Add Your Score — Based on the answers you have selected, tally your score. ☐ Total points

Step 3: Find Your Risk Profile — Based on your score, you will fall into one of the following five risk profiles:

Risk Profile	Score
Stable	44 – 56 points
Conservative Growth	30 – 43 points
Moderate Growth	22 – 29 points
Growth	16 – 21 points
Aggressive Growth	6 – 15 points

After determining your risk profile, read the portfolio descriptions to see if your result matches the type of investor you think you are.

Portfolios	Description
Stable	This portfolio is appropriate for investors whose primary objective is safety of principal. The majority of assets in this portfolio are allocated to short-term investments such as cash and fixed-income securities.
Conservative Growth	This portfolio is appropriate for investors who prefer current income over long-term capital appreciation, but are willing to accept some volatility associated with equity investments. The assets in this portfolio are allocated primarily to fixed-income securities.
Moderate Growth	This portfolio is appropriate for investors whose primary objective is growth, with secondary needs for current income. The assets in this portfolio are balanced among equities and fixed-income securities.
Growth	This portfolio is appropriate for investors whose primary objective is capital appreciation and who are willing to accept a higher level of risk. Assets in this portfolio are invested primarily in equity investments.
Aggressive Growth	This portfolio is appropriate for investors whose primary objective is long-term growth and who are willing to accept a high level of risk. Assets in this portfolio are invested entirely (or almost entirely) in equities.

Within each portfolio grouping there are various returns to choose from. For example, if you fall within the Conservative Growth risk profile, your expected before-tax return can range from 8.0% to 8.8%, with the 8.8% portfolio being approximately 25% riskier. So look at the risk, or volatility, of a specific portfolio before allocating your funds.

2002 Optimal Portfolio Allocations

Historical Before-Tax Return	Risk (+/–)	Risk/ Return Ratio	Cash Equivalents	Short-Term and Medium-Term Bonds	Large-Company Stock	Small-Company Stock	Foreign Stock
Stable Portfolios							
6.8%	5.0%	0.74	5%	89%	2%	2%	2%
7.2	5.2	0.72	5	82	5	4	4
7.6	5.5	0.72	5	75	9	6	5
Conservative Growth Portfolios							
8.0%	6.1%	0.76	5%	68%	13%	8%	6%
8.4	6.8	0.81	5	61	17	10	7
8.8	7.6	0.86	5	55	20	12	8
Moderate Growth Portfolios							
9.2%	8.5%	0.92	0%	54%	23%	14%	9%
9.6	9.4	0.98	0	47	27	16	10
10.0	10.4	1.04	0	40	30	18	12
Growth Portfolios							
10.4%	11.4%	1.10	0%	33%	34%	20%	13%
10.8	12.4	1.15	0	26	38	22	14
11.2	13.4	1.20	0	19	41	25	15
Aggressive Growth Portfolios							
11.5%	14.2%	1.23	0%	14%	44%	26%	16%
11.8	15.0	1.27	0	8	47	28	17
12.1	15.8	1.31	0	3	50	29	18

Evaluating the Expected Return and Expected Risk

The five portfolio group allocations help make up the efficient frontier of optimal portfolios. When choosing an expected rate of return in your given portfolio, keep the following in mind:

Historical Before-Tax Return — This figure is based solely on what has happened in the past and is not in any way a guarantee of what will happen in the future. For planning purposes, it's reasonable to look at this figure as the average return you reasonably can expect over a long period of time (*i.e.,* at least 10 years). However, you should also review the "Projected Results" table on the next page to see the potential impact of the variability of returns on your situation.

Risk — You can expect your return will vary up or down by this percentage two-thirds of the time. For example, with an 8.0% before-tax return and a 6.1% level of risk, you can expect your return to range from about 14.1% (8.0% return plus 6.1% risk) to 1.9% (8.0% return minus 6.1%) in approximately seven out of 10 years.

Risk/Return Ratio — Take the percent risk divided by the percent return. In the previous example that would be 6.1% ÷ 8.0% = 0.76. If the ratio is less than 1, your risk is less than the average. A more aggressive investor will have a ratio greater than 1.

Special Consideration:

Optimal Portfolio Allocation

The investment allocation to each asset class will change for each portfolio each year. In order to use this strategy effectively, you will need to review your allocations annually.

Review the Projected Results — Projected results for Ayco's *2002 Optimal Portfolio Allocations* are shown on the following page for time periods of 5, 10, 15 and 20 years. These tables are based on the assumption that $100 was invested according to the asset allocation shown. A statistical methodology known as Monte Carlo simulation was used to determine the likelihood that each portfolio will achieve a particular value. Monte Carlo simulation attempts to recreate a frequency distribution of potential outcomes by repeatedly choosing random values based on expected returns and risk. Ultimately, the program calculates an expected future value of a portfolio and a range of values within which its value is likely to fall over a given time frame.

For all time periods, there is a 90% chance that returns will fall between the 95th and 5th percentile. At the 95th percentile, investors have a 5% chance of achieving this or a higher value; 95% of all outcomes are lower than this value. You might want to think of this as your "best case." Your "worst case" is represented by the 5th percentile. Investors have a 95% chance of achieving this or a higher value; only 5% of all outcomes are lower than this amount. The expected value represents the growth of $100 at the stated rate of return. For example, after 10 years a moderate growth portfolio is expected to achieve a value of $250.10, and there is a 90% chance of it achieving between $148.04 and $366.64.

Projected Results

Stable Portfolio

- 5% Cash Equivalents
- 82% Short- and Medium-Term Bonds
- 5% Large-Company Stocks
- 4% Small-Company Stocks
- 4% Foreign Stocks

Year	"Worst Case" (5th Percentile)	Expected Value	"Best Case" (95th Percentile)
5	$117.00	$141.57	$167.22
10	150.28	200.42	251.15
15	201.54	283.74	373.15
20	269.22	401.69	548.16

7.2% Expected Return, +/– 5.2% Risk

Conservative Growth Portfolio

- 5% Cash Equivalents
- 61% Short- and Medium-Term Bonds
- 17% Large-Company Stocks
- 10% Small-Company Stocks
- 7% Foreign Stocks

Year	"Worst Case" (5th Percentile)	Expected Value	"Best Case" (95th Percentile)
5	$116.73	$149.67	$185.21
10	153.71	224.02	298.56
15	214.04	335.30	474.59
20	296.53	501.86	743.46

8.4% Expected Return, +/– 6.8% Risk

Moderate Growth Portfolio

- 0% Cash Equivalents
- 47% Short- and Medium-Term Bonds
- 27% Large-Company Stocks
- 16% Small-Company Stocks
- 10% Foreign Stocks

Year	"Worst Case" (5th Percentile)	Expected Value	"Best Case" (95th Percentile)
5	$112.05	$158.14	$ 210.53
10	148.04	250.10	366.64
15	211.09	395.51	626.43
20	298.89	625.48	1,049.12

9.6% Expected Return, +/– 9.4% Risk

Growth Portfolio

- 0% Cash Equivalents
- 26% Short- and Medium-Term Bonds
- 38% Large-Company Stocks
- 22% Small-Company Stocks
- 14% Foreign Stocks

Year	"Worst Case" (5th Percentile)	Expected Value	"Best Case" (95th Percentile)
5	$105.82	$166.99	$ 240.71
10	138.79	278.87	452.50
15	201.05	465.69	829.71
20	288.60	777.67	1,482.30

10.8% Expected Return, +/– 12.4% Risk

Aggressive Growth Portfolio

- 0% Cash Equivalents
- 8% Short- and Medium-Term Bonds
- 47% Large-Company Stocks
- 28% Small-Company Stocks
- 17% Foreign Stocks

Year	"Worst Case" (5th Percentile)	Expected Value	"Best Case" (95th Percentile)
5	$100.42	$174.67	$ 268.62
10	130.38	305.08	536.68
15	190.68	532.88	1,040.77
20	275.84	930.76	1,956.44

11.8% Expected Return, +/– 15.0% Risk

Investment Securities

Now that you're familiar with asset-allocation concepts, let's look at the investment vehicles available to implement your allocation. You have two basic choices when you invest: you can be a "loaner" (by lending money) or an "owner." You're a loaner whenever you invest in a fixed-income investment, such as a bond. With fixed-income investments you're promised a yield (interest rate), and, unless you're buying a "junk bond," your principal is relatively safe from the risk that it won't be paid back. *The tradeoff is that over the long term, the expected return on fixed-income investments is less than what you would expect to earn from stock ownership.*

Most of us will need to make our money grow substantially over the long term. That type of growth means investing in stocks or stock mutual funds as well as fixed-income investments. You're an "owner" when you invest in stock. Because you take more risk as an owner — the rate of return is uncertain — you can expect to earn more in the long run.

Historically, equity investments (stocks) have outpaced fixed-income investments (bonds). For example, if you had invested $1,000 in a diversified list of common stocks in 1951, left your money alone and reinvested the dividends, your $1,000 investment (disregarding taxes and any transaction costs) would be worth about $276,000 today! But if you had bought "safe" intermediate-term Treasury bonds at that time, you'd have only a little more than $23,000.

That's why you should consider placing a substantial portion of your investments in stocks — especially if you don't plan to draw on them for at least 10 years.

This record of returns doesn't mean, however, that *all* your money should be invested in stocks; bonds, for instance, also have performed well over the last 10 years. Different investment vehicles perform best in different economic cycles. So investing in both fixed-income investments and stocks is the best way to ensure good long-term performance with a manageable level of risk.

Bonds

Let's look first at the ways in which you can be a "loaner" using fixed-income investments. We define the fixed-income category broadly: as IOUs issued by corporations and governments. Investors buy bonds in return for regular interest payments, usually two per year. When the bond matures, the issuer pays back the original loan, called the principal or face value. Individual bonds sell for a minimum of $1,000 when newly issued, and are typically sold in "round" lots of 100, which cost $100,000.

If you're going to invest $250,000 or more in bonds, we recommend investing in individual bonds (rather than using bond mutual funds). Furthermore, we suggest laddering your maturities to provide diversification. This structures your bond portfolio so that the bonds mature at different times instead of all at once. For example, instead of having $250,000 maturing in five years, stagger or ladder the maturities so that $50,000 matures in one, two, three, four and five years. Then, when a bond matures, use the proceeds to purchase a five-year bond. This will protect you from being locked in at one interest rate for the life of your investment, and you will have access to some money every year.

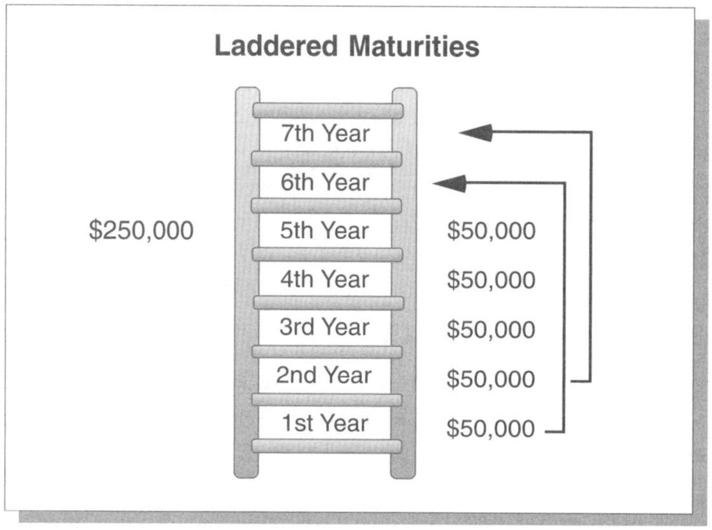

Most people realize that stock prices move up and down. But you face this same risk with the price of a bond if you want to sell it before it matures. Below is a list of risks to watch out for when investing in a bond:

Inflation Risk — As inflation increases, there's a risk your rate of return won't keep pace. Conservative investors who concentrate assets in bonds and money market investments (or other cash equivalents) should be aware they might face a substantial decrease in the purchasing power of their investments. For example, if your bond investments provide $1,000 of income per year, the $1,000 will not buy as much in the future if prices of goods and services increase due to inflation.

Interest-Rate Risk — As interest rates rise, the price of a bond will drop. This is because an investor can buy a newly issued bond with a higher coupon rate. On the other hand, as interest rates fall, the price of a bond will increase. Because of this relationship, if you sell a bond before it matures, you may have either a capital gain or loss. However, if you hold a bond until it matures, this type of risk will not affect you.

↑ Rates	↓ Bond price
↓ Rates	↑ Bond price

Call Risk — If you purchase a bond with a call provision, the issuing company can purchase it from you before the maturity date. If a company calls a bond from you, it usually pays you more money. Companies usually call a bond when the interest the bond is paying is greater than the current interest rates. Although you receive more money for your bond, your current income can decrease. For instance, assume you own $10,000 in bonds with a 10% coupon paying $1,000 per year. Let's assume the current interest rate is 8%, and the company decides to pay you $11,000 to call the bonds from you. Although you received more than your bonds' face value, when you reinvest the $11,000 at 8% you'll receive only $880 per year (and you might have incurred capital gains taxes by having to sell the bond).

Default Risk — If the bond issuer cannot pay you your interest or principal as scheduled, the issuer is said to have "defaulted." Debt issued by (and backed by the full faith and credit of) the U.S. government is considered to be the safest fixed-income investment, with virtually no default risk. Three primary rating services evaluate bond issues (other than U.S. Treasury debt) to help investors determine the likelihood that an issuer might default on a particular bond. The rating companies and their listings are presented on the following page.

Moody's	Standard & Poor's	Fitch	Interpretation
Aaa	AAA	AAA	Highest Grade
Aa	AA	AA	High Grade
A	A	A	Upper Medium; Medium Grade; Sound
Baa	BBB	BBB	Medium; Good Grade; Some Uncertainty
Ba	BB	BB	Fair to Good; Lower Medium; Uncertainty
B	B	B	Fair; Speculative Features
Caa		CCC	Outright Speculations; Poor Standing
Ca	C	CC	Outright Speculations; Marked Weakness
C		C	Best Defaulted Issue; Highly Speculative
		DDD	In Default
		DD	Assets of Little Value
		D	No Apparent Value

Generally speaking, bonds rated BBB (Baa by Moody's) or better are classified as investment-grade bonds. Bonds rated BB, Ba or B are speculative investments, while bonds rated CCC (Caa by Moody's) or lower are classified as "junk" bonds. Remember, the riskier the bond investment, the higher the bond's interest rate will be in order to compensate you for the additional risk. Conversely, the safer the bond, the lower the interest rate.

Municipal Bonds

You may want to consider investing in municipal bonds because the interest earned is usually exempt from federal, state and local income tax. Check your state's taxation of municipal bonds before you purchase any particular bond or bond fund. You can purchase municipal bonds individually, through a unit trust, or collectively, through a mutual fund.

Two categories reflect the tax treatment of municipal bonds issued after August 7, 1986:

Public-Purpose Bonds — This category includes securities issued by state or local governments meeting essential governmental functions. The interest from these bonds is fully tax-exempt.

Nonessential-Purpose Bonds — These pay tax-exempt interest, but the interest is a tax-preference item when calculating the Alternative Minimum Tax.

Bonds issued by a commonwealth, territory or possession of the United States are not subject to federal, state or local taxes. For example, the bonds issued by the Commonwealth of Puerto Rico, Guam and the U.S. Virgin Islands are triple tax-exempt.

Ginnie Mae, Fannie Mae and Freddie Mac

These are the street names for three agencies that issue mortgage-backed bonds. These agencies help banks raise money that can be loaned for mortgages. For example, Bill and Julie get a $100,000 mortgage from their local bank. Instead of holding the mortgage, the bank will sell their mortgage to one of these agencies. The bank takes the money from the sale and uses it to make another mortgage loan. The agency will then "bundle" a group of mortgages into "pass-through certificates." When Bill and Julie make their monthly mortgage payments, the interest and principal are passed through to holders of these securities. So when you buy one of these bonds, you are buying a piece of someone's mortgage.

In addition to the risk other bond investments have, Ginnie Maes, Fannie Maes and Freddie Macs also have prepayment and extension risk. Prepayment risk refers to a homeowner's ability to pay off a mortgage early. When this happens, investors in these securities don't receive the interest payments for as long as they expected. On the other hand, extension risk occurs when a mortgage is not paid off when anticipated, so investors don't get their principal back when they expect it. Keep in mind that extension risk is not the same as default risk. With extension risk you will get your principal back, but at a later date.

Collateralized Mortgage Obligations (CMOs) — This type of security is similar to those issued by Ginnie Mae, Fannie Mae and Freddie Mac because it, too, is a mortgage-backed security. All of these securities have interest rate, prepayment and extension risk. CMOs differ in that they are broken down into various tranches or classes. The CMO tranches range from the very conservative, with a defined maturity and a first claim on the principal and interest payments, to others having more risk because they are further down the payment line and receive payment only after other tranches have been paid off. Before investing in a CMO, know which tranche you're buying.

Institutional investors normally get the better CMOs. Before buying a CMO, ask your broker about the resale market. Traditionally, it has been difficult to resell a CMO, and the transaction costs have been high.

Cash-Equivalent Securities

These securities, which are essentially IOUs, have the lowest risk among investments. Since they mature in one year or less, your principal is only marginally affected by inflation. Because of the low risk associated with cash equivalents, the interest you'll earn is relatively low. Examples include:

- Checking accounts
- Savings accounts
- Money market instruments (either at a bank or through a mutual fund)
- Short-term CDs (one year or less)
- Commercial paper (short-term debt issued by corporations)
- U.S. Treasury bills

Stocks

Stocks represent ownership. When you buy stock, you own a portion of a company. There are two ways in which a stock can change in value. First, the price of the stock itself can increase or decrease. Second, the company may pay a dividend to stockholders on a per-share basis. Following is a description of different types of stock.

Common Stock — This is the most widespread type of stock issued by corporations, and the type referred to when we talk about owning stock. The growth potential is greater for this type of stock than any other type. An owner of common stock can vote on issues related to the general operations of a corporation and may receive dividend payments.

Preferred Stock — Many utility companies issue this type of stock. The dividend rate is fixed, and there is an implicit guarantee that a dividend will be paid. Investors wanting a steady stream of income with the possibility of growth may want to consider preferred stocks.

Convertible — Certain bonds and/or preferred stock can be exchanged for common stock. A convertible security provides an investor with a fixed rate of income, lower risk than a common-stock investment and the flexibility to switch to common stock. However, rising interest rates tend to reduce the market value of a convertible security.

In general, a stock investment is considered riskier than a cash-equivalent security or a bond investment. Not only do you have to be concerned with overall economic risks, as with any investment, you also have to be concerned with the business and financial risks of a particular company. Business risk refers to the revenue and expenses of a company, as well as its market position in the industry, while financial risk refers to the company's mix of debt and equity. Since you have no control over the direction of the economy, you'll want to choose companies that appear to have lower exposure to business and financial risks.

Mutual Funds

It can be both difficult and expensive for the average investor to manage a diversified stock and bond portfolio. Because a diversified portfolio should include 10 to 20 stock or bond issues, you would need to invest a significant sum of money to give yourself any degree of diversification. You would also have to deal with all of the buy-and-sell decisions and transaction costs associated with managing a portfolio.

Mutual funds provide an alternative to the purchase of individual securities because they pool money from thousands of investors and put it under one asset manager. You can invest and benefit from diversification and professional management — for as little as $50 per month. The funds also provide regular statements to shareholders reporting the value of their investments.

Selecting a Mutual Fund — There are thousands of mutual funds from which to choose. Mutual funds invest in all types of financial assets and can be classified from conservative to aggressive. To invest in a fund, you must call the fund or the broker who sells the fund and request an application and a prospectus. When you receive the information, read the prospectus. If you decide to invest in the fund, complete the application and send it with your check to the fund. You can also invest in mutual funds with the help of a stockbroker or investment representative.

You should be aware of the expenses associated with your investment. By law these expenses are listed in the fund's prospectus. Below is a list of common expenses:

- **Front-End Load** — A percentage of the initial investment that is paid to the mutual fund company and/or to the broker. These loads can be as high as 8.5% of your investment.
- **Back-End Load or Redemption Fee** — A percentage retained by the mutual fund when you make a withdrawal. Some funds will decrease the percentage charged over time so it disappears after a designated period of time.
- **12b-1 Fee** — An annual percentage of your account value withheld by fund management to be used for sales and promotional materials. The maximum fee is subject to SEC regulation and typically ranges up to .45%.
- **Management Fee** — An annual percentage charged for managing your investment. Such fees range from about 0.2% to 2.5% of the amount invested.

The prospectus will also detail the fund's expense ratio. This is the fund's total operating expenses for the fiscal year divided by its average net assets. Expenses include the management fee, nonmanagement fees and 12b-1 fees. The lower the expense ratio, the lower the cost to you as an investor.

Types of Mutual Funds

Money Market Funds — These funds all share one important feature. The net asset value — the price at which shares of the fund are bought and sold — is expected to remain constant at $1.00 per share. The fund's yield — the interest rate paid to investors — will fluctuate depending on current market interest rates, but your principal investment is expected to be safe.

The Securities and Exchange Commission (SEC) requires money market mutual funds to have average maturities of 90 days or less, and they can invest only in securities that mature in one year or less. This makes money market mutual funds the most secure type of mutual fund available.

Bond Funds — Mutual funds also offer the small investor a way to invest in the bond market. Before you invest in a bond fund, remember that interest-rate fluctuations will affect the price of its shares. So, unlike buying and holding an individual bond to maturity, there is no guarantee you will receive your total investment when you withdraw from a bond fund. When evaluating bond funds, stick with funds that invest in bonds that are rated at least A. (See pages 128 and 129.)

We recommend that investors avoid long-term bonds and bond funds (*i.e.,* with maturities of 12 or more years) because they can be as volatile as stocks. Instead, we recommend investing in short- and medium-term bonds or bond funds (average maturities of less than 12 years). A good general target is to have a bond portfolio with an average maturity of about five years.

Special Consideration:

SEC Yield

When evaluating a bond fund, be sure to ask for the "SEC Yield," a standard calculation that enables you to compare income yield among bond funds.

Stock Funds — Mutual funds provide an economical way to diversify a stock portfolio. A stock fund usually will invest in a particular type of stock. For instance, some funds focus their investments on large-company stocks, while others concentrate on small-company stocks. A fund's management style can be relatively conservative or aggressive. Since there are so many good stock funds to choose from, you should be able to find one that meets your investment objective.

In addition to investing in U.S. stocks, mutual funds offer a great opportunity for you to invest internationally. You should consider putting at least a small percentage of your investment money in foreign stocks, because they contribute to a well-diversified portfolio.

Balanced Funds — These funds invest in a mix of stocks and bonds. Generally, a balanced fund seeks to provide regular income and preserve capital.

Special Consideration:

Keep It Simple

If you don't understand an investment, and your broker cannot explain it to your satisfaction, you probably shouldn't invest in it. Before making any investment, make sure you're aware of all the risks involved.

Mutual-Fund Supermarkets

Many financial institutions have established programs that allow investors to purchase mutual funds from various families of funds within one account. For the investor, these "fund supermarkets" provide the convenience of having just one account statement, rather than multiple accounts with several different mutual-fund companies. Other advantages may include availability of quick switching of funds and easier accounting at tax time. Some funds offered through the supermarkets are sold on a "no-transaction-fee" basis; this means that buying the fund through the holding account would cost no more than making the investment directly. Others are sold with a fee for each transaction.

Not all fund supermarkets are created equal. Some offer more no-load or low-load, no-transaction-fee funds than others. That's why it's a good idea to comparison shop before making an investment.

The following is a listing of some mutual-fund supermarkets that you might consider.

Mutual-Fund Supermarkets

Sponsor	Telephone Number	Web Site
Accutrade	800/494-8939	accutrade.com
Ameritrade	800/454-9272	ameritrade.com
Bank of America	888/926-1111	bankofamerica.com
Charles Schwab	800/435-4000	schwab.com
CSFB Direct	800/825-5723	csfbdirect.com
Dreyfus	800/782-6620	dreyfus.com
E-Trade	800/387-2331	etrade.com
Fidelity Investments	800/343-3548	fidelity.com
Key Corp (McDonald Investments)	800/553-2240	key.com
Merrill Lynch	800/456-4587	ml.com
Muriel Siebert	800/872-0711	msiebert.com
Prudential Securities	800/225-1852	prufn.com
Quick & Reilly	800/793-8050	quickandreilly.com
Salomon Smith Barney	800/221-3636	salomonsmithbarney.com
TD Waterhouse	800/934-4448	tdwaterhouse.com
Vanguard	800/992-8327	vanguard.com

Online Trading

Online trading has become more and more popular with individual investors in recent years. Online trading is extremely convenient and can be a relatively inexpensive (in terms of commissions) way to buy and sell stocks. A few companies that offer online trading are: Ameritrade, E-Trade, Datek, CSFB Direct, Charles Schwab and Fidelity Investments. However, if you don't have the TWA (time, willingness and ability) to monitor your investments carefully, you probably will get better results by investing in stock mutual funds, which offer relatively low costs, diversification and professional investment management.

Step 5: Evaluate Your Rate of Return

At least once a year you should review your investments' performance. The easiest way to do this is to compare your results to an index. But make sure you're looking at the *right* index. For example, compare your stock investment results to the Standard and Poor's 500 or the Dow Jones Industrial indexes for large-company stocks and to the Russell 2000 for small-company stocks, not the Lehman Brothers Government/Corporate Bond index. This comparison will tell you if your investments are superior, average or below average.

Although most investment vehicles publish and report their returns, you can use the following worksheets to calculate your specific returns. The first or quarterly worksheet assumes all purchases and/or sales of investments occurred during the middle of each quarter of the year.

Quarterly Investment Result

		Example	Your Situation
Line 1:	What was the beginning value?	$10,000	________
Line 2:	Did you purchase any new investments during the quarter?*	$ 2,000	________
Line 3:	Did you sell any investments during the quarter?**	0	________
Line 4:	Subtract Line 3 from Line 2 to find the net additions or withdrawals ($2,000 – 0).	$ 2,000	________
Line 5:	What is the ending value?	$12,350	________
Line 6:	Multiply Line 4 by 0.5 ($2,000 x 0.5).	$ 1,000	________
Line 7:	Subtract Line 6 from Line 5 ($12,350 – $1,000).	$11,350	________
Line 8:	Add Line 1 to Line 6 ($10,000 + $1,000).	$11,000	________
Line 9:	Divide Line 7 by Line 8 ($11,350 ÷ $11,000).	1.032	________
Line 10:	Subtract 1 from Line 9 (1.032 – 1).	.032	________
Line 11:	Multiply Line 10 by 100 to find your quarterly result (.032 x 100).	3.2%	________

* For stock and bond investments, include the commissions and any reinvested dividends or interest. For mutual funds, *don't* include reinvested dividends or capital gains. Income taxes on dividends, interest and capital gains can be included on this line to find the after-tax rate of return.

** For stock and bond investments, include commissions and any dividends or interest you take. For mutual funds, include dividends and capital gains actually received.

After you've calculated one quarter's investment performance result, use the *Annual Investment Result* worksheet after calculating four quarterly results.

Annual Investment Result

		Example	Your Situation
Line 1:	Enter the first quarter's result.	3.20%	________
Line 2:	Enter the second quarter's result.	4.20%	________
Line 3:	Enter the third quarter's result.	– 2.00%	________
Line 4:	Enter the fourth quarter's result.	4.80%	________
Line 5:	Convert the quarterly percentage results to decimals:	________	
	First Quarter	0.032	________
	Second Quarter	0.042	________
	Third Quarter	– 0.020	________
	Fourth Quarter	0.048	________
Line 6:	Add 1 to the results on Line 5:		
	First Quarter	1.032	________
	Second Quarter	1.042	________
	Third Quarter	0.980	________
	Fourth Quarter	1.048	________
Line 7:	Multiply the answers on Line 6 together (1.032 x 1.042 x 0.98 x 1.048).	1.1044	________
Line 8:	Subtract 1 from Line 7 (1.1044 – 1).	.1044	________
Line 9:	Multiply Line 8 by 100 to find your annual investment result (.1044 x 100).	10.44%	________

Now that you've found your annual investment performance, compare it to the proper index and projected results for the optimal portfolios to see how your investments are doing. If you have to adjust your investment allocation, do it now.

How to Choose a Financial Planner

With many planning issues facing you, it's natural to seek out a professional financial planner. Working with a planner may lead to a recommendation that you also hire a more specialized professional such as an accountant, an estate-planning lawyer, or even a money manager.

It may be difficult to find a financial planner. You should do some homework and interview at least three planners to find the right one. Ask friends and business contacts for referrals, too.

While conducting an interview, listen and pay attention to what the planner believes is important about his or her background and what questions the planner asks you about your needs. Personal chemistry as well as professional competence is important.

We've provided 10 questions below that you should ask any planner you consider. We've also noted some guidelines to help you evaluate the answers.

1. *How are you compensated for financial planning services?*

   Financial planners earn a living in one of three ways:

   - They receive commissions based on selling financial products (such as stock or insurance);
   - They work on a fee basis (hourly or per-project); or
   - They receive a combination of both commissions and fees.

   Fee-based planners may be more objective about recommending an investment. On the other hand, they may not be as knowledgeable about certain investments because they're not paid commissions to know about them. It's important to know how the planner is compensated, the amount he or she receives, and whether you're comfortable with that method.

2. *How long have you been in this business?*

   There's no substitute for experience. We believe the minimum amount of experience should be five years. If the planner has had less than five years of experience, is s(he) part of an established planning firm and does s(he) have access to more experienced professionals in the firm?

3. *Do you do this full-time?*

   Determine if the person is a tax-return preparer doing financial planning "on the side," or a registered investment advisor. You can check to see if your planner is registered by calling the Securities and Exchange Commission at 800/732-0330.

4. *What's your background and education?*

   You'll want to know if the planner started out as an insurance salesperson, stockbroker, tax attorney, or accountant. Be on the lookout for bias. Ask whether the planner has ever been reprimanded or disciplined by regulatory or industry bodies.

   The North American Securities Administrators Association (NASAA) can tell you whom to contact in your state for a computer check of the complaints against a broker. Call NASAA at 202/737-0900 or visit their Web site at www.nasaa.org. The state, in turn, will check a database that will show complaints registered in all 50 states.

5. *How do you keep current with changes in the law and the market?*

   Try to select a professional who has 40 or more hours of continuing professional education every two years.

6. *With whom will I actually be working?*

   Find out if the person you'll be working with has a planner and/or an associate. If so, ask how that affects the fees.

7. *What will I get out of this process?*

   A written plan? A letter? Ask to see a sample of what you'll receive. Ask if the planner will recommend specific investments and insurance policies. Make sure you have a written agreement, including provisions regarding compensation and the nature of the relationship.

8. *Are there any clients you won't accept?*

   Try to find out whether the planner's style is unsuitable for certain types of clients: entrepreneurs, corporate employees, self-employed individuals, professionals. Does the planner specialize in working with clients at certain income levels?

9. *Can I see a list of referrals?*

   Talk to current and ex-clients for feedback about the planner.

10. *Am I comfortable with this person?*

    You and your planner must have a trusting and friendly relationship. Since many financial planners have a professional designation, below is a list of common designations and a brief description of the qualifications.

Designation	Abbreviation	Qualifications
Accredited Estate Planner	AEP	Title awarded by the National Association of Estate Planners to professionals who pass an exam and meet educational requirements.
Certified Financial Planner	CFP	Must pass a series of five modules and a 10-hour comprehensive exam. The exam covers various planning topics such as retirement planning, income taxes, estate and gift taxes, investments and insurance. Must meet continuing education requirements.
Certified Fund Specialist	CFS	Must pass a sixty-hour course and exam on mutual funds sponsored by the Institute of Certified Fund Specialists.
Certified Retirement Planner	CRP	Must pass an exam offered by the American Institute of Retirement Planners. Must meet continuing education requirements.
Chartered Financial Consultant	ChFC	Certified by the American College of Bryn Mawr as being proficient in investments, real estate ventures and tax shelters. Must pass a series of 10 exams. Must meet continuing education requirements.
Chartered Life Underwriter	CLU	Most holders of this designation are in the life insurance industry. They must pass a series of 10 exams that cover various planning issues as estate and gift taxes, income tax, investment and retirement. Must meet continuing education requirements.
Chartered Mutual Fund Consultant	CMFC	Must complete a course and exam sponsored by the National Endowment for Financial Education and the Investment Company Institute (a trade group for mutual funds).
Enrolled Agent	EA	Designation conferred by the IRS to income tax specialists who pass an exam.
Personal Financial Specialist	PFS	A CPA who has proven financial planning experience receives this designation after passing a six-hour examination. Must meet continuing education requirements.
Registered Financial Consultant	RFC	Title awarded by the International Association of Registered Financial Consultants to professionals who meet educational and experience requirements.
Registered Investment Advisor	RIA	Registration varies from state to state. Must pass an exam. An RIA is regulated by the states in most cases and by the SEC. There is no educational requirement.

In addition to going to a financial planner, you might also talk to a stockbroker. In order to help you understand more about the services and some types of accounts stockbrokers offer, use the following table.

	Advantages	Disadvantages
Mutual Funds	❖ Professional money manager ❖ Total costs are low	❖ Must do own asset allocation strategy ❖ Must do own research for fund selection decision
Full-Service Broker	❖ Ability to select individual securities, custom-design portfolio to fit personal circumstances ❖ Availability of brokerage firm research	❖ Broker's income based on frequency and size of trades ❖ Higher trading costs than discount brokers ❖ Must depend on individual broker's competence
Discount Broker	❖ No pressure to trade ❖ Ability to select individual securities, custom-design portfolio to fit personal circumstances ❖ Total costs held to absolute minimum	❖ Must do own asset allocation and research ❖ Investment knowledge necessary
Wrap Accounts	❖ Professional money management ❖ No incentive for the broker to make frequent trades	❖ Total costs are high. Usually 3% of annual account value. ❖ Manager-selection criteria not always explicit ❖ Must depend on individual broker's competence for manager selection and performance monitoring ❖ Choice of managers limited to those offered by firm and followed by broker

Commissions on a $10,000 Investment

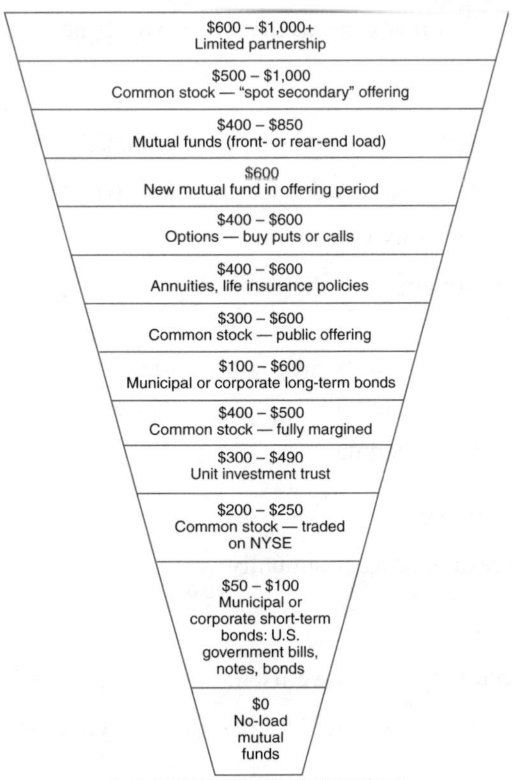

Source: "The Guide to Investor Protection" by Mary Calhoun

Items for Action

Don't discount the importance of your investment allocation and your rate of return. You should consider your investment returns as another source of income, much like your salary. This additional income can help you reach your goals.

Use the following Items for Action to ensure that your investment allocation, rate of return and goals are appropriate for your personal circumstances.

For each of the following items, assign a priority based on its importance to you: A (highest), B (medium) or C (lowest). Then check off each item as it is completed.

	Priority	Completed
Step 1: Establish Financial Goals		
❖ Contribute at least 10% to your company's saving or thrift plan.	_______	❑
❖ Eliminate high-interest personal debt.	_______	❑
❖ Save for your children's education.	_______	❑
Step 2: Identify Your Constraints		
❖ If your time horizon is more than five years, a majority of your investments should be in stock.	_______	❑
❖ If your time horizon is less than five years, invest for safety.	_______	❑
Step 3: Diversify, Diversify, Diversify		
❖ Diversify *among* asset categories and *within* asset categories.	_______	❑
❖ Invest in both value stocks and growth stocks to enhance diversification.	_______	❑
❖ Use dollar-cost averaging when investing to diversify over time.	_______	❑
Step 4: Determine Your Investment Mix		
❖ Understand the risk and rewards of any investment you make.	_______	❑
❖ Take the Risk Tolerance Test so you can determine your investor profile.	_______	❑
❖ Select an optimal portfolio that suits your investor profile.	_______	❑
❖ Reallocate your current investment portfolio over an 18- to 24-month time period.	_______	❑
❖ Invest in short-term and medium-term bonds, not long-term bonds.	_______	❑
❖ If investing more than $250,000 in bonds, purchase individual bonds with a laddered maturity schedule.	_______	❑
Step 5: Evaluate Your Rate of Return		
❖ Evaluate your investment results at least annually.	_______	❑
Choosing a Financial Planner		
❖ Ask family or friends whom they may have used.	_______	❑
❖ Use the 10 questions and answers as a guide when interviewing a potential planner.	_______	❑

Resources

American Association of Individual Investors (AAII)

625 N. Michigan Ave.
Chicago, IL 60611-3110
800/428-2244
www.aaii.com

The AAII is an "independent, nonprofit corporation formed for the purpose of assisting individuals in becoming effective managers of their own assets through programs of education, information and research." For a $49 annual membership fee, you receive a monthly magazine and an annual mutual fund review and can attend local investment meetings.

American Institute of Certified Public Accountants (AICPA)

PFS Division
1211 Avenue of the Americas
New York, NY 10036
888/777-7077
www.cpapfs.org

For information and a list of personal financial specialists in your area.

Bureau of the Public Debt

Savings Bond Operations Office
Parkersburg, WV 26106-1328

For additional information on investing in U.S. savings bonds, including current rate information, visit the Bureau's Web site at **www.publicdebt.treas.gov** or call **800/4US-BOND** (800/487-2663). The Web site includes a calculator called the "Savings Bond Wizard" to help you track the value of your bonds. A similar calculator is also available at the New York Federal Reserve Bank's Web site (**http://app.ny.frb.org/sbr**).

The Financial Planning Association (FPA)

3801 East Florida Avenue, #708
Denver, CO 80210
800/282-PLAN
www.fpanet.org

You can contact the FPA to obtain a list of CFP practitioners in your area and free brochures about financial planning.

Magazines and Newspapers

These newspapers and magazines can help you learn more about investing and business. Many of them can be found in your local library or at a newsstand.

The Wall Street Journal (www.wsj.com) is the most widely read business newspaper. It also has daily articles about investing and money matters.

Barron's (www.barrons.com) is a weekly newspaper that reviews the stock markets. The Lipper Analytical Services' mutual fund performance ratings are included on a quarterly basis. There are also frequent articles on mutual-fund investing.

Investors Business Daily (www.investors.com) is a daily newspaper that focuses on investment (rather than business) news and information.

Forbes (www.forbes.com)
A bi-weekly investment magazine that looks at news from an investment point of view, *Forbes* has an annual mutual fund survey usually published in August.

Morningstar, Inc.

225 West Wacker Drive
Chicago, IL 60606
800/735-0700
www.morningstar.com

Morningstar provides data on more than 10,000 mutual funds (including load, no-load, equity and fixed-income), 8,000 stocks and 5,000 variable annuity/life subaccounts. Its five-star rating system measures both risk and return.

National Association of Personal Financial Advisors (NAPFA)

355 West Dundee Road, Suite 200
Buffalo Grove, IL 60089
888/FEE-ONLY
www.napfa.org

This association provides a free brochure containing questions that you should ask when interviewing potential planners. The questions particularly stress disclosure. In addition, it will supply you with a list of *fee-only* planners in your area.

The National Association of Securities Dealers (NASD)

P.O. Box 9401
Gaithersburg, MD 20898-9401
800/289-9999
www.nasdr.com

The association reports disciplinary and pending actions by industry, federal and state securities regulators against, as well as convictions of, brokers and their firms. In addition to this organization, you may want to contact a state agency.

North American Securities Administrators Association (NASAA)

1 Massachusetts Ave., N.W., Suite 310
Washington, DC 20001
202/737-0900
www.nasaa.org

Made up of state securities regulators, this organization can help you find the agency in your state that handles disciplinary actions against brokers and their firms.

Securities and Exchange Commission (SEC)

Office of Consumer Affairs and Information Services
450 Fifth St., N.W.
Washington, DC 20549
800/732-0330
www.sec.gov

The SEC can tell you if your financial planner is a registered investment advisor.

Value Line, Inc.

220 East 42nd Street
New York, NY 10017
800/535-8760
www.valueline.com

Value Line reviews approximately 1,700 stocks and 2,000 mutual funds. The service rates securities and funds for risk potential and timeliness using a computer model based on the issuing company's earnings momentum.

Web Sites — Information on Bonds

www.publicdebt.treas.gov — Results of recent Treasury auctions, dates for upcoming auctions, explanations of how to buy Treasury securities and news on savings bonds.

www.bonds-online.com — News on U.S. government, corporate and municipal bonds, with market commentary.

www.moodys.com — Bond ratings and research.

www.economeister.com — Daily U.S. and international news from Market News International, Inc., a wire service for bond investors.

www.mysavingsbonds.com — For U.S. savings bonds: Plug in the face value, month and year issued and redemption year, and the calculator will tell you the value of your bond.

www.financenter.com — Lets you perform customized bond calculations; includes a feature that allows you to calculate an after-tax return, based on your federal and state tax rates.

Web Sites — Information on Mutual Funds

www.brill.com — Mutual-fund basics, fund profiles, analysis.

www.mfea.com — Links to more than 40 no-load fund groups, educational materials, investing tips.

www.fundalarm.com — Tough commentary on funds with high fees, bloated assets or mediocre returns.

www.greenmoney.com — Lists of socially responsible funds and money-management firms, articles and research on socially responsible investing.

Web Sites — Information on Stocks

www.bloomberg.com — Stock quotes, commodity prices and interest rates (as well as headlines and sports).

www.briefing.com — The day's biggest winners and losers, updated stock indexes, market commentary (for people who can't wait until the morning for the prior day's trading news).

www.cnnfn.com — Review from CNNfn of the day's business and market news.

www.investools.com — Cafeteria of more than 30 financial newsletters that you can buy piecemeal.

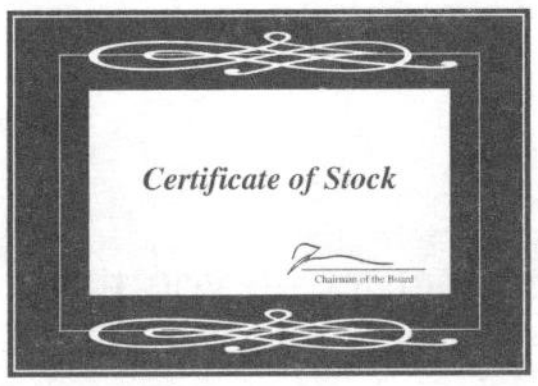

Company Stock Options

Investors dream of the perfect opportunity — minimum risk, minimum cash outlay and maximum return. In effect, stock options granted by a company to an employee can deliver this kind of opportunity. If you have been granted such options, it is important to understand both financial and tax considerations in order to maximize the value of the options.

A stock option gives you the right to purchase your employer's common stock at a specified price for a certain period of time. The option price, or purchase price (sometimes called the exercise price), is generally equal to the fair-market value of the common stock on the date the stock option was granted. The time period over which the stock may be purchased — the option term — begins with the date the stock option is awarded and typically ends 10 years later. The process of purchasing stock with your stock option is known as exercising the option.

There is generally a waiting (or vesting) period before any stock option can be exercised. In addition, there may be other conditions (*e.g.*, stock-price appreciation) that must be met before stock can be purchased. An example of a vesting schedule is found in the table to the right.

Sample Vesting Schedule

Anniversary of Award Date	Percentage of Award Vested
1st	25%
2nd	50%
3rd	75%
4th	100%

Most often, the right to purchase shares is cumulative. Based on the vesting schedule at right, if your award was for 1,000 shares, you could purchase up to a maximum of 250 shares beginning on the first anniversary of the option award; up to 500 shares beginning on the second anniversary; up to 750 shares on the third anniversary; and the entire 1,000 shares beginning on the fourth anniversary.

The specific terms of your options will be found in the documents you received at the time of your award. They may include an option agreement, prospectus and plan documents. These documents will tell you the number of shares you have a right to purchase, the option price, option term and other provisions that control the timing and manner in which the option can be exercised (for example, what happens upon retirement or other separation from service). Receiving stock options does not result in immediate federal-income-tax consequences.

Special Consideration:

Stock Splits

When your company stock splits, the same split will apply to all outstanding and unexercised stock-option awards. In a two-for-one stock split, for example, you'll have two option shares for every one option previously held, and the option price after the split will be half of the option price prior to the split. The total value of your award will not be affected directly as a result of any stock split.

Understanding the Value

The underlying value of your stock options comes from a unique combination of factors — you have the opportunity to benefit from any price appreciation that your company's stock may experience over the option term without any cash outlay on your part. When the stock's fair-market value rises above the option price during the option term (and all conditions for exercise stated in the option documents are met), you may purchase stock at the option price even though the fair-market value is higher. The difference between the fair-market value of the stock at any given time and the option price represents your profit (before taxes) and is called the spread. Generally, if the stock's fair-market value were to fall below the option price, the option should not be exercised.

In addition to the spread, stock options have another element of value — time value. Although difficult to measure, the time-value element represents the potential for additional stock-price appreciation over the remaining option term. As you can see in the chart at right, time value declines over the option term. When you exercise options you capture the spread at that time but give up the time-value element.

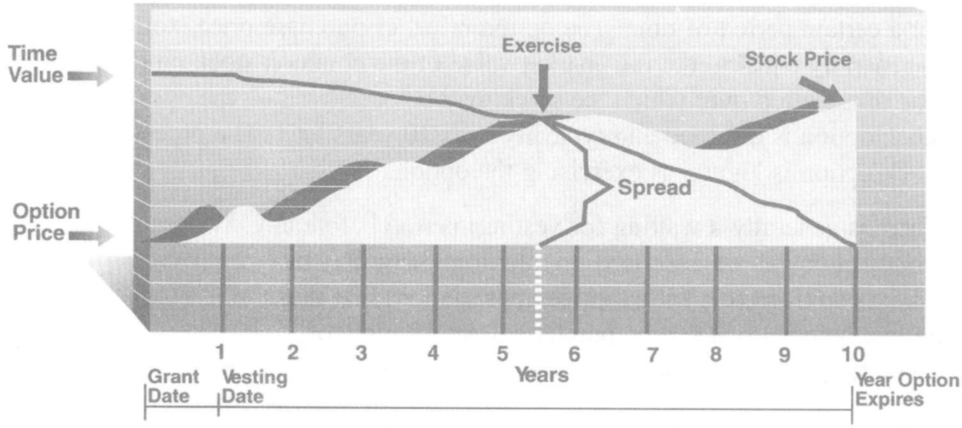

Valuing Your Options

Use this worksheet to track the value of your stock options.

1	2	3	4	5	6	7	8
Grant Date	Number of Shares Granted	Number of Shares Exercised	Number of Shares Unexercised 2 – 3	Today's Stock Price	Option Price	Spread 5 – 6	Value of Unexercised Options 4 x 7

Methods for Exercising Options

The steps you'll need to follow to exercise your vested and exercisable stock options generally are straightforward. Your company will provide you with the necessary forms and instructions. There are three basic ways to exercise options, although all three may not be available in any given situation.

Cash — With this method, you pay the option price and any taxes due in cash. A cash exercise generally is attractive if you wish to exercise your option and hold the maximum number of shares available under the option. However, a potential drawback of this exercise method is that you must have sufficient cash to pay the option price on the shares being exercised.

Stock Swap — A second way in which stock options can be exercised is to trade in shares of company stock you already own that have a value equal to the option price due to complete the exercise. This method, sometimes referred to as a stock-for-stock exercise, is an attractive way to increase your share ownership while minimizing cash outlay. Your company also may allow you to use a combination of cash and stock to cover the cost of exercising.

Cashless — By using this popular method, you can exercise your stock options through a stockbroker using funds advanced by the broker. You sell all or part of the option shares exercised to cover the full cost to exercise, and you keep the balance of the shares or sell them to generate cash for yourself. You'll also pay the applicable broker fees and any interest incurred. Sometimes this method is facilitated by an established arrangement between the company and a brokerage firm, but in all instances you must establish your own account with the brokerage before exercising your options.

Non-qualified Stock Options

There are two types of stock-option awards — non-qualified stock options (NQSOs) and incentive stock options (ISOs). The primary difference between them is the tax consequence upon exercising. In addition to NQSOs and ISOs, sometimes stock-appreciation rights (SARs) may be awarded under a stock plan. We will limit our discussion here to NQSOs and ISOs.

Cost to Exercise

The amount you pay when you exercise non-qualified stock options equals the sum of:

- ❖ The option price per share multiplied by the number of shares you're purchasing; and
- ❖ The tax withholding required to satisfy federal, state and, if applicable, local income taxes, as well as Social Security and Medicare taxes.

The difference between the fair-market value of the stock at the time you exercise the option and the option price (*i.e.*, the spread) will be considered taxable compensation income. Your company is required to withhold the applicable taxes based on the spread at the time of exercise. Current law requires federal income taxes to be withheld at a rate of at least 27%. Depending upon the location of your work and/or residence, your company may be required to withhold a percentage for state and local taxes as well. Social Security taxes are withheld at a rate of 6.2% on compensation income up to the Social Security wage base, and Medicare taxes are withheld at a rate of 1.45% on all compensation.

Cost to Exercise NQSOs

You want to purchase 100 shares from a non-qualified option award with an exercise price of $10 per share. The fair-market value (FMV) of a share of common stock on the day you exercise your option is $20. How much would it cost you to exercise your option for 100 shares?

FMV at Exercise (100 x $20)	$2,000
Option Price (100 x $10)	(1,000)
Taxable Income or Spread	$1,000
Tax-Withholding Rate*	x 38.65%
Tax Withholding	$ 387

Option Price (100 x $10)	$1,000
Tax Withholding	387
Total Cost to Exercise =	**$1,387**

* Assumed 27% federal, 3% state, 1% city, 6.2% Social Security and 1.45% Medicare.

Your actual tax liability due as a result of exercising your options may be larger than the tax paid through withholding. Any additional liability, while not necessarily due at the time of exercise, is part of your overall cost to exercise as well. Further, if you incur transaction fees in the process of exercising your options, these fees should also be thought of as part of your cost to exercise.

Tax Basis of NQSO Shares

For tax purposes, the value used as the starting point in figuring gain or loss on the sale of stock is called its cost basis or tax basis. Shares received from the cash or cashless exercise of non-qualified stock options will have a basis equal to the fair-market value of your company stock on the date you exercised your option. The holding period (the length of time you are considered to have owned the shares for tax purposes) for these shares begins on the date of exercise.

The basis of the shares acquired through the exercise of stock options using company stock that you already owned (a stock-swap exercise) is not as straightforward. The new shares equal in number to the number of already-owned shares used in the option exercise will retain the original tax basis and holding period of the shares swapped. The additional shares acquired in your swap exercise will have a tax basis equal to the fair-market value of your company stock on the date of exercise. The holding period of these additional newly acquired shares begins on the date of exercise.

Stock-Swap Exercise of NQSOs

You swap 50 shares having a basis of $5 per share in order to exercise an option to purchase 100 shares at $10 per share when the fair-market value of your company stock is $20 per share. You receive 100 shares as a result of the exercise. Fifty of these shares will retain the basis of the swapped shares ($5 per share) and 50 newly acquired shares will have a basis of $20 per share (the fair-market value as of the date of exercise).

Your holding period for the 50 shares with a $5 basis will be the same as that of the 50 already-owned shares that were swapped. Your holding period for the additional 50 newly acquired shares with a $20 basis begins on the exercise date.

Selling NQSO Shares

If you choose to sell shares you've acquired through the exercise of non-qualified stock options, your taxable gain or loss will be the difference between their tax basis and the sales price. You'll have a capital gain if you sell your company stock at a price higher than the tax basis, and you'll have a capital loss if you sell at a price lower than the tax basis.

The length of your holding period will determine whether your gain or loss is classified as "long-term" or "short-term." If it is more than one year, the gain or loss on the stock will be classified as long-term.

Under current law, short-term capital gains are taxed at the same rates as all other income. However, a long-term gain will be taxed at a rate of no more than 20%.

If you sell your stock at a loss, the loss can be used to offset taxable capital gains that you report on your income-tax return. Additionally, if your capital losses exceed your reportable capital gains, they can be used to offset up to $3,000 of other income annually. Any losses that can't be used can be carried forward to future years. Wash-sale rules prohibit you from taking a loss on the sale of stock if you acquire the same stock within 30 days of the sale.

Incentive Stock Options

Incentive stock options (ISOs), like non-qualified stock options, give you the opportunity to benefit from any appreciation in your company's stock price during the option term. ISOs, however, are eligible for advantageous tax treatment, provided certain holding-period requirements are met. The exercise of an ISO (other than by the cashless exercise method) generally doesn't create immediate income for regular tax purposes (although it does result in income for alternative-minimum-tax purposes — see discussion below). Consequently, the cost to exercise ISOs generally is only the option price.

ISOs and the Alternative Minimum Tax

The U.S. Internal Revenue Code provides for a secondary tax system called the alternative minimum tax (AMT). AMT was designed to ensure that high-income taxpayers pay their "fair share" of income tax. This system takes your regular taxable income and adds back items that are otherwise deductible or excluded from income. Then, it takes the resulting larger amount of taxable income and subjects it to a tax rate of 26% or 28%. If the resulting tax is more than your regular tax, you owe the difference. What items are added back? They're called preferences and adjustments, and they include real-estate taxes, state income taxes, interest on home-equity loans *and the spread on the exercise of an ISO.*

You must pay AMT to the extent it exceeds your regular tax liability. However, to the extent you incur an AMT liability in one year due to certain preferences or adjustments (such as the ISO spread), a credit for AMT paid may be available to offset your regular tax liability in succeeding years when there is no AMT liability.

ISOs and the Alternative Minimum Tax

Regular Tax

Adjusted Gross Income		$80,000
Exemptions		(12,000)
Itemized Deductions		
Contributions	$5,000	
Real-Estate Taxes	3,000	
Mortgage Interest	9,000	
Total		(17,000)
Taxable Income		$51,000
Regular Tax		$ 7,566

Alternative Minimum Tax

Taxable Income		$51,000
Preferences and Adjustments		
Exemptions	$12,000	
Real-Estate Taxes	3,000	
Spread on ISOs	15,000	
Total		30,000
Exemption		(49,000)
AMT Income		$32,000
Tentative Minimum Tax (26%)		$ 8,320

Alternative Minimum Tax = $754

Note: This example assumes four personal and dependency exemptions, no state income tax and the exercise of 1,500 ISO shares having a spread of $10 per share in 2002.

Tax Basis of ISO Shares

When you eventually sell your shares of company stock, you will need to compute the gain or loss resulting from the sale. To do so, you must know your cost or tax basis. In most cases, basis is calculated differently for ISO shares than for NQSO shares and varies with the method you used to exercise your options.

Cash — Quite simply, your basis for regular tax purposes on shares acquired through a cash exercise is the price you paid to exercise the incentive stock option — the option price.

Stock Swap — Like the swap exercise of NQSOs, the number of shares swapped to cover the cost to exercise the ISO (*i.e.*, the option price) retain their original basis and capital gains holding period. Because there is no taxable income as a result of the ISO exercise, the total basis of the newly acquired shares is equal to the amount of cash you paid to exercise the option. In most cases, this amount is zero or a relatively small amount.

Special Consideration:

Gifting Zero- or Low-Basis ISO Shares

Zero- or low-basis ISO shares acquired in a stock swap can be attractive for gifting to charity, a child age 14 or over, or another low-rate taxpayer. Once the required holding period has been met (see discussion of "disqualifying disposition" below), you won't recognize any of the gain as taxable income when you gift your ISO shares. If the gift is to a charity, you'll also get a charitable tax deduction for the full fair-market value of the stock as of the date of the gift.

Let's consider an example. If you gave a charity one share of zero- or low-basis stock with a fair-market value of $20, you essentially would be giving away $20 of gain assuming the holding-period requirements have been met. However, if the stock was acquired with a cash exercise for $10 per share, you would be giving away only $10 of gain. In either case, you could deduct the full $20 value of the stock as a charitable deduction on *Schedule A* of your IRS *Form 1040*.

Cashless — To the extent shares are sold immediately upon exercise of an ISO, a "disqualifying disposition" occurs and the spread will be treated as ordinary income, subject to tax withholding (see the discussion of disqualifying dispositions that follows). The retained shares will have a tax basis equal to the option price.

Disposition of Stock

In order for shares of stock purchased through the exercise of an ISO to retain their favorable tax treatment, you must not dispose of them until you've held them for at least a year after exercising *and* at least two years after the options were granted to you. Consequently, if you sell the stock after the end of the required holding period, the difference between your tax basis and the sale price will be treated as long-term capital gain or loss for tax purposes.

The disposition of ISO shares within one year of exercise or within two years of the date the options were granted to you will be deemed a "disqualifying disposition" of those shares, according to IRS rules. As a result, you must recognize ordinary income (rather than capital-gain income) equal to the difference between the option price and the fair-market value of the stock on the exercise date — the spread — or the actual price on the date of disposition, if less. At the time the option is "disqualified," applicable federal, state and local taxes may be due on the amount of the ordinary income. If the fair-market value of the stock on the date of disposition exceeds the value on the exercise date, the difference between these values will be treated as either long-term or short-term capital gain, depending upon your holding period.

Disqualifying dispositions can result from the sale or gift of ISO shares, in addition to the cashless exercise of ISOs. Also, if ISO shares are swapped to exercise an incentive stock option before the required holding period has been ended, a disqualifying disposition will result. However, you may swap in ISO shares to exercise a NQSO without triggering a disqualifying disposition.

Stock-Option Strategies — NQSOs

Exercising stock options is relatively simple. Deciding *when* to exercise is the problem. You have the same problem when deciding to sell stock on the open market: What are your expectations for the price of the company's stock? In addition, you must consider two elements unique to stock options:

- How much time remains in the option term?
- Will future income-tax rates increase? Decrease? Stabilize?

You don't have to exercise all your options at once. In fact, it may be prudent to exercise the options over time (*i.e.,* 35% or 50% at a time). This is a form of diversification using time.

Of course, exercising a stock option doesn't necessarily mean a sale of stock. You may exercise the option and then hold the stock. Or you may exercise to establish your cost basis. Then, assuming the stock appreciates, you can make a gift of it to others without tax consequences on the appreciated amount. But keep in mind that this approach requires sufficient capital to exercise the option *and* to pay the taxes due on the difference between the option price and the exercise price.

The following strategies represent two common approaches to exercising stock options. In Strategy 1, you exercise right away and sell the stock. In Strategy 2, you wait a year to exercise, then sell. Consider the *loan* aspect of a stock-option grant when reviewing these strategies. Theoretically, you've been granted an interest-free loan to buy stock in your company. Each year that you don't exercise the options, you have the use of that interest-free loan for one more year. Potentially this allows the stock to continue to appreciate.

Strategy 1: Current exercise and immediate sale — In this strategy, you exercise an option that costs $27.94 to buy a share of stock that's worth $45. You sell the stock immediately to realize an after-tax profit of $11.43. You invest this $11.43 at 3%, and, after one year, it would have grown to $11.77.

Exercise, Sell and Invest Proceeds

Stock price	$45.00
Option price	(27.94)
Taxable income	$17.06
Subtract income taxes (33% assumed)	(5.63)
After-tax profit per share	$11.43
Proceeds (per share) in one year from sale of shares at a simple interest of 3% after-tax	$11.77

Current price of the stock

What the option costs you

Profit from the immediate sale

Strategy 2: Deferred exercise and immediate sale — This strategy assumes you'll hold the option (defer exercise) for one year, then exercise and immediately sell the shares.

The following table shows what happens when you defer, then sell. It also shows how changes in the value per share affect your profit. For example, if the stock increases just 3% to $46.35 (see column 3), your profit per share — if you wait a year, exercise, and then sell the stock — is $12.33. This is more than the $11.77 you earned in Strategy 1 when you exercised, sold immediately and invested elsewhere, earning 3% after taxes.

In column 4 you can see that a larger increase in the stock price (compared to the current value of $45) increases your profit per share by 24% to $14.14. So a 24% increase in the after-tax profit results from a mere 9% increase in the stock's price. You'd have to invest your after-tax profit of $11.43 (from Strategy 1) at 24% after taxes to end up with $14.14. Of course, if the stock price declines while you're deferring the option, so does your after-tax profit.

These illustrations show that you have to analyze investment options each time you consider exercising. Develop your own comparison — similar to what we've done here — before you make a decision.

Wait One Year to Exercise, Then Sell

	Change in value per share of stock			
Market Value	Down 5%	Same	Up 3%	Up 9%
Stock price	$42.75	$45.00	$46.35	$49.05
Subtract cost of option	(27.94)	(27.94)	(27.94)	(27.94)
Taxable income	$14.81	$17.06	$18.41	$21.11
Subtract income taxes (33%)	(4.89)	(5.63)	(6.08)	(6.97)
After-tax profit/share	$ 9.92	$11.43	$12.33	$14.14

When Should You Exercise?

You generally should exercise your stock option(s) in stages (diversify over time). Think about exercising when:

- The stock price has increased by 2 to 2.5 times the initial option price
- You're in the second half of your option term (especially in years 7 to 9)
- The dividend rate (as a percentage of the after-tax cost to exercise the option) is more than prevailing interest rates (either your borrowing rate or the lowest rate you earn on money-market-type investments).

Special Considerations for the Exercise of ISOs

In general, the recommended strategy for exercising incentive stock options (ISOs) is the same as for NQSOs — wait for the stock price to increase by 2 to 2.5 times the initial option price and exercise in stages during the second half of your option term. However, there are special considerations for the exercise of ISOs due to the unique tax treatment that they receive.

Determine Your AMT "Opportunity" — Although a credit may be available to the extent you pay AMT, it's generally advisable to avoid being subject to the alternative tax system. Before exercising ISOs, determine your AMT "opportunity" (or have a financial professional do this for you). This is the difference between your regular income tax and your alternative minimum tax. If your regular tax is greater than your AMT, you have the opportunity to exercise ISOs without owing any additional tax.

Let's consider an example. Assume that the projected difference between your regular tax and AMT before including ISO spread is $3,000. If you're in the 26% AMT bracket, you may be able to exercise ISOs having a spread of $11,500 without incurring any additional tax.

Additionally, you may want to consider exercising both NQSOs and ISOs in the same tax year if you've been granted both types of options. By exercising NQSOs (or disqualifying ISOs) you increase your regular taxable income by the amount of the spread and, consequently, your regular tax due. This additional regular tax will increase your AMT "opportunity" and allow you to exercise additional ISOs without incurring any AMT. Likewise, the sale of ISO shares acquired during a previous option exercise might allow you to recognize more ISO spread currently without incurring AMT. Before implementing these strategies, carefully review their tax implications with your financial advisor.

Consider Exercising Early — If you're optimistic about the future performance of your company's stock and intend to hold your ISO shares as a long-term investment after exercising your options, you might consider exercising early in the option term rather than later. What will this strategy do for you? Assuming limited price appreciation as of the exercise date, you limit the amount of spread that must be included in your AMT income. As illustrated in the example earlier in this chapter, even a middle-class taxpayer with a modest spread on ISOs can be faced with AMT. Consequently, this strategy can potentially lower your tax bill at the time you exercise your options. The downside of this strategy is that you forgo the interest-free-loan aspect of your option by paying the option price when you exercise.

When Option Shares Have Lost Value — If you've exercised and held ISOs this year that have since dropped in value, you should consider the following question: Should you sell the ISO shares before year end to reduce or eliminate AMT, or should you continue to hold them with the hope that the stock's price will bounce back? Remember, a sale prior to the end of the calendar year would be a disqualifying disposition of ISO shares and the difference between the option price and the sale price must be recognized as ordinary income.

Let's assume you've exercised an option with a price of $10 per share when the fair-market value per share was $50. If you are subject to the AMT, you may have to pay $10.40 or more per share exercised in additional tax on the $40 AMT spread. However, if you sold the stock before year-end when the fair-market value was only $20 per share, the $10 difference (between the sale price and the option price) would be taxed at your regular tax rate (let's assume 27%) and you would pay only $2.70 per share in additional tax. On the other hand, if you had waited to sell the ISO share, a credit for the AMT paid in the year of exercise may be available in subsequent years to reduce the regular tax due. Additionally, if the stock price recovered and was sold at $50, you would be much further ahead by selling at $50 instead of at $20.

In this situation, consider selling if you don't expect the stock price to recover adequately or if you don't have the cash to pay the AMT. However, if you have the funds to pay the additional tax and you expect the stock's price to appreciate substantially, waiting to sell may be the best choice.

The tax issues associated with ISOs are complex, while the potential benefit of ISOs is high. Each person's tax and financial circumstances are unique. Therefore, it is impossible to lay out guidelines for the exercise of ISOs that will be appropriate for everyone who has been granted them. Nonetheless, the following summary lists significant issues to consider. Although concise in format, these issues can be complex and deserve your thorough consideration. In general, the more of these to which you can reply "yes," the more likely a current exercise of the ISO is appropriate.

- ❖ Do you feel the stock will move upward significantly in the future?
- ❖ Do you want to hold the stock for at least one year following the exercise?
- ❖ Do you have sufficient cash available to pay the exercise price? Or do you have shares of stock in your possession that you can use to swap to pay the exercise price?
- ❖ Do you want to give shares of stock to charity or to a lower-bracket taxpayer?
- ❖ Can you exercise without incurring the AMT? If not, do you have cash available to pay the AMT?
- ❖ Do you have other ISO grants outstanding?
- ❖ Are you near retirement or is it likely that you will leave your current employer in the near future?

Given the complexity of stock options and the significant income they could potentially provide you, consider obtaining the advice of a financial planner or other qualified professional before exercising your options.

Items for Action

If used properly, your company stock-option grant may provide you with substantial value. Consequently, it is very important to understand the terms of the stock options you've been granted and how they work. It's equally important to establish a *strategy* for exercising your options. Use the Items for Action below to get started.

For each of the following items, assign a priority based on its importance to you: A (highest), B (medium) or C (lowest). Then check off each item as it is completed.

	Priority	Completed
❖ Review and understand how your stock options work, including the exercise methods available and the potential tax consequences.	_______	❑
❖ Review your expectations for tax rates and growth of your company stock.	_______	❑
❖ Establish a timetable for exercising your options.	_______	❑
❖ Determine the appropriate exercise method for your situation (*i.e.*, cash, stock swap or cashless exercise).	_______	❑

Resources

Books

Consider Your Options: Get the Most from Your Equity Compensation
Thomas, Kaye A.; Fairmark Press Inc.; 2000; 248 pages; $23.95
Described as a plain-language guide to getting the maximum value from your equity compensation, this book offers guidance on stock grants and employee stock-purchase plans, as well as incentive and non-qualified options.

Stock Options; An Authoritative Guide to Incentive and Nonqualified Stock Options (2nd edition)
Pastore, Robert R.; PCM Capital Publishing; 1999; 150 pages; $39.95
This book offers professionals as well as the layperson concise guidance on employee stock options. The author spends considerable time on tax issues, detailing the ramifications of long-term capital gains, AMT and disqualifying dispositions of stock.

myStockOptions.com

This Web site offers a variety of stock-option education resources, such as a global tax guide and glossary of terms. The site also includes useful calculators and modeling tools. If you're looking for informative articles, **myStockOptions.com** includes extensive links to articles ranging in topic from AMT to year-end planning.

Risk Protection

Most financial catastrophes are the result of overborrowing, overspending and underdiversifying. But there is another pitfall to be avoided: underinsuring. Many people hesitate to purchase insurance or fail to purchase the right insurance because it seems too complicated or too costly. If you take the time to master a few simple principles, however, you can protect your family at a reasonable cost. This section will show you how.

Life Insurance

"Do I have enough life insurance?" This is a common worry. On the next page you'll find a worksheet, *Determine Your Life-Insurance Needs,* to help you calculate how much life insurance you need.

Consider your goals as you fill out the worksheet. Most people buy life insurance to provide income to survivors. If you cannot identify your goals for your family, you won't truly be able to determine how much money you'll need to satisfy them. If you have ambitious goals and fail to spell them out, you may end up being underinsured. If your goals are more modest, you could easily be overinsured, which means you'll be paying too much in insurance premiums. Knowing your goals will help you reach your most cost-effective level of coverage.

The following three steps will help you determine how much life insurance you need:

Step 1: Add Up Your Investable Assets and Estimate Your Survivors' Sources of Income

How much income will your survivors need? This general question is hard to answer. Break it down into specific questions like these:

- Can my surviving spouse replace all or part of my lost earnings or return to the job market? (Be realistic!)
- How long must the replacement income last: Until the children finish school? For the life of my surviving spouse?
- Will my spouse benefit from life insurance, my employer's survivor benefits, Social Security, or other benefits? Will it be enough?

The answers to these and other questions should give you a more accurate picture of your surviving spouse's sources of income.

Determine Your Life-Insurance Needs

			Example	Your Situation
Line 1.	**Sources of survivors' annual income**			
	A. Value of your savings, investments and liquid assets. Include retirement plan savings, company savings plan, IRA or Keogh (and pension plan if available after your death in a lump sum)		$ 100,000	$
	B. Multiply the total from line A by 2% to show the estimated annual income from these assets after taxes and inflation		$ 2,000	$
	C. Spouse's wages (if applicable) — include only 50% to adjust for taxes and eventual retirement		$ 0	$
	D. Social Security (see Table A) — include only 85% to adjust for taxes		$ 27,115[1]	$
	E. Other income — *e.g.,* pension survivor benefit — include only 40% to adjust for inflation		$ 0	$
	Total annual income available (add lines B, C, D, E)		$ 29,115	$
Line 2.	**Family living expenses** (excluding mortgage, but including property taxes)			
	Be careful here! Most people underestimate living expenses for their survivors.		$ 37,500	$
		Excess	$	$
Line 3.	**Annual income: excess or shortfall** (Line 2 minus total from Line 1)	*Shortfall*	$ 8,385	$

If total in Line 3 is a **shortfall**, complete Line 4, Line 5 and Line 6; if it is an **excess**, complete Line 5 and Line 6 only.

			Example	Your Situation
Line 4.	**Principal needed to provide required annual income**			
	Total from Line 3 above		$ 8,385	$
	Multiply by life insurance estimator factor[2] (see Table B)		x 27.36	x
	Subtotal		$ 229,414	$
Line 5.	**Estimated cash needs**			
	Remaining mortgage		$ 50,000	$
	College education expenses (years x annual cost)		$ 40,000	$
	Outstanding debts		$ 3,000	$
	Funeral costs		$ 6,000	$
	Estate administration		$ 3,000	$
	Cash reserves		$ 10,000	$
	Total cash needs		$ 112,000	$
Line 6.	**Insurance needed**			
	Add: Subtotal Line 4 plus total Line 5		$ 341,414	$
	Subtract: Group life insurance		$ 75,000	$
	Subtract: Personal life insurance		$	$
		Excess	$	$
Line 7.	**Amount of insurance coverage** (excess or shortfall)	*Shortfall*	$ 266,414[3]	$

[1] The total Social Security benefit is estimated to be $31,900 for a deceased 45-year-old employee who earns $50,000 and expects to leave a spouse and two children. If your surviving spouse expects to continue working, his/her benefit (but not the children's) would be reduced based on the Social Security earnings limitation.

[2] Based on the surviving spouse age 45, estimated to live until age 85. It is best to assume you will live until at least age 85. If you want to be more conservative, assume an even longer life span. Approximately 15% of men are likely to live to age 90 and 16% of women to age 95. In this example, we have assumed a 40-year life span.

[3] Typically you should round up the size of the insurance policy to the next $50,000 increment; in this example, the need for an additional $300,000 of life insurance is indicated.

Table A: Approximate Social Security Survivor Benefits

Your Annual Income	Spouse *(No Children)* Benefits Begin at Age 60	Annual Social Security Benefit: Child; Spouse Caring for Child	Annual Social Security Benefit: Maximum Family Benefit
$35,000	$10,200	$10,700	$26,200
$50,000	$13,000	$13,700	$31,900
$65,000	$14,500	$15,200	$35,500
$84,900 +	$16,300	$17,100	$39,900

Table B: Life Insurance Estimator

Years Required	Income Factor*
5	4.71
10	8.98
15	12.85
20	16.35
25	19.52
30	22.40
35	25.00
40	27.36
45	29.49
50	31.32
60	34.76

* Based on the present value of a $1 annual annuity earning a 2% real rate of return.

Step 2: Understand Your Social Security Benefits

These benefits may be important to your survivors' financial well-being. If you have young children, your surviving spouse will receive benefits until your youngest child is 16 years old. Each of your children receives a benefit until he or she is 18 years old or graduates from high school. If your children are older than 16, your surviving spouse will have to wait until age 60 before collecting a survivor benefit.

If your surviving spouse contributed to Social Security, he/she will receive the greater of your survivor benefit or his/her retirement benefit. See Table A for an estimate of your survivor benefit.

If you and your spouse are currently receiving Social Security benefits, you should consider how much your spouse's income will drop after your death. For instance, you receive $800 a month and your spouse is receiving a portion of your benefit — say, $400. When you die, your spouse's Social Security check will increase to the amount you were receiving: $800. Even though your spouse's check increased, the combined income dropped from $1,200 ($800 + $400) to $800. Or take another example: If both you and your spouse are receiving Social Security benefits because you both worked, your spouse's total income will drop by the amount of your Social Security check. Realizing how much your spouse's income will decrease because he/she will no longer receive benefits from a combined Social Security income is an important consideration in determining your life-insurance needs.

Step 3: Estimate Your Survivors' Living Expenses

Identify which living expenses might decrease (for instance, car-maintenance bills and life-insurance premiums) and which might increase (child care, psychological counseling, educational expenses, future medical premiums). Many people also factor in an additional $6,000 to $8,000 each year for medical insurance premiums for their survivors, regardless of their employer's current policies, because medical coverage is always subject to change.

Put This Worksheet to Use

No single worksheet can cover all the factors that influence how much life insurance you'll need, but you can review your projections with your life insurance agent. Carefully examine all your assumptions and play "What if?" by altering your estimate of inflation rates, changes in your earnings, etc.

Also, don't concentrate just on *your* life insurance needs. Consider your spouse, too. If he/she is employed, his/her death may result in a long-term loss of income. Even if your spouse doesn't work outside the home, but provides services to the family you would have to replace (for instance, child care), that increase in living expenses must be covered.

Types of Life Insurance

Once you've determined your insurance needs, you should choose the type of life insurance best suited for your situation. Will you need insurance coverage for your lifetime or for a specific period of time? Insurance can be very costly, so look at the various options and related costs before choosing a policy.

There are two basic types of insurance: temporary and permanent. There are many variations within each type, too.

Temporary (Term) Insurance

As a general rule, people purchase term-insurance policies to insure their families for a given period of time, usually no longer than 15–20 years. For instance, term insurance is often purchased by homeowners carrying a mortgage or by parents of young children. Term insurance is pure insurance — it consists of a death benefit only. It's inexpensive in comparison with other types of life insurance offering the same protection, but premiums increase as you get older.

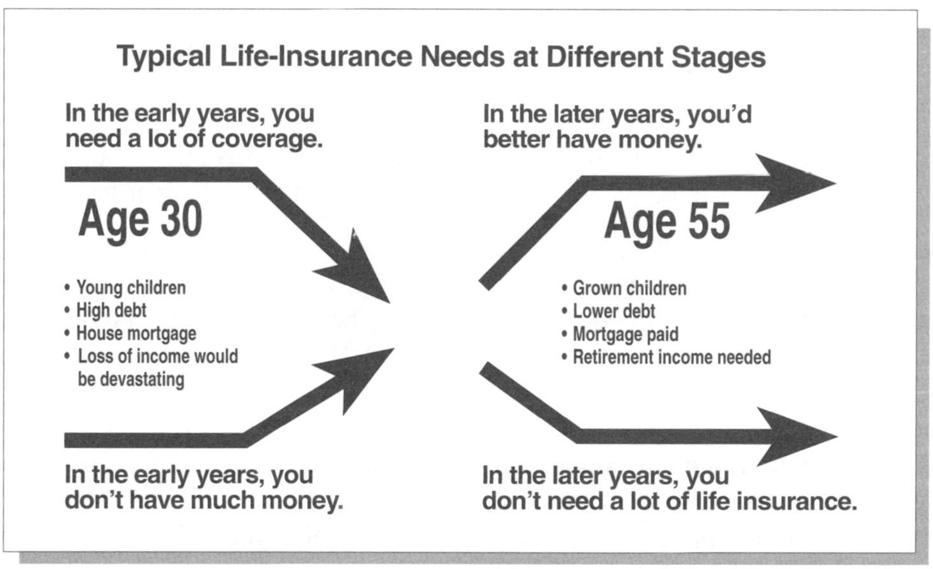

Because term policies don't pay dividends or accumulate cash value, you can compare policies covering the same amount of time easily using the "net payment index," an interest-adjusted measurement reflecting the long-term annual cost of term insurance. All things being equal, the term policy with the lowest net payment index value offers you a better deal. Ask your insurance agent for the net-payment-index values on any term policy you're considering.

Special Consideration:

Individual Term Insurance Quotes

Besides going to your own insurance agent, you may want to check out the following services:

SelectQuote Insurance Services	**InsuranceQuote Services**
800/670-3214	800/972-1104
www.selectquote.com	www.iquote.com

Both services will provide free quotes.

Types of Term Insurance

Yearly renewable — This type of coverage is priced for one year at a time, and its price increases every year. The insurer must keep the policy in effect — regardless of your health status — as long as your premiums are paid. But there's no guarantee that the premiums won't be increased. Widely used for short-term protection, this type of insurance typically provides inexpensive coverage for young adults but can be costly for individuals in their middle years and beyond.

Level or multi-year renewable — Many companies offer terms that range from 5 to 25 years. During the time period selected, the yearly premium will remain the same. At the end of the term, the premiums may be increased substantially if the policy is renewed.

Term to a specified age — Some policies are geared to last until a specified age has been attained, typically 65 or 70. The premium will remain level during the term. Policies like these generally are not renewable but are usually convertible to whole-life coverage.

Straight term — This covers you for the time provided in the policy. Continuing coverage can be obtained only by renewing the policy (subject to insurability) for another period of time and paying the new, higher premium for your new age.

Decreasing term — The face value decreases over the term of the policy while the premium remains the same. Mortgage insurance, which pays off the principal due on a mortgage upon the death of the insured, is a form of decreasing term insurance. Although this term coverage is aimed at matching your insurance needs with the amount of coverage, it tends to be expensive. Renewable and level-term policies offer a more cost-effective alternative.

Permanent Insurance

If your insurance needs are longer than approximately 20 years, it's usually more cost effective to use a "permanent" life-insurance policy. Whole life, universal life and variable life are common types of permanent life insurance. Here's some information to help you compare these policies with term insurance:

Cost — Cash-value policies generally cost much more than term policies with a comparable death benefit. There are two reasons for this: 1) You are buying a death benefit as well as making an investment, and 2) the agent's commissions are higher than with term insurance.

Comparing the cost of permanent policies is complicated because you must factor in the accumulated cash value plus any loan features and dividends (used either to purchase additional coverage, pay premiums or receive in cash). Careful evaluation also should include a review of how the insurance company's past projections compare with actual results.

Flexibility — Cash-value insurance may be used to accumulate savings on a tax-deferred basis. The cash value may be used as collateral for a loan and may eventually pay the policy premiums. From an investment perspective, however, these policies can be inflexible. With many policies, you can't control how your money is invested. Your returns will depend on the insurance company's investment experience, its overhead costs and the size of your agent's commissions.

Indefinite periods — Coverage continues indefinitely as long as the premiums are paid. Unlike term, it doesn't lapse after a specified time period, so renewability and re-entry don't apply.

Borrowing — You can borrow against a cash-value policy, but you're just borrowing your own money, usually at current interest rates. Most policies also contain an automatic premium loan provision.

Tax benefits — The investment portion of the cash-value policy grows tax-deferred, and money you borrow from it is not taxed. Furthermore, the cash value paid to a beneficiary* as part of a death benefit is not taxable to the beneficiary. Generally, benefits payable to a beneficiary from a life-insurance policy are not subject to taxation under federal tax law, except if benefits are composed, in part, of interest on policy proceeds.

Types of Permanent Insurance

Traditional whole life — This type of policy is known as endowment insurance. You pay a fixed premium every year. You earn interest on the cash value, and your beneficiaries receive a fixed benefit if you die. The contract lasts until the insured is 100 years old or dies. If the insured lives to 100, the benefits are paid to the insured. Keep in mind: Whole life is rarely appropriate unless purchased to pay estate taxes, mainly because it is not flexible.

Individual Universal Insurance — Universal life is a permanent insurance plan offering a combination of flexible premiums and adjustable insurance. The death benefit can be increased or decreased as needed, subject to insurability requirements. In addition, the policy allows the tax-deferred growth of its cash value at rates competitive with those of outside cash-equivalent investments.

The cost of a universal policy also will be affected by which type of death benefit you elect. You can choose either a level death benefit (Option A) or an increasing death benefit (Option B). Premiums usually are higher if you select an increasing death benefit.

Finally, the premium for a universal life policy is based upon the insurance company's current interest rate. If the rate were to drop, your annual premium could increase or the policy would lapse before you reached age 95. Ask your agent to show you an illustration with a lower and/or the *guaranteed* minimum interest rate for the contract.

* The named beneficiary on a whole life insurance policy would receive the greater of the cash value or the face amount of the policy. In almost all instances, the face value of the policy exceeds the cash value.

Special Consideration:

Life-Insurance Illustrations

Life-insurance agents sometimes use graphics illustrating premiums and death benefits when selling a policy. *These illustrations are not guarantees of future premiums and/or benefits.* They are based on assumptions. Your actual results will be different.

Group Universal Insurance — With a group universal policy, either you or your employer pay the premium. If *you* pay the premium, you have the option of purchasing the term life-insurance portion and the cash-accumulation portion of the group universal life policy. When purchasing *only* the term-life portion, the annual cost may increase as you become older, and when you stop making payments, your insurance coverage ends.

However, if you elect to contribute to the cash-accumulation fund as well as the term-life portion, your money grows tax-deferred at an interest rate offered by the insurance carrier. The funds can then be used to purchase insurance, or for any other cash need you may have.

Variable Universal Life — This type of insurance (commonly referred to by the initials VUL) differs from the universal life insurance described previously in terms of how the cash value is invested. Unlike the universal policy described earlier, the VUL policy allows the insured to choose the investments to be made with the cash value. The available investments typically include mutual funds that invest in stocks, bonds and cash equivalents.

The combination of investment flexibility and tax-deferred growth can appear attractive. However, because of expenses associated with the typical VUL policy, it generally is necessary for the policy to be in place — with premiums being paid each year and no loans or withdrawals — for 15–20 years before the tax benefits are likely to be significant.

If you need permanent insurance, VUL is an option to consider, especially if you're an aggressive investor who will monitor the investments in the policy carefully. In addition, you should maximize contributions to retirement plans (*e.g.*, company savings plan, IRA) before purchasing a VUL policy. Finally, a VUL policy isn't likely to be appropriate unless you plan to withdraw or borrow from it at some time beginning 10–20 years after issuance.

Special Consideration:

Universal Life Quotes

Call Ameritas at 800/555-4655 for quotes on low-cost universal insurance. These quotes can then be compared to what your agent provides you. Ameritas is a subsidiary of Ameritas Life Insurance Company (www.ameritas.com), which is rated A+ by A.M. Best.

Selecting a Life-Insurance Company

Several companies rate the financial strength of insurance companies and their ability to pay claims. The most widely used is the A.M. Best Company (www.ambest.com). You can find Best's ratings at your local library. In addition to A.M. Best, two other companies, Standard & Poor's (www.standardandpoors.com) and Moody's Investors Service (www.moodys.com), also rate insurance companies.

When considering a policy, look at two or more highly rated (A or better) insurance companies. This table shows some of the top-rated companies in the industry. It is not a complete listing of all the insurance companies, so your carrier may not be on this list.

Highly Rated Insurance Companies (April 2001)

Company	Best	S&P	Moody's
Northwestern Mutual	A++	AAA	Aaa
Jefferson Pilot	A++	AAA	Aa2
American General	A+	AA+	Aa3
Pacific Life	A++	AA+	Aa3
TransAmerica Occidental	A+	AA+	Aa3
Principal Life	A+	AA	Aa2
Travelers	A++	AA	Aa3
State Farm	A++	AAA	Aaa
New York Life	A++	AA+	Aa1
First Colony	A++	AA	Aa2
Equitable	A+	AA	Aa3
Hartford Life	A+	AA	Aa3

Note: Although The Ayco Company, L.P., deals only with top-rated companies, this is *not* an exhaustive list of quality insurance firms. This list is also subject to change.

Life Insurance *vs.* Survivor-Annuity Election

An insurance agent may suggest you buy life insurance rather than elect a joint-and-survivor annuity under a company pension plan. If you elect an annuity, you will receive a specified payment for the rest of your life. This is a single-life annuity. A joint-and-survivor annuity pays you and your beneficiary a fixed sum as long as one of you lives. Because a joint-and-survivor annuity usually is paid out over a longer time period than a single-life annuity, the amount of the joint-and-survivor annuity is less.

If you elect a joint-and-survivor annuity, you've ensured your survivor's income after your death. If you choose a single-life annuity, your survivor won't receive any income after your death. However, you can provide for your survivor with a life-insurance policy. Your own preferences and goals must be taken into account when considering these options. So it's important to find out whether your beneficiary wants to receive an insurance check or a monthly survivor annuity.

Before you make your decision, consider the following: First, you won't have the entire annual difference between the single-life annuity and the joint-and-survivor annuity to spend on life-insurance coverage, only the after-tax amount. For example, let's say your single-life annuity is $12,000 per year and the joint-and-survivor annuity is $11,500 per year. You won't have $500 extra for an insurance premium. You'll have to subtract income taxes from the $500. Furthermore, under the terms of the pension plan, the survivor annuity may be *guaranteed* for your beneficiary's life, regardless of how long that may be. Many find it comforting to know their beneficiary will receive a check every month for the rest of his or her lifetime.

If you decide to purchase a life-insurance policy, be sure to buy enough coverage. For instance, a $150,000 policy may be enough insurance if you die in 20 years. But if you die in six months, you may need $500,000 of coverage to provide enough money for your beneficiary. Also, a life-insurance policy is usually paid in a lump-sum amount. If your beneficiary doesn't want the responsibility of managing a large amount of money, ask your agent to discuss other payment options.

Life Insurance: Items to Consider

Buy Supplemental Coverage — If you project, after completing the *Determine Your Life-Insurance Needs* worksheet or a similar calculation, that your survivors would need more income, you should buy additional insurance.

First, look at your company's group insurance, which is convenient and may be a bargain, depending on your underwriting status. But company-sponsored insurance usually terminates if you leave your job. You may be able to convert from a group term to an individual whole-life policy, but this is *rarely* cost-effective.

If you're in good health, you'll probably save money by purchasing insurance outside of your company's plan. Buying coverage from an external source allows you to maintain the policy no matter where you work. Consider all the alternatives, then find a reputable agent.

Check Your Beneficiary Designations — Always designate both a primary and contingent (or secondary) beneficiary. Review these designations periodically to be sure they are current, as well as coordinated with your will and trusts. Many people with estates greater than $1 million have inappropriate beneficiary designations. Typically, a spouse is named as beneficiary of a life-insurance policy when perhaps a trust or, in some situations, your estate should have been named. Check with your estate-planning attorney.

Consider Dependent Life Insurance — Adequate insurance on the life of a wage-earner will pay expenses at death and fill any financial gap. If your spouse also earns an income — or if you think you'll need to hire someone to care for your children if your spouse dies — you should insure your spouse's life as well.

Usually, however, it's not necessary to insure the life of a child. Most people have more pressing priorities for their money. If you decide to insure your child's life, ask your agent about a guaranteed insurance rider on your policy as well as an increasing whole- or variable-life policy.

Avoid Accidental Death Insurance — Although accidental death and dismemberment insurance (AD&D) is extremely inexpensive, it generally should be avoided. That's because, regardless of the circumstances of your death, you'll want to have the right amount of life insurance to support your survivors. In other words, the circumstances of your death are less important than having the right level of coverage. AD&D will pay only if the cause of death or dismemberment is accidental.

Plan for the Future — After an employee dies, medical coverage may continue for the surviving spouse and eligible dependents. But company medical plans vary and are always subject to change. It isn't prudent to assume your employer will pay certain medical expenses or share the costs of future premiums on the same basis as today.

Disability Insurance

Disability insurance is designed to replace money lost during times when an illness or injury prevents you from earning an income. Statistics show that during their working years, people are more likely to become disabled — at least for a while — than they are to die.

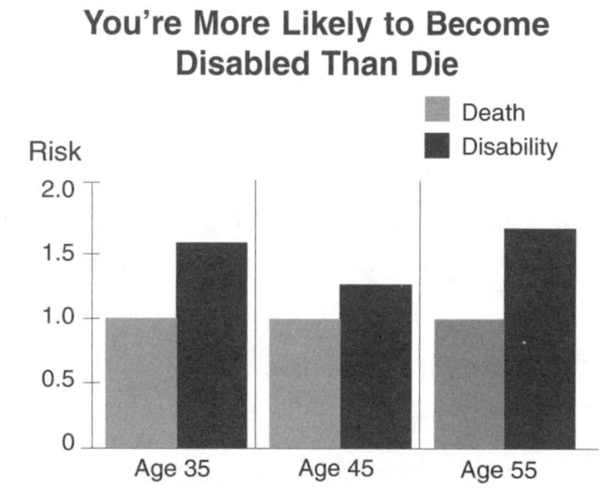

Example: For every 35-year-old who dies, 1.74 35-year-olds become disabled.

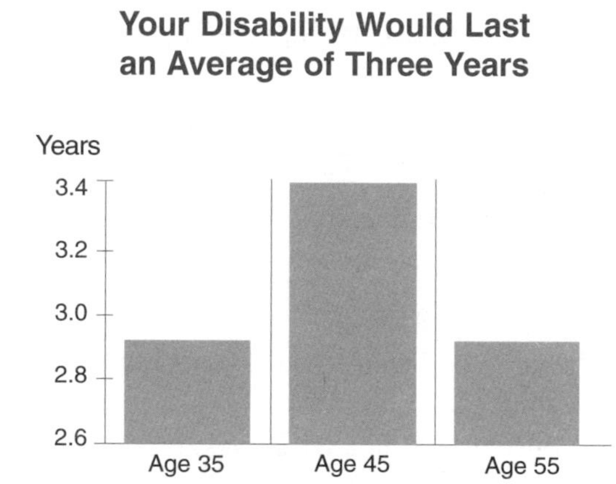

Example: The average disability for a 35-year-old lasts about 2.9 years.

Virtually all employees still risk the loss of income despite their company-provided long-term disability coverage. This is because most company policies aren't indexed for inflation. And most are limited only to a percentage (such as 50–60%) of your base salary and don't cover additional income from sources such as an annual bonus. Furthermore, insurance for a partial disability, which provides coverage when you can work only on a limited basis, typically isn't available through your employer.

Although many employees can get a better policy outside an employer's plan, disability insurance through your employer is usually far less expensive than comparable individual insurance. Buy as much group-disability insurance from your employer as you can before looking to supplement it from outside sources.

A single parent may decide that additional disability insurance is critical. Most people decide not to fill this gap, however, because purchasing additional coverage outside the company plan usually is very expensive.

If you want to explore additional disability coverage, get a quotation from a reputable insurance company. And if you belong to a professional or social organization, find out if a group-disability policy is offered to members. Although those policies may have a restrictive definition of disability as well as other limitations, they do afford some additional protection.

Protecting Your Earnings

Make Sure You Have Adequate Disability Coverage — The disability benefits from your company policy, together with other sources such as Workers' Compensation and Social Security, are designed to replace a portion of your income. The benefits from company policies often are limited to a maximum of 70% of your base salary only and aren't indexed for inflation. Consequently, you might consider purchasing a supplemental policy that will replace more of your income, including compensation other than base salary. Life-insurance companies usually also sell personal disability policies.

Sample Annual Disability Premiums for an Employee with $30,000 Annual Income — Monthly Benefit $650

Age (non-smoker)	Annual Premium
25	$224
35	$306
45	$450
55	$583

These premiums are calculated for a policy with a six-month waiting period before benefits begin and having an "own occupation" clause. The monthly amount is paid until age 65, with an inflation rider benefit increasing the payout by up to 5% per year; a rider permits future purchases of more disability insurance depending on income.

Set Up a Cash Reserve — As financial self-defense, you should establish a reserve fund equal to at least three months of living expenses. A six-month reserve, however, is better because many long-term disability policies begin paying after six months. Consider the kind of lifestyle you'd want to maintain during a period of disability.

Manage Your Debt — If you become disabled, you'll be glad your financial obligations are at a minimum. A good rule of thumb is to limit total debt to no more than twice your annual income including your mortgage. You should strive to eliminate any debt other than your mortgage or a home-equity line of credit.

Access Your Company's Savings Plan as a Source of Disability Funds — Your savings plan account should be one of your most substantial investments. If you become disabled, these funds usually become accessible. You won't have to pay the 10% additional tax for an early withdrawal, although you will have to pay income taxes on any taxable amount withdrawn. Keep in mind, however, that withdrawal of these funds may jeopardize your long-term retirement planning.

Consider Coverage for Your Spouse — Disability insurance can protect only against the risk of losing income. If a spouse doesn't work outside the home and becomes disabled, the family may have to rely on its cash reserve and make changes in its lifestyle. If this situation might apply to your family, make sure you're properly self-insured for this risk (*i.e.,* have a cash reserve and keep debt to a minimum, as discussed above).

Homeowner's Insurance

The three most important steps in buying homeowner's insurance are Shop! Shop! Shop! Premiums vary greatly from one insurer to another. Nonetheless, don't overlook the importance of your agent's service. You may decide to pay more for coverage if the service is worth the difference.

Types of Policies

HO-3 *vs.* Other Policies — Homeowner's insurance covers three primary areas: the dwelling, the contents and liability. There are two main levels of coverage: *named peril* and *open peril*. With the named-peril coverage of an HO-2 policy, a loss isn't covered unless it falls within the scope of a peril specifically *included* in the policy. Under an open-perils form, a loss is covered unless it is specifically *excluded*. Historically, this coverage has been called "all-risk" coverage. An HO-3 policy provides open-peril coverage on the dwelling, with named-peril coverage on personal property.

Often you'll find that named-peril coverage is more limited than you would anticipate. Read your policy carefully to see which risks are omitted. (Does your policy cover damage due to sump-pump failure, water back-up or wind-driven rain?) Also, find out what limits apply.

In order to extend the HO-3 policy one step further to provide open-peril coverage on contents, purchase the homeowner's special personal-property-coverage endorsement (HO-15). The combination of the HO-3 plus the HO-15 covers all risks (except those specifically excluded) and offers the most extensive coverage.

As with any type of insurance, you should check the rating of your property and casualty insurer. Be sure to select highly rated companies.

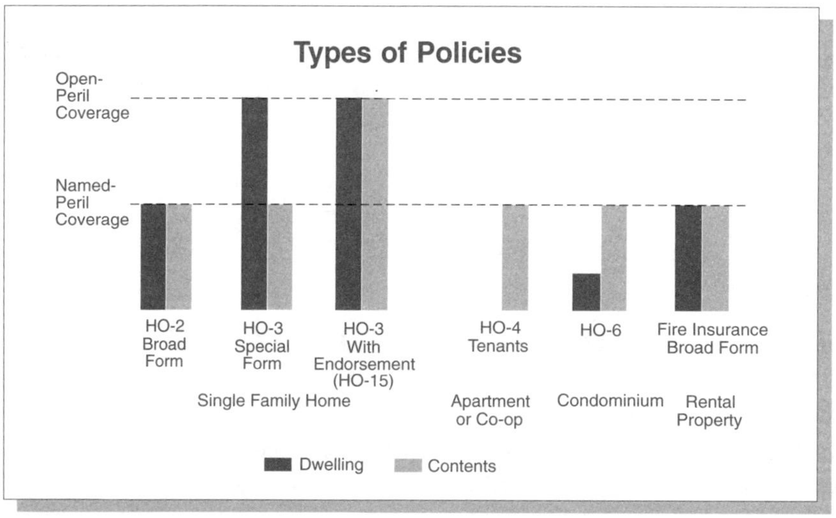

Homeowner's Coverage for Condominiums — Buy an HO-6 policy to cover interior walls as well as any improvements, personal property, additional living expenses and liability coverage. Your condominium association's master policy will pay to rebuild the exterior of the building in the event of a fire and also may include comprehensive personal liability coverage. *Be sure to check this out!* Verify that your HO-6 policy is coordinated with your building's master insurance policy.

Any improvement that condominium owners make to their units — such as moldings, built-in bookshelves, fireplaces and custom doors — become a part of the property. These improvements, known in insurance jargon as "Additions and Alterations" or "Improvements and Betterments," should be properly insured. Many standard condominium policies may not cover the entire value of these improvements. You can eliminate the potential for underinsurance by purchasing an endorsement for increased "Additions and Alterations" coverage.

If your condominium association files a claim for a loss that exceeds its coverage, unit owners may be asked to make up the difference. Even in cases in which the loss is less than the condominium's coverage, owners can be assessed to pay the deductible. You can purchase loss-assessment insurance to pay for these expenses, usually $1,000 for the deductible and as high as $50,000 for excess loss. However, the loss must be the result of a peril covered under your own owner's policy.

Homeowner's for Tenants — Buy an HO-4 policy to cover both contents and personal liability. Even if you're renting, you can be sued if your dog bites a neighbor, a tipsy guest wrecks a car or your tee shot hits another player on the golf course. An HO-4 policy provides coverage on a "named-peril" basis for personal property and additional living expenses.

Specific Areas of Coverage

Replacement-Cost Endorsement on the Dwelling — Remember, what's important to you is the real replacement cost of your home. You should be sure that your homeowner's policy includes a guaranteed-replacement-cost rider, which covers the actual cost to replace your home. Replacement cost is *not* the current market value, but the amount it would actually cost to rebuild your home from the ground up, excluding the value of the land and the foundation. Note that some companies have withdrawn the replacement-cost guarantee or limited the dollar amount payable (*e.g.,* 120% of face amount of coverage) in the event of a loss. Check with your agent for details.

Rebuilding to Code — An older structure, or even one built just a few years ago, might not meet building codes in force today. If such a structure is damaged or destroyed, the building-code provisions now in effect could add significantly to the cost of repairing or replacing the structure. In some cases, standard homeowner's coverage doesn't provide payment for ordinance-mandated changes in design or materials. You should investigate the need to purchase an endorsement or enhanced policy.

Replacement-Cost Endorsement on Depreciating Contents — Both owners and tenants should have a replacement-cost rider to cover depreciating contents such as furniture, electronic equipment and clothing. Without this coverage, the contents are insured only for the actual cash value (*i.e.,* the depreciated value) up to the policy limits for personal property. Any "scheduled personal property" listed on a personal articles floater, rider or endorsement is insured up to the amount of its stated value.

Liability Coverage — Get at least $300,000 of coverage or, more importantly, the minimum required by your personal excess-liability (umbrella) policy (see "Excess-Liability Insurance" later in this chapter).

Personal-Articles Floater for Appreciating Contents — Check your homeowner's policy's sub-limits on items such as jewelry, watches, furs, coins, stamps, silverware and musical instruments. If those limits are too low to cover the value of your possessions, consider an endorsement to your policy. The endorsement will increase the homeowner's sub-limits so all of the items are insured up to the higher limit.

In addition to an endorsement raising your sub-limits, you may have personal property that would represent a catastrophic financial loss — not just a sentimental loss — if lost. If this is the case, have the item(s) appraised, and then add a personal-articles floater (sometimes called an "inland marine" policy). There is usually no deductible associated with a personal-articles floater, and the typical annual premium for $1,000 of jewelry is $30.

Household Help — It's your responsibility to provide worker's compensation for any household help you employ, such as a housekeeper, babysitter, nanny or handyman. You may need an endorsement or separate policy to cover this exposure.

Document Your "Instruments of Harm" — Let your agent know in writing of any recreational activities, possessions or features of your home/property that could give rise to claims (*e.g.*, a swimming pool, pond or lake, fountains, firearms, dogs, off-road recreational vehicles). Ask your agent whether an additional rider or endorsement is necessary.

Inventory Your Possessions — Make a list of the type and value of your possessions and store it with a visual record in a safe-deposit box or another safe place outside your home. A more practical approach is to take photographs or make a videotape of your belongings.

Business Losses — Accidents arising from home-based businesses are usually excluded from homeowner's coverage. Rental real estate also may require special provisions. Check with your agent.

Flood Insurance — If your community participates in the National Flood Insurance Program (NFIP), you'll be able to purchase flood insurance. If your community hasn't joined the program, you, as an individual, are ineligible to buy NFIP protection. Be careful to purchase the full amount of NFIP flood insurance available before you buy supplemental flood insurance from another carrier. If you don't, you may pay substantial out-of-pocket expenses in case of a claim.

Earthquake insurance — Depending on where you live, it can cost quite a bit to protect against earthquake damage. In California, earthquake coverage is almost as expensive as a basic homeowner's policy. The deductible is usually very large and is stated as a percentage of the limits of liability for property damage. If you believe that it's better to be safe than sorry, purchase coverage before a small quake hits nearby. Insurance companies have been known to suspend coverage on the theory that smaller earthquakes are warnings of bigger things to follow.

Windstorms — Hurricane Andrew proved the need for windstorm insurance in Florida and other areas subject to hurricanes and tornadoes.

Deductibles — Each year when you renew your policy ask your agent how raising or lowering your deductibles could affect your premiums. Usually you should have at least a $250 deductible, and a $500 deductible may be more appropriate.

Maintain Adequate Coverage — Insurance coverage on real estate and personal possessions can become inadequate in only a few years. Make it a habit to review your coverage periodically — at least every two years — to ensure it still meets your needs. Consider adding an inflation-guard endorsement to your homeowner's policy.

Auto Insurance

More than any other type of property and casualty coverage, automobile insurance is an area where it really pays to shop insurers, increase your deductibles and be careful not to buy any unnecessary coverage. Also, buy from a reputable and well-established agent and look at high-quality companies with competitive premiums.

Fault or No-Fault? — Whether your state of residence is a "fault" or "no-fault" state* is a significant factor with regard to how you are covered. If you live in a "fault" state and are hurt in an auto accident that is the other driver's fault, you collect from the other driver's insurance company. This assumes the other driver has insurance — and has enough of it. If you caused the accident, you will probably collect nothing from your insurance for your own injuries. If you're partly at fault, state law dictates to what extent your policy pays.

* No-fault states include Colorado, Florida, Hawaii, Kansas, Kentucky, Massachusetts, Michigan, Minnesota, New Jersey, New York, North Dakota, Pennsylvania and Utah.

If you live in a "no-fault" state and are hurt in an auto accident, you collect from your own insurance company — even if the accident was entirely your fault.

Bodily-Injury Liability — This coverage pays claims resulting from injuries to passengers in your car or in other cars or to pedestrians. It covers other drivers when they use your car with your permission. It covers both you and your family members when driving someone else's car with permission.

You should have coverage equal to at least $250,000 per person and $500,000 per accident. You may need higher limit amounts if your state requires it. If you elect these amounts, $250,000 will be the maximum your insurance company will pay toward a judgment against you for the injury or death of one person; $500,000 will be the maximum aggregate payment if more than one person is injured in the same accident.

Medical-Expense Payments — These pay for medical expenses resulting from accidental injuries involving you, your family members and passengers in your car. In addition, coverage is provided for injuries sustained by your family members while riding in another car or walking. If your state has "no-fault" auto insurance, your injuries may be covered by personal injury protection or PIP, rather than medical expense payments.

Property Damage — This pays the cost of claims resulting from damages to property caused by your car. You and your family members are covered, either while driving your car or another car with the owner's permission. Buy $50,000 to $100,000 of coverage, since the typical $25,000 coverage may not be enough. What if you hit a Mercedes or a BMW?

Uninsured and Underinsured Motorists Coverage — These categories of coverage pay up to the limits of the policy for judgments resulting from injuries caused by an uninsured or underinsured driver. As a general rule, get the same amount of insurance in this category as your liability coverage. Also, ask whether your excess-liability or umbrella policy can include uninsured/underinsured coverage for the limits of the policy.

Collision Coverage — This insurance category pays for damages to your automobile resulting either from a collision with another vehicle or object or from rolling over. Ask your agent how much you would receive from the insurance company if your car were completely destroyed, then compare that risk with the premium payment. Is the coverage worth the amount you'll pay for collision insurance? And if you feel your car is worth more, ask your agent about an "agreed-value" endorsement, although not all insurers offer this additional coverage.

If the annual premium for collision coverage is greater than 10% of the "blue book" value of your car (minus the deductible), you might decide the cost of collision coverage isn't worth the price. In that situation, consider dropping the collision coverage or increasing the deductible.

Collision Deductible — The higher the deductible (usually ranging between $100 and $1,000), the lower the premium. Many people buy insurance with low deductibles, yet never submit small claims for fear their premiums will go up or the insurance company will drop them. If you had a $250 accident, would you file a claim? If not, get a $500 (or better yet, a $1,000) deductible — just be sure to set money aside to cover minor damages to your vehicle!

Comprehensive Physical Damage — This insurance pays for damages resulting from incidents "other than collision" such as theft, malicious mischief, fire, falling objects, glass breakage, explosion, wind, hail, flood, earthquake or contact with a bird or animal. You'll want to have at least a $500 deductible, but make sure you have "full-glass" coverage.

Planning for the Future — Your automobile coverage is not a long-term decision, so you should revisit it every year. Be sure to:

- ❖ Pay premiums annually rather than monthly, quarterly or semiannually. This protects you against midyear rate increases and typically reduces the premium.
- ❖ Increase your deductibles.
- ❖ Consider premium costs before purchasing an automobile.
- ❖ Require your teenagers (and possibly all adult family members) to pass a safe-driver course to reduce your premiums.
- ❖ Ask your agent whether you or other family members qualify for any discounts. Typical discounts include:
  - multicar, for two or more cars insured with the same company
  - passive restraints
  - successful completion of an accredited driver-training course
  - mature drivers credit for those over 55
  - good student or students who live more than 100 miles from home
  - anti-theft devices
  - anti-lock brakes
  - car pool for commuters

Excess-Liability Insurance: an "Umbrella" Policy

Excess-liability or "umbrella" policies are standardized so you don't have to choose among different types. If your total household income is more than $50,000 or if you own a rental property, you should have an umbrella policy. In fact, some advisors recommend that everyone—regardless of his or her income or assets — should carry this type of policy. The annual premium for minimum coverage of $1 million is generally between $150 to $400. In these days of seven-figure judgments, an excess-liability/umbrella policy is essential for anyone with even a modest financial situation. Remember, if your household income is $60,000 or more, you are in the top 25% of wage earners in the United States.

Umbrella Policy: Items to Consider

Assess Needs — Review your total household income to determine whether you should have an umbrella policy and discuss this with your agent. Remember, you have additional risks if you:

- ❖ drive a car
- ❖ own a boat, an RV or a snowmobile
- ❖ own a swimming pool
- ❖ have a teenager who drives
- ❖ hire domestic help (including babysitters)

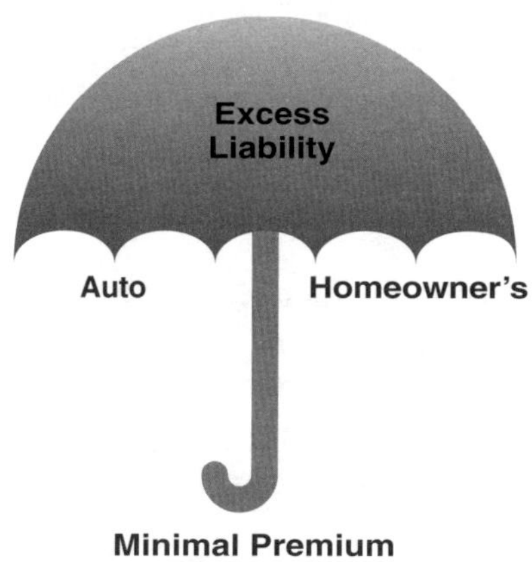

Buying Liability Insurance — The first place to shop for your umbrella policy is with the insurance company carrying your homeowner's and/or auto insurance. Most insurance companies will not write just your liability coverage—they want your other business as well.

Coordinate Policies — An umbrella policy requires you to carry certain minimum amounts of liability coverage on your homeowner's and auto policies — usually $300,000 on your homeowner's policy and between $300,000 to $500,000 on auto policies. To avoid a gap in coverage, make sure you meet these minimums. The umbrella policy will then cover you against excess liability up to the policy's limit (*e.g.,* $1 million) in addition to the amounts provided under your homeowner's or automobile policy.

Liability for directors and officers of nonprofit organizations — Directors and officers of nonprofit organizations are subject to the same kind of liability as directors and officers of for-profit organizations. They can be cited for nonmanagement or mismanagement in a variety of areas stemming from suits brought by employees, government entities, donors, beneficiaries, other related parties or the general public. These suits can jeopardize the directors' and officers' personal property, and may require them to pay their own legal fees. If you are a director or officer of a nonprofit organization, you should consult your insurance agent to determine if your current coverage is adequate. Availability of coverage will vary, depending on your organization's activities.

Errors and omissions — Many professionals — accountants, architects, engineers, lawyers, stockbrokers and travel agents, among others — are faced with the possibility of having to pay damages resulting from the rendering or failure to render professional services.

Errors and omissions insurance coverage is tailored to the duties required by a specific profession. Check with your insurance agent if you think you may be exposed to this type of liability.

Insurance on Your Financial Assets

Brokerage Accounts

The Securities Investor Protection Corporation (SIPC) is a federally sponsored agency designed to provide investors with safety and insurance for their securities and funds held in brokerage accounts in the event the brokerage firm holding them fails.

Through SIPC, each brokerage account is insured up to $500,000, with a $100,000 limit on cash. In addition to the SIPC coverage, many brokerage firms carry extra coverage, typically $1 million per account. If a firm defaults and a client's account is greater than these limits, the balance is a bankruptcy claim. Individuals cannot buy SIPC insurance, so contact your broker to see if your account is insured through the SIPC and whether any coverage applies above the SIPC limit.

SIPC regulations don't cover precious metals, commodity contracts, unregistered partnerships, futures or currencies. SIPC doesn't cover cash or securities considered part of the capital of a firm. Therefore, accounts of general partners, officers and directors of the failed firm wouldn't be protected by SIPC coverage. SIPC covers stock options but not commodity options. It also covers securities bought on margin. Basically, SIPC covers registered rather than unregistered securities.

For more information on SIPC, ask your broker or write or call SIPC at:

Securities Investor Protection Corporation
805 15th St. N.W., Suite 800
Washington, DC 20005-2215
202/371-8300
www.sipc.org

Bank and Credit-Union Accounts

The Federal Deposit Insurance Corporation (FDIC) and National Credit Union Administration (NCUA) are government-funded agencies providing protection to lenders, depositors or investors against losing their money due to a bank or credit-union failure. Each of these agencies provides protection up to $100,000 per insured account. If you are planning to keep $100,000 or more in an account for longer than two months, it's a good idea to keep only $90,000 in any single account so interest earnings will not push you above the threshold for protection.

Special Consideration:

Bank Ratings

The FDIC never releases its ratings on the safety and soundness of banks and thrift institutions to the public. However, there are private companies that provide their own ratings of these institutions. One such company, Veribanc, offers instant ratings by phone for $10 for the first rating and $5 for each additional rating. They rate all U.S. banks, savings and loans and credit unions.

Veribanc, Inc.
P.O. Box 461
Wakefield, MA 01880
800/837-4226
www.veribanc.com

Pension Insurance

The Pension Benefit Guaranty Corporation (PBGC) is a U.S. government agency established by the Employee Retirement Income Security Act of 1974 (ERISA). The PBGC administers two insurance programs guaranteeing the payment of basic retirement benefits, within specified limitations, to participants of certain private pension plans. PBGC programs are financed with premiums paid by covered plans.

PBGC guarantees "basic benefits" — those vested monthly pension benefits providing income at retirement. Basic benefits begin at normal retirement age and include certain early retirement and disability benefits for survivors of deceased plan participants. However, all benefits provided by a pension plan may not be guaranteed under the PBGC insurance program — for example, special incentives to retire early.

Although the amount of benefit paid by PBGC depends on each pension plan, there is a maximum benefit limit. The pension-benefit guarantee is set annually by law under provisions of ERISA. For 2002, the single-life annuity limit is $3,579.55 per month ($42,954.60 annually) for someone who begins receiving benefits at age 65. The maximum guaranteed benefit is reduced 7/12% per month (7% annually) for those who begin receiving benefits between ages 60 and 65; 4/12% per month (4% annually) between ages 55 and 60; and 2/12% per month (2% annually) between ages 50 and 55. If you receive a benefit before age 50, the PBGC will determine the maximum guaranteed benefit on a case-by-case basis.

Maximum Annual Guaranteed Retirement Benefits

Benefits Starting in 2002

Age	Guaranteed Benefit
65	$42,955
62	$33,934
60	$27,921
55	$19,330
50	$15,034

Individuals eligible for additional benefits in excess of the guaranteed amount will receive them, provided the terminated plan has enough funds to pay the benefits.

For more information on the PBGC: Pension Benefit Guaranty Corporation
1200 K Street, NW
Washington, DC 20005-4026
800/400-7242
www.pbgc.gov

Items for Action

Insurance is a necessity, not a luxury. Adequate levels of life, disability, property and casualty insurance play an important role in every family's financial planning. It's critical that you evaluate your insurance needs and compare the results to your current coverage. Use the Items for Action below to get started.

For each of the following items, assign a priority based on its importance to you: A (highest), B (medium) or C (lowest). Then check off each item as it is completed.

	Priority	Completed
Life Insurance		
❖ Find out how much insurance you need on your life and on your spouse's life (if applicable).	______	❑
❖ Call Social Security at 800/772-1213 and request *Form SSA-7004* to obtain a customized Social Security statement or visit Social Security's Web site at www.ssa.gov to request a statement.	______	❑
❖ Use the *Determine Your Life-Insurance Needs* worksheet to experiment with different scenarios.	______	❑
❖ Weigh the options between term and permanent life insurance.	______	❑
❖ Contact your life-insurance agent to review your policies.	______	❑
❖ Get a quotation from an outside company *(e.g.,* SelectQuote at 800/670-3214, www.selectquote.com or InsuranceQuote at 800/972-1104, www.iquote.com) for term insurance, or universal life insurance through Ameritas at 800/555-4655.	______	❑
❖ Consider employer-provided coverage (review cost and portability).	______	❑
Disability Insurance		
❖ Determine how much income you'd lose if you or your spouse became disabled.	______	❑
❖ Discuss additional insurance, if available, from your employer or through other group coverage.	______	❑
❖ Build a cash reserve, reduce debt and contribute to your savings/thrift plan to self-insure.	______	❑

Items for Action (continued)

	Priority	Completed
Homeowner's Insurance		
Call your homeowner's insurance agent and		
❖ Discuss whether open-peril coverage is cost-effective for you.	_______	❑
❖ Examine replacement cost riders on both contents and dwelling; ask about a replacement-cost endorsement.	_______	❑
❖ Determine adequate liability coverage ($300,000 minimum).	_______	❑
❖ Consider a personal-articles floater.	_______	❑
❖ Ask about water-back-up or "sump-pump" insurance (check whether limits apply).	_______	❑
❖ Ask about a worker's compensation rider to insure household help.	_______	❑
❖ Re-examine deductibles: $250 minimum.	_______	❑
❖ Take photographs or a videotape of your possessions.	_______	❑
❖ Document any "instruments of harm."	_______	❑
❖ Consider flood and/or earthquake coverage.	_______	❑
Auto Insurance		
❖ Re-examine liability coverage: $250,000 per person/ $500,000 per accident minimum.	_______	❑
❖ Review uninsured/underinsured coverage.	_______	❑
❖ Increase deductible (for example, to $500) with "full-glass" coverage.	_______	❑
Excess-Liability Insurance		
❖ Consider purchasing a $1 million umbrella policy.	_______	❑
❖ Coordinate underlying coverages on your car and homeowner's insurance.	_______	❑
Insurance for Your Financial Assets		
❖ Ask your stockbroker for the maximum amount of insurance on your account.	_______	❑
❖ If holding a large amount of money in a bank for more than two months, only deposit up to $90,000 in each insured account.	_______	❑

Resources

American Council of Life Insurers

1001 Pennsylvania Avenue, NW
Washington, DC 20004-2599
www.acli.com

Tips on buying insurance products online.

Insurance Information Inc.

23 Route 134
South Dennis, MA 02660
800/472-5800

This service will search for the company with the best rates on term insurance for you.

Life and Health Insurance Foundation for Education (LIFE)

2175 K Street, NW
Suite 250
Washington, DC 20037
202/464-5000

The foundation is a non-profit organization designed to address the need for information and education on life, health and disability insurance. Visit their Web site (**www.life-line.org**) to learn about insurance or to order LIFE's education materials.

Life Insurance Advisors Association

2822 A Drive
West Bloomfield, MI 48324
800/521-4578

For referrals to fee-only insurance advisors.

National Insurance Consumer Helpline

Insurance Information Institute (sponsor)
110 William Street
New York, NY 10038
www.iii.org

This toll-free number (**800/942-4242**) allows you to talk to an insurance expert about a problem with your auto, home or business insurance. They can also answer your questions about life insurance.

Estate Planning

Despite common misconceptions, estate planning really is for everyone. While the rich may need complicated strategies to avoid federal and state death taxes, even the not-so-rich require some planning to pass property to their heirs. Having a simple will might be all the estate planning you need, but it's still important.

Through estate planning you can:

- ❖ ensure the assets you accumulated during your lifetime are distributed upon your death exactly as you would wish
- ❖ nominate a guardian for minor children or other legally dependent persons
- ❖ name an executor to carry out your wishes
- ❖ minimize or eliminate taxes and expenses
- ❖ name someone to make decisions about your medical treatment if you aren't able to make them yourself
- ❖ make known your wishes about medical treatment if you become seriously ill, injured or incapacitated

Please note: *This chapter discusses federal estate-tax laws. Since state laws vary on this topic, consult an estate-planning attorney when drafting a will and/or trust document.*

On June 7, 2001, the President signed into law the Economic Growth and Tax Relief Act of 2001 (2001 Act). This legislation reduces the federal estate and gift taxes between 2002 and 2009 and repeals the estate tax in 2010. However, you should note that the 2001 Act's provisions are scheduled to end after 2010; consequently, unless Congress takes further action, all of the estate tax provisions that were effective prior to these recent changes will be reinstated in 2011.

How Assets are Distributed at Death

Your assets will be passed on in one of two ways. *Nonprobate* assets will be distributed without reference to your will. What are nonprobate assets? (1) Assets owned jointly with a right of survivorship, (2) assets for which a beneficiary has been named (*e.g.,* your benefit plans, life-insurance proceeds, IRAs — including Roth IRAs, SEPs, Keoghs) and (3) assets held in trust.

Typically, all other property is categorized as (4) *probate* property, which will be distributed according to the terms of your will, or if there is no will, by your state's intestacy laws. Probate property includes individually owned (*i.e.,* not held in joint tenancy) real and personal property, assets for which your estate has been named as beneficiary and any assets for which a beneficiary has not been named.

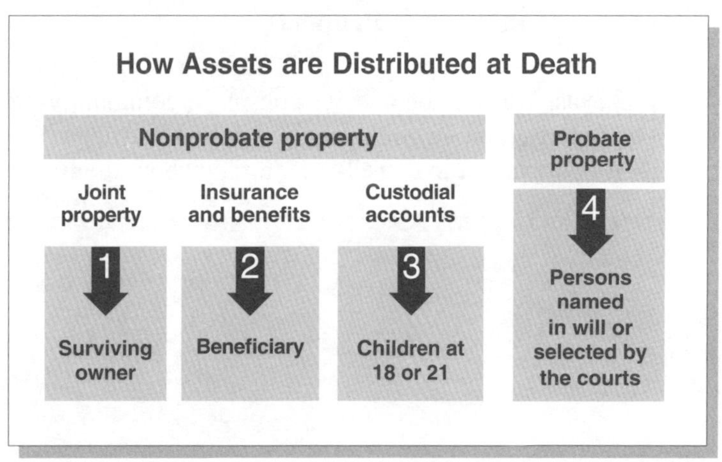

1) **Joint Property** — Any property held in joint tenancy with the right of survivorship (JTWROS) automatically passes to the surviving owner, regardless of what the will or trust specifies. This does not include property held as "tenants in common."

2) **Insurance and Benefits**

❖ **Group and personal insurance** — Proceeds from any company-sponsored insurance plans are passed on to the current beneficiary designated on the form on file at your personnel or human resources department. Likewise, any proceeds from personal life insurance you own will pass to the named beneficiary. Now is the perfect time to make sure these designations are up to date, and it would be wise to review them annually from now on.

If your estate includes a trust, it's often best to name your trustee as beneficiary of a life-insurance policy. That way the provisions of the trust document will determine who receives the proceeds.

❖ **Company savings plan, ESOP, deferred-compensation plans, stock options, IRAs, Keoghs and SEPs** — These assets pass to the beneficiary designated on the appropriate form, usually the surviving spouse. While qualified distributions from a Roth IRA are exempt from federal income tax, Roth IRAs are an includable asset for estate-tax purposes and are subject to estate tax. Typically, you cannot designate a beneficiary for any employer-provided stock options that you may hold at the time of your death. In that instance, subject to the terms of the plan, your executor is entitled to exercise the stock options.

❖ **Pension** — In some circumstances, survivor benefits may be paid to a beneficiary. If applicable, you can request the details from your personnel or human resources department.

3) **Custodial Accounts** — When assets are placed in a custodial account, an irrevocable gift is made. If you act as custodian and you contributed assets to the account, your contributions are considered part of your estate for tax purposes until the recipient reaches either age 18 or 21, depending on state law.

4) **Probate Property** — The balance of your personal property — titled in your name alone or in tenancy-in-common — is your probate assets. These assets pass to the beneficiaries — individuals, trusts or charities — named in your will. If you don't have a will, this property passes according to state intestacy laws. If you are single with children, you need to pay particular attention to beneficiary designations and testamentary documents. Leaving assets outright to minor children could actually circumvent your intentions to provide funds when most needed.

Special Consideration:

Community Property

Community-property states include Arizona, California, Idaho, Louisiana, Nevada, New Mexico, Texas, Washington and Wisconsin. In community-property states, each spouse owns half of any property (and income) acquired during marriage. Due to the unique nature of community property, it is important to consult an attorney about the impact on your estate plan.

Why You Need a Will

Everyone should have a current will prepared by an attorney. This allows you, at the very least, to:

- ❖ Appoint an executor to eliminate the fees of a court-appointed administrator.
- ❖ Clarify your intent rather than relying on the provisions of state law.
- ❖ Name a guardian for minor children.
- ❖ Make specific bequests (*e.g.,* $25,000 to your friend or a pearl necklace to a niece).
- ❖ Consider a two-share trust if your estate is worth at least $1,000,000.
- ❖ Have a provision to remove the trustee and appoint a successor.

ESTATE PLANNING

Controlling Distribution of Property

A will ensures your property will be distributed where and when you wish. If you don't have a will, you die intestate, and your assets will be distributed according to your state's intestacy rules. In many states the intestacy laws will split your assets between your children and your spouse, even if you want to leave most of your assets to your spouse.

Minimizing Expenses

If you die intestate, a state probate court will appoint an administrator to settle your estate, performing the executor's duties. These duties include collecting all the assets, paying all debts, settling all claims, filing tax returns and hiring an attorney or another individual to perform these services. People who don't have wills typically also have disorganized estates, so administrators may have to spend a lot of time — at $100 an hour or more — settling your affairs. One Michigan administrator spent more than 11 years settling a $50,000 estate!

If you have a will, you can stipulate whether you want your executor to post a bond or surety, verifying that he/she will not run off with your assets. But if you die intestate, you will not have named an executor, and the court-appointed administrator must post a bond. This means additional costs to your estate, both in time and money.

You can help your executor and survivors by providing them with the information they need to carry out their tasks efficiently. Use the *Document Locator* found later in this chapter.

Naming a Guardian

The most frequent reason parents with children procrastinate about drawing up a will is the inability to agree on a guardian. However, this is probably one of the most important reasons to have a will. If you haven't named a guardian for your minor children, the local probate judge will make the decision without your input. Be sure to name both a guardian and a contingent guardian. Consider naming just one person — not a couple. That way you avoid a custody battle over your children in the event of the guardian's divorce. Also, if your estate plan includes a trust, write a letter providing direction to the trustee about reimbursing expenses for the guardian.

Selecting an Executor

The executor is the person responsible for taking charge of your affairs, carrying out your wishes, distributing your property and settling your estate. The executor's role largely entails collecting information, but whomever you name to fill this role shouldn't have to make decisions alone. Generally, you'll want a close family member or trusted friend to be your executor. If your spouse is comfortable with the idea, you can name him or her as executor to lower estate-administration costs. *Also name a successor executor who will step in if your executor is unable or unwilling to serve.*

Explain to whomever you name as executor that you don't expect him or her to settle your estate *but to hire and oversee an attorney* to handle the process. The attorney will work with the executor to provide procedural and technical advice. That way your friend or family member can negotiate the fee and have some control over the process.

You also may want to consider naming an entity — such as a law firm, trust company or bank — as your executor, but you'll be charged either an hourly fee or a percentage of the estate's value. If your estate is complicated, it may be worth it. Moreover, unless your will states otherwise, family members won't be able to fire an executor with whom they're unhappy. The executor is entitled to be paid a fee from your estate assets for services rendered. As you can see in the table at right, fees can be costly. If your spouse is named executor, he or she normally will waive this fee since it's subject to income taxes. However, in estates with significant assets, it might be appropriate for a family member serving as executor to receive fees, which might be taxable at an ordinary income tax rate lower than the estate's marginal estate tax rate.

Typical Executor's Fees

Size of estate		Fees (% of estate)
First	$ 200,000	5%
Next	$ 800,000	3%
Over	$1,000,000	2% (or less)

Twelve Events Requiring Revision of Your Will

A change in your personal circumstances, such as a birth, marriage, divorce or death, could affect the way you want your personal property divided. Likewise, a change in your financial situation could affect the value of your estate. For these reasons, it's a good idea to review your will periodically to make sure it reflects your current wishes. Consider whether you need a new will or maybe just a codicil (an amendment, addition or qualification to your existing will).

It's important to review your will periodically — but especially if:

- your spouse or other close relative dies or becomes seriously ill
- the witnesses aren't alive or can't be found and your will is not self-proving
- the laws on estate taxes change
- your current will is more than five years old
- a beneficiary named in your will dies
- you failed to nominate a guardian
- you marry, divorce or begin a new significant relationship
- you become a parent
- you inherit substantial funds or valuable property
- you buy additional life insurance
- you change your mind about the disposition of your property
- you move to a new state. (The laws vary from state to state.)

Note: Never make changes directly on your will — that would invalidate it. The best way to make a change is either to draft a new will or add a codicil to incorporate the changes. Since a codicil must meet the same legal requirements as a will, have an attorney help you.

You'll want to review your will — including trusts and beneficiary designations — with your estate-planning attorney *at least* every five years *or* whenever your family or financial situation changes materially. If federal or estate tax laws change, review them sooner. Your attorney is a critical part of this process. Too many people will end up wasting large sums of money tomorrow because they're reluctant to pay for an estate checkup today!

How You Can Find an Estate-Planning Attorney

As mentioned earlier, you're not legally required to use an attorney to draw up a will. In fact, you can write your will yourself. However, there can be many problems with do-it-yourself or "boilerplate" wills. And because of the importance of your will and the complexity of the laws, it's well worth spending a little extra money to obtain the advice and expertise of an estate-planning attorney.

Using the attorney who handled the closing on your house may not be the wisest choice if you have an estate worth more than the credit exemption amount ($1,000,000 in 2002). You may have to do a little research to find an estate-planning specialist. Here are possible sources:

- Contact your county or state bar association for names of attorneys on the estate-planning, probate or trust committees. (Also request any relevant literature the association publishes.) Even if they have more legal expertise than you need or can afford, they may be able to refer you to someone in your price range.
- Interview a trust officer from a local bank that has a well-established reputation for managing trusts. Ask for a referral to an estate-planning attorney. If you're impressed with the trust company, consider naming it in your will as a successor trustee.
- Interview two attorneys to get a sense of their fees and their approach. Be prepared to discuss the size of your estate and any arrangements you'd like to make. Fees can range anywhere from $100 for a simple will to thousands for a more complex estate plan.

Do your homework. Before you meet with an attorney, consider the questions outlined under Items for Action and be prepared to discuss your answers. Being prepared will save you time and money.

Do You Need a Trust?

Your estate plan may well require the use of trusts, which frequently are drafted in conjunction with wills. The unique concept of the trust was developed during the Crusades, when an estate owner would ask a friend to manage property during the owner's absence. The relationship between the person who owned the assets and the person who managed them was called a trust relationship. The trust has become an important aspect of estate planning since it offers tax advantages and provides asset management long after the trust's creator has died.

The person who creates or establishes a trust is called the settlor or grantor. The manager is called the trustee or fiduciary. If there is more than one trustee, each one is called a "co-trustee." When a trustee declines to serve or resigns his or her appointment, the trustee who succeeds is called the "successor trustee."

You need a trust to:

- help ensure that your money and property are managed wisely or spent for your children as you would wish until they reach a certain age
- support a disabled child
- possibly reduce taxes if you have a large estate (typically greater than $1,000,000)

Regardless of whether you need a trust, *you should always have a will.*

Types of Trusts

A trust is said to be either a testamentary or living trust. The testamentary trust is part of a will — it can take effect only at death. A living trust, which is separate from a will, can take effect during the grantor's lifetime (*e.g.,* if the grantor is disabled) or at death. An important type of living trust is called a declaration of trust, in which the grantor declares himself/herself trustee. The grantor has total control over the trust and pays no fees until resignation or death. Typically, the grantor's spouse is the successor trustee. And a corporate trustee, such as a bank, is usually named as successor trustee to the spouse.

A living trust can further be described as revocable or irrevocable. A revocable trust provides the grantor with control over the assets in the trust. As a result, assets held in a revocable trust are included in the grantor's estate. The grantor has no control over the assets of an irrevocable trust. Due to the lack of control, assets held in this type of trust usually are not included in your estate. Banks can offer very valuable trustee services. Interview a bank's trust officers to get a sense of their professionalism.

How a Living Trust Can Help if You Become Incapacitated

Suppose you have, in your name alone, $100,000 or more in stocks or mutual funds outside an employer's savings or thrift plan, and you suffer a stroke. Who will decide when and if these assets should be sold? If you're married, your spouse can step in, but first he or she may have to go to court and be appointed guardian of your estate. This may mean additional expenses and delays at a time when quick action is needed.

If you and your spouse hold the property in joint tenancy at the time of your stroke, it's possible that your spouse could act without court approval. As we'll discuss later in this chapter, if your total assets exceed $1,000,000, it usually isn't a good idea to hold assets — other than your home and one checking account — in joint tenancy.

So what should you do? Make sure you've given a *general durable power of attorney* to someone you trust. A durable power of attorney legally authorizes someone to act on your behalf if you're incapacitated. Yet even though they're helpful, powers of attorney aren't always honored — at least, not immediately.

So consider holding those assets in trust and name yourself as trustee. Then a successor trustee, such as your spouse or an adult child, could take over — as directed by the trust document — if someone you trusted (*e.g.,* your spouse) and a physician certify that you are incapacitated or legally incompetent. This would ensure that your financial affairs would continue to be managed while you're incapacitated. The trust then becomes irrevocable and is managed by the successor trustee.

How Trusts Can Help After Your Death

Administrative Convenience — If you don't have a trust, your executor will collect your assets by contacting all of the institutions that hold them. To do this, the executor furnishes a copy of the death certificate and proves his/her appointment with a "letter of office." The institutions then re-register the accounts or securities in the name of your estate and return them to the executor, who will eventually disburse them to your beneficiaries. This is a time-consuming and often expensive process that can take a year or more, depending on how organized your affairs are when you die.

If you create a living trust, you can place your assets within it during your lifetime. You will find it is a simple, although somewhat tedious, process. When you purchase new securities, simply purchase them as "John Doe as Trustee Under the John Doe Trust Dated January 1, 2001," rather than in your name. Upon your death, the successor trustee — for example, your spouse or child — does not have to collect any assets because they are already in the trust. Unless taxes are due, the successor trustee simply disburses the assets. So a living trust simplifies the administration of your estate — saving time, money and aggravation. However, there is a cost when you establish a living trust because you will want an attorney to draft it for you. This cost should be weighed against the potential cost savings of avoiding probate.

More Sophisticated Asset Disposition — Asset disposition (*i.e.,* who gets the property and when) is facilitated by *either* a living or testamentary trust. There are a variety of names for these trusts. (See the discussion about the two-share plan later in this chapter.) Typically, for a married person, income from a trust will be paid to the surviving spouse for the spouse's lifetime; the spouse is the income beneficiary and is said to have a "life estate." Usually, if there are children, they receive the remainder (principal) of the estate and are called the remaindermen.

Control and Professional Asset Management — Many individuals want a professional to invest large sums of money from insurance proceeds and retirement plan distributions. This can be accomplished by placing funds in a trust and naming a bank, trust company or money manager as trustee.

Trusts are also frequently used to control and manage property for children. It's common to hold property in trust until the child reaches a certain age or completes his/her education. Or you might want to specify that your children have staggered rights of withdrawal at specific ages (*e.g.,* ages 25, 30 and 35). Some people like to give their money to their children sooner, others later, and some never!

Special trusts can be created for special situations, too. For example, a trust can ensure appropriate care will be given to a handicapped child or elderly parent.

Other Types of Trusts

Grantor-Retained Income Trusts (GRITs) are irrevocable. They are used to:

- remove assets from an estate;
- reduce gift taxes; and
- allow the grantor to retain the right to income for a set period of time.

The grantor must outlive the trust for assets to pass to a beneficiary during his or her lifetime. Income-producing assets and residences are most suitable for GRITs.

Spendthrift Trusts (also called Minor's Trusts) limit investment decisions and assure prudent use of assets earmarked for a minor or financially naive beneficiary. The principal must be distributed eventually.

Life-Insurance Trusts are ideal for large estates. The trust should own the grantor's life insurance and be its beneficiary to avoid taxation. Typically, these irrevocable trusts are designed to pay the estate taxes. If a policy is transferred to this kind of trust, the grantor must live at least three more years to avoid taxation of the policy's proceeds at death. Also, depending on the type of insurance policy transferred to the trust, there may be a gift tax due.

Generation-Skipping Trusts transfer assets to second or later generations and bypass children's estates.

Qualified Domestic Trusts (Q-DOTs) allow a non-U.S. citizen to take advantage of the marital deduction. Setting up this kind of trust involves a very complex process.

Charitable Remainder Trusts provide income to a non-charitable beneficiary for a stated period of time (or for life), after which the remainder of the trust assets transfer to a charity.

Charitable Lead Trusts provide income to a charity from an asset for a specified time period. The asset then is returned to the grantor, typically after the grantor has retired and may be in a lower tax bracket, or some other beneficiary.

Special Needs Trusts are used to retain eligibility for Medicaid and Supplemental Security Income (SSI) benefits. Assets bypass probate and can be used for extras, but not for essentials such as food, clothing and shelter.

Understanding the Federal Estate Tax

A federal estate tax, with rates that effectively range from 41% to 50% in 2002, is levied upon the transfer of property at death. Under the 2001 Act, the top estate-tax rate was reduced in 2002 to 50% from 55% and is gradually reduced to 45% for deaths occurring in 2007 through 2009. After 2009, the federal estate tax is repealed.

Currently, estate-tax liability is determined by applying the tax-rate schedule to the value of the gross estate — including certain post-1976 lifetime gifts — minus specific deductions and credits. This section focuses only on federal estate and gift taxes, but bear in mind that most states have either an estate or an inheritance tax.

Your gross estate includes the value of all property owned at death. *It isn't the same as your net worth.* The estate-tax value of your assets is likely to be far greater than your net worth, and it shouldn't be confused with the probate estate. Because your estate includes all your life-insurance proceeds and your home, you may be surprised at how large it is. An individual's *gross* estate for tax purposes includes *both* probate and nonprobate assets.

An individual's gross estate also is entitled to deductions for administrative costs and "last expenses," including medical and funeral costs. As an alternative, some administrative expenses can be deducted from the federal income taxes owed by the estate. So if the estate has income (*e.g.,* from employee stock options), the executor can choose to offset that income with deductions for administrative expenses. Using the *Estate Tax Balance Sheet*, you can estimate the value of your estate.

Federal Estate Taxes for Deaths Occurring in 2002

Taxable Estate	Estate Tax After Federal Credit	Tax Rate on Excess
Up to $1,000,000	$ 0	41%
1,250,000	102,500	43%
1,500,000	210,000	45%
2,000,000	435,000	49%
2,500,000	680,000	50%

Special Consideration:

Qualified State Tuition Programs

When you fund a qualified state tuition program (also known as a 529 plan), you generally retain control over the account as the owner. Any asset that you own normally will be included in your estate for federal estate-tax purposes. However, qualified state tuition accounts are specifically excluded from the account owner's taxable estate, unless the grantor/owner made a one-time gift in excess of $11,000 and elected to treat the gift as having been made over five years and died before the end of the five-year period.

Three provisions in the tax laws can significantly reduce — or even eliminate — federal estate and gift taxes: the unlimited marital deduction, the unified credit and lifetime gifts.

The Unlimited Marital Deduction

If a married individual wants a spouse to inherit some or all of the estate, using the marital deduction is the easiest way to defer federal estate taxes. To qualify for this deduction, property must benefit the spouse in one of two ways: Either the assets must pass directly to the spouse or be held in a trust that benefits the spouse or the spouse's estate exclusively. Under current law, if one of these requirements is met, an individual may leave a surviving spouse as much property as desired without incurring any federal estate tax. The unlimited marital deduction may not apply if your spouse is not a citizen of the United States. Please see an estate-planning attorney about creating a Qualified Domestic Trust (QDOT) to qualify for the marital deduction if either you or your spouse is not a U.S. citizen.

ESTATE PLANNING

Estate and Gift Tax Credits

Each person is entitled to a credit against taxes for gifts during a lifetime and/or transfers upon death. In 2002, the credit is the same for either type of transfer and shelters assets up to $1,000,000 from federal estate and gift taxes. After 2002, the credit for lifetime gifts will remain at $1,000,000 but the credit for transfers at death will increase. Estate planning for couples often focuses on ensuring each spouse takes full advantage of his/her credit for transfers at death. The 2001 Act provided for future increases in the credit exemption amount for transfers at death as follows:

Year	Credit Exemption Amount (Transfers at Death)
2002 – 2003	$1,000,000
2004 – 2005	$1,500,000
2006 – 2008	$2,000,000
2009	$3,500,000
2010	Taxes Repealed

Given the credit, only people with larger estates will pay any federal estate tax.

Understand Lifetime Gift Rules

Good estate planning often involves an effective and orderly gift program. Although the credit for transfers upon death will shield up to $1,000,000 or more of assets from federal estate taxes, inflation and actual growth in the value of assets may increase the value of lifetime giving. The systematic use of gifts can help control expenses by removing assets from an estate.

Still, most people cannot afford to give away property to save estate or death taxes. They might run out of money during their lifetimes — that's the greater risk. But if you choose to make gifts, probably for personal reasons, you should understand the rules.

Each individual may make a gift of property or cash with a fair market value of up to $11,000 per year to an unlimited number of recipients without incurring any federal gift tax as long as the recipient has a present interest in the property. In addition, an unlimited dollar amount is allowed for gifts made *directly* to a school or medical institution that are designated for either tuition payments (not room and board) or medical expenses. Finally, the $11,000 annual gift-tax exclusion is subject to indexing for inflation. However, it will only be indexed in increments of $1,000.

Donors won't be entitled to an income-tax deduction for gifts unless they were made to charities. Donees (recipients) won't pay income tax on any gifts received but will assume the donor's cost basis (or market value at the time of the gift, if lower) and holding period if they receive property.

Gifts by married individuals to a third party may be treated as a "split gift": two separate gifts, one from each spouse (provided both spouses consent). As a result, married couples can make a gift of up to $22,000 per recipient without paying tax. In this situation, a gift-tax return (IRS *Form 709* or *709*-A) must be filed. (Gifts exceeding $11,000 made to any donee — including a charity — require the filing of a gift-tax form.)

Some states also have a gift tax. At this point, states with a gift tax are Connecticut, Louisiana, North Carolina and Tennessee. Puerto Rico also has a gift tax.

Although significant tax advantages can result from lifetime giving, prospective donors should keep in mind that *gifts of property are irrevocable*. Before a gift is made, it's vital to evaluate the estate's composition, the nature of the gift property and the relationship with the intended recipient.

Estate-Tax Balance Sheet

Use the following worksheets to value your estate. If you're married, you should each complete your own worksheets, so make a photocopy before you start. Also, note that any jointly owned assets or community property should be divided equally between husband and wife. For example, if a couple owns a home valued at $100,000 with a mortgage of $60,000, half of the home's value ($50,000) and half of the mortgage ($30,000) is listed on each balance sheet. The same applies to all joint accounts such as checking, mutual funds, etc. When completing the worksheet, be sure to indicate how the property is held (*i.e.,* joint, separate or community).

Estate-Tax Balance Sheet Summary

Assets		Liabilities	
Cash	$__________	Funeral and Estate Administration Expenses	$__________
Securities	$__________	Mortgages, Liens, Property Taxes	$__________
Life Insurance	$__________	Loans	$__________
Pensions, Annuities, Retirement Plans, Profit Sharing, IRAs, Keoghs	$__________		
Real Estate	$__________		
Business Interests	$__________		
Debts Due the Estate	$__________		
Personal Property	$__________		
Total Assets	$__________	**Total Liabilities**	$__________
Taxable Estate*	$__________		

* Total assets minus total liabilities.

ESTATE PLANNING

Estate Assets Worksheet*

Cash *(bank, credit union, savings & loan, checking, money market, CDs, Christmas club, etc.)*

Financial Institution Name/Phone	Type of Account	Account No.	Ownership Sole – Joint	Amount
				$
				$
				$
				$
			Total Value	$

Securities *(stocks, bonds, mutual funds, unit trusts, government securities)*

Institution-Broker Name/Phone	Account No.	Ownership Sole – Joint	Cost Basis	Value
			$	$
			$	$
			$	$
			$	$
			$	$
			$	$
			$	$
			$	$
			Total Value	$

* Source: *The Widow's Handbook*

Estate Assets Worksheet *(continued)*

Life Insurance

Company Name/Phone	Policy No.	Beneficiary(ies)	Cash Value*	Face Amount
______	______	______	$ ______	$ ______
______	______	______	$ ______	$ ______
______	______	______	$ ______	$ ______
______	______	______	$ ______	$ ______
______	______	______	$ ______	$ ______
______	______	______	$ ______	$ ______
			Total Value	$ ______

Pensions, Annuities, Retirement Plans, Profit Sharing, IRAs, Keoghs

Description and Location (Firm Name)	Account No.	Value of Survivor Benefits (If Any)
______	______	$ ______
______	______	$ ______
______	______	$ ______
______	______	$ ______
______	______	$ ______
______	______	$ ______
	Total Value	$ ______

* Accumulated dividends, credit for unused premiums, etc.

Estate Assets Worksheet *(continued)*

Real Estate

Description and Location	Purchase Date – Price	Ownership Sole – Joint	Cost Basis	Appraised Value
______________________ ______________________	__________	__________	$ __________	$ __________
______________________ ______________________	__________	__________	$ __________	$ __________
______________________ ______________________	__________	__________	$ __________	$ __________
______________________ ______________________	__________	__________	$ __________	$ __________
			Total Value	$ __________

Business Interests *(corporations, partnerships, sole proprietorships)*

Firm Name Address/Phone	Type of Business	Cost Basis	Appraised Value
______________________ ______________________	__________	$ __________	$ __________
______________________ ______________________	__________	$ __________	$ __________
______________________ ______________________	__________	$ __________	$ __________
______________________ ______________________	__________	$ __________	$ __________
______________________ ______________________	__________	$ __________	$ __________
______________________ ______________________	__________	$ __________	$ __________
		Total Value	$ __________

ESTATE PLANNING

Estate Assets Worksheet *(continued)*

Debts Due the Estate *(notes, mortgages, royalties, patents, etc.)*

Name of Person/ Firm Owing	Address/ Phone	Ownership Sole – Joint	Date Due	Amount
				$
				$
				$
				$
			Total Value	$

Personal Property *(automobiles, jewelry, furniture, collections, etc.)*

Description	Location	Approximate Current Value
		$
		$
		$
		$
		$
		$
		$
		$
		$
		$
	Total Value	$
	Total Value of All Assets	$

Estate Liabilities Worksheet*

Funeral and Estate Administration Expenses

Description	Date Incurred	To Whom Paid	Amount
			$
			$
			$
			$
			$
		Total Value	$

Mortgages, Liens, Property Taxes

Description	To Whom Owed	Date Owed	Amount
			$
			$
			$
			$
		Total Value	$

Loans *(automobile, personal, insurance, credit cards, etc.)*

Description	To Whom Owed	Address/ Phone	Amount
			$
			$
			$
			$
			$
			$
		Total Value	$
		Total Value of All Liabilities	$

* Source: The Widow's Handbook.

ESTATE PLANNING

Choosing the Most Appropriate Estate Plan

Once you determine the value of your estate, you can choose the estate plan that will meet your distribution goals and minimize your estate taxes.

Simple or Outright "I Love You" Will

Single People — A simple will is appropriate for singles with estates valued at $1,000,000 or less. The federal credit against taxes for transfers upon death allows assets to pass on to any beneficiary, either directly or through a trust, free of estate taxes.

Married Couples — Simple wills also are appropriate for married couples with *combined* estates of less than $1,000,000. With this approach most (if not all) assets pass on to the surviving spouse, either directly or in trust. The marital deduction prevents the imposition of federal estate taxes upon the death of the first spouse. When the surviving spouse dies, the federal tax credit for transfers upon death also allows up to $1,000,000 of assets to pass to the survivor's beneficiaries free of federal estate taxes.

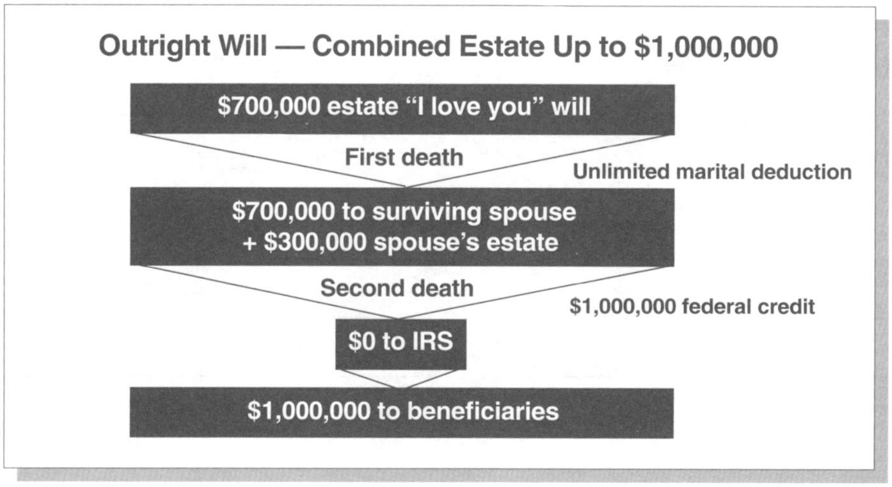

Although a simple outright "I love you" will is the most common choice for married couples, it can be disastrous if their combined estates are worth more than $1,000,000.

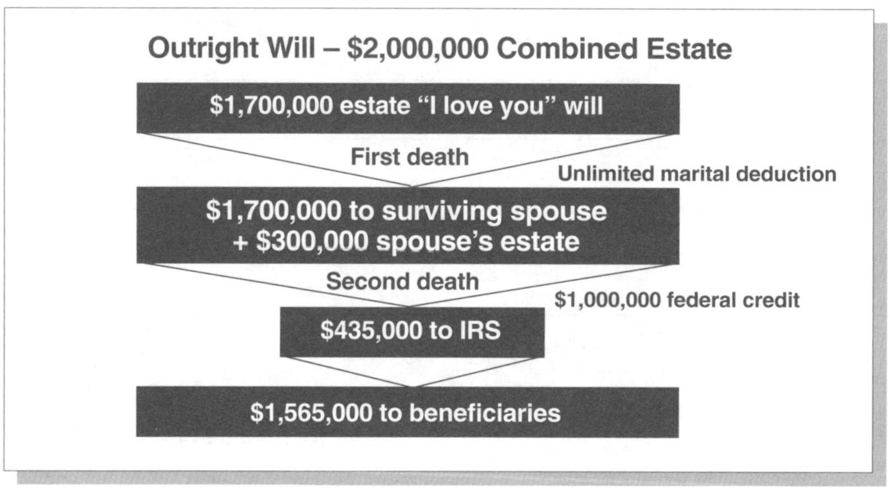

Two-Share Plan for Married Couples

To take full advantage of the federal tax credit for transfers upon death in each estate, married individuals with combined estates valued over $1,000,000 should consider a two-share plan. You can set up a two-share plan either in a will (a testamentary trust) or through the combination of a will and a separate living trust.

A two-share plan is designed to ensure that the estate of the first spouse to die takes full advantage of the federal credit, minimizing the taxes due at the second death. This is accomplished by "splitting" a married couple's combined estates into two parts: a marital share and a nonmarital or family share. A two-share plan allows a married couple to pass up to $2,000,000 (more in future years) to beneficiaries free of federal estate taxes.

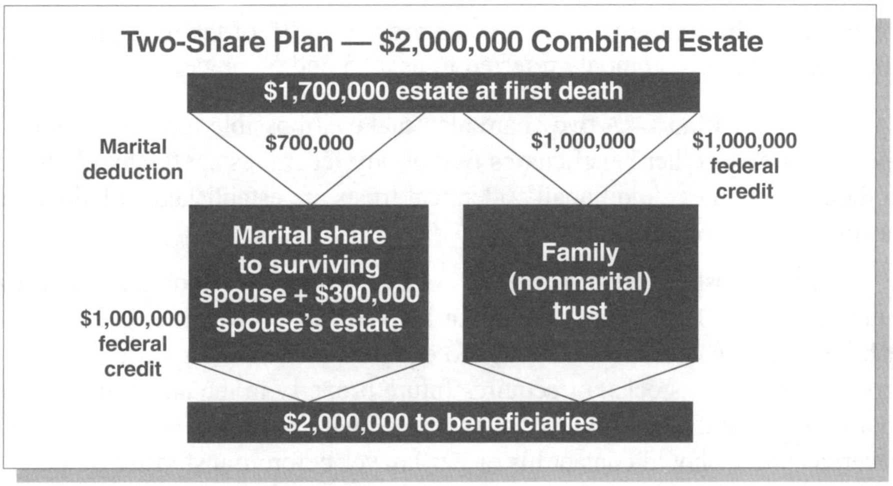

Marital Share — This share can either pass outright to the surviving spouse or it can be held in trust for the surviving spouse's benefit. If the assets are placed in trust, the surviving spouse has access to income as well as trust principal. The main reasons to place marital assets in trust are for professional management and to control the ultimate distribution of the trust property.

Special Consideration:

Q-TIP Marital Trust

A qualified terminable interest property trust (Q-TIP) is a marital trust that qualifies for the estate- or gift-tax marital deduction. A Q-TIP trust typically provides for income to be paid to the surviving spouse. But when the surviving spouse dies, the remaining assets are directed to a beneficiary named by the first spouse. Typically, the children or the family trust are named as the beneficiary.

Q-TIP trusts are often used in second-marriage situations because they can prevent the disinheritance of children from a prior marriage. They are also used in first marriages when both spouses are eager to protect marital assets. If a Q-TIP trust is properly drafted and implemented, it can protect assets from shifting to a new spouse if the surviving spouse remarries. If the Q-TIP trust appeals to you, discuss it carefully with your attorney. And be sure to coordinate your beneficiary designations. If all property is held in joint tenancy and the spouse is the beneficiary of all the insurance and company benefit plans, there might not be anything in the Q-TIP trust to protect!

Nonmarital or Family Share — At the first spouse's death, an amount equal to the credit exemption amount, *i.e.,* $1,000,000 in 2002, is placed in the nonmarital trust. This trust may go by a number of names: a credit shelter trust, a bypass trust, a credit equivalent bypass trust, a B-trust or a nonmarital trust. When the surviving spouse dies, the assets held in this trust will not be included in his or her estate, so the estate taxes are lowered. The surviving spouse and children usually are named as trust beneficiaries and can have fairly liberal, but not unlimited, access to trust property.

Common provisions of this trust include:

- Rights to all income generated by the trust for the spouse.
- Access to trust principal if, in the opinion of the trustee, funds are needed for the beneficiaries' health, education, maintenance or support.
- A provision allowing the spouse to withdraw the greater of 5% of the trust principal or $5,000 on an annual basis. This is commonly referred to as a "5 and 5" power.

Implementing a Two-Share Plan — A two-share plan makes it possible for a married couple to pass $2,000,000 to their children or other beneficiaries free of any federal estate tax, but both spouses must own property in their own names. Additionally, identical trusts are established so federal taxes can be avoided or reduced regardless of who dies first.

For a two-share plan to be most effective, the estates of the two spouses should be "equalized." Ideally, each spouse would have $1,000,000 or more in his or her respective name, not in joint tenancy (excluding their home and one checking account). To equalize estates, the spouse with the larger amount of assets transfers property (*e.g.,* stocks) or acquires future property in the name of the other spouse so that the other spouse has up to $1,000,000 in that spouse's own name (*i.e.,* not in joint tenancy). Generally, however, a spouse should contact his or her lawyer before transferring property brought into the marriage or acquired by inheritance. Such property, if kept separate, typically would not be deemed marital property that is split up upon divorce.

Outright Will With Disclaimer

As an alternative to the two-share plan, consider using an outright will with a disclaimer to build in flexibility. You can set up your estate so the entire amount is left to the surviving spouse, who has the option of creating a family share when the first spouse dies. Within nine months of the date of death, the surviving spouse can disclaim all or any portion of his/her interest in the estate. However, be careful about disclaiming property. Disclaimed assets will pass according to the will provisions that control the distribution of assets at the first death, and, depending upon those provisions, the assets may not pass to the family (nonmarital) trust. Assuming the disclaimed amount passes outside of the marital share, it will escape tax upon the survivor's subsequent death. If the size of your combined estates is between $1,000,000 and $2,000,000, and if you want to give your spouse as much flexibility as possible, this is a useful provision. But it's very complicated — you'll need expert legal advice.

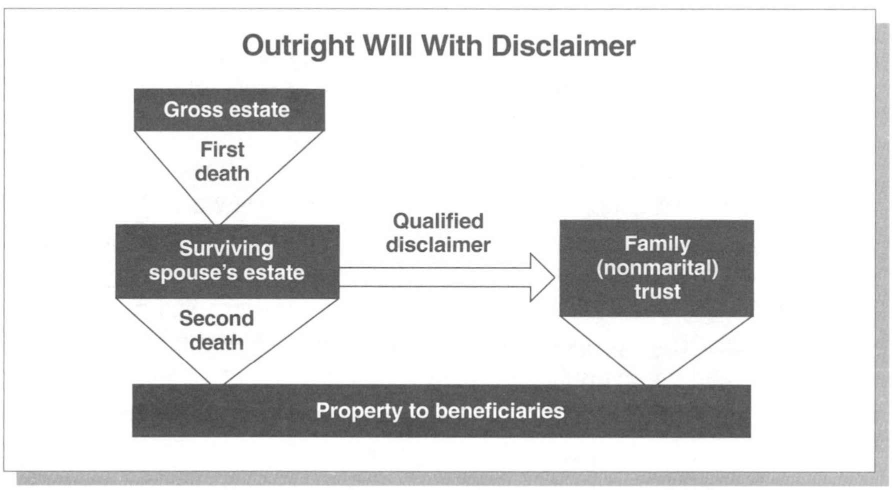

Irrevocable Trust

Most people aren't interested in designing an estate plan that decreases lifetime flexibility. But if you have a very large estate (singles over $1,000,000 or married couples over $2,000,000) and have a stable financial and personal situation (*e.g.,* marriage, relationship with children), then adding an irrevocable trust to your estate plan may be appropriate. To avoid estate taxes, you can transfer the ownership of your life insurance to an irrevocable trust. If you outlive this transfer by three years, the insurance proceeds will not be subject to estate tax when you die. But be careful, because the gift is irrevocable. If you have a sizable estate, discuss this strategy with your estate-planning attorney.

Four Steps to Planning Your Estate

Step 1: Decide Who Should Receive the Assets

If you were to die today, who should receive your property? If you have children, you should decide when and how they would receive their share. Develop a list of who should receive personal property, such as jewelry. Be sure to discuss your estate plan with your loved ones.

Step 2: Get the Basics in Place

The right estate plan for you and your family depends on your personal objectives and the size of your estate. You should have an attorney licensed in your state draft a detailed document for you. However, you can save time and money by understanding your options before meeting with the attorney.

Ownership — If you don't live in a community-property state, you should know how your assets are titled. Are they in your name alone? In joint tenancy? Or are they held in tenancy-in-common (less typical than tenancy by the entirety)? For larger estates (over $1,000,000), this information is critical if you want to take advantage of your federal credit for transfers upon death. For smaller estates (under $1,000,000) — or in situations when either avoiding probate or reducing legal fees is important — consider joint ownership.

Beneficiary Designations — Make sure you know the beneficiary designations on all life-insurance policies, company benefit plans and IRAs. Bring the appropriate forms to change your beneficiary designations when you meet with your attorney.

Life insurance — The proceeds from your life-insurance policy (personal or group) will be included in your estate. Transferring life-insurance ownership to an irrevocable trust will remove the proceeds from your estate if you survive the transfer by at least three years. However, if the trust is the initial owner and beneficiary, then the proceeds are never a part of the estate. The suitability of an irrevocable trust to own insurance on your life will depend on the value of your estate as well as your age and objectives.

Step 3: Value Your Estate

Before selecting the right estate plan, you must know the value of your estate. Your gross estate is the value of all the assets you own at the time of your death — it's *not* the same as your net worth. For example, your estate value includes the proceeds from life-insurance policies. Bring your completed *Estate Tax Balance Sheet* with you when you meet with your attorney.

Step 4: Understand the Effect of Relevant Tax Laws

Many people aren't interested in leaving an estate to their heirs. Instead, they prefer to use the money during their lifetime. Despite this intent, assets usually remain after death because most people don't want to die in poverty. At death, assets will go either to the IRS (and the state) or to selected beneficiaries. Given that choice, most people want to ensure that their heirs receive the bulk of their estate. If you're married and your estate is valued at over $1,000,000, be sure you're familiar with the two-share plan discussed earlier.

Special Consideration:

Income Taxes at Death on Appreciated Property

Under current tax law, a "step-up in basis" at death allows you (that is, your estate or beneficiary) to avoid paying income taxes on most appreciated property included in your estate. The rule states that your share of a home, shares of stock or any other capital asset that would result in capital-gains taxes if sold the day before you die escapes income taxes on the increase in value up to your date of death if sold after your death. So, before selling or transferring the property of someone on his or her death bed, talk with a tax attorney about both the estate tax *and* capital-gains tax implications.

Once the estate tax has been repealed in 2010, the current rules for "step-up in basis" will end. Your estate, however, will be entitled to a set-up in basis of up to $1.3 million, but no more than the fair market value of the assets. Additionally, if you're maried your estate will have up to an additional $3 million to allocate to the basis of property passing to your surviving spouse.

Advance Directives

Making decisions about medical care can be difficult, especially because tremendous advances in medicine and technology now make it possible to prolong life beyond the point where people are capable of making decisions or expressing their desires.

For this reason you should put a series of advance directives about your health-care preferences in writing now. Legal documents such as a living will, health-care power of attorney and general durable powers of attorney allow you to retain control by recording your preferences for medical care in advance. They ensure your values and wishes are considered when decisions must be made.

Living Will

A living will isn't the type of will used in estate planning. It's a legal document allowing you to express your wishes as to health-care treatment. A living will makes clear what measures you want taken — or not taken — to keep you alive if you're seriously ill or injured and cannot survive without mechanical means. State laws usually require you to notify your physician so a copy of the living will can be included in your medical records, but you can always revoke the document by making an oral request. It's important that a living will be drafted according to state law.

Health-Care Power of Attorney

This legal document is a health-care proxy that allows you to appoint someone — a family member or close friend — to make medical decisions should you become unable to make them for yourself. The powerholder decides what treatment you should receive and when the treatment should stop. Therefore, it's important to make sure the person you designate to make these critical decisions understands and will consider your beliefs and values about life, sickness, medical treatment, suffering and death. Furthermore, it's important that a health-care power of attorney be drafted according to state law. This document differs from a living will, which typically is designed to avoid the undesired prolongation of life.

ESTATE PLANNING

General Durable Power of Attorney

Consider giving a family member or trusted friend a general durable power of attorney allowing him or her to make decisions on your behalf should it ever become necessary. A "springing power" may be appropriate, since it springs into existence only after a specified event — such as a legal incompetency — occurs. Be explicit regarding any company benefit plans — especially about authorizing the power-holder to make decisions. You also may ask your attorney to hold the power documents until they're needed. Show a copy of the power of attorney to whomever you expect to honor it, including an employer. Most importantly, do not execute a power of attorney if you do not trust the powerholder *completely.* If you own property in another state, you'll need a power of attorney from that jurisdiction as well.

Special Consideration:

Partnership for Caring

Call Partnership for Caring at 800/989-9455 or visit their Web site at www.partnershipforcaring.org to receive a sample of a living will and health-care power of attorney for your state. A donation is requested for obtaining these copies. You should complete new copies of these forms every five years. This will show that your intentions haven't changed.

ADVANCE DIRECTIVE
Living Will and Health-Care Proxy

Death is a part of life. It is a reality like birth, growth and aging. I am using this advance directive to convey my wishes about medical care to my doctors and other people looking after me at the end of my life. It is called an advance directive because it gives instructions in advance about what I want to happen to me in the future. It expresses my wishes about medical treatment that might keep me alive. I want this to be legally binding.

If I cannot make or communicate decisions about my medical care, those around me should rely on this document for instructions about measures that could keep me alive.

I do not want medical treatment (including feeding and water by tube) that will keep me alive if:

- I am unconscious and there is no reasonable prospect that I will ever be conscious again (even if I am not going to die soon in my medical condition), *or*
- I am near death from an illness or injury with no reasonable prospect of recovery.

I do want medicine and other care to make me more comfortable and to take care of pain and suffering. I want this even if the pain medicine makes me die sooner.

I want to give some extra instructions: [*Here list any special instructions,* e.g., *some people fear being kept alive after a debilitating stroke. If you have wishes about this or any other conditions, please write them here.*]

____

____

The legal language in the box that follows is a health-care proxy. It gives another person the power to make medical decisions for me.

I hereby name ______________________________,

who lives at ______________________________

______________________, phone number ______________________,

to make medical decisions for me if I cannot make them myself. This person is called a health-care "surrogate," "agent," "proxy" or "attorney in fact." This power of attorney shall become effective when I become incapable of making or communicating decisions about my medical care. This means that this document stays legal when and if I lose the power to speak for myself, for instance, if I am in a coma or have Alzheimer's disease.

My health-care proxy has power to tell others what my advance directive means. This person also has power to make decisions for me, based either on what I would have wanted or, if this is not known, on what he or she thinks is best for me.

If my first choice health-care proxy cannot or decides not to act for me, I name ______________

______________________ address ______________________,

____,

phone number ______________, as my second choice.

(continued on next page)

I have discussed my wishes with my health-care proxy and with my second choice if I have chosen to appoint a second person. My proxy(ies) has (have) agreed to act for me.

I have thought about this advance directive carefully. I know what it means and want to sign it. I have chosen two witnesses, neither of whom is a member of my family nor will inherit from me when I die. My witnesses are not the same people as those I named as my health-care proxies. I understand that this form should be notarized if I use the box to name (a) health-care proxy(ies).

Signature ______________________________

Date ______________________________

Address ______________________________

Witness' signature ______________________________

Witness' printed name ______________________________

Address ______________________________

Witness' signature ______________________________

Witness' printed name ______________________________

Address ______________________________

Notary [to be used if proxy is appointed] ______________________________

Drafted and distributed by Partnership for Caring: America's Voice for the Dying. Partnership for Caring is a national not-for-profit organization that works for the rights of patients at the end of life. In addition to this generic advance directive, Partnership for Caring distributes advance directives that conform to each state's specific legal requirements and maintains a national Living Will Registry for completed documents.

Partnership for Caring:
America's Voice for the Dying
1620 Eye Street, NW, Washington D.C. 20006
800/989-9455
www.partnershipforcaring.org

Letter of Instruction

The final step in completing your estate plan is to prepare a letter of instruction. This letter will help your family settle your affairs by letting them know what you want. Usually, this is not a legal document, but it should be consistent with the terms of your will. As an alternative to a written letter, you can record your letter of instruction on audio or video tape.

Consider the following items as you develop your outline:

- ❖ **People to Notify** — Certain people and institutions must be contacted upon your death, including your attorney, executor, trustee and tax specialist. Providing names, titles, addresses and telephone numbers now will make it easier for the person who will contact these individuals.
- ❖ **Funeral Arrangements** — If you've made your own arrangements or have special requests, communicate them clearly and provide the necessary details. Include a reminder for the funeral director to provide multiple copies of the death certificate for transferring property and processing insurance and Social Security claims.
- ❖ **Location of Personal Papers** — Use the Document Locator to record the exact location of your personal documents.
- ❖ **Letter to Trustee** — Specify how you want your guardian reimbursed for expenses incurred while caring for your children.
- ❖ **Valuables** — Maintain a complete list of all your jewelry and other valuables (china, glassware, art collections, antiques, etc.), including their location. You also may include the names of those to whom the articles should be given. This list is sometimes part of the will itself, or itemized on a separate personal-property list. Some states allow a letter of instruction to be a binding part of your will through incorporation by reference. Check with your estate-planning attorney for more information.
- ❖ **Special Assets** — List any special assets, such as stock options, requiring action by your executor within a specific time frame.
- ❖ **Trusts** — List any trusts you've established, including the name and address of the trustees and the contents of the trusts.
- ❖ **Special Survivors' Benefits** — List possible sources of benefits not mentioned in your will, such as: Social Security, veterans' organizations, employee, pension and retirement plans, fraternal associations. Otherwise these benefits might be overlooked.
- ❖ **Notes/Letters** — Because wills and trusts tend to be tightly sealed, somber legal documents, consider including personal thoughts and messages for your beneficiaries. For example, you can name whom you want to receive grandmother's brooch or grandfather's watch, as well as a bit of history relating to each memento. It is often awkward to ask relatives for items you have lent them previously. This is your last opportunity to retrieve those items and pass on the property to whomever you wish. While this is not binding, most last requests will be honored.
- ❖ **Create a Personal Legacy** — Consider conducting annual interviews on audio or video tape, dictating stories or writing letters to convey autobiographical information for future generations. This is especially important when you have young children. Interview grandparents, too, or have them read a holiday story on a separate tape.

Settling an Estate

Getting Organized — A Guide for Survivors
"There's So Much Paperwork — Where Do I Begin?"

Survivors are inundated with mail from insurance companies, the decedent's employer, banks, etc. Combine this with the mountain of paperwork that needs to be filled out and the supporting documentation required to claim benefits, and it all looks overwhelming!

If you're not organized, important documents could get lost, or worse yet, you could miss important deadlines. While you may not be ready to deal with all the correspondence yet, it will prove extremely beneficial to be organized for when you are.

The first rule is: "Don't Throw Anything Away!" Not at first, anyway. What may not look like something important now always seems to be essential in one way or another in a month.

A relatively simple way to organize all the mail, documentation and paperwork is to start a file. Your file can be anything from manila folders in a box to a filing cabinet, or anything in between. What is important is that your documents are in a safe place where you can quickly and easily put your finger on them when needed. And, your filing system can be as general or as specific as you want it to be.

The following is a list of general categories — each one can be a file label — followed by documents that should be located and filed. This may take some time to set up, but it will undoubtedly prove to be an invaluable investment of your time. Then, every day when the mail arrives, sort it and promptly file each piece in the appropriate area. Make new files as necessary.

- **Estate Documents**
  Wills, codicils, supporting memoranda
  Trust agreements
  Powers of attorney
  Powers of appointment
- **Life Insurance**
  Life insurance policies
  Copy of claim forms
  IRS *Form 712*
- **Correspondence From Employer**
  Benefit-claim forms
  Stubs from checks you receive
  Current benefit-plan statements
  Record of claims
- **Tax Information**
  Copies of tax returns from three previous years' *W-2* and *1099* forms
  Receipts for other taxes paid
  Charitable-contribution receipts
  Other deductible items
- **Business-Related**
  Partnership agreements
  Joint-venture agreements
  Contracts
- **Credit-Card Statements**
- **Unpaid Bills**
  List of bills to be paid
  List of bills paid
- **Household**
  Homeowner's insurance policy
  Property deed
  Appraisals
  Records and receipts for home improvements
- **Automobile Papers**
  Title
  Automobile insurance policy
  Registration
- **Correspondence From Banks**
  Savings-account statements and passbook
  Checking-account statements and register
  Canceled checks
- **Decedent's Personal Documentation**
  Death certificates
  Birth certificate
  Social Security card
  Military papers

ESTATE PLANNING

- **Family's Personal Documentation**
  - Birth certificates
  - Social Security numbers
  - Marriage certificate
  - Divorce agreement

- **Investment Information**
  - Brokerage-account statements
  - Money-market accounts
  - Certificates of deposit
  - Stock certificates
  - Bonds
  - Mutual funds
  - IRAs
  - Credit-union accounts
  - U.S. savings bonds
  - U.S. Treasury securities

Locating These Documents

If this information is not readily available, begin by reviewing the decedent's checkbook register for payments to credit-card companies, insurance companies, financial advisors, etc. To assist in the search for important documents, look in family hiding places, closets, drawers, briefcases, strong boxes, home and office desks, safe-deposit boxes, etc.

Another invaluable tool you may wish to use to help you get organized and stay organized is the Document Locator found later in this chapter. You can use the Document Locator for your personal information, too.

"Do I Need to Do Anything With the Will?"

One of your most immediate concerns and, quite possibly, responsibilities, will be finalizing the affairs of the decedent's estate. It's common practice for spouses to name each other as the executor (or executrix, for a female) of their respective estates. In the case of intestacy (dying without a will) the court will appoint an administrator who has the same responsibilities as an executor.

An executor or administrator is the person legally responsible for administering the will or, in the absence of a will, administering the estate. Regardless of how large or small the estate is, and whether or not there is a will, the affairs of the decedent need to be finalized.

"Settling the estate" is a term of art used to describe the process of distributing the decedent's property according to the terms of the will, or in the case of intestacy, distributing the decedent's property as dictated by state law. Settling the estate is not to be confused with "probate," which is the court procedure by which a will is proved to be valid or invalid.

However, in recent years, the term probate has been expanded to include all matters pertaining to settling the estate. "Estate" refers to the total property owned at death and prior to distribution.

The responsibilities and powers of an executor vary from state to state, but generally the executor is responsible for making a list of the estate's assets, managing its affairs, paying its bills and collecting its debts and communicating with, and distributing property to, the appropriate beneficiaries. Specific additional powers may be granted in the will.

While it is common practice to hire an attorney for guidance in settling the estate, it isn't mandatory. However, as executor, you should be aware of your responsibilities. In addition, you can save money on legal fees by settling some of the issues yourself. As you complete each of the following items, cross it off the list.

Estate Settlement Checklist

Immediate Duties of the Executor

- ❖ **Funeral Arrangements** — Locate written funeral or burial instructions and make arrangements.
- ❖ **Retain Necessary and Appropriate Advisors** — Evaluate your needs and retain appropriate professionals: attorney, accountant, broker, etc.
- ❖ **Financial Accounts** — Accounts owned jointly with a right of survivorship should be changed to the name of the surviving owner. If your spouse had an Individual Retirement Account (IRA) and you are the beneficiary and are under age 59½, *don't automatically transfer the name on the account to your own*. As a surviving spouse, you're allowed to take money from the account without suffering the 10% additional tax.
- ❖ **Locate the Will and Other Significant Documents** — Locate key documents including the *original* will and codicils (amendments to the will), trust agreements, marriage certificate, divorce agreement (if applicable), insurance policies, bankbooks, stock and bond certificates, Social Security numbers and birth certificates for all family members, property titles, deeds, powers of attorney, military service papers, etc. Also, the Document Locator provided later in this chapter will prove helpful.

  If you don't have originals or certified copies of marriage or birth certificates, divorce agreements, military service papers or Social Security cards, all states have offices where you can obtain certified copies. Check your phone book for the Office or Department of Vital Records or Statistics.
- ❖ **Secure Assets** — Take possession of the property (especially movable items) of the estate, collect rents, etc. Check to see whether the decedent's residence is secure.
- ❖ **Safeguard Assets** — Take necessary steps to protect the estate's interest in an ongoing business.
- ❖ **Establish Records** — It's important to keep a list of all property, income, debts and expenses of the estate. Keeping receipts will prove useful when closing the estate.
- ❖ **Organize Correspondence** — Retain and keep a list of all mail and correspondence. *Don't* throw anything away!
- ❖ **Obtain Death Certificates** — You will need certified Death Certificates to file claims for life insurance, survivor benefits and to change the title of property and financial accounts. These may be obtained from your funeral director or the county coroner.
- ❖ **Collect Employee Benefits** — File claims for and collect benefits due and owing to the estate and survivors from employee benefit plans sponsored by the current employer and all former employers. File a claim for accrued vacation pay, unpaid salary and accumulated sick pay, as well as any worker's compensation benefits.

  Surviving spouses are permitted to make a tax-free *rollover* of certain employee benefit plans into IRAs. The tax law gives you 60 days from when you receive the funds to roll them over into the IRA. Rather than making this rollover yourself, ask for a *direct rollover* to avoid the mandatory federal 20% tax withholding.

  If your deceased spouse worked for a long period of time for another employer, there may be benefits payable. Be sure to contact that employer also.
- ❖ **Continue or Convert Employer-Provided Health Insurance** — You'll need to decide whether or not to *continue* or *convert* any existing hospitalization, medical or dental insurance under which you and other dependents were covered. Putting off this decision could have very costly consequences.

Most group hospitalization/medical plans continue for a fixed number of months after the person covered by the insurance passes away. A federal law known as COBRA lets you, as surviving spouse, continue to buy medical insurance through your spouse's employer's plan for up to 36 months. This is called *continuation,* which is different from *conversion.*

Most group plans also allow the surviving dependents to *convert* to individual policies without a medical exam. They may also cover pre-existing conditions. Converting a policy can be expensive. It may be cheaper to buy your own individual policy elsewhere. In any case, it's important that you make a decision.

Make sure you file claims for any bills incurred by your spouse. Ask your spouse's employer if your spouse had a medical-care "flex" or reimbursement account. If so, how much is the balance? Can you still use it?

❖ **Collect Life-Insurance Benefits** — File claims for life insurance. If your spouse was covered by personally owned life insurance, write to either the insurance company whose name and address are on the policy or the agent who sold the policy or call the insurance company's local office.

If you're the policy beneficiary, you'll prepare a statement of claim and provide the following to the insurance company:

1. A copy of the death certificate
2. The policy number
3. The policy amount (sometimes called the death benefit or face value)
4. Name and address of your spouse
5. Your spouse's occupation and last day of work
6. Your spouse's birth certificate (or other birth documentation) and possibly yours, depending on how you want the proceeds to be paid

The insurance company may ask for additional specific information about the cause of death, such as an attending physician's statement or a police report. Since the insurer is required to file information on taxable payments with the federal government, the company also will need your age, address and Social Security number. However, remember that life-insurance proceeds aren't taxable to the beneficiary. Also, if the estate has to file an estate-tax return (IRS *Form 706*) ask the insurance company for a Life Insurance Statement, IRS *Form 712.*

Many social organizations, professional associations and unions have group life-insurance plans for members that provide special benefits for surviving spouses. Contact these organizations and tell them of the death of a member and ask for information on possible insurance proceeds or other benefits. Also, check to see if there was life insurance on loans, mortgages and credit cards.

❖ **Collect Social Security Benefits** — Be sure to apply for Social Security benefits as soon as practicable. Social Security benefits are paid to widows, widowers, children and other surviving family members. When a worker dies, the funeral director usually notifies the Social Security Administration. This is not a formal claim for benefits. You must file a benefits claim by contacting the nearest Social Security office, whose address and phone number you can find in your telephone book under "U.S. Government, Department of Health and Human Services." For more information, phone the Social Security Administration at 800/772-1213.

❖ **Collect Veteran's Benefits** — Benefits available to spouses and children of veterans include reimbursement of some burial-plot expenses, pension payments and education assistance. Payments depend on whether the veteran died from causes connected with military service; whether the veteran served in war or peacetime; whether the discharge was honorable or other than honorable;

and the family's financial circumstances. To check on benefits, call 800/827-1000 or visit the Veterans' Administration (VA) office in your area. If you don't have a local VA office, contact local veterans' organizations (such as the Veterans of Foreign Wars or the American Legion) or the American Red Cross for assistance.

The VA will need either a veteran's claim number (called a "C" number) or a copy of a discharge from military service certificate (*DD Form 214*), military service number or branch of service, and dates served. In addition, a death certificate, marriage certificate(s) and birth certificates for children may be required.

Families of certain peacetime veterans and of veterans who served in wartime are eligible for a $150 burial-expense payment. Both wartime and peacetime veterans are eligible for free grave markers or headstones.

A widow or widower and some unmarried children of a veteran are eligible for monthly pension payments from the VA if a veteran's death is connected with military service. Spouses of veterans whose deaths or disabilities were connected with military service can apply for educational benefits for themselves and their children. Widows and widowers (who have not remarried) of veterans of World War II, Korea and Vietnam who died of service-connected disabilities are eligible for GI loans to acquire a home. Surviving spouses also may be eligible for an "aid-and-assistance" benefit if they are patients in a nursing home, helpless, blind, or require the regular aid of a person in the home.

- **Notify Creditors** — Contact all creditors and check for insurance on outstanding loans, mortgages and credit cards. Your spouse may have carried *credit life insurance* on those borrowings. Check with the banks and other lenders (*e.g.,* department stores) to determine if those payments are covered by insurance.

Probate of the Will

- **Submit Will to Probate** — The procedures for probate that govern the transfer of property and assets of the decedent vary by state. Therefore, it is wise to contact the Probate Court (also referred to as the Surrogate's Court, Register or Registry of Wills) in your county to ask the clerk the necessary procedures to follow.

Probate is the legal procedure followed by courts to prove the validity of a written will. This is necessary to authorize distribution of property according to the will's provisions.

If you need to probate the will, you may need to hire an attorney to assist you. There are a number of rules you must follow when probating a will. Sometimes the local probate court may be unwilling to provide you with assistance, particularly if you reside in a metropolitan area.

Special Consideration:

Absence of a Valid Will

Administration in lieu of probate occurs when there is no valid will. The Court will issue "Letters of Administration" that authorize the administrator to settle the estate. Each state has what are called *laws of descent* that dictate the distribution of an estate if there is no valid will. These laws usually provide for the surviving spouse and children to receive shares of the estate. For example, in some states a surviving spouse with one child receives half of the estate and the child the other half. If there is more than one child, the surviving spouse receives a third and the children share equally in the remaining two-thirds. Also, in some states, the parent(s) of the decedent will receive a portion of the estate if the decedent has no children.

If there is a valid will, you or your attorney should start the probate process by filing it with the Probate Court. The court will then formally appoint the executor named in the will and issue "Letters Testamentary," which authorize the executor to begin settlement procedures. Your duties as executor include making a list of all your spouse's assets, collecting debts owed to your spouse, paying debts owed by your spouse, managing and distributing property, and submitting a *final accounting* to the court.

In addition to the will, the court will need the names and addresses of children and a list of the estate's assets. It also may require copies of a marriage certificate and documents on any previous marriage(s).

During the legal sorting-out period, bank accounts and other assets may be frozen, safe-deposit boxes sealed, and other steps taken to protect the interests of heirs and to conserve assets subject to estate taxes. There are also numerous forms to be completed and fees to be paid. Banks will often allow a widowed spouse to withdraw funds to meet daily expenses until the estate is settled. When the bank doesn't allow any assets to be withdrawn, the court can order the release of assets from the estate to the spouse to meet daily living expenses.

Not all assets are subject to probate. The clerk of the Probate Court can provide general information on assets that should — or should not — be included in probate. Although laws vary among states, many exclude property that passes with a right of survivorship — for example, a jointly owned home or bank account. Beneficiary-designated assets, such as life-insurance proceeds, that are payable to an individual (and not the estate) aren't included in the probate estate.

Special Consideration:

Small Estates

In small, uncomplicated estates, it may be possible to handle probate without legal assistance. If the decedent's probate estate is smaller than the amount established for small estates by the laws of the applicable state, then the estate often can be settled by filing an affidavit with the Probate Court or entity holding an asset instead of by probate of the will. Legal assistance usually is still advisable.

- **Open Estate Account** — Open a separate checking account to deposit checks received. Apply for a Taxpayer Identification Number (TIN) for the estate using IRS *Form SS-4*.
- **Inventory Assets** — Locate and make a list of the assets of the estate including bank accounts, property in safe-deposit boxes, stocks and bonds, titles, deeds, life insurance policies, automobiles, jewelry, business agreements and out-of-state property. (You'll find it helpful to use the *Estate Assets Worksheet* earlier in this section.)
- **Appraisal and Valuation** — Arrange for appraisal and valuation of estate assets as of date of death and the alternate valuation date (six months after date of death.)
- **Notify Heirs and Beneficiaries** — Contact all heirs, beneficiaries and other interested parties who will receive assets from the estate. Keep a list of their names, addresses, birth dates, Social Security numbers and telephone numbers.
- **Distribution of Assets** — Consult with appropriate heirs and beneficiaries on the orderly distribution of estate assets.

Active Management of the Estate

- **Review Insurance Coverage** — Establish, keep in force, and if necessary improve fire, rent, title, liability, property and casualty, or other insurance to protect the estate's property. Notify the automobile and/or homeowner's insurance carrier of a change in coverage to activate the adjustment.
- **Title Transfer** — Change the name on any bank account, mutual-fund account, etc., that was held jointly with the decedent or solely by the decedent. This can be accomplished by taking a copy of the death certificate to the financial institution and filing for a change. Any stocks and bonds that were specifically bequeathed (distributed under the will according to the decedent's instructions) must be reregistered in the name of the beneficiary. Additionally, you may need to update or change title to real property, *e.g.,* your primary home or vacation home. Depending on the state, this may require filing an affidavit at the County Clerk's office or drafting a new deed. You should check with your county clerk's office or consult with an attorney on this issue.
- **Collect Debts** — Collect all debts owed to the decedent or the estate.
- **Pay Bills** — Receive all claims against the estate. After determining their validity, pay them according to the priority established by state law. You may need to consult with an attorney on this issue, particularly with regard to your personal obligation to pay for your spouse's debts. You may or may not have such an obligation depending on the type of debt and the state in which you reside. It's wise to keep a list of bills paid.
- **Determine Estate-Tax Liability** — The IRS requires *Form 706 — United States Estate Tax Return* to be filed by the estate's executor or administrator, or if there is neither, any person in possession of any property of the decedent, of a decedent whose gross estate valued at the date of death, plus adjustable taxable gifts (made by the decedent during his or her lifetime) and specific exemptions, is more than $1,000,000. *Form 706* must be filed within nine months of the decedent's date of death. **The gross estate includes life-insurance proceeds, even though they are payable to beneficiaries other than the estate, other beneficiary-designation assets and jointly owned property with a right of survivorship even though these assets are not part of the probate estate.** In addition, ask your attorney or tax preparer if there is a state filing requirement.

  To help you determine the value of the gross estate, we suggest you complete the *Estate-Tax Balance Sheet Summary* earlier in this section. *When completing the worksheet, make sure you include the correct amounts*. For example, if you and the decedent each owned 50% of a $100,000 home with a $40,000 mortgage, the amount included on the worksheet is $50,000 for the home and $20,000 for the mortgage. The proportional value of jointly owned assets, usually 50%, is included in the decedent's gross estate. However, the full value of life insurance proceeds, employee benefits *and assets or debts owed solely in the decedent's name* will be included on the worksheet.
- **Determine Estate Income-Tax Liability** — The IRS requires *Form 1041 — Income Tax Return for Trusts and Estates* to be filed by the authorized representative (*i.e.,* executor or administrator) of the estate of a decedent whose estate has gross income of $600 or more during a taxable year. Gross income includes dividends, interest, rents, royalties, capital gains and income from businesses, partnerships, trusts and other sources. In addition, ask your attorney or tax preparer if there is a state filing requirement.

Document Locator

Insurance Policies

Life *(attach schedule if necessary)*

____

____

Accident/Health ________________

____

____

Disability ____________________

Property/Casualty ______________

Major Medical _________________

Other ________________________

Marriage Certificate

____

Medical and Dental Information

____

____

____

Power of Attorney

____

____

Safe-Deposit Box

Location _____________________

Box Number ___________________

Other Persons Having Access to Box ____

____

Location of Keys ______________

____

Contents _____________________

____

____

Safe-Deposit Box

Location _____________________

Box Number ___________________

Other Persons Having Access to Box ____

____

Location of Keys ______________

Contents _____________________

Securities Certificates *(attach schedule if necessary)*

Stocks _______________________

____

____

Bonds ________________________

____

____

Money-Market Funds ____________

____

____

Other ________________________

Social Security Cards

____

Wills/ Trust Agreements

Original ______________________

Conformed copies ______________

Automobile Papers

1. Registration ____________________
   Bill of Sale ____________________
   Finance Agreement/Lease ____________
2. Registration ____________________
   Bill of Sale ____________________
   Finance Agreement/Lease ____________

Bank-Account Books and Papers

Checking Acct. # ____________________

Bank & Address ____________________

____

Other Signature ____________________

Checking Acct. # ____________________

Bank & Address ____________________

____

Other Signature ____________________

Savings Acct. # ____________________

Bank & Address ____________________

____

Other Signature ____________________

Savings Acct. # ____________________

Bank & Address ____________________

____

Other Signature ____________________

Cert. of Deposit ____________________

Bank & Address ____________________

____

Other Signature ____________________

Cert. of Deposit ____________________

Bank & Address ____________________

____

Other Signature ____________________

Baptismal Certificate

____

____

Birth Certificate

____

____

Burial Instructions

____

____

Deeds

Primary Residence ____________________

Secondary Residence ____________________

Mortgage – Primary ____________________

Mortgage – Secondary ____________________

Leases ____________________

Cemetery Plot ____________________

Divorce Papers

____

____

Employee-Benefit Data

Group-Insurance Plans ____________________

Pension Plan ____________________

Savings/Profit-Sharing Plan ____________________

Other Employee Benefits ____________________

Income-Tax Returns

Federal ____________________

State ____________________

Other ____________________

Document Locator

Organization is half of the financial planning process. In order to help you with this task, a document locator has been provided. Take time to complete it now, and update it every six or 12 months. Keeping the document locator current will help you get a better understanding of your financial picture and help your executor settle your estate faster.

Name: ______________________________

Social Security Number: ____________________

Date: ______________________________

Directions:

- ❖ Each adult should complete the following questions individually.
- ❖ Leave blank any item that does not apply to you. Include the *location* and a brief *description* of those items that apply to you.
- ❖ This record should be kept in a secure location known to husband or wife, if married; or to a friend or relative, if not married.
- ❖ Complete the information now and bring it up to date at least annually.

Note the following *important* information:

1) I have written a personal letter to ______________________________ .

   The letter is located ______________________________ .

2) I have made a living will: Yes ____ No ____.

   The following people have copies of this will: ____________________ .

3) I have made arrangements to donate ______________________________

   for transplant. Please call ______________________________

   immediately in case of death.

4) Other important documents ______________________________ .

The following are to be contacted in the event of my death:

Attorney ______________________________

Phone ______________________________

Tax Advisor ______________________________

Phone ______________________________

Executor ______________________________

Phone ______________________________

Trustee ______________________________

Phone ______________________________

Employee Benefit Manager ____________________

Phone ______________________________

I belong to the following organizations, which I would want notified in the event of my death:

____

____

____

____

Items for Action

We concentrate most of our financial planning efforts on accumulating wealth. Unfortunately, many fail to protect that wealth in the event of death. An estate plan is merely a contingency plan — what do you want to happen in the event of your death? An appropriate estate plan will serve not only to protect your wealth but will prove useful in other areas as well. Who will be the guardian for your children or the trustee for your trust? These individuals are named in your estate-planning documents. Use the Action Items below to get started.

For each of the following items, assign a priority based on its importance to you: A (highest), B (medium) or C (lowest). Then check off each item as it is completed.

	Priority	Completed
Complete the Estate-Tax Balance Sheet		
Select an estate-planning attorney.	______	❑
Do your homework. Before meeting with the attorney, consider the following questions:		
❖ What is the value of your estate? (Give your attorney a copy of your *Estate Tax Balance Sheet.*)	______	❑
❖ Who are the current primary and contingent beneficiaries of your employee benefit plans, life insurance (group and personal) and IRA? Ask your lawyer to revise beneficiary designations as appropriate.	______	❑
❖ Who should be your children's guardian? The contingent guardian? Consider writing a letter to the trustee regarding reimbursement of expenses to the guardian.	______	❑
❖ Consider naming an executor of your estate. **Note:** Think first of a family member. If the family member should die, then who should be named?	______	❑
❖ Should you have a living trust in case you become disabled?	______	❑
❖ Do you want to name a school or charity in your plan if your family should predecease you?	______	❑
❖ Who should receive your personal property?	______	❑
❖ Have you prepared letters, audio or video tapes to children and other loved ones?	______	❑

Items for Action (continued)

Priority | Completed

Lifetime Planning

When you contact an attorney to help with your estate plan, discuss three lifetime-planning techniques:

- ❖ A general durable power of attorney — perhaps a "springing" power. ______ ❑
- ❖ Call Partnership for Caring at **800/989-9455** or visit their Web site at **www.partnershipforcaring.org** to obtain a sample living will and health-care power of attorney for your state. ______ ❑
- ❖ Write letters of instruction regarding people to notify, funeral arrangements, etc. ______ ❑

Planning for Your Parents

You may wish to raise certain issues with your parents:

- ❖ A general durable power of attorney. ______ ❑
- ❖ Organization of information relating to their financial affairs (a document locator). ______ ❑
- ❖ The importance of a current will. ______ ❑
- ❖ Creation of a living will and health-care power of attorney. ______ ❑
- ❖ Taking steps to reduce the estate-tax bill. ______ ❑

Resources

Books

Clifford, Denis and Jordan, Cora. *Plan Your Estate: Absolutely Everything You Need to Know to Protect Your Loved Ones.* Nolo Press, Berkeley, CA, 2000. ($39.95).

Schumacher, Vickie and Jim. *Understanding Living Trusts: How You Can Avoid Probate, Save Taxes and Enjoy Peace of Mind.* Schumacher & Company, Los Angeles, CA, 1999. ($24.95).

Shenkman, Martin M. *The Complete Probate Guide*. John Wiley & Sons, New York, 1999. ($22.95).

Federal Trade Commission

Consumer Response Center
600 Pennsylvania Avenue, NW
Washington, DC 20580

The Commission makes available numerous free or low-cost publications including *Funerals: A Consumer Guide*. Call the Public Reference Branch at **202/326-2222** and ask for a free copy or download the publication from the FTC Web site (**www.ftc.gov**).

Funeral Consumers Alliance

PO Box 10
Hinesburg, VT 05461
800/765-0107

To find a nonprofit funeral consumer group in your area, call FCA or visit their Web site at **www.funerals.org**.

Internal Revenue Service

You can get free telephone assistance by calling **800/829-1040**. Additionally, the IRS's Publication 559, *Survivors, Executors, and Administrators*, is available without charge by calling the IRS at **800/829-3676** or at the IRS's Web site (**www.irs.gov**).

Military-Specific Information

Army and Air Force Mutual Aid Association
800/336-4538
Officers' Benefits and Estate-Tax Planning

Navy Mutual Aid Association
800/628-6011

A veterans' benefit group for personnel and families of the U.S. Navy, Marine Corps, Coast Guard, Public Health and NOAA.

For additional information on pensions and payouts from the military, contact **Military District of Washington** — Survivor Assistance Office, Fort Meyer, VA 22211. Fax: 703/696-3236.

For your local office of the **Department of Veterans' Affairs**, call **800/827-1000**.

For veterans information on **National Service Life Insurance**, write to P.O. Box 42954, Philadelphia, PA 19101, or call **800/669-8477**.

National Association of Financial and Estate Planning

525 East 4500 South, #F-100
Salt Lake City, UT 84107
801/266-9900

This organization's Web site (**www.nafep.com**) includes free and useful information to help you with estate planning, business entity planning, charitable foundations and more.

Education Funding

Whether you have a child about to enter college or a newborn baby, you're probably concerned about funding your son's or daughter's college education. Because college costs have skyrocketed, proper planning is critical. Since 1991, college costs — including tuition, fees, room and board — have increased at an average annual rate between 5 and 8%. This is approximately twice the rate of inflation. Most parents would like to be able to pay for their children's entire college cost, but it may be impossible. Experts say if you can fund half of the expected cost of college, you're doing great!

You can prepare for these future expenses by following this step-by-step process. Since long-term planning is difficult because of changes in interest rates, inflation, tax laws and your child's eligibility for scholarships, you should revisit this process every two to three years.

Step 1: Estimate the Cost

How much does it cost to attend college? The answer to this commonly asked question depends upon where your child goes. On average it costs $11,980 per year for a four-year public college if you are a resident of the state, $26,070 per year for a private college and $36,690 per year for an Ivy League education. Most forecasters predict the rate of increase in education expenses, at both private and public schools, will continue to outpace inflation.

Average College Costs
2001 – 2002 Academic Year

	Tuition and Fees Only	Total Costs
4-Year Public	$ 3,750	$11,980
4-Year Private	$17,120	$26,070
Ivy League	$26,330	$36,690

Source: The College Board, New York, NY.

As a parent (or grandparent), keep college prices in perspective — more than 40% of students attended four-year colleges that charged less than $4,000 for tuition and fees in the 2001 – 2002 academic year! Additionally, while college costs seem high, the cost of not attending college might be even higher. Based on 2000 U.S. Census statistics, the average annual income of a college graduate with a bachelor's degree only was more than 85% higher than that of a high school graduate. Clearly, a college education continues to be a great value.

Your first step is to do a little research and get a sense of what it will cost to educate your child today. Once you have an estimate of annual expenses in today's dollars, you can calculate how much you should save each month in order to accumulate enough money by the time your child reaches college age.

Step 2: Pre-Fund a Portion

Given today's college costs, many parents find themselves paralyzed by the sheer magnitude of the potential expense. Most financial planners stress the need to start early and attempt to "pre-fund" or save in advance for a child's education.

Monthly Education Calculator

The Monthly Education Calculator provides you with an estimate of how much you need to save each month to pay for a four-year college education. When you look at the chart, don't panic — few people can afford to put aside the full amount each month. The important thing is that you start to invest something — even as little as $50 — each month.

If you have already started setting aside some funds, use the *Accumulated Savings* worksheet to adjust your monthly savings amount. Then revisit your calculations every three years to make sure that your investment return is keeping up with inflation. When using the Monthly Education Calculator, you should be aware that it is based on three significant assumptions:

- the expected average annual after-tax rate of return on your investment is 8%;
- the expected inflation rate for college expenses is 5%;
- payments will be required until your child is 22 years old.

Monthly Education Calculator

How much will you need to invest each month to afford the college of your choice?

	Annual Cost (Today's Dollars)				
Age	$5,000	$10,000	$15,000	$20,000	$25,000
Newborn	$ 90	$179	$ 269	$ 358	$ 448
1	94	188	282	376	470
2	99	198	297	396	495
3	105	209	314	418	523
4	111	222	333	444	555
5	118	235	353	470	588
6	126	251	377	502	628
7	134	268	402	536	670
8	144	288	432	576	720
9	156	312	468	624	780
10	170	339	509	678	848
11	186	372	558	744	930
12	206	411	617	822	1,028
13	231	461	692	922	1,153
14	262	524	786	1,048	1,310
15	304	608	912	1,216	1,520
16	363	725	1,088	1,450	1,813

Accumulated Savings

	Example	Your Situation
1. Amount saved.	$ 5,000	$
2. Current four-year cost ($10,000 x 4).	$ 40,000	$
3. Divide Line 1 by Line 2 ($5,000 ÷ $40,000).	.125	
4. Amount from ***Monthly Education Calculator***.	$ 198*	$
5. Multiply Line 3 by Line 4 (.125 x $198).	$ 25	$
6. Subtract Line 5 from Line 4 to find the adjusted monthly savings needed ($198 – $25).	$ 173	$

* Assumed age 2.

Putting aside money may be difficult. Most families are trying to cope with other financial commitments at the same time — like buying a home or car or simply feeding or clothing a young family. Rather than saying "We can't afford to save $198 per month for our child's education," (that would be the amount necessary to fund a $10,000-per-year education for a two-year-old), you should examine your living expenses closely to determine how much you can realistically save. Then do what you can — put aside whatever you can each month and increase it later if possible. *Remember, partial pre-funding of college costs is better than none at all.*

If your child is not in high school yet, disciplined savings is the easiest way to accumulate college funds. Put your education pre-funding program on "automatic pilot" by setting aside money periodically. Arrange to transfer money from your checking account on a monthly or quarterly basis to mutual funds or other investments. These small periodic investments will add up over the years.

Also, look to other sources — "found money" — that can be used to pre-fund your child's education. Unexpected cash amounts like bonuses, inheritances, insurance payouts and tax refunds are all potential sources. Or, if you reach the maximum FICA wage base before year-end, deposit those extra dollars from each paycheck into your education fund.

The "Kiddie Tax"

To save taxes, it may make sense to put enough assets in a child's name to generate up to $1,500 of unearned income each year. This is income from dividends, interest and capital gains. For children under the age of 14, you will not pay any taxes on the first $750 and only 10% on the next $750. Unearned income over $1,500 is taxed at the parents' highest marginal tax rate. But these "kiddie tax" rules apply only to children under age 14. Children age 14 and older pay taxes on both earned and unearned income based on their marginal tax rate (for 2002, 10% on the first $6,000 and 15% on the next $21,950 of taxable ordinary income but as low as an 8% rate on long-term capital gains).

Special Consideration:

Gifts of Appreciated Stock

For children age 14 and over, consider using gifts of appreciated stock to finance education expenses. This allows the gain on those securities to be taxed at the child's rather than the parents' tax rate. Here is an example:

Mr. and Mrs. Smith own 100 shares of stock (that they have held for at least 12 months) that have increased in value.

Tax basis (cost) of $40/share	$4,000
Current fair market value of $85/share	$8,500

Look at the difference in income taxes if the Smiths, who are taxed at the maximum long-term capital-gains rate of 20%, sell the shares, *vs.* if they give the shares to their daughter, who is in a 10% bracket, to sell:

	Taxes at Sale	
	Parents	**Daughter**
Fair Market Value	$8,500	$8,500
Tax Basis	(4,000)	(4,000)
Taxable Gain	$4,500	$4,500
Federal Income Taxes	$ 900	$ 450
Tax Savings	**$ 450**	

If the Smiths' daughter has no other income in the year she sells the stock, her standard deduction would reduce her tax bill to $375, meaning the family would have saved $525 in income taxes by transferring the stock to her. Further, for a sale of an asset that has been held for at least five years, the long-term capital-gain rate will be 8% instead of 10% for taxpayers in the lowest marginal tax bracket.

Custodial Accounts

A custodial account is a simple vehicle for accumulating investments for a minor child. The child pays taxes on any income or gain from the account (subject to the "kiddie tax" rules) unless it is used to fulfill child-support obligations. These accounts are established either under your state's Uniform Gift to Minors Act (UGMA) or the Uniform Transfer to Minors Act (UTMA) because minors usually cannot buy and sell property directly, but an adult custodian can on their behalf. Custodial accounts can be opened at banks, mutual fund companies, brokerage firms or other financial institutions.

Custodial accounts make sense for those who want to earmark funds for their children's college education and at the same time save some income taxes. But there is a drawback. When you transfer funds to a custodial account, you're making an irrevocable gift to your child. Before the child reaches legal age, the custodian can withdraw funds from the account only for the child's benefit. Then between the ages of 18 and 21, depending on your state's law, the account legally becomes the child's property. Although your intent may be to provide education funds, some children might have other ideas about how to spend the money.

Special Consideration:

Financial Aid

If you expect to qualify for financial aid, accumulate education funds in *your* name, not your child's (or a custodial account for a child). Why? Under current federal rules 35% of the student's assets — as opposed to 5.6% of the parents' assets — are included in financial aid calculations for the "expected family contribution."

Coverdell Education Savings Accounts (ESAs)

The rules for these education savings accounts, formerly called education IRAs, have been liberalized beginning in 2002. Subject to income limitations, you can now set up an ESA and make nondeductible contributions of up to $2,000 per year for each child younger than age 18. Eligibility to contribute to an ESA is phased out at AGI of $110,000 for a single taxpayer and $220,000 for a married couple filing a joint return. Education Savings Accounts must be funded with cash and can be established at banks, brokerage firms, insurance companies and other financial institutions. You control the investment of the account.

Distributions from the ESA that are used to pay "qualified education expenses" will not be subject to income taxes (or the 10% additional tax). Qualified education expenses include not only expenses for undergraduate and graduate-level education but also elementary and secondary public, private or religious school tuition and expenses.

Any balance remaining in an ESA when the beneficiary reaches age 30 must be distributed, and any earnings will be subject to income tax and the 10% additional tax at that time. However, before a beneficiary reaches age 30, the account balance can be transferred tax-free to an ESA for the benefit of another member of the beneficiary's family.

For federal financial-aid purposes, a Coverdell ESA is included as an asset of the student in the calculation of the family's expected contribution.

Qualified State Tuition Programs

In recent years, state-sponsored college savings programs, also called 529 Plans after the IRC section authorizing them, have become quite common and are popular with many families. There are two types of programs prepaid tuition programs and college savings plans. Prepaid tuition programs let you lock in today's tuition rates by allowing you to purchase credits or units of tuition in today's dollars for your children or grandchildren to use when they actually attend college at some future date. Generally, you may purchase amounts of tuition through a one-time, lump-sum purchase or monthly installments.

The more common program, however, is the college savings plan. Contribution amounts can vary, and minimum contributions are generally very low. Until late in 2001, IRS rules prohibited either you or the student beneficiary from changing the investment strategy of the account once it was established. New rules, however, permit the plans to give participants the opportunity to change their investment strategy once every year. The plans offer a variable rate of return, although some guarantee a minimum. Funds in the account can be used for tuition, fees, room and board, books, supplies and equipment required for enrollment.

Qualified state tuition programs offer you the opportunity to invest for a child's education on a tax-advantaged basis. For federal tax purposes, earnings on investments accumulate tax-deferred and, when used to pay qualified education expenses, are excluded from taxation. Many states also exempt earnings and distributions from taxation and some even allow a deduction for the contributions you make. Payments made from a state tuition program for a purpose other than education expenses will be included in the account owner's federal taxable income and, beginning in 2002, will be subject to an additional 10% tax. This penalty may be in addition to any imposed by the plan for non-qualifying payouts.

These programs also offer a gift-tax advantage. Generally, if you make gifts to any person in any tax year in excess of an annual exclusion amount ($11,000 in 2002), the amount of the gift in excess of the exclusion amount will be subject to federal gift tax. However, gifts to a qualified state tuition program in excess of the annual exclusion amount may be treated as if they had been made over five years. Therefore, you could contribute $55,000 to one of these accounts in 2002 and report the gift as $11,000 in 2002 and each of the four succeeding years.

If the student beneficiary does not attend college, you may choose to continue to hold the investment in the qualified state tuition program until a later date, when the student may decide to attend college. Or you may transfer the account to another member of the student's family, including a first cousin of the student. You also may request a refund according to the program's provisions. The 10% penalty tax will be assessed for refunds, except in the case of the student's death, disability or receipt of a scholarship.

The treatment of qualified state tuition programs for federal financial aid purposes depends upon the type of plan. Prepaid tuition programs are not treated as assets of either the parents or the student for purposes of calculating the family's expected contribution. However, the college or university will consider prepaid contracts a resource that reduces the student's financial need on a dollar-for-dollar basis. On the other hand, guidance from the U.S. Department of Education indicates that college savings plans will be considered assets of the parent or other account owner for purposes of financial aid.

The specific provisions of the plans vary from state to state. Therefore, you should consult the plan document for the particular program of interest to you. A listing of the prepaid tuition and college savings programs currently offered is provided in the following pages.

Qualified State Tuition Programs – by State

State	Name of Program	Type of Program	Telephone Number	Website
Alabama	Prepaid Affordable College Tuition Program	Prepaid tuition	800/252-7228	www.treasury.state.al.us
Alaska	College Savings Plan	Savings plan	866/277-1005	www.uacollegesavings.com
Arizona	Family College Savings Program	Savings plan	602/229-2591	www.acpe.asu.edu
Arkansas	GIFT College Investing Plan	Savings plan	877/442-6553	www.thegiftplan.com
California	Golden State Scholarshare Trust	Savings plan	877/728-4338	www.scholarshare.com
Colorado	CollegeInvest	Prepaid tuition	800/478-5651	www.collegeinvest.org
	Scholars Choice^{sm}	Savings plan	888/572-4652	www.scholars-choice.com
Connecticut	Higher Education Trust	Savings plan	888/799-2438	www.aboutchet.com
Delaware	College Investment Plan	Savings plan	800/292-7935	personal100.fidelity.com/planning/college/content/delaware.html
Florida	Prepaid College Program	Prepaid tuition	800/552-4723	www.fsba.state.fl.us/prepaid
Georgia	College Savings Plan	Savings plan	404/656-2168	www2.state.ga.us/OTFS
Hawaii	College Savings Program	Savings plan	808/586-1518	www.state.hi.us/budget/college/college.htm
Idaho	Ideal College Savings Program	Savings plan	208/334-3200	www.idsaves.org
Illinois	College Illinois!	Prepaid tuition	877/877-3724	www.collegeillinois.com
	Bright Start Savings	Savings plan	877/432-7444	www.brightstartsavings.com
Indiana	Family College Savings Plan	Savings plan	888/814-6800	www.incollegesave.com
Iowa	College Savings Iowa	Savings plan	888/672-9116	www.collegesavingsiowa.com
Kansas	Learning Quest Education Savings Program	Savings plan	800/579-2203	www.learningquestsavings.com
Kentucky	Affordable Prepaid Tuition Plan	Prepaid tuition	888/919-5278	www.getkapt.com
	Education Savings Plan Trust	Savings plan	877/598-7878	www.kentuckytrust.org
Louisiana	START Savings Program	Savings plan	800/259-5626	www.osfa.state.la.us
Maine	NextGen College Investing Plan	Savings plan	877/463-9843	www.nextgenplan.com
Maryland	Prepaid College Trust	Prepaid tuition	888/463-4723	www.collegesavingsmd.org
Massachusetts	U.Plan*	Prepaid tuition	800/449-6332	www.mefa.org
	U.Fund	Savings plan	800/449-6332	www.mefa.org
Michigan	Education Trust	Prepaid tuition	800/638-4543	www.treas.state.mi.us/met/metindex.htm
	Education Savings Program	Savings plan	877/861-6377	www.misaves.com
Minnesota	College Savings Plan	Savings plan	877/338-4646	www.mnsaves.org
Mississippi	Prepaid Affordable College Tuition Program	Prepaid tuition	800/987-4450	www.treasury.state.ms.us.mpact.htm
	Affordable College Savings Program	Savings plan	800/486-3670	www.collegesavingsms.com

* The Massachusetts U.Plan does not meet the requirements of a "qualified state tuition program" under IRC§529.

Qualified State Tuition Programs – by State (continued)

State	Name of Program	Type of Program	Telephone Number	Website
Missouri	Saving for Tuition Program	Savings plan	888/414-6678	www.missourimost.org
Montana	Family Education Savings Program	Savings plan	800/888-2723	montana.collegesavings.com
Nebraska	College Savings Plan	Savings plan	888/993-3746	www.planforcollegenow.com
Nevada	America's College Savings Plan	Prepaid tuition/	877/529-5295	nevedatreasurer.com/prepaid
		Savings plan	877/529-5295	www.estrong.com/strongweb/strong/jsp/nevada/index.jsp
New Hampshire	UNIQUE College Investing Plan	Savings plan	800/544-1722	personal100.fidelity.com/planning/college/content/unique.html
New Jersey	Better Educational Savings Trust (BEST)	Savings plan	877/465-2378	www.hesaa.org/njbest
New Mexico	Prepaid Tuition Program	Prepaid tuition	800/449-7581	www.tepnm.com
	College Savings Program	Savings plan	800/449-7581	www.tepnm.com
New York	College Savings Program	Savings plan	877/697-2837	www.nysaves.org
North Carolina	College Vision Fund	Savings plan	800/600-3453	www.collegevisionfund.org
North Dakota	College SAVE	Savings plan	800/472-2166	www.collegesave4u.com
Ohio	CollegeAdvantage™ Savings Plan	Savings plan	800/233-6734	www.collegeadvantage.com
Oklahoma	College Savings Plan	Savings plan	877/654-7284	www.ok4saving.org
Oregon	College Savings Plan	Savings plan	866/772-8464	www.estrong.com/strongweb/strong/jsp/oregon/index.jsp
Pennsylvania	Tuition Account Program	Prepaid tuition	800/440-4000	www.patap.org
Rhode Island	CollegeBound*fund*℠	Savings plan	888/324-5057	www.collegeboundfund.com
South Carolina	Tuition Prepayment Program	Prepaid tuition	888/772-4723	www.state.sc.us/tpp
Tennessee	BEST Prepaid Tuition Plan	Prepaid tuition	888/486-2378	www.tnbest.org
	BEST Savings Plan	Savings plan	888/486-2378	www.tnbest.org
Texas	Tomorrow Fund	Prepaid tuition	800/445-4723	www.texastomorrowfund.org
Utah	Educational Savings Plan Trust	Savings plan	800/418-2551	www.uesp.org
Vermont	Higher Education Investment Plan	Savings plan	800/637-5860	www.vsac.org/investment_plan/main.htm
Virginia	Prepaid Education Program	Prepaid tuition	888/567-0540	www.vpep.state.va.us
	Education Savings Trust	Savings plan	888/567-0540	www.vpep.state.va.us
Washington	Guaranteed Education Tuition Program	Prepaid tuition	877/438-8848	www.get.wa.gov
West Virginia	Prepaid College Plan	Prepaid tuition	800/307-4701	www.wvtreasury.com/prepaid.htm
Wisconsin	EdVest	Savings plan	888/338-3789	www.estrong.com/strongweb/strong/jsp/edvest/index.jsp
Wyoming	College Achievement Plan℠	Savings plan	877/529-2655	www.collegeachievementplan.com

Note: Additional programs are pending implementation in the states of Alabama, Florida, Maine, Maryland, Pennsylvania, South Carolina, South Dakota, Texas, Washington and West Virginia, as well as the District of Columbia.

Source: The College Savings Plans Network of the National Association of State Treasurers.

Step 3: Put Together an Investment Plan

Many people who use the Monthly Education Calculator find they cannot set aside as much as needed to fully fund their child's education. If you find yourself in that situation and your children are young, look to invest for greater return in growth-oriented securities like stock mutual funds, which over time are likely to produce better than an 8% after-tax return on investment.

Stock Mutual Funds

If your children are under age 14 — and especially if they are under age 10 — invest for growth through stocks or stock mutual funds. Growth-oriented mutual funds are risky as a short-term investment. But those with a proven track record may be an ideal investment vehicle for accumulating education funds over the long term. As a general rule, the younger the child, the more aggressive the portfolio. Then, as your child approaches college age, you should reallocate the portfolio into fixed-income securities like short-term, high-quality bond funds or money market funds. This reduces investment volatility and protects principal.

Special Consideration:

Putting Your Investment Program on "Automatic Pilot"

Some mutual funds will allow you to invest as little as $50 a month. Setting up an automatic investment plan is an excellent way to buy shares at a lower average price and save for your child's education.

Fixed-Income Investments

Zero-coupon bonds — Zero-coupon bonds are sold at a deep discount to their face value. This feature makes them more affordable for most parents. You receive the accrued interest and the bond's face value when the bond matures. Bear in mind, however, that you'll be responsible for paying taxes each year on the interest earned, but not received. If you decide to purchase zero-coupon bonds, time the maturities to coincide with your tuition payments.

Baccalaureate bonds — These are general obligation zero-coupon bonds. Unlike other municipal bonds, they are usually non-callable and tax-exempt—important bonuses for the purchaser. They may offer other special features that may make them more attractive than most municipal bonds. Check with your stockbroker for more information and to find out whether they are offered in your state.

CollegeSure® CD — One response to escalating college expenses is a program offered by the College Savings Bank® of Princeton, NJ. The CollegeSure CD is a certificate of deposit indexed to college costs and designed to meet future college tuition, fees and room and board. The CDs are sold in units or partial units and mature in one to 25 years. The CDs are also available within the Montana and Arizona qualified state tuition programs. For more information call 800/888-2723 or visit the College Savings Bank's Web site at www.collegesavings.com.

Series EE savings bonds — Savings bond rates are announced semi-annually on May 1 and November 1. The amount of interest credited, and the timing of the crediting of interest, vary depending on when the EE bond was issued. Call 800/4US-BOND (800/487-2663) for current interest-rate information.

Inflation-indexed bonds (Series I bonds) — Since 1998, the U.S. Treasury has sold inflation-indexed notes and savings bonds (Series I). I bonds are sold at face value and grow in value with inflation for up to 30 years. The earnings rate of an I bond is a combination of two separate rates: a fixed rate of return and a variable semi-annual inflation rate. Like the interest rate for Series EE bonds, the fixed rate of return is announced each May and November for bonds issued during the following six months and is fixed for the life of the bond. The semi-annual inflation rate is also announced each May and November and is used to adjust the value of the bond monthly for the next six months. Any change in the principal value will result in an adjustment to the next semi-annual interest payment.

Special Consideration:

Using Savings Bonds to Pay for College

You can choose when to pay tax on the interest from a savings bond (Series EE or I). You can elect either to defer the taxes until the bonds are redeemed (sold or gifted), or you can pay taxes on the interest annually as it accrues. If you choose to defer the tax, no action is required until redemption. Remember, if you purchase savings bonds in your child's name, consider the "kiddie tax rules" before cashing in the bonds.

Parents may qualify for a tax break on savings bonds used to pay for college expenses (tuition, not room and board). Interest on bonds issued after December 31, 1989, is not taxable if your income is below a certain threshold when you redeem the bonds. For 2002, parents' modified adjusted gross income (MAGI), including interest from the bonds, must be less than $86,400 ($57,600 for single taxpayers). As you earn more than the limitation amount, this income exclusion gradually phases out. To determine your exclusion and to compute your MAGI, use IRS *Form 8815,* "Exclusion of Interest From Series EE and I U.S. Savings Bonds Issued After 1989." To keep a written record of the post-1989 bonds that you redeem, use IRS *Form 8818*, "Optional Form to Record Redemption of Series EE and I U.S. Savings Bonds Issued After 1989."

Investing for College

We have described which investments would be appropriate for your child's education savings. However, to find out what the mix of investment assets should be, use the three-question quiz below.

	Points	Score
1. *What is the age of the child for whom the investment will be made?*		☐
2. *What are your expectations for the future value of your portfolio over your investment time horizon?*	Points	
I want to preserve principal and keep pace with the current inflation rate...	*16*	
I expect my portfolio to earn a conservative rate of return that is higher than inflation and lower than the stock market...	*12*	
I expect my portfolio to increase at the same rate as the stock market...	*8*	
I expect my portfolio to outperform the stock market...	*1*	☐
3. *How long are you willing to sustain a loss in your investment portfolio?*	Points	
I'm not willing to sustain any loss...	*20*	
One year or less...	*14*	
One – two years...	*8*	
More than two years...	*1*	☐
	Total Score	☐

After totaling your score, look at the chart below and match your total score to the portfolio indicated. The sample portfolios provide a guide as to which investment mix you should use.

Total Score	Sample Portfolio
More than 36 points	Stable
26 to 35 points	Conservative Growth
16 to 25 points	Moderate Growth
9 to 15 points	Growth
2 to 8 points	Aggressive Growth

Sample Portfolios for Education Investments

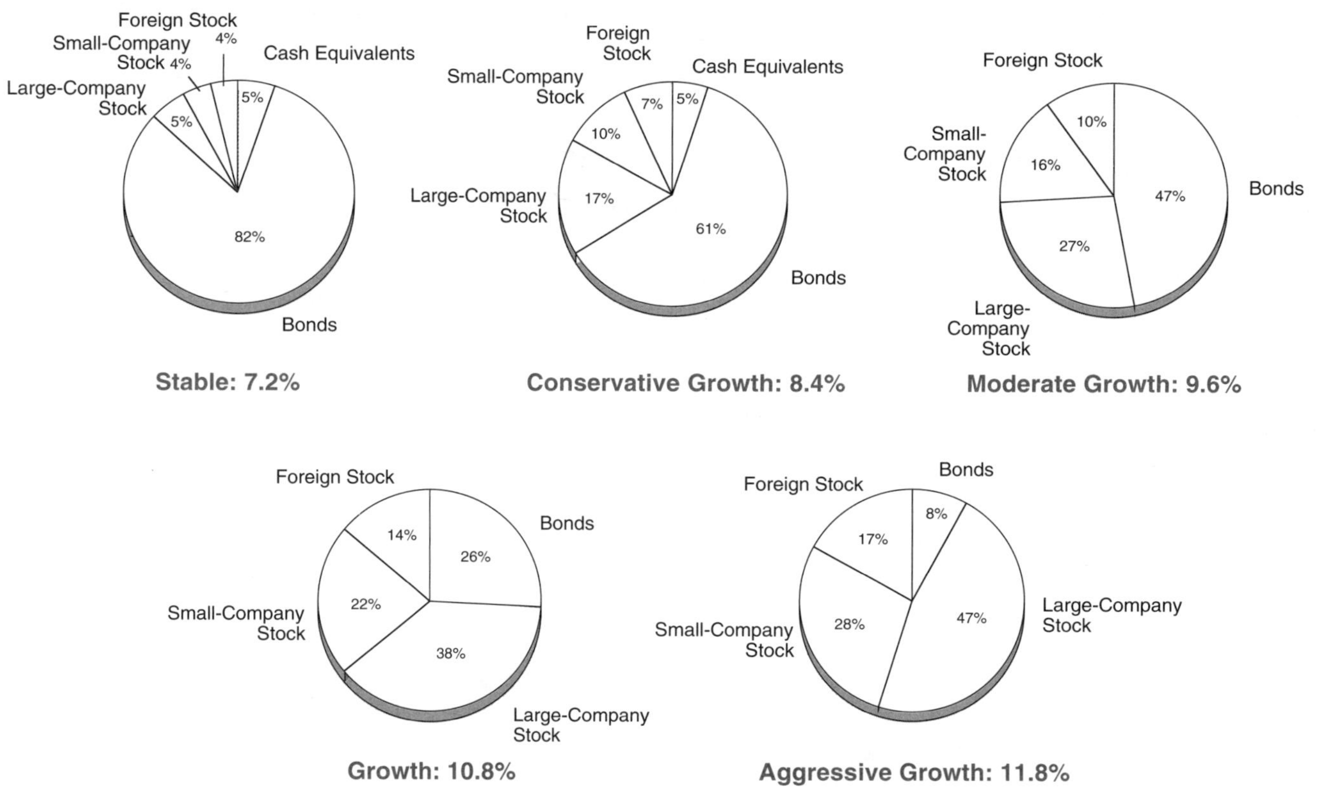

Note: Allocations are based on long-term risk and return data for the various asset classes and are subject to change annually. The projected returns are not guaranteed. If you anticipate using your education fund within the next two years, consider allocating additional funds to cash equivalents in lieu of bonds in order to satisfy imminent cash-flow needs.

Step 4: Post-Fund the Difference

If you are in a situation where it is too late either to pre-fund or set up an investment plan, you need immediate resources to meet college expenses. You should look at all alternatives to find the least costly.

Financial Aid

Over $74 billion of student aid was awarded in the 2000 – 2001 academic year, with the federal government providing approximately 70%. Financial aid comes in two main forms: grants and loans. A grant is an outright gift of funds to be used toward education and related expenses, and a loan must be repaid. In recent years, loans have comprised approximately 60% of the total aid awarded.

Both grants and loans are available on the basis of financial need, which means the student's and his or her family's ability (or inability) to pay college costs. Financial need is determined by subtracting the amount your family is expected to contribute from the anticipated cost of attendance. Any gap represents the student's financial need and the potential amount of need-based financial aid.

Determining Financial Need

Expected Cost of Attendance
– Your Expected Family Contribution (EFC)
Your Financial Need

For federal financial-aid programs and many others, need analysis uses a formula that evaluates your family's financial situation based on a method developed by the U.S. Congress. It's therefore called the "Federal Methodology."

The Federal Methodology looks at need on a relative basis. For example, your need would be greater if your child attended a $20,000-per-year school than it would be for a $10,000-per-year school. It also would be greater if you had four children in college instead of one.

The calculation of the amount your family is expected to contribute (*i.e.,* your EFC) is based on the assets and income of both you (the parents) and the child, the number of family members and the number of children in college. Assets that are counted in the calculation include cash, savings and checking accounts and the net worth of investments (including real estate and Education IRAs), businesses and farms. Company-sponsored retirement plans, non-Education IRAs, prepaid tuition plans, your personal residence and the value of life insurance and annuity contracts are excluded. In addition to taxable income, the calculation also takes into consideration non-taxable income such as non-taxed Social Security benefits, child-support payments, tax-exempt interest income and income deferred under either a 401(k) or 403(b) arrangement.

The formula for calculating expected family contribution allows you to keep some income available for things like housing, taxes, retirement and transportation. This is called the "Income Protection Allowance." Unfortunately, the numbers are based on the Department of Labor's "low-budget standard," which may not reflect the reality of your budget. For example, the allowance for basic living expenses for a family of five with one child in college is approximately $24,000 per year.

It's important to understand that the financial-aid process takes into account the cost of attendance as part of the evaluation. The cost of attendance includes tuition, fees, room and board, recreation, travel and personal expenses. Each school has its own estimate of its cost of attendance.

Using the table on the next page, you can estimate your EFC. This number is "fixed." What isn't fixed is the cost of attending different colleges. The reason need is relative is because, if the expected family contribution is $3,000 per student per year and the cost of attendance is $10,000 per year, the financial-aid potential is $7,000; if the cost of attendance is $20,000, your potential aid jumps to $17,000.

Your Expected Annual Contribution as a Parent

*Here's an estimate of what you may be expected you to pay each year toward one child's college education.**

Assets**	Number of Children***	Parents' Adjusted Gross Income $30,000	$40,000	$50,000	$60,000	$80,000	$100,000	$120,000
$40,000	1	$1,863	$3,666	$6,251	$9,706	$15,608	$21,993	$28,390
	2	1,239	2,913	5,135	8,374	14,446	20,831	27,228
	3	658	2,297	4,243	7,140	13,383	19,768	26,165
	4	0	1,630	3,358	5,827	12,127	18,512	24,909
$60,000	1	2,391	4,387	7,340	10,834	16,736	23,121	29,518
	2	1,767	3,540	6,077	9,502	15,574	21,959	28,356
	3	1,186	2,857	5,059	8,268	14,511	20,896	27,293
	4	291	2,158	4,054	6,842	13,255	19,640	26,037
$80,000	1	2,963	5,203	8,468	11,962	17,864	24,249	30,646
	2	2,295	4,239	7,135	10,630	16,702	23,087	29,484
	3	1,714	3,474	5,987	9,396	15,639	22,024	28,421
	4	819	2,698	4,843	7,970	14,383	20,768	27,165
$100,000†	1	3,598	6,157	9,596	13,090	18,992	25,377	31,774
	2	2,854	5,055	8,263	11,758	17,830	24,215	30,612
	3	2,242	4,170	7,030	10,524	16,767	23,152	29,549
	4	1,347	3,298	5,733	9,098	15,511	21,896	28,293

* Assumes two parents in household with one parent working and one child in college.

** Families with adjusted gross income under $50,000 and who are not required to file IRS *Form 1040* do not need to report parental assets to determine eligibility for federal programs such as the Stafford loan. However, the assets may be considered in making other awards, including the college's own funds.

*** Total number of children in your family.

† Once assets exceed $100,000, the "expected family contribution" usually increases by 5.6% of the additional assets.

Competition for most financial aid begins January 1 of each year. You begin the process by submitting a Free Application for Federal Student Aid (or FAFSA) form to the federal processing center as soon as possible on or after January 1. Applications postmarked before January 1 will not be considered.

The FAFSA form is available at most high schools and colleges beginning in late fall. It also may be requested directly from the U.S. Department of Education (800/433-3243). A free software program called "FAFSA Express" allows the student to apply for federal student aid from a home or school computer. Alternatively, the student can apply online. Both of these electronic options are available at the Department of Education's Web site (www.ed.gov/offices/OSFAP/students/apply/express.html).

Many private colleges and universities use their own methodology instead of the Federal Methodology when determining financial need. They may include in their calculation of expected family contribution assets that would otherwise be excluded, such as the equity in your home, employer-sponsored retirement plans and the cash value of life insurance and annuity contracts. These schools will require you to submit an additional application for financial aid on their own form or the College Scholarship Service's PROFILE form (available by calling 800/778-6888 or online at http://profileonline.cbreston.org).

As you can see, the rules for obtaining aid are complicated. Your chances of receiving aid should improve if you do the following:

Start early — You and your child should begin to discuss college choices and the costs of attending various colleges early on — the junior year of high school at the latest. Also, submit the FAFSA form for processing as soon as possible after January 1 and comply with all deadlines that colleges may impose for submitting aid applications.

Take advantage of free resources — A variety of free information is available from federal and state governments, and your high school guidance counselor should be able to help out. A plethora of information is available on the Web as well. Check out the resources at the end of this chapter.

Buy or borrow *Don't Miss Out: The Ambitious Student's Guide to Financial Aid* — Published by Octameron Associates (703/836-5480 or online at www.thinktuition.com), this 200-page guide is packed with valuable information. Updated annually, it costs $10 (plus shipping and handling).

Be neat, accurate and well-organized when completing forms and applications. An omitted or incorrect item on an application could cause unnecessary delays and result in less aid. Also, make sure you are using current forms and applications since they are generally revised annually.

Shift income — If you have control over when you'll receive income (bonuses, capital gains, commissions, business income, stock-option income, etc.), realize that more or less income in any given tax year could affect potential aid significantly. Keep in mind that financial-aid eligibility for the upcoming or current school year (2002 – 2003) is based on information from the preceding tax year (2001).

Shift assets — It may help to shift assets away from the student and toward the parents (since the student's contribution percentage is expected to be larger), but don't concentrate too much effort on this because the Federal Methodology looks more at income than assets.

Special considerations — Death in the family, divorce, loss of job earnings, medical expenses, etc., will affect eligibility for and amount of aid.

Claim independent status if possible — The requirements for independent status are rigorous but, if the student has unusual circumstances, he or she should talk to the school's financial aid administrator. If the administrator determines that the student's circumstances warrant independent status, only the student's assets and income (as well as his or her spouse's) will be considered for purposes of the aid calculation.

Apply for aid every year even if previously denied.

Use cash/assets to reduce non-housing debt — You can't deduct personal, non-housing debt in arriving at your net assets for purposes of calculating your expected family contribution. So consider paying off these debts using cash and other assets. This will reduce your reportable assets, decrease your expected family contribution and increase your potential financial aid. As stated earlier, some schools, especially the private ones, may take into consideration the equity in your home when calculating the amount your family is expected to contribute. At the same time, they do not allow for the deduction of non-housing debt in the calculation. Therefore, you may also wish to consider paying off these debts with a home-equity line of credit to increase your aid potential by decreasing the value of your assets. You also give yourself a tax break when you deduct the interest on the loan.

Pay cash for major purchases — If you use cash instead of borrowing for a major purchase like a car or appliance, you will reduce your available assets and increase your aid potential by a percentage of what you spend. Of course, *you should do this only if you need a car.* Also, restructure savings strategies by maximizing contributions to retirement plans — these are not used in financial-aid calculations, although your before-tax contributions will be added back to your total income for the year.

Do not offer information that is not mandated.

EDUCATION FUNDING

Loans

Interest on student loans has been deductible since 1998, subject to an income test and a maximum deduction amount. Prior to 2002, the interest paid must have been part of the payments for the first 60 months in which payments on the loan were required to be made. The maximum deductible interest now is $2,500. The deduction is available if AGI is less than $65,000 for a single taxpayer or $130,000 for a married couple filing a joint return.

Federally Sponsored Loans — There are several low-interest loans for which either parents or their children can apply. They include Stafford Loans, Perkins Loans and PLUS Loans for parents. Additionally, the following campus-based loan programs are available for students studying to enter the health-care profession: Loans for Disadvantaged Students (LDS), Primary Care Loan (PCL) and the Nursing Student Loan (NSL). Additional information on these loan programs may be obtained either from the Department of Education or from your college financial aid office.

State-Sponsored Loans — About 20 states offer low-cost educational loans. For more information, talk to your child's high school counselor as well as the financial aid staff at the college(s) you have selected. For links to a specific state's educational assistance program, visit the Department of Education's Web site at www.ed.gov/programs/bastmp/SHEA.htm.

School-Sponsored Loans — Many universities will lend parents as much as the full cost of a four-year education. Some of these institutions will even allow you to lock in the cost at current prices by establishing a line of credit to cover up to four years' expenses.

ConSern Education Program® — Since 1987, this program, run by the Servus Financial Corporation, has been providing education-financing benefits to the families of the sponsoring companies' employees. Unlike federal programs, this private loan program will lend up to $25,000 annually based on the credit of the borrower — not need. The benefits of this program include low monthly payments, no application fees, generous repayment terms and the flexibility to defer payments until after graduation. Currently, over 525 companies are part of the ConSern Education Program. To see if your employer participates in this program, contact your Human Resources department.

Home Equity — Because there is only a limited tax deduction for interest on student loans, home equity might continue to be one of your first sources for borrowing to meet college expenses. Be careful, however, not to over-extend — your house is at stake. By using a home-equity line of credit, you can borrow up to $100,000 against the equity in your home, and the interest is tax-deductible in most states. When shopping for a home-equity loan, take the time to compare fees and rates to get the best deal.

Your Company's Savings/Thrift Plan — If you are vested in your company's savings/thrift plan, most plans allow you to take a loan from your account. Based on IRS rules, you can borrow up to the lesser of one-half your account balance or $50,000. The interest rates for these loans often are more favorable than from outside sources. Generally, interest on a savings/thrift plan loan is not deductible unless it can be traced to qualified education expenses. After a home-equity loan, this is usually the next-best borrowing alternative.

Margin Loans — You can borrow against your securities by establishing a margin account with your broker. To the extent the loan can be traced to qualified education expenses the interest expense may be deductible, subject to the income test and the maximum deduction amount. There is risk involved if you are highly leveraged and your investments drop drastically in value. In this instance, you may be forced to sell to meet the margin requirements.

Annuities — If you own annuities that were purchased before August 14, 1982, you will be able to withdraw your initial investment first, which will be tax-exempt. Withdrawals from an annuity purchased after August 13, 1982, would be taxable.

Life Insurance Loans — These are available from permanent-type life insurance policies. Typically, the interest compounds and is subtracted from your policy's cash value. If you do not pay the money back or die while the loan is outstanding, the amount of the loan will reduce the death benefit. Remember that the interest is only deductible to the extent it qualifies as an education loan, subject to the limits, and that the interest cost might be more than the nominal interest rate cited by the insurer. If either the dividends or increases in cash value are reduced, that's part of the cost to borrow, too.

Education Tax Credits

Either of two tax credits might be available for qualified education expenses (tuition, fees, books, supplies but not room and board): the HOPE credit or the lifetime learning credit.

- The HOPE credit is equal to 100% of the first $1,000 of qualified education expenses, and 50% of the next $1,000. Consequently, the maximum credit is $1,500 per student per year. The HOPE credit is available only with respect to the first two years of a child's post-secondary education.
- The lifetime learning credit is equal to 20% of the family's first $5,000 of tuition and fees, so the maximum credit is $1,000 per family per year. (Beginning in 2003, the credit will be 20% of the first $10,000 of expenses, so the maximum credit will then become $2,000.)

Either credit is available for expenses of the taxpayer, the taxpayer's spouse or dependent child. An income test applies in determining eligibility for the credit: if AGI exceeds $102,000 on a joint return ($51,000 for other filers), the credit is not available.

Special Consideration:

Education Credits, State Tuition Programs and Coverdell ESAs

You will be able to claim either the Hope or lifetime learning credits in a tax year when excluded distributions are made from a qualified state tuition account and/or a Coverdell ESA for the student as long as credits aren't claimed for expenses paid with tax-free distributions. Also, if distributions from ESAs and qualified state tuition programs exceed the beneficiary's education expenses after reduction by amounts used in claiming either of the education credits, the beneficiary will have to allocate the expenses between the distributions to determine the amount to be included in taxable income.

New Deduction for Higher-Education Expenses

In tax years 2002 through 2005, you may be able to claim a deduction for qualified education expenses (as defined above). The maximum deduction is $3,000 in 2002 and 2003 and $4,000 in 2004 and 2005 for taxpayers whose AGI doesn't exceed $65,000 ($130,000 for married taxpayers filing a joint return). In 2004 and 2005, the maximum deduction is $2,000 for taxpayers whose AGI doesn't exceed $80,000 ($160,000 for married taxpayers filing jointly). The deduction is not available after 2005. It is also not available in any year in which the Hope or lifetime learning credit is claimed for any of the student's expenses.

Additionally, the tuition deduction generally cannot be claimed for expenses that were paid with tax-free withdrawals from a Coverdell ESA or qualified state tuition programs, or that were used to determine the amount of excluded interest on the redemption of certain U.S. savings bonds. Withdrawals from state tuition programs that represent contributions to the plan, however, will not be counted in determining the amount of the deduction.

Step 5: Manage the Expense

The last element in your education plan is to manage the expense by selecting a school that represents a good value. This might mean a less-expensive school or one where, based on grades and test scores, your child places in the top 25% of the entering class. Also explore whether your child's athletic, musical or other skills might motivate a school to offer financial aid, a grant or a favorable loan package.

Look for Discounts — Many schools offer discounts in one form or another (*e.g.,* students over age 25, multiple students, children of alumni). Contact the admissions office to see if any discounts exist.

Community Colleges — Starting a college education by attending a community college for a few years is an inexpensive route to a four-year degree, especially if your child is uncertain of his/her career choice. However, make sure the student can transfer credits to the four-year school in which they have an interest.

Many four-year schools now have pre-arranged programs with affiliated two-year and four-year colleges. Students entering these programs complete the first two or three years of their degree program at the lower-cost affiliated school, then transfer to the target college or university to complete their degree. Generally, the student must maintain some level of academic performance in order to be accepted by the target school after the first few years of study.

Military — More than 2,300 colleges offer Reserve Officer Training Corps (ROTC) scholarships sponsored by the Army, Navy and Air Force. These scholarships pay full tuition (Army ROTC up to $16,000), fees, books and laboratory costs plus a monthly stipend. In return, the student must serve eight years after graduation in active duty, the Reserves or both. For more information, contact the university's ROTC office or a representative at your local military recruiting center.

One of the U.S. service academies or the National Guards are possible options, too. Contact either for more information.

Part-Time Jobs — Have your child visit the campus student employment center. A work-study program can tailor an on- or off-campus job to fit your child's class and study schedule. Some schools help arrange co-op programs so students can work in career-related jobs and receive either a salary or college credit.

Items for Action

The funds you'll need to pay for your children's education will represent one of your largest capital commitments. You must begin today! Don't hope for financial aid or scholarships. Use the Action Items below to estimate the cost and put together an investment plan. Your children's futures will be more secure, and so will yours.

For each of the following items, assign a priority based on its importance to you: A (highest), B (medium) or C (lowest). Then check off each item as it is completed.

	Priority	Completed
❖ Ask your child (age 16 or over) to read this chapter.	______	❑
Step 1: Estimate the Cost		
❖ Review current college cost and trends and settle on a target level of funding for your child.	______	❑
Step 2: Pre-Fund a Portion		
❖ Use the *"Monthly Education Calculator"* to estimate how much you'll need to set aside each month.	______	❑
❖ Review your spending patterns and find money you can have automatically withdrawn each month from your paycheck or bank account.	______	❑
❖ Save any "found money" from bonuses, tax refunds, inheritances, etc.	______	❑
❖ Consider "kiddie tax" rules and comply with tax-reporting rules.	______	❑
❖ Consider shifting income through gifts of appreciated stocks held for more than one year.	______	❑
Step 3: Put Together an Investment Plan		
❖ For children under age 14, invest primarily in growth mutual funds.	______	❑
❖ For children age 14 or older, invest in federally insured CDs (including the *CollegeSure CD)* or zero-coupon bonds with maturities that match your time frame.	______	❑
❖ Keep annual summaries of mutual-fund statements.	______	❑

Items for Action (continued)

	Priority	Completed
Step 4: Post-Fund the Difference		
❖ Review whether you will qualify for financial aid and the amounts you will qualify for. Shop lenders, because loan-origination and insurance fees vary.	______	❑
❖ Submit a FAFSA as soon after January 1 as possible.	______	❑
❖ Work with a high school counselor to qualify for loans and grants.	______	❑
❖ Work with the college financial aid counselor.	______	❑
❖ Borrow money to pay the difference.	______	❑

Source	Amount You Can Borrow	Priority	Completed
– Federally sponsored loans	$ ________	______	❑
– State-sponsored loans	$ ________	______	❑
– School-sponsored loans	$ ________	______	❑
– Home	$ ________	______	❑
– Employer's savings/thrift plan (not more than $50,000 or 50% of balance)	$ ________	______	❑
– Margin loans	$ ________	______	❑

	Priority	Completed
Step 5: Manage the Expense		
❖ Carefully evaluate the cost/value relationship.	______	❑
❖ Encourage your child to get a part-time job or in some way share the financial responsibility of the college expenses, (*e.g.*, IOUs).	______	❑
❖ Consider		
– Community Colleges	______	❑
– Military	______	❑
– Government internships or fellowships	______	❑
❖ Review this checklist each year.	______	❑

Resources

The College Board

45 Columbus Avenue
New York, NY 10023-6992
212/713-8000

The College Board is an excellent resource to research college costs. Visit their Web site at **www.collegeboard.com** for a profile of the colleges of interest to your child. Additionally, the Board publishes *The College Board College Costs & Financial Aid Handbook* annually ($22.95). This handy guide can be ordered online or by calling **800/323-7155**. Additional services available through The College Board's Web site include a scholarship search, an expected family contribution (EFC) calculator and registration for the PROFILE financial aid application.

College Savings Bank®

5 Vaughn Drive
Princeton, NJ 08540

The College Savings Bank offers the CollegeSure® CD, a certificate of deposit indexed to college costs and guaranteed to meet future tuition, fees, room and board. Applications for this product and others, as well as additional college planning resources are available at the Bank's Web site (**www.collegesavings.com**) or by calling **800/888-2723**.

College Savings Plan Network

P.O. Box 11910
Lexington, KY 40578-1910

For information on qualified state tuition programs, visit the College Savings Plan Network's Web site at **www.collegesavings.org**. Additionally, you can obtain information about a specific state's college savings program by visiting the Network's Web site or calling **877/CSPN-4-YOU** (877/277-6496).

U.S. Department of Education

Federal Student Aid Information Center
P.O. Box 84
Washington, DC 20044-0084

For general information about the federal student financial assistance programs, assistance with the application process or to obtain federal student aid publications, including *The Student Guide*, call the Department's information center at **800/4-FED-AID** (800/433-3243) or visit the Department's Web site at **www.ed.gov**.

FinAid Page, LLC

P.O. Box 81620
Pittsburgh, PA 15217
412/422-6189 (fax)

This award-winning Web site (**www.finaid.org**) has grown into one of the most comprehensive collections of student financial aid information on the Web. Here you'll find information on student loans, scholarships, military aid and other types of aid. Additionally, this site includes helpful hints for completing financial aid applications, various financial calculators and a free scholarship search.

Internal Revenue Service

You can get free telephone assistance by calling **800/829-1040**. Additionally, the following publications are available without charge by calling the IRS at **800/829-3676** or at the IRS's Web site (**www.irs.gov**):

- ❖ Publication 520, *Scholarships and Fellowships*
- ❖ Publication 550, *Investment Income and Expenses*
- ❖ Publication 564, *Mutual Fund Distributions*
- ❖ Publication 590, *Individual Retirement Arrangements (IRAs) (Including Roth IRAs and Education IRAs)*
- ❖ Publication 929, *Tax Rules for Children and Dependents*
- ❖ Publication 970, *Tax Benefits for Higher Education*

Octameron Associates

P.O. Box 2748
Alexandria, VA 22301-2748

Octameron offers a wide variety of publications, software, videos and services that will help you plan for college. Visit their Web site at **www.thinktuition.com** to review the products and services they offer or call **703/836-5480** to request a catalog.

Bureau of the Public Debt

Savings Bond Operations Office
Parkersburg, WV 26106-1328

For additional information on investing in U.S. savings bonds, including current rate information, visit the Bureau's Web site at **www.publicdebt.treas.gov** or call **800/4US-BOND** (800/487-2663). The Web site includes a calculator called the "Savings Bond Wizard" to help you track the value of your bonds. A similar calculator is also available at the New York Federal Reserve Bank's Web site (**www.ny.frb.org/pihome/svg_bnds/sb_val.html**).

Savingforcollege.com, LLC

Corporate Crossings Office Park
171 Sully's Trail, Suite 201
Pittsford, NY 14534
800/400-9113

At its Web site (**www.savingsforcollege.com**) you can learn more about qualified state tuition programs (529 plans), including the latest developments. The site also rates each of the plans for state residents and non-residents using its "5-cap" rating system.

Social Security

For the past 65 years, the Social Security system has provided partial income replacement to cover three different events: retirement, disability and death. The federal program of social insurance (OASDI) currently provides benefits to more than 45 million people. In planning for your financial future, it's important to remember that these benefits were never meant to replace lost earnings totally but rather to supplement income.

More than one member of a family may be eligible to receive Social Security benefits. A family maximum — the total annual amount payable to all family members together, which varies with each program (*i.e.,* retirement, disability or death) — is established based on an employee's primary benefit. The family maximum applies only when benefits are collected from the same account.

When a person becomes entitled to two separate benefits, *i.e.,* as an employee and as the spouse (or ex-spouse) of another employee, the higher of the two benefits will always be paid, but not both.

Special Consideration:

Benefit Calculation

Social Security does not automatically calculate each separate benefit to which you are entitled. If you qualify in more ways than on your own earnings, request a calculation of each at the time you are applying for your benefit. You should receive the highest benefit amount.

The higher your income has been throughout your working career, the smaller the percentage of income Social Security replaces at retirement. You may receive more money than someone who earned less, but it will replace a smaller portion of your income. The table below will give you some idea of how this works.

Social Security Benefits

Average Earnings	Estimated Percentage of Pay Replaced by Social Security Benefits at Normal Retirement Age
$30,000	41%
$50,000	30%
$85,000 or more	25%*

* Of that portion of your pay subject to Social Security tax.

You can turn to the following resources for information on the Social Security system:

- Free brochures available from your local Social Security office.
- The Social Security Hotline at 800/772-1213 is a source for answers to common questions.
- A Social Security statement will help you to make sure your Social Security wages are correct. Your Social Security wages can be found on your *Form W-2*. You will receive a Social Security Statement approximately three months prior to your birthday each year or you may request a statement using *Form SSA-7004*. Visit the Social Security web site at www.ssa.gov to request a statement or additional information.

Social Security Contributions

Since 1937, employees have been taxed on a portion of their earnings, and this amount has been matched by their employer. The maximum taxable wage base, which is calculated on wage-level increases, changes annually.

The Social Security tax rates are established by federal law. Since 1965, these percentages reflect a combined rate that includes the Medicare tax (HI).

Self-employed individuals have been taxed since 1951 at a higher rate. The self-employed amount paid to Social Security equals the combined employer/employee contribution. Half of this amount is an adjustment to their income as a business expense for self-employed individuals.

Social Security Employee Contributions Over the Years

Date	Rate	Max. Wages	Max. Tax
1937	1.00%	$3,000	$30.00
1951	1.50	3,600	54.00
1960	3.00	4,800	144.00
1966	4.20	6,600	277.20
1970	4.80	7,800	374.40
1972	5.20	9,000	468.00
1975	5.85	14,100	824.85
1979	6.13	22,900	1,403.77
1980	6.13	25,900	1,587.67
1981	6.65	29,700	1,975.05
1982	6.70	32,400	2,170.80
1983	6.70	35,700	2,391.90
1984	7.00	37,800	2,532.60
1985	7.05	39,600	2,791.08
1986	7.15	42,000	3,003.00
1987	7.15	43,800	3,131.70
1988	7.51	45,000	3,379.50
1989	7.51	48,000	3,604.80
1990	7.65	51,300	3,924.45
1991	7.65	53,400*	4,085.10
1992	7.65	55,500*	4,245.75
1993	7.65	57,600*	4,406.40
1994	7.65	60,600**	4,635.90
1995	7.65	61,200**	4,681.80
1996	7.65	62,700**	4,796.55
1997	7.65	65,400**	5,003.10
1998	7.65	68,400**	5,232.60
1999	7.65	72,600**	5,553.90
2000	7.65	76,200**	5,829.30
2001	7.65	80,400**	6,150.60
2002	7.65	84,900**	6,494.85

* Medicare tax (HI) of 1.45% continued on wages until a separate Medicare wage limit was reached.

** The Medicare tax of 1.45% continues on *all* wages above this amount.

Application Procedures

You can call or visit any one of the more than 1,300 local Social Security offices to start the application process. It's a good idea to start the process early, so contact your local office approximately three months before you want to begin receiving your benefit. You will need to submit original documents or copies certified by the issuer. Social Security will make photocopies and return your documents.

Information You Will Need:

- Social Security number;
- birth certificate;
- proof of U.S. citizenship or lawful alien status if not born in the United States;
- military discharge papers if you had military service;
- *Form W-2* or self-employment tax return for last year;
- checking or savings account information to arrange direct deposit; and,
- in the case of disability, a statement from the physician projecting 12 consecutive months of anticipated disability.

Dependents Who Qualify Will Need:

- birth certificate or other proof of age;
- Social Security number;
- marriage license and/or divorce decree to prove the period of marriage (if applicable); and,
- in the case of an employee's death, a death certificate.

Applicants may file for retirement benefits online at the Social Security Administration's Web site instead of applying at a local Social Security office. To use this service, you must be at least age 61 years and nine months and plan to start receiving benefits within four months. You also must reside in the United States or one of its territories, have a working printer connected to your computer and agree to receive your benefits by direct deposit.

If you use Social Security's Web site to apply for benefits, you must fill out the online application and send the information electronically to the agency. You then must print a copy of the completed application form, sign it and mail it or bring it to the address provided by the agency, along with other required documents such as your birth certificate. You may go to www.ssa.gov/applytoretire/ to start the online application process.

Additionally, when you call Social Security's toll-free number, you may be able to apply for retirement or survivor benefits immediately, without making an appointment or visiting a local office. To take advantage of this service, you must agree to receive your benefits by direct deposit. When applying for retirement benefits you must have the following documents in hand when you call: your birth certificate, your most recent *Form W-2* or tax return and your bank account information. Similarly, applicants for survivor benefits are required to have the following documentation: the deceased worker's Social Security number, proof of marriage (marriage certificate), death certificate, the surviving spouse's proof of age (birth certificate), divorce papers if applicable and bank-account information. Call the Social Security Administration at 800/772-1213 from 7 a.m. to 7 p.m., Monday through Friday, to apply for benefits by telephone.

Retirement Benefits

Benefit Entitlement

To qualify for any Social Security retirement benefit, you must have accumulated a minimum of 40 "work credits" over your working career. These credits are accrued by paying Social Security tax on a portion of your earnings. The dollar amount needed to earn a credit changes annually, reflecting increases in average wages.

A maximum of four credits can be earned each year. Once you have 40 credits (or 10 years of contributions), you will be considered fully insured and entitled to a retirement benefit. The amount of benefit is individually determined based on several factors including your age and Social Security taxable earnings history. These factors are used to compute your primary insurance amount or PIA.

Age Eligibility

The age you begin collecting the retirement benefit determines the percentage of the PIA you will receive. If you were born before 1938, you can collect 100% of your Social Security benefit at age 65. Reduced benefits are available as early as age 62. However, if you collect benefits early, a permanent reduction of 5/9 of 1% applies for each month you collect before age 65.

Annualized Benefit For Those Born Before 1938

Age Benefits Begin	% Benefit Collected
65	100%
64	93%
63	87%
62	80%

Eventually, the age a person can retire with no reduction in benefits will increase to 67. The increase is being phased in gradually and affects workers born after 1937. You can still receive a benefit at age 62, but if you retire in 2022 or later, and are 62, you will receive only 70% of the full benefit rather than 80%. As the table below shows, the reduction (from 80% to 70%) occurs in stages between the years 2000 and 2022.

If You Were Born in	Reduced PIA Benefit at Age 62	Your Age for Full Benefits Is
1937 or earlier	80.0%	65 yrs.
1938	79.2	65 yrs., 2 mos.
1939	78.3	65 yrs., 4 mos.
1940	77.5	65 yrs., 6 mos.
1941	76.7	65 yrs., 8 mos.
1942	75.8	65 yrs., 10 mos.
1943-1954	75.0	66 yrs.
1955	74.2	66 yrs., 2 mos.
1956	73.3	66 yrs., 4 mos.
1957	72.5	66 yrs., 6 mos.
1958	71.7	66 yrs., 8 mos.
1959	70.8	66 yrs., 10 mos.
1960 or later	70.0	67 yrs.

Is it better to wait until your full retirement age to collect an unreduced PIA benefit? There are several factors to consider:

Do you need the income? You may be forced to retire before your full retirement age and find that you need additional cash flow or you may need to pay off debts. In either case starting Social Security benefits before your full retirement age might be appropriate.

Will you still be earning income from part-time or full-time work? Due to the Social Security earnings limitation, if you continue to earn income while collecting Social Security before age 65 you may be forfeiting some or all of your benefit. If this is the case, you generally should wait to apply until age 65.

How is your health? If you're in poor health, you may want to take the money and run. Although the benefit will be reduced, you will be receiving payments that you may not ever receive if you wait until your full retirement age. For those in good health, however, it may be worthwhile to wait. Generally, the longer you live the more financially beneficial it will be to have waited to begin your benefit.

The Delayed Credit

If you delay receiving benefits, for any month after your full retirement age through age 70, you will receive an extra amount when you do collect. The rate of the delayed credit varies according to your year of birth.

If you decide to delay the start of retirement benefits past age 65, be sure to sign up for Medicare at age 65. In some circumstances, medical insurance costs more if you delay applying for it.

Delayed Retirement Credit Rates

If You Were Born in	Monthly Percentage	Yearly Percentage
1917 to 1924	1/4 of 1%	3.0%
1925 or 1926	7/24 of 1%	3.5%
1927 or 1928	1/3 of 1%	4.0%
1929 or 1930	3/8 of 1%	4.5%
1931 or 1932	5/12 of 1%	5.0%
1933 or 1934	11/24 of 1%	5.5%
1935 or 1936	1/2 of 1%	6.0%
1937 or 1938	13/24 of 1%	6.5%
1939 or 1940	7/12 of 1%	7.0%
1941 or 1942	5/8 of 1%	7.5%
1943 or later	2/3 of 1%	8.0%

COLA Increases Over the Years

Year	Increase
1984	3.5%
1985	3.5%
1986	3.1%
1987	1.3%
1988	4.2%
1989	4.0%
1990	4.7%
1991	5.4%
1992	3.7%
1993	3.0%
1994	2.6%
1995	2.8%
1996	2.6%
1997	2.9%
1998	2.1%
1999	1.3%
2000	2.4%
2001	3.5%
2002	2.6%

Cost-of-Living Adjustment

Under the current law, your basic Social Security benefit for retirement, disability or death will increase annually by a cost-of-living adjustment (COLA) beginning when you are first entitled to benefits and every year thereafter, whether or not the benefit is actually collected. The annual COLA benefit is determined at the end of the year and begins with the January check. The percentages shown in the table at left represent the increase for that year's benefit compared to the prior year. For example, benefit payments in 2002 are 2.6% higher than in 2001.

Payment of Benefits

All Social Security recipients are encouraged to receive their benefits through direct deposit to their bank, savings and loan or credit union account. Direct deposit gets your benefit into your account conveniently and safely. The U.S. Treasury sends an electronic message to your bank, savings and loan or credit union crediting your account with the exact amount of your benefit. You can then withdraw money, put some in savings or pay bills just like you'd do if you had received a check. If you do not have a checking or savings account or do not wish to have your payment made by direct deposit, you can still receive your Social Security benefit by check.

Family Benefits

Once you begin receiving Social Security, other eligible family members may then begin to collect. These dependent benefits are based on your full PIA, and the total paid is subject to an annual family maximum.

Spouse — If your spouse is not entitled to a benefit based on his/her own earnings, he or she still will be entitled to a spousal benefit based on your earnings. A spouse born before 1938 will be entitled at age 65 to the full spousal benefit, 50% of your PIA. A permanent reduction factor of 25/36 of 1% is applied to the spouse's benefit for each month the benefit is received before the full benefit age.

Spouse Retirement Benefit

Full Benefit Age	Percent Received at Full Benefit Age	Percent Received at Age 62
65	50%	37.5%
66	50%	35.0%
67	50%	32.5%

Future age adjustments will be made depending on the year of birth. A spouse at any age caring for dependent children under age 16 is entitled to a 50% monthly benefit.

Special Consideration:

Potential Offset

A spouse who receives a federal, state or Railroad System retirement benefit may face an offset to his or her Social Security benefit. Check with Social Security for more information and a projection of the spouse's Social Security benefit.

Other Eligible Dependents — The following dependents may receive benefits equal to 50% of your PIA:

- dependent children under age 18 (including age 18 if in high school);
- child disabled before age 22 with continued disability; and,
- dependent grandchildren (if their parents are deceased) to age 18.

A divorced spouse who was married at least 10 years and has not remarried qualifies for the same benefits as the current spouse (see above) but is not included in the family maximum.

How Work Affects Your Benefits

Social Security benefits may be limited annually by any earnings you received from work (*W-2* wages) or self-employment. Pension income, IRA distributions, interest, dividends and capital gains, to name a few, are not included in the definition of earnings. The reduction will only apply until you reach full retirement age (currently age 65). Starting with the month you reach full retirement age, you can receive your full benefits with no limit on your earnings.

If you're under full retirement age when you begin receiving your Social Security benefits, $1 in benefits will be deducted for each $2 you earn above the annual limit. In 2002, the limit is $11,280. A special monthly limit ($940 in 2002) applies to earnings in the first calendar year you collect Social Security retirement benefits. This special rule allows you to retire during the year and receive your unreduced benefit (after any adjustment due to your age) each month for the rest of the year as long as your earnings each month are less than one-twelfth of the annual maximum. Beginning in January of the year following your retirement, the annual limit applies.

In the year you reach your full retirement age, $1 in benefits will be deducted for each $3 you earn above a different limit, but only counting earnings before the month you reach full retirement age. That limit for 2002 is $30,000.

Special Consideration:

Earnings Limits in the Year You Reach Full Retirement Age

Let's say that you've begun receiving a monthly benefit of $900 in January 2002, but won't reach your full retirement age (age 65) until October 2002. You earn $50,000 during 2002, with $37,500 of it in the first nine months from January through September. Your benefits for the first nine months of the year would be reduced by $2,500 [($37,500 – $30,000) ÷ 3]. You would still receive $8,300 of your Social Security benefits for the year. Starting in October, when you reached age 65, you would receive your full benefits no matter how much you earned.

If your wages are going to exceed the annual earnings limitation, contact the Social Security Administration so they can adjust your current benefit. If you do not contact Social Security by April 15 of the next year, Social Security will notify you about a collection of the overpayment, and you will have to repay the amount in one of several ways.

The worksheet on the following page will help you estimate your net income from wages while receiving a Social Security benefit.

Special Consideration:

Prorated Reductions

If you are receiving a Social Security benefit and are going to have wages exceeding the Social Security earnings limit, you can have reductions in your monthly Social Security benefit made on a prorated basis over the year by notifying Social Security right away. Otherwise, the government's recovery of the overages after April 15th of the following year may actually eliminate the Social Security benefit for several months. This does not apply during the first year because of the special earnings rule.

Calculating Retirement Benefits

Retirement-benefit calculations are now determined by the Index Method. Actual earnings taxed by Social Security for a 40-year period (ages 22 to 62) are "indexed" or adjusted to reflect inflation. A formula is then applied to the 35 highest of these indexed years to determine the PIA or basic benefit. The set of index factors applied is developed annually from the preceding year's average wage-level increase.

The system is equitable and based on your contributions and the year you become 62. If you continue to work and contribute to Social Security past age 62, your benefit will be recalculated to account for your additional years of Social Security contributions.

Since the Social Security benefit amount is based on your earnings averaged over most of your working career, higher lifetime earnings will result in a higher benefit. To receive the maximum benefit, you must pay in the maximum. Each year has its own maximum for contributions and benefits.

Worksheet
Calculating Net Income From Earnings From Employment While Receiving Social Security Benefits*

Use this worksheet to help estimate your net (spendable) income from wages earned while receiving a Social Security benefit. (Do not use this worksheet if you are 65 or older — none of your Social Security benefits is subject to reduction.)

	Example		Your Situation
A. Estimated earnings from work	$15,000	A.	________
B. Current earnings limit	$11,280	B.	________
C. Subtract B from A (enter on line C)	3,720	C.	________
D. If C is greater than zero, multiply it by .5 (50%)	$ 1,860	D.	________

Your Social Security benefit will be reduced by this amount (D).

Additional considerations in calculating net income from earnings while receiving a Social Security benefit:

1. All earnings are subject to FICA tax, up to the maximum for the year.
2. Earnings are subject to federal, state and local taxes.
3. Some of the Social Security benefit may be subject to federal tax if total income from all sources, (*i.e.,* AGI or adjusted gross income) exceeds the current limits.

In summary, to project more accurately the amount of spendable income from employment while receiving a Social Security benefit, your calculation should follow these guidelines:

	Example	Your Situation
E. Enter gross amount of earnings:	$15,000	________
F. Calculate and subtract any reduction in Social Security benefit (line D from top of page):	(1,860)	(________)
G. Subtract estimated tax (FICA, federal, state, local) from gross earnings:	(5,948)**	(________)
H. Net income from earnings***:	$ 7,192	________
I. Net income as % of gross earnings (Line H divided by line E)	48 %	________

* Note: Different rule for first *calendar* year to receive Social Security benefit when subject to *monthly* earnings limits.
** Assumes 7.65% FICA/FICM withholding, 27% federal tax, and 5% state/local tax.
*** Does not account for any additional income taxes that might be due on Social Security benefits because of the earned income.

Early Retirement Considerations

If you leave work early, you may not have 35 years of earnings to be used in the Social Security retirement benefit calculation. The result may be a lower Social Security benefit. On the other hand, your contributions to the Social Security system also would be less. Call Social Security and request *Form SSA 7004* to get a benefit estimate or request an estimate on line at www.ssa.gov. The following table estimates the comparative cost of early retirement (as measured by the projected decrease in your age-62 monthly Social Security benefit) with the associated savings (as measured by the FICA payroll tax you won't pay because you've retired). The tax savings far outweigh the relatively nominal loss in benefit. Conversely, if you work until age 62, your monthly Social Security benefit should increase, but not to a level sufficient to recoup the additional FICA taxes you'll pay until then, *unless you live a very, very long time!* Consequently, people who work past age 62 should be working for reasons other than increasing their benefit.

How Does Early Retirement Affect Your Benefit?

Age at Retirement	Approximate Loss in Monthly Benefits at Age 62	Extra FICA Tax Paid If Worked Until Age 62	Approximate Years to Recoup Additional FICA Taxes
58			
Maximum Earnings	N/A	$25,979	N/A
Average Earnings	N/A	$ 9,180	N/A
55			
Maximum Earnings	$ 45	$45,464	83
Average Earnings	$ 34	$16,065	39
50			
Maximum Earnings	$159	$77,938	41
Average Earnings	$120	$27,540	19

Maximum Earnings = $84,900 Average Earnings = $30,000

Additional Social Security Benefits

Survivor Benefits

Social Security benefits payable to your survivors may include both a monthly benefit and a one-time lump-sum death benefit of $255. The lump-sum death benefit is payable only to a qualifying current spouse or dependent child. Monthly survivor benefits are based on your PIA on the date of your death and the current age of the widowed person. The following table summarizes the monthly survivor benefits that may be payable if you die in 2002.

To qualify for a survivor benefit, your spouse must have been married to you for at least nine months before your death, or be the parent of your natural or adopted child.

Survivor Benefits if You Die in 2002

Beneficiary	Percent of Your PIA
Spouse, age 65	100.0%
Spouse, age 60	71.5%
Disabled spouse, age 50 – 59	71.5%
Spouse under age 61 with eligible child who is under age 16 or disabled	75.0%
Each eligible child	75.0%

Currently, a monthly surviving spouse benefit beginning at a spouse's age 65 would equal 100% of your PIA or a smaller amount if you had begun receiving retirement benefits before your full retirement age. (The age for a full benefit will begin to rise after 2002 as the full retirement age for workers rises.) Alternatively, a surviving spouse could begin receiving a benefit equal to 71.5% of your PIA as early as age 60. If a benefit begins after a spouse's age 60 and before full retirement age, it is prorated for each month between age 60 and a spouse's full retirement age. A disabled spouse could collect a benefit equal to 71.5% of your PIA as early as age 50. The family maximum and earnings limitation apply to this benefit.

If you are a divorced surviving spouse who qualifies (10 years of marriage to the deceased worker and not remarried), you are entitled to the same benefits as the current widowed person, except for the lump-sum death benefit. The surviving spouse or divorced surviving spouse may remarry after age 60 and still collect the monthly survivor benefit.

The same dependents qualify for survivor benefits as qualify for retirement benefits and are entitled to 75% of your PIA within the family maximum. In addition, parents (age 62 or older) who received at least half of their support from the deceased worker may be eligible for benefits.

Disability Benefits

In addition to retirement and survivor benefits, Social Security will pay a benefit to people who are unable to work for a year or more because of severe physical or mental impairment. To be eligible, your disability must be expected to last a year or to result in death. You will be considered disabled if you cannot do the work you did before you became disabled or you cannot adjust to other work because of your medical condition. This is a strict definition of disability.

To qualify for Social Security disability benefits you must have earned the number of work credits required for your age. Generally, the older you are the more work credits will be required for qualifying.

If qualified, you can receive a monthly disability benefit from Social Security equal to 100% of your PIA at the time that the disability occurs. Additionally, members of your family may qualify for benefits. The maximum family benefit is 150% of your PIA. There is a five-month waiting period before disability benefits begin.

The Social Security Administration can provide more details on all these programs.

Taxation of Benefit

Whether you pay income taxes on your Social Security benefit depends on your taxable sources of income, including pension benefits, IRA withdrawals, interest, dividends, capital gains, rental income and *W-2* earnings.

All of these items are included in your adjusted gross income (AGI) on your federal income tax return. You must also include tax-free interest income, such as that derived from municipal bonds, in determining whether your Social Security benefit is subject to taxes. Based upon the current law, the maximum amount subject to income tax is 85% of your Social Security benefit.

Use the following worksheet to determine whether you will owe federal income taxes on your benefit. Also, check to see if your Social Security benefit is taxed in your state.

Benefit Taxation Worksheet

		Example	Your Situation
Line 1:	Enter your Social Security benefit. If you are married, include your spouse's benefits, too.	$ 8,000	(1) ________
Line 2:	Enter 1/2 of Line 1.	4,000	(2) ________
Line 3:	Enter the AGI from your federal tax return. Do not include your Social Security benefits.	42,000	(3) ________
Line 4:	Enter any tax-exempt interest. This figure can be found on your tax return.	1,000	(4) ________
Line 5:	Add Lines 2, 3 and 4 ($4,000 + $42,000 + $1,000).	47,000	(5) ________

If the amount on Line 5 is less than $32,000 if married ($25,000 if single,) you will not owe income tax on your Social Security benefit and do not need to proceed further. Otherwise, proceed with Lines 6 through 17.

		Example	Your Situation
Line 6:	Enter $32,000 if married ($25,000 if single).	32,000	(6) ________
Line 7:	Subtract Line 6 from Line 5 ($47,000 – $32,000).	15,000	(7) ________
Line 8:	Enter 1/2 of Line 7.	7,500	(8) ________
Line 9:	Enter the smaller of Line 2 or Line 8. If Line 5 is less than $44,000 if married ($34,000 if single), this is your taxable Social Security benefit. If not, please continue.	4,000	(9) ________
Line 10:	Enter $6,000 if married, $4,500 if single.	6,000	(10) ________
Line 11:	Enter the smaller of Line 9 or Line 10.	4,000	(11) ________
Line 12:	Enter $44,000 if married, $34,000 if single.	44,000	(12) ________
Line 13:	Subtract Line 12 from Line 5 ($47,000 – $44,000).	3,000	(13) ________
Line 14:	Multiply Line 13 by 85% ($3,000 X .85).	2,550	(14) ________
Line 15:	Add Line 11 to Line 14 ($4,000 + $2,550).	6,550	(15) ________
Line 16:	Multiply Line 1 by 85% ($8,000 X .85).	6,800	(16) ________
Line 17:	Enter the smaller of Line 15 or Line 16. This is your taxable Social Security benefit.	6,550	(17) ________

2002 Annual Highlights

Contributions

- ❖ A combined tax rate of 7.65% will be levied on a taxable wage base up to $84,900 in 2002.

6.20%	Social Security (OASDI)	$5,263.80
1.45%	Medicare (HI)	1,231.05
7.65%	Combined	$6,494.85

- ❖ In addition, the 1.45% rate applies to all earnings above $84,900.
- ❖ Self-employed individuals pay combined employer/employee rates up to the same wage base for Social Security and Medicare listed above. Federal income tax Schedule SE must be filed. Half of the Social Security tax is treated as an adjustment on your federal income tax return.
- ❖ No further rate increases are scheduled under current law. Maximum taxable earnings are subject to annual adjustment.

Credits

- ❖ For 2002 one work credit equals $870 of earned income. The annual maximum of four credits is given with $3,480 of earnings.

Maximum Benefits at Retirement*

- ❖ Age 65 retiree — $1,660 per month.
- ❖ Retiree and spouse, ages 65 — $2,490-per-month joint benefit.
- ❖ A cost-of-living (COLA) increase of 2.6% was added in January 2002.

Earnings Limitations

- ❖ Over age 65 — no limit.
- ❖ Year individual reaches age 65 — $30,000 annual earnings limit; $3:$1 reduction above this limit applies only to months prior to attaining age 65.
- ❖ Under age 65 — $11,280 annual earnings limit ($940/month); $2:$1 reduction above this limit.

* In 2002 the average benefit for a retiree is $874 per month.

Items for Action

Social Security was designed to replace a portion of your income in retirement. Since participation is automatic and there are no decisions to make until retirement, the only recommendation is to review your Social Security statement each year.

If you are age 62 and retired, the only decision you have to make is when to start your benefit. Most analyses will prove it is to your advantage to start your benefit as early as possible.

For each of the following items, assign a priority based on its importance to you: A (highest), B (medium) or C (lowest). Then check off each item as it is completed.

	Priority	Completed
❖ Call Social Security at 800/772-1213 and request *Form SSA 7004* to obtain a customized Social Security statement or visit Social Security's Web site at www.ssa.gov to request a statement.	_______	❑
❖ Call Social Security whenever you need information or visit the Social Security Administration's Web site at www.ssa.gov. If calling, call before 9 a.m. and after 5 p.m. to avoid the busiest times.	_______	❑
❖ Use the age eligibility chart to determine the percentage of Social Security retirement benefit you will receive at age 62 based upon your year of birth.	_______	❑
❖ Submit your application two or three months before you plan to receive benefits to ensure sufficient processing time.	_______	❑
❖ Complete the Benefit Taxation Worksheet to see if any of your Social Security benefit will be taxable.	_______	❑
❖ Request the updated brochures each year so you will have accurate information on this annually changing system.	_______	❑

Resources

Internal Revenue Service

You can get free telephone assistance by calling **800/829-1040**. For Publication 554, *Older Americans' Tax Guide*, or Publication 915, *Social Security and Equivalent Railroad Retirement Benefits*, call the IRS at **800/829-3676** or visit the IRS's Web site: **www.irs.gov**. IRS publications are free.

Social Security Administration

Office of Public Inquiries
6401 Security Boulevard
Room 4-C-5 Annex
Baltimore, MD 21235-6401

Social Security has a toll-free number that operates from 7 a.m. to 7 p.m., Monday to Friday: **800/772-1213**. If you have a touch-tone phone, recorded information and services are available 24 hours a day, including weekends and holidays. Additionally, you may obtain information (including several publications), access retirement planners and request a Social Security statement online at the Social Security Administration's Web site: **www.ssa.gov**.

Free publications available from the Social Security Administration include:

- *Social Security—Retirement Benefits* (Pub. No. 05-10035)
- *Social Security—Understanding the Benefits* (Pub. No. 05-10024)
- *Social Security—Survivors Benefits* (Pub. No. 05-10084)
- *Social Security—Disability Benefits* (Pub. No. 05-10029)
- *How Work Affects Your Benefits* (Pub. No. 05-10069)
- *Your Payments While You Are Outside the United States* (Pub. No. 05-10137)

William M. Mercer, Incorporated

462 South Fourth Avenue
Suite 1500
Louisville, KY 40202-3431
502/561-4541

Mercer's *2002 Guide to Social Security and Medicare* provides a thorough overview of the Social Security and Medicare programs for the layman. To receive a copy, send a check for $19 to the above address.

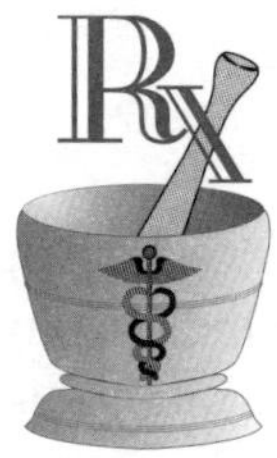

Health-Care Coverage

Health insurance has become increasingly important as medical costs continue to skyrocket. Most of us expect that our employers will provide group coverage at an affordable price. Unfortunately, group health insurance and the government programs supplementing them are becoming more difficult to fund as the costs of medical services increase.

Health insurance and government programs were never intended to pay all our medical bills, but rather cushion the costs when they became excessive. In truth, although we rely on insurance companies and the government to pay these bills, we also supply the funds by paying insurance premiums and through our taxes. The best way to reduce these costs is to be smart consumers when using medical services or purchasing health-care coverage and to practice ongoing personal health management.

Consumer Issues

To be smart consumers of health care we must make thoughtful decisions about our options, considering both quality and cost, as well as our own personal and family circumstances.

Consider Your Choices

Many companies now offer a choice of health-care plans. To encourage sound personal decisions, they provide information through booklets, newsletters and presentations. Informational hotlines and personal meetings often are available to help you understand the options. It's important to review your individual and family changes, as well as health-care costs, each year. The open-enrollment period for your company affords an excellent opportunity to make appropriate changes.

Cost Containment

Everyone benefits from the appropriate use of medical services. Companies institute guidelines (*e.g.*, providing networks and precertification requirements) to ensure that dollars are well spent. Following these guidelines should maximize medical benefits for everyone.

Flexible Spending Accounts

At many companies employees can contribute before-tax dollars to a health-care reimbursement account. The money can be used to pay for out-of-pocket expenses — deductibles, co-insurance and certain medical expenses not covered by your health insurance — incurred in a calendar year. Companies may also offer a separate before-tax account for dependent care. If a flexible spending account is available to you, it's important to maximize your use of it to manage your medical expenditures more efficiently.

With a health-care reimbursement account you can claim the entire account balance even before it's fully funded for the year. For example, you can elect during your company's open enrollment to contribute $120 through payroll deduction over the following year to an account because you need new prescription glasses and frames that will cost that amount. Then, in January of the following year, you can claim a reimbursement for the entire $120 if you purchase the glasses at that time. The advance-reimbursement feature of the health-care account is a very important component.

Two-Income Couple

If you and your spouse both have health-insurance coverage available through your employers, you should take a close look at the provisions of these plans to ensure that you're maximizing the effectiveness and minimizing the cost of one or both plans. Generally, both plans will contain a coordination-of-benefits provision, which means you won't be reimbursed for more than 100% of covered expenses.

Adult Children

Depending on your policy, health-insurance coverage may cease when children reach a certain age and/or when they're no longer full-time students. Make sure you understand your policy's limitations as well as options for continued coverage. These options include coverage under COBRA (see discussion below), individual comprehensive major medical, and temporary or conversion medical policies.

Planning Strategies

Adequate health-insurance coverage should be a major consideration in financial planning. Without such coverage, you run the risk of financial ruin in the event of a catastrophic illness. When planning, you must consider various "what-if" situations to be prepared for possible eventualities.

COBRA/HIPAA

If you change jobs or retire, you may lose your group coverage. The Consolidated Omnibus Budget Reconciliation Act of 1986 (COBRA) is a federal law requiring, under certain circumstances, your group health-insurance coverage to be continued for you and your dependents. You'll be required to pay your employer's full premium cost plus 2% to cover administrative costs. Also, the amount of time you can extend the group medical coverage will be either 18 or 36 months, depending upon the qualifying life event. Your company's summary plan description or benefits representative can provide you with details.

The Health Insurance Portability and Accountability Act of 1996 (HIPAA) includes provisions to enhance the portability of health-care benefits and continued coverage for pre-existing conditions.

Conversion

Once COBRA coverage ends, you may have the right to convert to an individual plan. These conversion policies usually offer "scaled-down benefits" at a higher premium cost, so consider this option as a last resort when coverage cannot be found anywhere else.

Special Consideration:

Retiree Medical Insurance

Unlike a pension plan, in which the benefit is guaranteed by your employer and federal law, a group (or individual) health-insurance policy and/or premium payment can change or the policy may be terminated after you retire. Any change in your medical insurance would happen to the entire group, not just you.

Group Insurance *vs.* Individual Coverage

Group coverage usually provides the most comprehensive benefits at the most affordable price because the risk is spread over a large group. Besides being available from your employer, group health insurance may also be offered by fraternal or professional associations, alumni organizations, etc. Individual policies usually are more expensive and difficult to obtain if you have a chronic condition. However, HIPAA is generating changes that should allow an individual in any state to obtain health insurance regardless of his or her health condition.

Medicare

Created by the federal government in 1965 as part of Social Security, Medicare is one of the largest insurance programs in the world. It is designed primarily to provide hospital and medical services for individuals age 65 and older. It also covers individuals at any age with permanent kidney failure and those with certain lengthy disabilities.

The Balanced Budget Act of 1997 created new health-care options called Medicare Plus Choice (Medicare + Choice). Added to the existing health-insurance options, more managed-care options and the opportunity to have private insurance or a Medicare Medical Spending Account (MSA) now are available.

The Social Security Administration processes Medicare applications and claims. The Centers for Medicare & Medicaid Services (CMS) set the standards and policies used to certify service providers. The services offered are the same nationwide, but levels of reimbursement may differ according to regional fee structures. Benefits usually aren't paid for services furnished outside the United States.

Medicare programs are financed by Social Security taxes, appropriated federal revenue, premium contributions for Part B coverage, deductibles and copayments. For more information on Medicare, call Medicare customer service at 800/633-4227 weekdays from 8 a.m. to 8 p.m., visit the Medicare website at www.medicare.gov or go to your local Social Security Administration office for pamphlets.

What is the Original Medicare Plan?

The Original Medicare Plan is the traditional pay-per-visit arrangement. It has two parts: Part A (Hospital Insurance) and Part B (Medical Insurance). An individual can go to any doctor, hospital, or other health-care provider who accepts Medicare. The individual must pay the deductible. Medicare then pays its share. There are also certain co-insurance payments in Part A and Part B.

Federal regulations require physicians and suppliers to submit bills to the Medicare carrier without charges, which eases the burden of paperwork for the patient.

What is Part A?

Part A (Hospital Insurance) helps pay for care in hospitals and skilled-nursing facilities, and for home health and hospice care. If you (or your spouse) qualify for Social Security benefits, no premium is required for the Part A coverage. If you don't qualify for premium-free Part A, and you're age 65 or older, you may be able to buy it. You can obtain this information by contacting Social Security.

The benefit period is the key to understanding the time parameters of hospital coverage. It consists of the period of time beginning with admission to a hospital and ending with the 60th consecutive day after discharge from a hospital and/or a skilled-nursing facility. There's no limit to the number of benefit periods an individual may have in a lifetime.

Example of a Benefit Period:

- ❖ **1st Day** — Hospital inpatient incurs a deductible.
- ❖ **Inpatient Days 2 through 60** — Most services covered in full.
- ❖ **Days 61 through 90** — Inpatient coverage continues with a daily co-insurance payment of one-fourth the initial deductible.
- ❖ **60 Reserve Days** — (Lifetime benefit) may be added after 90 consecutive inpatient days are used. Daily co-insurance cost of one-half the initial deductible. Reserve days aren't renewable.

Hospitalization must be in a Medicare-approved facility and deemed appropriate and necessary to be covered by Medicare. Admission and continued stay are reviewed.

Skilled-Nursing Facility — In some cases, extending care in a skilled-nursing facility may be more appropriate. After an inpatient hospital stay of at least three consecutive days (not counting the day of discharge), the patient will be entitled to coverage for care as an inpatient in a skilled-nursing facility if:

1. The care required is considered skilled or rehabilitative under doctor's orders.
2. Admission to the facility is within 30 days of hospital discharge.

If these two requirements are met, up to 100 days in the benefit period are available as an inpatient in a skilled-nursing facility.

- ❖ **Days 1 through 20** — Most services covered by Medicare.
- ❖ **Days 21 through 100** — Continued coverage with a co-insurance payment of one-eighth the initial hospital deductible.

Hospice Care — Pain-and-symptom relief and supportive services for the management of a terminal illness are provided in a facility or in the home.

Home Health Care — Skilled nursing care, physical or speech therapy, home health-aide services, medical equipment and supplies and other services are provided.

What is Part B?

Part B (Medical Insurance) helps pay for doctors, outpatient hospital care and some other medical services such as physical and occupational therapy. Part B covers all medically necessary doctor services in any setting. These services may be received in a hospital, doctor's office or clinic, a nursing home or at home. You're automatically eligible for Part B if you're eligible for premium-free Part A. You're also eligible if you're a U.S. citizen or permanent resident age 65 or older.

Part B Payments — There is a required monthly premium for Part B, and an annual deductible must be met in "approved charges" for covered services. Medicare then pays for 80% of approved charges incurred in the calendar year. The patient pays any fees above the approved charges.

Though Part B is "voluntary," it's a necessary component of complete health-care insurance coverage. Almost all company-sponsored supplements to Medicare for retirees assume the retiree is enrolled in Part B and pay benefits as though Medicare Part B benefits have already been paid. Further, if you don't take Part B when eligible, you'll pay a higher premium on an ongoing basis when you do elect it. The more serious consequence is that doctor's services and other services covered under Part B can become out-of-pocket expenses. Both Part A and Part B are required before Medigap insurance may be purchased or Medicare managed care or Medical Spending Account (MSA) options may be elected.

Special Enrollment Period (Part B) — If you didn't enroll in Part B because you or your spouse currently works and has group health coverage through an employer, you can sign up for Part B upon retirement with no penalty. Medicare allows an eight-month open-enrollment period for Part B, starting from the date of retirement. However, most company plans expect immediate enrollment in Part B upon retirement for Medicare-eligible retirees.

Special Consideration:

Open Enrollment

Federal laws require insurance carriers who offer Medigap policies to offer all plans that they market in your state of residence regardless of pre-existing conditions during an open-enrollment period. The open-enrollment period begins when you enroll in Part B. If you or your spouse are covered under an employer plan that is primary to Medicare in paying medical bills, it would be wise to wait to buy Part B to delay triggering the Medigap open-enrollment period.

What is Assignment?

Some physicians and other health-care providers participate in an agreement to accept Medicare's approved amount as their fee. If you select providers who don't participate in assignment, you're responsible for your 20% of the approved charges plus the amount of the extra charges up to the federal limit, which is 15% above the approved charge. Ask your providers if they accept assignment or consult directories available through your local Department of Aging or Social Security offices to find out.

Is Medicare Enough?

There are health-care costs that Medicare either doesn't pay in full or doesn't pay at all. There are deductibles and co-pays for hospital stays as well as doctor and other services. Therefore, it's wise to have an additional plan that will cover a significant portion of these costs. Usually, it isn't necessary to have more than one source of additional coverage. For many retirees, this source is the company-sponsored plan, which becomes secondary to Medicare when the retiree reaches age 65.

Options for Health Insurance for Individuals on Medicare

Currently, an individual eligible for Medicare has the following choices (however, not all of these choices may be available in your area):

- The Original Medicare (Fee-for-Service) Plan, comprising Part A and Part B
- The Original Medicare with a supplemental insurance policy (an individual's company-sponsored plan or a purchased Medigap or Medigap Select policy)
- A Medicare Health Maintenance Organization (HMO)
- HMOs with Point-of-Service Option (POS)
- Provider-Sponsored Organizations (PSOs)
- Preferred-Provider Organizations (PPOs)
- Private Fee-for-Service Plans
- Medicare Medical Savings Account Plans (MSAs).

Special Consideration:

Medicare Part A and Part B

Both Medicare Part A and Part B are the base for all options. In order to purchase a Medigap policy or other private insurance, have full coverage from most company-sponsored plans, participate in a managed care plan, or elect an MSA, an individual must have enrolled in Medicare Part A and Part B.

Choosing a Medicare Coverage

Changes in the health-care delivery system, corporate benefits, and in Medicare can make the process of selecting coverage confusing. However, helpful information is available through Medicare, the health-care plan provider, and/or the sponsoring company's Human Resources department. It's important to understand the types of plans and coverage options within each. The following is a brief overview:

Fee-for-Service Plans — You can go to any doctor or hospital that accepts Medicare. You or the provider submit claims to Medicare. You pay any charges that Medicare, a Medigap insurance policy or your company-sponsored plan doesn't cover. ***If you choose a private insurance plan that accepts Medicare beneficiaries, the insurance plan — not the Medicare program — decides how much to reimburse for the services you receive.***

Managed-Care Plans — These consist of groups of doctors, hospitals and other health-care providers who have agreed to provide care to Medicare beneficiaries in exchange for a fixed amount of money from Medicare every month. Managed-Care Plans include HMOs, HMOs with a PSO option, PSOs, and PPOs. Plan members retain all of their Medicare protections and appeal rights. There are usually premiums and small copayments for services. You don't pay Medicare's deductibles and co-insurance. Often these include benefits for health-care services that Medicare doesn't cover, such as vision, dental and prescriptions.

Medicare Medical Savings Account (MSA) Plans — These are comprised of two parts: a special type of savings account and a Medicare MSA Health Policy. The account is approved and funded by Medicare, and although you choose the policy, it must have been approved by Medicare. These policies have high deductibles (though limited by Medicare to no more than $6,000). Once set up, Medicare makes an annual contribution to the account and pays the policy premium to the insurance company. The funds in the account are used to meet the deductible and can be used to pay for other health-care costs. ***There are two primary cautions in using a Medicare MSA: (1) the MSA may not have enough in the account for medical expenses since there is a high deductible and, (2) the Medicare limits on what providers can charge you above the amount paid by Medicare doesn't apply.*** People who are covered by a company-sponsored plan aren't eligible for a Medicare MSA, and some other exclusions apply. As of this writing, no MSA plans exist.

Special Consideration:

Medicare

Corporate benefit plans that become secondary to Medicare when a retiree reaches age 65 can be either a fee-for-service or managed-care plan. It's important to understand your company-sponsored plan's provisions. This information is available from the company or the health-plan provider.

Strategies to Maximize Benefits

Medicare was never designed to pay the full costs of medical care and currently covers somewhat less than half of incurred costs. Gaps exist not only in the amounts paid but in the services offered. Presently, Medicare does not cover the following:

- private-duty nursing
- physical exams
- some preventive measures
- routine dental care/dentures
- routine foot care
- routine immunizations
- outpatient prescription drugs
- custodial nursing-home care
- care received outside the United States
- eye exams/glasses
- hearing exams/hearing aids

Having a cash reserve on hand to cover these costs is advisable, but you may also want to purchase supplemental insurance. When considering a Medicare supplement or medigap policy, a single comprehensive policy is better than several polices that may overlap or duplicate coverage. Begin by checking availability through your employer.

A very important component of health maintenance is prudent health screening and disease prevention. Medicare provides coverage for the following services:

- mammograms
- pap smears, including pelvic and breast exams
- colorectal cancer screening
- diabetes glucose monitoring
- diabetes education
- bone-mass measurements
- flu and pneumococcal pneumonia shots.

Some of these services are covered without having to meet the Part B deductible, some are free, and some can be used more frequently by high-risk individuals. Be sure to ask your health-care provider if any of these services would be right for you.

2002 Medicare Highlights

Part A — Hospital and Related Services

Hospital:

- ❖ Initial deductible — $812
- ❖ Coverage through day 60
- ❖ Days 61 through 90, inpatient co-insurance of $203 per day
- ❖ 60 reserve days, inpatient co-insurance of $406 per day

Skilled-nursing facility:

- ❖ Coverage through day 20
- ❖ Days 21 through 100, inpatient co-insurance of $101.50 per day

Part B — Medicare Services

- ❖ Monthly premium — $54 per person
- ❖ Annual deductible — $100 for approved charges
- ❖ After deductible, Medicare pays 80% of approved charges
- ❖ You're responsible for the remaining 20% and costs above approved amounts as well as the full amount for services not covered by Medicare.

Doctors who accept Medicare patients may not charge more than 115% of the Medicare-approved charge in your area. Some states have imposed more stringent regulations.

Personal Medicare Supplement or Medigap Policies

These policies are subject to extensive federal and state regulations. Also, the National Association of Insurance Commissioners (NAIC) has made it easier to shop for policies by creating 10 standardized packages of coverage, designated by letters A through J. Although each standardized plan is identical from insurer to insurer, prices may differ. The Medicare call center (800/633-4227) can provide more information on these plans. An insurance company may not carry each policy, so you may have to call four or five companies to compare costs. If a retiree has supplemental health insurance through a prior employer, it's unlikely that a Medigap (or Medigap Select) policy is needed. Medigap policies are appropriate for individuals whose only insurance is Medicare.

Standardized Medigap Plans

CORE BENEFITS	A	B	C	D	E	F	G	H	I	J
Part A Hospital (Days 61-90)	ALL 10 PLANS COVER THESE CORE BENEFITS									
Lifetime Reserve Days (91-150)										
365 Life Hosp. Days - 100%										
Parts A and B Blood										
Part B Co-insurance - 20%										
ADDITIONAL BENEFITS	**A**	**B**	**C**	**D**	**E**	**F**	**G**	**H**	**I**	**J**
Skilled-Nursing Facility Co-insurance (Days 21-100)			x	x	x	x	x	x	x	x
Part A Deductible		x	x	x	x	x	x	x	x	x
Part B Deductible			x			x				x
Part B Excess Charges						100%	80%		100%	100%
Foreign Travel Emergency			x	x	x	x	x	x	x	x
At-Home Recovery			x			x			x	x
Prescription Drugs								1	1	2
Preventive Medical Care					x					x

[1] A "basic" benefit with $250 annual deductible, 50% co-insurance and a $1,250 maximum annual benefit (Plans H and I above).

[2] An "extended" benefit (Plan J above) containing a $250 annual deductible, 50% co-insurance and a $3,000 maximum annual benefit.

Note: Medigap Select policies are the same as Medigap policies in every respect except that you must use network hospitals and in some cases network doctors to be eligible for full benefits. Medigap Select policies are usually less expensive than Medigap policies, but they are not available in all states nor are they offered by all insurers.

Medicaid

Medicaid is a joint federal and state program designed to help pay medical-related expenses for people of all ages with limited income and assets. Since the federal government also contributes, it has established minimum standards for coverage in all states. Generally speaking, people who receive Supplemental Security Income or public assistance (welfare) checks are eligible.

Many states provide benefits for other groups through medical assistance. Eligibility for medical assistance varies from state to state but usually covers low-income individuals and families where medical costs are unaffordable. Medicaid also can pay nursing-home costs for the elderly poor. Income limitations often follow federal guidelines, and assets such as checking and savings accounts are reviewed to ensure they're not greater than qualifying limits. Federal law prevents the transfer of assets within 36 months (60 months if transferred to a trust) before receiving Medicaid, but legal protection does exist to prevent spousal impoverishment. These time limits are known as "look-back" periods.

It's possible to have Medicare and be eligible for Medicaid. Under the Qualified Medicare Beneficiary (QMB) benefit, Medicaid may pay for Medicare premiums, deductibles and co-insurance costs for low-income persons.

Special Consideration:

Long-Term Care

There are stringent financial requirements for Medicaid, but once a person qualifies, most of the costs of long-term care are paid. It's wise to check with the particular state and county to understand its eligibility requirements, coverage and procedures.

Long-Term Care Issues

Americans are living longer. Concerns arise, however, about whether their later years will be lived independently or whether care will be required for them. Long-term care implies care that is *custodial*, not medical. Many mid-life adults today are not only projecting their own needs, but are often addressing these issues on behalf of elderly parents.

The good news is that Americans are not only living longer but are also healthier. Most will function independently their entire lives. Frailties that can come with advanced age don't in themselves necessitate nursing-home care.

Support Services

Personal care and community programs that help maintain an older person's independence and avoid the total-care environment of a nursing home are becoming more common. Resources often are available to provide home assistance. These resources include community-based support programs such as "Meals on Wheels," homemaker and health-aide services, chore workers, friendly visitors, telephone reassurance, day care and shopping assistance. Service contacts can be made through the Area Agency on Aging, churches, family physicians and social workers. Most phone directories group these resources in a guide to "human services."

The AARP special projects section has developed several excellent booklets on home-based support services that include extensive references.

Coordinating Services

In our mobile society, people often find themselves living a long way from their elderly parents and frustrated by the difficulty of arranging for appropriate care. Many companies have expanded their employee assistance programs to include caregiver information and referral. Check with your employee assistance or human resource representative.

Another alternative is Elder Care Locator, which is now available locally and on a nationwide basis. This service of the U.S. Administration on Aging provides professional assessment and matches the appropriate services with the needs of the individual through a nationwide network of clinical social workers. For more information on Elder Care Locator, call 800/677-1116 or visit its Web site at www.eldercare.gov.

Long-Term Care Insurance

Long-term care (LTC) insurance is designed specifically to cover the cost of care for those unable to care for themselves. Medicaid is currently the only government program that provides long-term care, and then only if an individual meets certain federal- and state-mandated income and asset guidelines. Though some employers provide an opportunity for employees to purchase LTC insurance, no corporate or private health-insurance plan provides benefits for custodial care. Similarly, Medicare doesn't cover the cost of custodial care.

LTC polices pay a daily or monthly benefit (usually $20 to $300 per day) for care you receive in a qualified nursing home, assisted-living facility, adult day-care center or your own home. Payment for these services begins after a qualification, or waiting, period, usually from 20 to 90 days. This period is similar to the deductible on a medical policy or the waiting period on a disability policy.

The policy's daily benefit is paid either for a stated period of time — usually three to six years (lifetime coverage is available) — or up to a stated dollar amount ("pool of money" option). Most policies also provide inflation-protection coverage, which will automatically increase the value of the coverage. The inflation-protection feature is available for an additional cost.

Benefit eligibility is usually based on functional or cognitive impairment. Functional impairment is the inability to perform necessary activities of daily living (ADLs), such as: eating, bathing, dressing, remaining continent, using the toilet, walking and transferring (getting in and out of a chair or bed). Cognitive impairment is the deterioration or loss of mental functions. A third benefit trigger, a doctor's order or recommendation, may be part of policies issued before January 1, 1997. This benefit trigger was eliminated by the Health Insurance Portability and Accountability Act of 1996 (HIPAA). Policies purchased after January 1, 1997, may include this trigger, but if they do, the insured won't be eligible for the favorable tax features implemented by HIPAA.

Government Regulations

Though HIPAA became effective July 1, 1997, related regulations are still being written. In general, HIPAA identified very specific provisions that must be included in LTC policies. Policies that meet the HIPAA guidelines are called tax-qualified (TQ) policies. There are two major potential tax benefits: LTC policy premiums may be deductible as a medical expense for those who itemize, subject to limitations; and LTC insurance benefits will be tax-free to the recipient, subject to limitations. Any LTC policy purchased before January 1, 1997, regardless of its provisions, was grandfathered into these tax benefits.

Special Consideration:

"Materially Altered"

It's unclear whether making changes to a policy purchased before January 1, 1997, would mean that it has been "materially altered" and thus no longer eligible to be considered grandfathered into the favorable tax benefits. It would be wise not to make changes to existing policies until it is certain what effect the changes would have.

Evaluating the Need for LTC Insurance

Determining whether there is a need to purchase LTC insurance is not easy. Though protecting *assets* is the primary reason to purchase an LTC policy, some people purchase such policies because they think they will also ensure "choice" and a high quality of care should the need for long-term care arise. *But LTC insurance does not ensure quality of care.* Before purchasing LTC insurance, it's critical to project what your future income and assets will be. Consider the following guidelines when assessing the need for LTC insurance.

When to Purchase LTC Insurance

The usual age to purchase LTC insurance is between 55 and 65. Though the premiums are lower for younger purchasers, the length of time a person would pay premiums makes this an expensive venture. Consider also that while actively employed, a person generally relies on a steady flow of earned income. Purchasing disability insurance to provide an income source addresses a more likely risk and generally would be a wiser use of resources.

LTC Policy *vs.* Self-Insurance

Planning for the possibility of needing long-term care may or may not include purchasing LTC insurance. Assuming an average three-to-four-year stay in a nursing home at $40,000 per year, targeting a $160,000 investment that would average a rate of return at or above the inflation rate could address this potential need. Then, if long-term care were not needed, this resource would be available for other uses.

Generally speaking, LTC premiums shouldn't exceed 5 – 7% of annual income. Be sure to consider this measure in terms of *both current and future premiums* in comparison to income. As noted below, *you should expect the premium to increase over the lifetime of the policy.*

For those who have or would have assets (not including their home) of below $150,000 for couples and $75,000 for individuals, the heavy cost of premiums *vs.* the potential benefit seems not to justify the purchase of LTC insurance. Those individuals whose assets are between $300,000 and $1.5 million and who wish to leave assets for a spouse or an heir rather than spend available assets while alive might want to consider this insurance. While the premiums appear very costly compared to the potential benefit for those whose assets are below $300,000, those with assets over $1.5 million should be able to absorb any long-term care expenses that might arise.

Evaluating LTC Policies

When shopping for a long-term care policy, be familiar with the following terms and policy provisions. Most good policies already met or exceeded the HIPAA guidelines when they were enacted.

Guaranteed Renewable — This means that an insurance carrier cannot cancel your policy as long as the payments are made on a timely basis. It also means an insurer cannot increase premiums based on an individual's age or health *unless it does so for a whole class or category of policy holders*. Expect to have periodic increases in the premium and anticipate that group increases most likely will happen a number of times through the life of a policy. *It would not be unusual for a premium to increase 50% or more over a period of years.*

Hospital Requirements — Benefit eligibility shouldn't require that the insured be *hospitalized* immediately before admission to a nursing home. Most policies purchased over the last 10 years wouldn't require a preceding hospitalization. HIPAA mandates that hospitalization cannot be a requirement in policies eligible for favorable tax treatment unless the requirement was part of a grandfathered policy.

Benefit Eligibility

- ❑ **Functional Impairment** — HIPAA mandates that an individual be certified by a professional health-care provider as needing assistance in two of five or six activities of daily living (ADLs) for at least 90 days. An older policy grandfathered under HIPAA might vary in the number and/or specific ADLs that make the insured eligible for policy benefits.

> **Special Consideration:**
>
> **ADLs**
>
> Bathing has been identified as the first activity of daily living (ADL) with which a person usually needs assistance. If ADLs are specified, a policy holder would want bathing to be listed.

- ❑ **Cognitive Impairment** — This is defined as mental confusion that puts a person's safety or the safety of others at risk. The HIPAA mandate that a professional health-care provider certify that the condition will last at least 90 days is also applicable.
- ❑ **Medical Necessity** — This trigger was eliminated by HIPAA, but if it is included in a "grandfathered" policy, it remains valid. This means that the need for care can be validated by a doctor's written recommendation or order. It would be wise to measure this feature carefully before changing or eliminating an old policy, since it has proven to be a frequent trigger for nursing-home benefits.

Benefit-Increase Option or Inflation Coverage — This coverage is critical, since most people who buy LTC policies don't expect to need them for at least 10 and maybe as many as 30 years. HIPAA requires that this option be made available in TQ policies. However, this rider may increase the premium cost by 30-50%. A policy offering *5% compounded* annual inflation coverage is the most effective.

Daily Benefit Amount — This can range from a benefit of $20-$300 per day. Some policies pay all covered services up to policy limits. Still another type is a "pool of money" option that covers charges for services whenever and wherever needed until the fixed benefit amount is exhausted.

Coverage Options — Policies can be purchased for nursing-home care only or for care provided in any setting. Realistic consideration should be given to such things as health, gender, marital status, retirement location, projected support systems, etc. Though most people would prefer to be in their own homes, the cost of 24-hour home care could be double the daily cost of nursing-home care, thus rapidly depleting policy benefits. Many policies limit benefits for home care to 60% to 70% of the daily nursing home benefit. The gap in coverage could be considerable.

Term Length — This feature determines how long the policy will pay for care. One- to six-year policies or a lifetime benefit may be purchased. Term length is a significant cost factor. The average length of stay in a nursing home is three to four years.

Waiting Period — Policies require a waiting period before benefits start. This is usually 20-90 days or longer. The waiting period is like a deductible in that it affects the cost of the coverage.

Non-Forfeiture — This feature preserves some of the benefit even if the policy lapses. Usually, there is a requirement that the premium be paid for a minimum number of years. The policy holder is then eligible for a partial benefit.

Special Consideration:

Additional Features

Additional features are available in LTC policies. When comparing them, make certain that you're comparing "apples to apples." Additions can be costly without adding much value. Be an informed consumer and select a strong, reputable carrier.

"Living-Needs Benefits"

Living-needs benefits allow some people to access the money from life-insurance policies before their death. These benefits are for people who are terminally ill (*i.e.,* death is expected within 24 months) or chronically ill (a person who has severe cognitive impairment, or who is unable to perform two ADLs). Living benefits make it possible to pay for costly medical care or other expenses. Two common options are:

Accelerated Death Benefits — This feature gives the insured person access to a portion of the face value of his or her life-insurance policy, which can be taken as a lump-sum payment or in a series of installments before death. The life-insurance company pays the face value to the insured after a deduction to compensate for the early payout.

Viatical Settlements — In these situations, a third-party investor (the viatical settlement company) purchases the life-insurance policy of a terminally ill person by making a lump-sum payment to the insured, generally paying around 60% of the face amount. In return, the viatical company becomes the irrevocable beneficiary, collecting the full death benefit when the individual dies. The viatical company is also the policy owner and is responsible for paying the premium. Check with your state's insurance commissioner for information and regulations.

Just as life-insurance benefits are excluded from the beneficiary's personal income taxes, accelerated death benefits and viatical settlements are excluded from the policyholder's income taxes.

Items for Action

For each of the following items, assign a priority based on its importance to you: A (highest), B (medium) or C (lowest). Then check off each item as it is completed.

Priority | Completed

- ❖ Make before-tax contributions to your flexible spending accounts. ______ ❑
- ❖ If you and your spouse both work and have no dependents, see which course of action provides the most appropriate insurance for the money: single health-care coverage with your respective employers or family coverage with one employer. ______ ❑
- ❖ Always elect COBRA coverage if you leave your job and don't have health insurance. ______ ❑
- ❖ Review whether adult children have adequate insurance coverage. If they don't, they could become a "contingent liability" for you — not a legal liability, but a personal one. ______ ❑
- ❖ Evaluate your post-retirement insurance coverages to determine whether they're adequate. ______ ❑
- ❖ Review the Medicare section, and determine if the provisions apply to you or someone you know. ______ ❑
- ❖ If you work past age 65, enroll in Medicare Part A at 65. ______ ❑
- ❖ Consider obtaining a Medigap policy to supplement your Medicare coverage if you do not have a company-sponsored retiree medical plan. ______ ❑
- ❖ Review long-term care coverage issues. ______ ❑
- ❖ If you decide not to buy a long-term care insurance policy, consider investing an amount comparable to an LTC premium in a mutual fund or funds and earmark these funds for long-term care coverage. ______ ❑

Resources

AARP

601 E Street, NW
Washington, DC 20049
202/434-2277

Anyone age 50 or over can join AARP for $10 per year. For membership information call **800/424-3410** or see **www.aarp.org**. Information and research on long-term care and Medigap policies are available from AARP.

Centers for Medicare & Medicaid Services

7500 Security Boulevard
Baltimore, MD 21244-1850

For specific information about Medicare, contact Medicare customer service at **800/633-4227** or at its Web site, **www.medicare.gov**. Request the following publications:

Medicare and You 2002
Publication No. 10050

2001 Guide to Health Insurance for People with Medicare: Choosing a Medigap Policy
Publication No. 02110

Guide to Choosing a Nursing Home
Publication No. 02174

Life Management

A New Perspective

So much has changed over the past 50 years. Roles and career choices are no longer defined by gender or age. You can be president of your company in your 20s and go to college in your 80s. Money management once meant putting part of your salary in the bank to live on later. It now includes rollovers, tax deferral, risk protection, two-shares and a diversified investment portfolio. No wonder financial planning has become a business.

Independence has replaced conformity. People now are supposed to chart their own careers rather than assume they will unfold naturally within one company. We live longer and healthier. Have you kept up with the changes? Are you taking advantage of them? While all of this can be overwhelming, it's also exciting.

The previous pages of this book showed how the tools of assessment and planning can be applied to managing finances. This section shows how these tools can be applied to managing other significant aspects of life. Effective money management requires accurate assessment, good organization, valid, up-to-date information and well-defined goals. Successful management provides control and stability as well as protection against an unpredictable future. These same principles apply to life management.

Life management is a relatively new concept. In the past, adult issues were left to discovery. A generation ago, very little information was available about predictable events in adulthood. Now, this information provides opportunities to understand and direct life rather than simply react as it unfolds. The choices people make each day influence the rest of their lives. So, the management of all aspects of life must be an active, ongoing process.

The Fundamentals of Life-Management Planning

This workbook began with a planning process that is applicable to any question or problem. The following steps apply this process to life management.

❖ **Identify Your Psychological or Personality Profile**
What are your personal strengths and potential weaknesses? Are you maximizing innate strengths?

❖ **Identify Your Values and Relate Them to Your Goals**
What do you value? What is important to you? To your family? Are you on a path toward accomplishment of your goals? Have you taken the time to celebrate past or current achievements? Are lofty as well as lesser goals in place?

❖ **Organize**
Define areas of your life other than finances that will influence your future. List things you want to:

- Change — *e.g.,* health, relationships, occupation, location, activities, goals
- Initiate — *e.g.,* education, relationships, career-related objectives
- Complete — *e.g.,* education, hobbies, projects, current career goals
- Maintain — *e.g.,* health, relationships, career status, financial success, momentum toward goals, balance.

❖ **Get the Facts**
Realistically assess your current situation and make projections for the future. How do you rate your situation in the major life areas? Is there balance?

❖ **Play "What If?"**
What does the future hold? What if you were faced with a job change, the opportunity for early retirement, or a new career? Contemplate the effects of these scenarios on yourself, your spouse, others or your lifestyle. What impact would a significant change in any major life area have?

❖ **Write it Down**
An important component of the planning process is having a written plan. It aids in the assessment process, and in defining goals, identifying tasks, setting priorities and defining time frames. A "life map" is an invaluable tool.

❖ **Focus on What is Important**
What is important to you now? Could that change? If so, how? Are you satisfied with your current management of what is important? If not, what action will you take to improve it?

❖ **Identify and Use Your Resources**
Company benefits, libraries, friends, business associates, mentors, placement services, local colleges, etc.

❖ **Diversify**
Are you achieving balance between the demands and desires in your life? Does your schedule include recreation, leisure, and social, religious, volunteer and family activities?

❖ **Take Control of Your Own Life**
Are your goals providing direction and momentum in your life? Or are you primarily responding to the demands placed on you? Take responsibility for yourself. No one is better qualified to manage your life than you are.

❖ **Do It Now!**
The demands of work, family and other commitments often leave only enough time to manage what we *must* do, not what we would *like* to do. But, daily, we go about the business of making not only a career, but a life. Invest in yourself for a lifetime.

Dynamics of Change

Change is the fresh air of life and an essential part of the life process. You move, the winds of change move, and the process is called LIFE. A popular poster reads, "I cannot change the wind but I can adjust the sails." It is attitude that determines success at change. Viewing change as an opportunity rather than a frustration frees creative energy to be focused on productive actions.

Forms of Change

Change comes in several forms. Sudden, unsolicited change is the most difficult to deal with because there is no time to prepare; no control over what is happening. Gradual change is the type of change folks are best at accepting and managing. The third form of change is the kind a person initiates. A decision is made to change something and then, on his or her own or with help, (s)he makes the desired change.

Characteristics of Change

Regardless of the form of change, or whether it is regarded as positive or negative, change has three elements: *anxiety*, *excitement* and *time*. Anxiety is the first response. People tend to be cautious and uncomfortable with the unknown. On the other hand, human beings are creatures of hope. The idea of newness is exciting. Decisions usually find you rocking between these two elements. The third element is time. All changes take time to work through. The bigger the change, the more time it takes. Think back to major changes you've made in your life, like relocation, marriage or a new job. Over time, you were able to adjust. Change always evokes feelings. Dealing with change requires that you also acknowledge and deal with whatever feelings are associated with it.

Managing Change

Expect Change. Develop contingency plans by using "what-if?" scenarios in a planning process. "What if I were faced with a job change, the opportunity for early retirement, my spouse becoming employed or unemployed or changes in my personal situation?" If you think this is a waste of time, consider the term "job security." Job security at any level in any field is almost nonexistent today except, perhaps, in parenting. According to recent studies, an employee today can expect to work for three or four companies during his or her career. At least one of these job changes will be involuntary. Therefore, it's wise to consider career direction and alternatives on an ongoing basis.

Accept Change. Change is inevitable. How many changes in your life so far did you actually choose to make? Most people make far fewer changes than are made for them. How many times did what at first appeared to be the worst thing that could be happening turn out to be for the best? Did you get the position you hold now by careful planning or by chance? How did you find your first job? Did the timing of the birth of your children coincide with having all of the required time, money and energy for the task? Probably not. Did you do a good job anyway? Probably.

Assess Change. Weigh the pros and cons of opportunities or change. Reflect on the changes that have occurred over time in your life. How do you think you managed your way through them? Use the following worksheet to assess — as well as project — changes in your life. Since gradual changes are easier to manage, can you predict some changes and begin preparations now?

Managing Change

Changes I want

Now ______________________________

Future ______________________________

Changes I don't want

Now ______________________________

Future ______________________________

Changes I expect (good or bad)

Now ______________________________

Future ______________________________

What is my plan to make the desired changes happen and the undesired not happen?

Target Dates

Start	**Assess Progress**

Values Assessment

Whether or not you anticipate a change in your current job status or personal situation, and regardless of your age, the assessment worksheets that follow are valuable tools for the life-management process. Successful life management requires an ongoing, realistic and accurate assessment process similar to managing finances. Whether a change would have you seeking re-employment of any kind, retirement, volunteer opportunities, a new career or development of other interests, the key to managing is to have prepared for — or at least considered — these prospects in advance. A positive attitude and planning contribute to self-confidence and a sense of control both today and in the future.

The Time of Your Life

Life can be a wonderful experience if enjoyed to its fullest. However, balancing a full and productive career with a satisfying family life, leisure activities and friendships can be overwhelming. What is important may often be set aside for what is urgent. What is urgent (deadlines, preparations for meetings, evaluations, etc.) is not always what is really important. Answering the following questions and completing the balance sheets that follow may provide new insights into your use of time.

In what activities do you spend the most time?

What would you like to do if you had time?

What would your priorities be if you had only six months to live?

What would you like to be doing in three years? five years? ten years?

Weekday Balance Sheet

Instructions: Ten typical activities are listed in the first column. In the second column, identify the number of hours per day you spend on each activity. Represent the entire 24-hour day. Make sure the total for the 10 activities adds up to 24 hours.

For each activity, multiply Column 2 by five and enter the result in Column 4. The total at the bottom should equal 120.

COLUMN 1 **Activity**	*COLUMN 2* **Total Hours Per Day**	*COLUMN 3* **Multiply By 5**	*COLUMN 4* **Total Hours Per Week**
1. Work/Work Related Activities (*e.g.,* commuting) Home Maker/Full-Time Parent		x 5 =	
2. Sleeping		x 5 =	
3. Activities of Daily Living (eating, bathing, dressing, etc.)		x 5 =	
4. Activities with Family/Significant Other (if done in conjunction with No. 3, divide between)		x 5 =	
5. Health Maintenance/Physical Exercise		x 5 =	
6. Home/Auto Maintenance		x 5 =	
7. Relationships (non-family)		x 5 =	
8. Spiritual activities		x 5 =	
9. Education/Self Improvement		x 5 =	
10. Leisure/Recreation		x 5 =	
Total			
	(Should be 24 hours)		(Should be 120 hours)

Weekend Balance Sheet

Instructions: Identify the times for the same 10 activities on a 24-hour basis. Assume the weekend to be a two-day, 48-hour period.

For each activity, multiply Column 2 times Column 3 and enter the result in Column 4.

COLUMN 1 **Activity**	*COLUMN 2* **Total Hours Per Day**	*COLUMN 3* **Multiply By 2**	*COLUMN 4* **Total Hours Per Week**
1. Work/Work Related Activities (*e.g.,* commuting) Home Maker/Full-Time Parent		x 2 =	
2. Sleeping		x 2 =	
3. Activities of Daily Living (eating, bathing, dressing, etc.)		x 2 =	
4. Activities with Family/Significant Other (if done in conjunction with No. 3, divide between)		x 2 =	
5. Health Maintenance/Physical Exercise		x 2 =	
6. Home/Auto Maintenance		x 2 =	
7. Relationships (non-family)		x 2 =	
8. Spiritual activities		x 2 =	
9. Education/Self Improvement		x 2 =	
10. Leisure/Recreation		x 2 =	
Total			
	(Should be 24 hours)		(Should be 48 hours)

LIFE MANAGEMENT

The Pie of Life

Write the activity or color-code with colored pencils on the pie graph for the equivalent hours computed on the Balance Sheet.

Place the weekday figures in the first pie graph and the weekend figures in the second.

Weekday

Each pie segment represents 10 hours. Write the activity or color-code the weekday pie graph with the figures from the Weekday Balance Sheet.

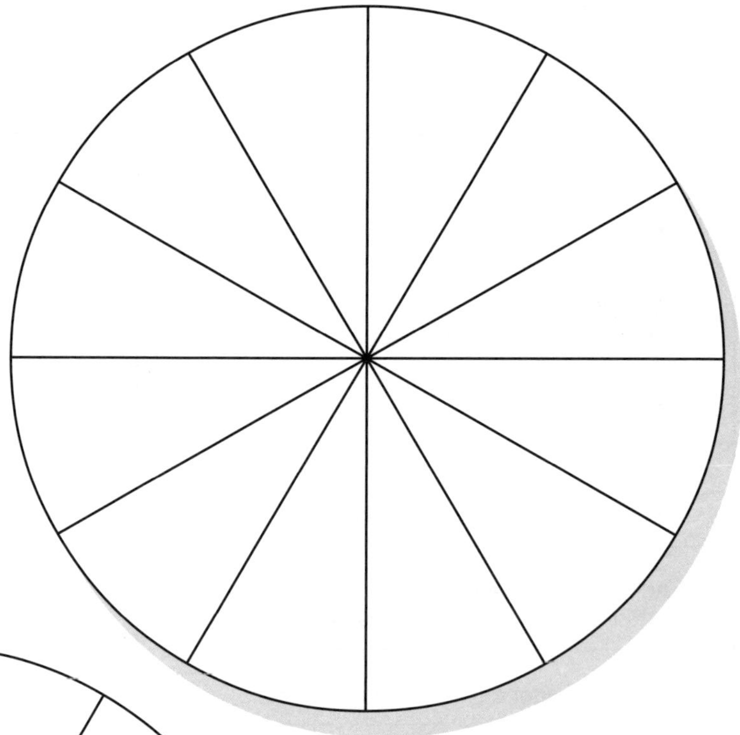

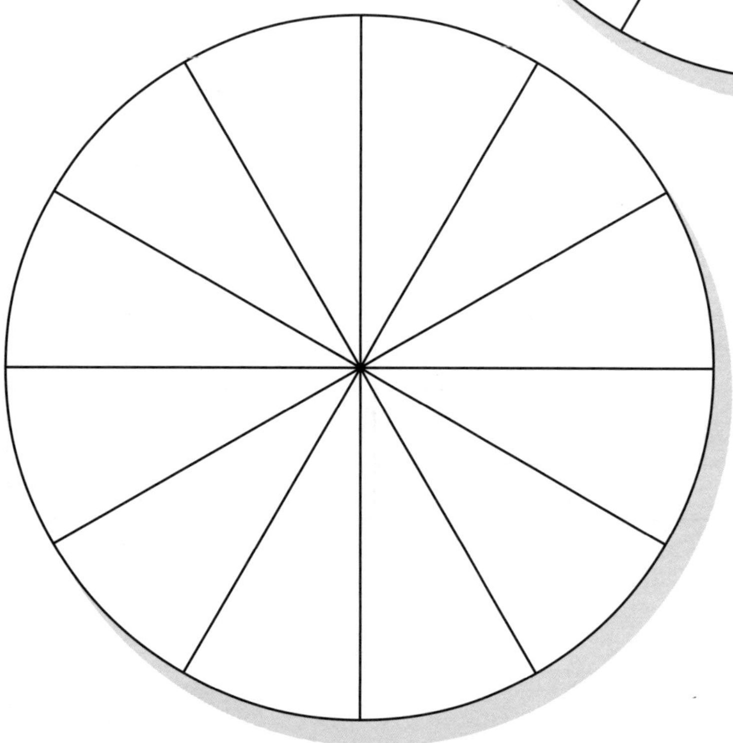

Weekend

Each pie segment represents four hours. Write the activity or color-code the weekend pie graph with the figures from the Weekend Balance Sheet.

Are you satisfied with how your time is currently allocated? If not, how can you achieve the desired balance in the use of your time? Read through the "Dynamics of Change" and "Managing Change" sections that follow and use the "Change Worksheet" to record desired specific changes and a plan of action.

Success Analysis

Success can be measured by more than just material and financial prosperity. Success can mean happiness, contentment, health, good relationships and use of talents and abilities. It also can mean integrity, faith or the ability to enjoy life. How do you measure success in your own life? What do you hope to accomplish in the future? As life progresses, what we view as important often changes. How has what is important changed for you? How might it change in the future? We build on past accomplishments and experiences but are not limited to the past to generate or predict success in the future.

My current success(es) is/are:

I have achieved my goal(s)/dream at this point in my career. Yes ❑ No ❑

My dream is to achieve/accomplish:

I have the possibility of realizing my dream at my present job. Yes ❑ No ❑

Doing what you enjoy brings ongoing career contentment. The ideal is to have it in place throughout life, not postpone it until retirement or some other future date. You're more likely to be good at what you enjoy doing.

If the answer to the last question is no, then use the *Recareering Process* worksheet to identify a career direction that will allow you to realize your dream. The *Recareering Process* worksheet is also a useful tool for those not seeking employment — simply skip the "Income Desired" line and proceed.

The Recareering Process

Objectives ____

Income Desired ____

Schedule ____

(full time/part time)

Areas of Interest	Opportunities to Market

Self-Assessment

Skills	Education	Experience	Obstacles

Requirements

Skills	Education	Experience	Obstacles

Additional Preparation

	Start Date	Completion Date

Personal Income Strategies

Important questions to consider in developing opportunities for employment:

I. "Do I need, or choose to earn, an income?" "How much?" Choose an amount.

II. "What skills or abilities are required?" "What new skills do I need to develop?"

III. "What would I enjoy doing?" "What makes me unique?"

IV. "What work schedule do I want? Full-time or part-time?"

The answers to these questions will help you create your own job description. Then you will be ready to pursue the job you desire. Begin to research the possibilities and develop the contacts now.

Options to Earn

I. Specialized Talents and Skills

Look for opportunities to use and build on your primary career focus through consulting, writing, teaching, or self-employment.

II. Basic Talents and Business Skills

Assess opportunities from previous experience. What basic skills do you have? Administrative, management, marketing, sales, secretarial, communication, financial, personnel, benefits? These skills are useful to smaller companies that often prefer part-time, experienced employees.

III. Individual Creative Assets

Hobbies and special skills can result in added income, especially if targeted to meet a specific need.

IV. New Frontiers

Adult education on all levels offers the opportunity to develop a second career focus. There are businesses and jobs today that did not exist even five years ago.

V. Business/Franchise

Contact the Small Business Administration or local businessmen for guidelines on starting your own business.

Health Strategies

Most people manage money to some extent, even if it is just reviewing account balances once a month. However, they're often too busy to consider health until it becomes a problem. Research shows that by using very simple strategies, people have the ability to preserve and even restore health. They can even slow the aging process.

Health is a person's greatest asset. Maintaining it should be a priority. Given a choice between money or health, most people would give up the money and keep the health. The older people get, the more certain they are of that choice. What do you have to lose? What do you have to gain?

If you don't already have a fitness routine, follow these simple but effective health strategies. *Moderation* and *consistency* are the guiding principles for health maintenance.

Nutrition

- ❖ Eat a well-balanced diet
- ❖ Avoid arbitrary use of dietary supplements
- ❖ Avoid "fad" diets

Exercise

- ❖ Schedule a physical exam
  - establish safe and optimal parameters
  - discover exercise alternatives if limitations exist
- ❖ Establish goals
  - choose aerobic exercise for cardiovascular benefit
  - choose an exercise that is enjoyable
  - reach the goal gradually
  - add activities for fun and variety
- ❖ Maintain a routine
  - 30 to 45 minutes duration
  - three to five days per week
- ❖ Expect results
  - more energy
  - better appearance
  - reduced stress
  - improved health
  - improved mental functioning

Moderation

- ❖ Maintain ideal body weight
- ❖ Control use of alcoholic beverages
- ❖ Eliminate or reduce smoking
- ❖ Use medications wisely
- ❖ Manage stress

Health Worksheet

Health in the past was defined only as the absence of disease. But research and the current interest in managing health and in healthy aging have resulted in a new definition: a "balance of physical, mental, social and spiritual well-being." To be healthy means not only having *focus*, but also having *balance* among these four areas. The principle of "use it or lose it" should guide health strategies. An inactive, sedentary lifestyle promotes rusting out rather than wearing out. Regardless of limitations, people should strive for improvement or the optimum potential within any limits they have. Robustness is possible in any or all of these areas. Answer the following questions to assess your current health status. Use the worksheet to develop a wellness plan.

I assess my health today as: **Excellent ❑** **Good ❑** **Average ❑** **Poor ❑**

My health concerns are:

____

____

Health Action Plan

	Action	Timing
Physical Wellness		
Nutrition		
Exercise		
Moderation		
Intellectual Growth		
Social Interaction		
Spiritual Beliefs		

Health Reflections

Use this worksheet to record significant information. Identify goals and monitor change.

Examinations	Date	Recommendations	Return Visit
Physical			
Dental			
Specialists			
Eye			

Have recommendations been implemented? Are examinations scheduled on a regular or required basis?

Baseline	Values	Goal	Date
Weight			
Blood Pressure			
Cholesterol			
Other			

Inform one pharmacist of all prescription and nonprescription medications you take regularly or frequently. Request information on safe usage.

Medications	
Prescription	Nonprescription

Health Quiz

Answer these questions (and compare your answers to the key at the bottom of the page) to determine your understanding of healthy aging.

1. Your family doctor is the person you consider most responsible for your health. T ______ F ______
2. To be healthy means not being sick. T ______ F ______
3. In general, most older people are pretty much alike. T ______ F ______
4. The changes of aging are disease changes. T ______ F ______
5. Functional cell loss occurs in all our systems as we age. T ______ F ______
6. Exercise is bad for older people. T ______ F ______
7. All five senses tend to decline with aging. T ______ F ______
8. Our nutritional needs change as we get older. T ______ F ______
9. It is wise to restrict our fluid intake as we age. T ______ F ______
10. With advancing years we need stronger doses of medicine for it to be effective. T ______ F ______
11. The majority of people past 70 are senile. T ______ F ______
12. Senility is rarely, if ever, reversible. T ______ F ______
13. Old people usually take longer to learn something new. T ______ F ______
14. Arteriosclerosis is the primary cause of senility. T ______ F ______
15. Most old people have no interest in, or capacity for, sexual relations. T ______ F ______

True: Number 5, 7, 8 (partially), and 13.
All others False.

Relationship Strategies

This workbook is focused primarily on individual planning to help you meet your goals. However, whether single or married, you are interdependent. A spouse or companion, family, friends and society at large influence to one degree or another the decisions you make. In some ways opportunities are enhanced, and in other ways restricted, by associations and relationships.

The people closest to you — husband, wife, mom, dad, son, daughter, friend — may stay the same. However, the way you relate to them changes. Indeed, as you grow through life's phases your interactions are changing because you are changing. Negotiating these changes is easier if you understand human behavior and development. Expectations become more realistic. In turn, relationships become richer, deeper and more rewarding.

Use this worksheet to describe your relationship goals with any or all of the people around you.

Spouse ______________________

Children ______________________

Grandchildren ______________________

Parents ______________________

Siblings ______________________

Friends ______________________

Neighbors ______________________

Associates ______________________

Residence Strategies

Most of the choices you make about where to live are dictated by your work, your family situation and your budget. You will have the opportunity to base your location and housing decisions more on the lifestyle you identify for retirement when family and work situations change.

If you're a corporate employee, you may have relocated several times during your career, giving you valuable experience and a greater appreciation of the issues involved.

The primary consideration should be the way you choose to live. Visualize your desired lifestyle for the next 10 years. There is no "magic" in relocating, especially in that first year. "Home" is far more than a physical structure or a particular locale. Take time to assess the tangible and intangible elements that create that special place for you. Can your present location be adapted to meet current and future changes in your lifestyle?

Location and housing are separate considerations in determining where to live. You'll need to gather information from many sources to provide a broad base for your decisions. There is no "Utopia." Consider the factors on the following page in assessing your plans.

Location Considerations

Climate

Seasonal/temperature variations
Humidity/weather patterns
Topography/altitude
Personal physical limitations

Cost of Living

Climate-related costs
Taxes
Housing, food, clothing
Travel-related expenses

Service Availability

Public transportation
Health care
Communication
Safety/protection

Involvement

Recreation/sports activities
Education/cultural opportunities
Supplemental income possibilities
Civic/church involvement

Relationships

Proximity to family/relatives
Established friendships
New friendships
Intergenerational mix
Ethnic groups
Social comfort level

Make Your Comparisons

Present Area	Option 1	Option 2

Housing Considerations

Suitability

Size/convenience/storage
Privacy/security
Adaptability/safety factors
Neighborhood

Maintenance

Routine needs
Interior
Exterior
Repair concerns

Costs

Affordable rent or mortgage
Property taxes/insurance
Maintenance/repairs
Utilities
Other service costs

Own or Rent

Single-family units
Mobile home
Manufactured housing
Condominiums/cooperatives
Adult communities
Life-care residency
Time-share ownership
Apartment rental

Make Your Comparisons

Present Area	Option 1	Option 2

Items for Action

For each of the following items, assign a priority based on its importance to you: A (highest), B (medium) or C (lowest). Then check off each item as it is completed.

	Priority	Completed
Life Management		
❖ Complete the worksheets to develop insight into the opportunities you have available.	______	❑
❖ Make a commitment to achieving a more balanced life.	______	❑
❖ Concentrate on a personal action plan with specific goals and target dates.	______	❑
Health Strategies		
❖ Maintain healthy eating patterns.	______	❑
❖ Schedule regular exercise activities.	______	❑
❖ Work not only to maintain, but to improve, your health.	______	❑
❖ Be responsible for your own health.	______	❑
❖ Watch for change.	______	❑
❖ Maintain focus and balance in all aspects of health.	______	❑
Growth Options		
❖ Broaden your interests with a new experience or activity — cultural, educational, athletic or creative.	______	❑
❖ Consider options to enhance your earning ability. What would be fun?	______	❑
❖ Develop open communication with your family and friends.	______	❑
❖ Commit time to people important to you.	______	❑
Residence Possibilities		
❖ Gather information from as many resource materials as you have available. Talk with professionals, friends, etc.	______	❑
❖ Research the options, focusing on several factors: • personal criteria • economic feasibility • health-care availability • social, cultural and educational opportunities	______	❑
❖ Explore selected areas personally to determine suitability.	______	❑
❖ Rent, rather than buy, for one year.	______	❑
❖ Consider redesigning current residence.	______	❑
❖ Coordinate with partner on all items.	______	❑

Resources

General

Bridges, William
Transitions: Making Sense of Life's Transitions
Addison-Wesley Pub. Co.

Bridges, William
Managing Transitions
Addison-Wesley Pub. Co.

Chopra, Depak, M.D.
Ageless Body, Timeless Mind
Harmony Books

Covey, Steven R.
First Things First
Simon & Schuster

Dychtwald, Ken
Age Wave
Jeremy P. Tarcher Inc.

Heilman, Joan R.
Unbelievably Good Deals & Great Adventures That You Absolutely Can't Get Unless You're Over 50
Contemporary Books

Johnson, Spencer, M.D.
One Minute for Myself
Avon Books

Peck, M. Scott
The Road Less Travelled
Simon & Schuster

Salwen, Judy
Solo Retirement
Dodd, Mead & Co.

Seskin, Jane
Alone, Not Lonely
AARP Books

Sheehy, Gail
New Passages
Random House

Tieger, Paul and Barbara B.
Do What You Are
Little Brown & Co.

Weaver, Peter
Strategies for the Second Half of Life
Franklin Watts

Career Transitions

Bird, Caroline
Second Careers: New Ways to Work After 50
Little Brown & Company

Bolles, Richard N.
The New Quick Job-Hunting Map
Ten Speed Press

The Three Boxes of Life
Ten Speed Press

What Color is Your Parachute? A Practical Manual for Job-Hunters and Career Changers
Ten Speed Press

Cetron, Marvin J.
Jobs of the Future
McGraw-Hill

Lamdin, Lois
Earn College Credit for What You Know
Kendall-Hunt

Lathrop, Richard
Who's Hiring Who?
Ten Speed Press

Marsh, DeLoss L.
Retirement Careers: Combining the Best of Work & Leisure
Williamson Publishing

Redd, Robert O.
Achievers Never Quit
Thornapple Publishing, Co.

Sernaque, Vivienne
Part Time Jobs
Ballantine Books

Tenenbaum, Frances
184 Businesses Anyone Can Start and Make a Lot of Money
The editors of *Entrepreneur*
Bantam Books

Other

CAEL (Council for the Advancement of Learning) — Career and education planning as well as guidance in obtaining college credit for non-academic experience.
800/497-5465

CLEP (College Level Examination Program) — CLEP exams are given regularly to people who want to test their knowledge in different areas and earn college credit without having to take courses. Contact local college for information.

Internet Contacts

Job Postings:
www.hotjobs.com
www.careermosaic.com
www.monster.com
www.careers.msn.com
www.careerbuilders.com

Research Corporations:
www.hoovers.com — Hoover Business Network

Salary Survey:
www.wsj.com — Wall Street Journal

Corporation Home Page:
www.cael.org — Verizon

Residence and Travel

Boyer, Richard, and David Savageau
Places Rated Retirement Guide
Rand-McNally & Co.

Dickinson, Peter A.
Guide to Academic Travel
Shaw Associates

Travel and Retirement Edens Abroad
An AARP book
Scott Foresman & Co.

Savageau, David
Retirement Places Rated
Prentice Hall

Shakman, Robert A
Where You Live May Be Hazardous to Your Health
Stein & Day, Scarborough House

Symons, Allene, and Jane Parker
Adventures Abroad: Exploring the Travel/Retirement Option
Gateway Books

Cool Works (www.coolworks.com/showme) lists paid and volunteer, seasonal and full-time jobs at parks, resorts, camps, dude ranches and cruise ships.

Caring for Elderly Parents

Jarvick, Lissy, and Gary Small
Parentcare
Crown Publishers

Kenny, Dennis E., and Elizabeth N. Oettinger
The Family CAREbook
CAREsource Program Development

Levin, Mora Jean
How to Care for Your Parents: A Handbook for Adult Children
Storm King Press

Mace, Nancy, and Peter Rapins
The 36-Hour Day
Warner Books

National Academy of Elder Law Attorneys, Inc.
1804 North Country Club Road
Tuscon, AZ 85716-3195
www.naela.org

Shapiro, Barbara A.
The Big Squeeze
Mells & Sanerson Publishing

Shelley, Florence D.
When Your Parents Grow Old
Harper & Row

Tomorrow's Choices
AARP Special Project

Caregivers Assistance

National Association of Area Agencies on Aging — This organization's mission is to "assist older Americans to maximize independence and independent living with dignity." It serves as a focal point in a nationwide system of elder-care services and resources. For information: www.n4a.org.

National Family Care Givers Association — offers information and support to all family caregivers. Small membership fee. *For information:* www.nfcacares.org.

The Well Spouse Foundation — offers support to the partners of chronically ill or disabled individuals. *For information:* www.wellspouse.org.

Retirement Opportunities

Peace Corps — provides professional and technical experts as well as other talents and experience to developing countries. Training is provided in language and culture. Fields such as agriculture, engineering, math/science, home economics, education, skilled trades, forestry, fisheries, and community development are typical areas of concentration. Living and travel expenses are covered by the Corps. Married couples are eligible and will be assigned together. *For information:*

Peace Corps, 1111 20th Street, North West, Washington, DC 20526
(800) 424-8580
www.peacecorps.com

Volunteers in Technical Assistance (VITA) — a non-profit international organization providing volunteer experts to developing countries. Interactions are done primarily by correspondence and address such issues as small-business development, energy applications, agriculture, reforestation, water supply, sanitation and low-cost housing. Other services include project planning, translations of publications, marketing strategies and more. A person must be retired to serve. Travel and living expenses are reimbursed for on-site consultation. *For information:*

Volunteers in Technical Assistance, 1600 Wilson Blvd., Suite 710, Arlington, VA 22209
(703) 276-1800

Operation ABLE (Ability Based on Long Experience) — a nonprofit organization affiliated with agencies to match job seeker with employer. The organization provides job counseling, on-the-job training, individual career assessment and guidance, and teaches job-hunting skills as well as providing a myriad of other services. It primarily serves metropolitan areas, though it is expanding. *For information:*

Operation ABLE, 16250 Northland Drive, Suite 102, Southfield, MI 78075-5226
(800) 922-4473
jobhotline.org/able.htm

Elder Craftsman — a non-profit organization that provides advice, training courses and a retail outlet for seniors age 55 and older who want to make and sell their own handcrafts. Handwork is marketed at an outlet with 60% of the price going to the crafter. In addition, the organization provides patterns and materials to skilled craftspeople who are then paid by the piece. *For information:*

The Elder Craftsman, Inc., 135 E. 65th Street, New York, NY 10021
(212) 319-8128

National Executive Service Corps — assists nonprofit organizations in solving problems through the use of retired executives with extensive corporate and professional experience. The Corps serves five basic types of organizations: education, health, arts, social services and religious. Volunteers' expenses are paid. *For information:*

National Executive Service Corps, 622 Third Ave., New York, NY 10017-6753
(212) 269-1234

National Senior Service Corps — provides training and placement in numerous programs. Retired Senior Volunteer program, Foster Grandparents Program, and the Senior Companion Program. *For information:*

1201 New York Avenue, NW, Washington, DC 20525
(800) 424-8867
www.cns.gov/senior/

Adult Space Academy — lets participants guide astronaut training simulators through a space shuttle mission and expand their knowledge of space science and history. *For information:*

U.S. Space Camp, One Tranquillity Base, Huntsville, AL 35805
(800) 63-SPACE
www.spacecamp.com

Shelter Institute — teaches participants the skills they need to create their own dream home. Classes include physics of materials, plumbing, carpentry and electrical wiring. Classes are conducted to promote understanding of the building process and more efficient use of contractors. Classes vary in length and cost. *For information:*

Shelter Institute, 38 Center Street, Bath, ME 04530
(207) 442-7938
www.shelterinstitute.com

Wooden Boat School — provides the opportunity to learn to build or sail a boat. Tuition varies. *For information:*

Wooden Boat School, Naskeag Road, Brooklin, ME 04616
(207) 359-4651
www.woodenboat.com

Special Interest

National Audubon Society (CT) — Natural-history programs in many states. *For information:*

(800) 274-4201 or (212) 979-3080
editor@audubon.org

University Vacation (Univac) — Universities in England, France, Italy and other countries provide morning classes with afternoons free for excursions. Lectures provided on a variety of topics. *For information:*

U.S. Headquarters, "Writers' Corner," 2660 Bongainville Road, Coconut Grove, FL 33133-6505
(800) 792-0100

Close-Up Foundation — daily briefings, presentations by representatives and senators and other officials, tours and theater are part of this educational vacation. *For information:*

44 Canal Center Plaza, Alexandria, VA 22314-1592
(800) 544-6087
www.closeup.org/resource.htm.com

Grandparents & Grandchildren Camps — located in the Adirondacks in Sagamore, NY. *For information:*

(315) 354-5311

Interhostel — University of NH. Trips for two or more weeks for older adults or older adults and their grandchildren. *For information:*

(800) 733-9753
www.learn.unh.edu/interhostel

Elderhostel — an educational adventure for older adults. Must be at least 55 years of age. *Request a catalog:*

75 Federal Street, Boston, MA 02110
(877) 426-8056

House Swapping — registry of national and international homes. Unique and less-expensive travel opportunity. *For information:*

Intervac – (800) 756-4663
The Invented City – (800) 788-2489

Glossary

Active Participation — When you make the decisions regarding the management of a rental property you own.

Adjusted Gross Estate — An individual's gross estate less allowable deductions for mortgages, bank loans, etc.

Adjusted Gross Income (AGI) — All income subject to tax less certain deductions permitted by law, such as unreimbursed business expenses, alimony, deductible contributions to IRAs, etc. It is used as a basis for determining the amounts deductible for miscellaneous deductions, casualty or theft losses and medical expenses.

Administrator — A person appointed by the court to supervise the handling of an individual's estate in the event no will has been executed.

Alternative Minimum Tax — An additional tax that applies to individuals, trusts and estates with certain tax-preference items.

Annuitant — The person who is covered by an annuity and who normally will receive its benefits.

Annuity —

1. The specified monthly or annual payment to a pensioner.
2. An investment contract that provides a series of payments either for life or another specified period.

Assignment — A transfer of the ownership rights of an insurance contract. In order to be valid when the claim is paid, any assignment must be filed in writing with the insurance company.

Automatic Premium Loan — A provision that allows an insurance company to use a life insurance policy's cash value automatically to meet premium payments.

Basis — For tax purposes, the value used as the starting point in figuring gain or loss.

Before-Tax Contributions — Payments to a retirement plan or flexible benefit plan made from payroll deductions prior to the calculation of federal and, generally, state income-tax withholding. (Flexible-benefit-plan contributions also are exempt from Social Security and Medicare withholding.) These payroll deductions are excluded from your reported *W-2* taxable earnings.

Beneficiary — The party who receives proceeds under an insurance policy, trust or will.

Callable Bond — A bond that may be redeemed under stated conditions by the issuing municipality or corporation prior to maturity.

Capital Asset — This term refers to any property, whether or not connected with a trade or business. A taxpayer's household furnishings, personal residence and automobile are capital assets. Although gain on the sale of this kind of property is treated as capital gain, no loss is recognized for income-tax purposes unless the property was held for the production of income.

Capital Gain or Loss — Gains and losses resulting from the sale of capital assets. They are classified as long-term or short-term, depending on the length of time the asset was held.

Cash-Balance Plans — Along with pension-equity plans, these retirement plans typically calculate lump-sum payouts rather than annuities. They also tend to feature a more even accrual rather than the seniority-weighted accrual of traditional pension plans and generally are more "portable," in the sense that vested employees can take the accrued lump sum with them whenever they leave employment.

Cash Value — The "savings element" in a permanent life insurance policy, which is the legal property of the policy owner.

Certificate of Deposit — A time deposit with a specified maturity date.

Codicil — A brief document that amends a will.

CollegeSure CD — a certificate of deposit designed to pay (upon maturity) the average cost of a year's tuition, general fees, and room and board at a four-year private college in the United States.

Community Property — Property owned "in common" (both persons owning it all) by a husband and wife that is acquired while residing in a community-property state.

Coupon Bond — A bond with interest coupons attached. Coupons are clipped as they come due and are presented to the issuer for payment.

Credit Exemption Amount — That portion of a decedent's estate that is sheltered from federal estate taxes by the credit for transfers upon death. In 2002 and 2003, this amount is $1,000,000 and increases to $1,500,000 in 2004.

Death Benefit — The proceeds of the policy that will be paid after the death of the insured.

Decedent — A person who has died recently.

Dependent — In 2002, a person is a dependent if the following conditions are met:

1. His or her gross income is less than $3,000. However, if the individual is a child of the taxpayer and is either a student or under 19, the $3,000 gross-income rule is waived.
2. Taxpayer supplies over half of the support of the dependent; and
3. The dependent is either a close relative of the taxpayer or has his principal place of abode with the taxpayer.

Dependent Student — For federal student financial aid, a student who is 23 years old or younger and dependent on his or her parents for financial support.

Depreciation — An annual deduction allowed by the Internal Revenue Code for a portion of the cost or other basis of capital assets used during the year in a trade or business or held for the production of income.

Disclaimer — The refusal, rejection or renunciation of a claim, power or property.

Diversification — A key concept in investing that means not having "all your eggs in one basket." Investors can diversify portfolios in at least three different ways: *among asset categories* (cash, stocks, fixed-income investments), *within asset categories* (using different asset classes) and *over time* (through dollar-cost averaging).

Dividend —

1. A portion of a corporation's profits that is distributed to stockholders. The amount of the dividend is determined by the corporation's board of directors. (Not all stocks pay dividends.)
2. A portion of a mutual fund paid to its shareholders.
3. Return of premium on a life insurance policy (not taxable).

Domicile — An individual's permanent home.

Endowment Insurance — A permanent life-insurance policy that offers death protection for a specified period of time. If the insured lives past the period specified, the contract pays the face amount of the policy to the insured.

Estate Tax — A tax paid on property that is owned at an individual's death. The tax is paid on the property as a whole before it is distributed.

Estate-Tax Balance Sheet — A summary of all property that an individual has an interest in at his or her death (our term for the Federal Estate Tax Return, *Form 706*).

Executor — An individual appointed through a will to administer and distribute property upon the testator's death.

Exemption — An amount for you and each of your dependents by which you are allowed to reduce your income subject to tax. In 2002, each exemption is worth $3,000. Exemptions are phased out for high-income taxpayers.

Expected Family Contribution (EFC) — The amount that a student's family would be expected to contribute to the cost of a college education. This figure includes parental contribution as well as the student's contributions from earnings and assets.

Fiduciary — An individual who manages property or acts for another individual and is placed in a position of trust.

Financial Need — The difference between the total cost of college attendance and the expected family contribution.

Flexible Spending Accounts — Employer-sponsored savings accounts that allow you to set aside money with before-tax contributions for health-care and dependent-care expenses.

Form W-4 — An employee's withholding allowance certificate. The form is filed with the employer so that the employer can withhold federal income tax from pay. *Form W-4* remains in effect until the employee changes it. By correctly completing this form, the employee can match the amount of tax withheld from wages to his or her tax liability.

401(k) Savings Plan — An employer-sponsored savings (or thrift) plan offered as a retirement savings vehicle. The maximum amount an employee can contribute to the plan each year is dictated by tax laws and the plan's rules. Investment options vary by company.

Free Application for Federal Student Aid (FAFSA) — The form required to determine eligibility for all federal financial aid programs.

Gift — Any willing transfer of money or property without payment. There must be a showing of "detached and disinterested generosity."

Gift Tax — A tax imposed on the transfer of money or property through gifts made by an individual.

Grantor — A person who establishes a trust and makes a gift. Also called a settlor.

Grants — Financial aid awards that do not have to be repaid.

Guardian — An individual who has the legal right and duty to take care of another person or his or her property because that person cannot legally take care of himself or herself.

Home-Equity Loan or Line of Credit — A form of second mortgage secured by the excess equity (*i.e.,* equity over the balance of the first mortgage) in a home. Interest paid on these loans generally is tax-deductible.

Income Beneficiary — A trust beneficiary who can receive income (as opposed to principal) from trust assets.

Incompetency — Refers to individuals who lack the ability or legal right to manage their own affairs.

Independent Student — For federal student financial aid, a student who is either 24 years old by December 31 of the academic year in which he or she wants to receive aid, married, a graduate or professional student, someone with legal dependents other than a spouse, an orphan or ward of the court, or a veteran.

Individual Retirement Account (IRA) — A tax-sheltered investment vehicle designed primarily for the purpose of putting aside money for use later in life (*i.e.,* retirement).

Inflation — A rise in the cost of goods and services corresponding to a decreasing value of currency, usually measured by the Consumer Price Index (CPI).

Inheritance Tax — A tax on money or property that an individual inherits.

Intangible Drilling Costs — An operator's expense for wages, fuel, repairs, hauling and supplies incurred in the preparation and drilling of oil and gas wells.

Interest — A charge for borrowing money, paid by the issuer of a security (usually a bond) to the lender. If you're the lender, you *earn* interest; if you're the borrower, you *pay* interest.

Inter Vivos — Between the living; from one living person to another.

Intestate — Dying without having made a valid will.

Irrevocable Trust — A trust that cannot be changed, altered or revoked.

Itemized Deductions — Deductions from adjusted gross income for various taxes, interest paid, charitable contributions and miscellaneous. If a taxpayer's deductions are less than the standard deductions, the taxpayer uses the standard deductions. Otherwise, the taxpayer uses his/her total itemized deductions.

Joint-and-Survivor Annuity — Periodic payments that are made to two beneficiaries. At the death of the first beneficiary, the survivor will continue to receive payments.

Joint Ownership — Ownership of property by more than one person.

Joint Tenancy — A form of joint ownership in which, if one of the owners dies, his or her interest in the property automatically passes to the other joint owner(s).

Keogh Plan — A self-funded, tax-sheltered retirement plan available for self-employed individuals if they have net self-employment income (*i.e.,* a profit from self-employment activity).

Legal Age — The age at which an individual becomes old enough to make a contract, generally 18 to 21 in most states.

Legatee — A person who inherits property by will.

Life Estate — A property right, the duration of which is limited to the life of a person holding it.

Living Trust — A trust that can take effect while you're alive; the chief benefit is its asset-management potential while the beneficiary is still alive but legally incapacitated. Also valuable as a way to organize and collect assets before death, saving time and administration expenses after death. See also Inter vivos.

Load Fund — A mutual fund that charges a sales fee for buying or selling shares.

Margin — The amount paid by the customer when broker's credit is used to purchase securities.

Marital Deduction — A deduction allowed under certain conditions for federal estate-tax purposes for property left to a surviving spouse.

Maturity Date — The date on which a loan or bond comes due and is to be paid off.

Net-Payment Index — A method of comparing the cost of term life-insurance policies developed and formalized by the National Association of Insurance Commissioners.

No-Load Fund — A mutual fund that doesn't charge a sales fee for buying or selling shares.

Nonprobate Property — Property that passes without reference to a will.

Passive Activity — An investment, trade or business in which the taxpayer does not participate materially. In order to materially participate, the taxpayer must be involved in the activity on a regular, continuous and substantial basis. Limited-partnership interests and rental activities are passive activities by definition.

Personal Interest — Interest on credit cards, automobile loans and other personal debt. This interest generally is not tax-deductible.

Power of Appointment — A part of an individual's will, deed or trust document that gives someone the right to decide who will receive property or how the property will be used.

Power of Attorney — A document that authorizes someone to act on someone else's behalf.

Preference Items — Certain income and deduction items that receive preferential tax treatment, for example, accelerated depreciation. These preference items are added to income to determine whether the taxpayer is subject to the Alternative Minimum Tax.

Preferred Stock — A class of stock with a claim to the company's earnings before payment to common stockholders can be made.

Principal — The face value of the debt.

Probate — 1) The process of proving that a will is genuine; 2) distributing property that passes according to the terms of a will.

Qualified State Tuition Programs — State-sponsored, prepaid-tuition and college-savings plans that qualify for special tax treatment under §529 of the Internal Revenue Code.

Remaindermen — Typically, a trust beneficiary who receives the "remainder" (*i.e.,* the property remaining) upon the death of the income beneficiary.

Return — An investor's profits, whether through interest, dividends or capital appreciation.

Revocable — Susceptible to being altered, modified or cancelled.

Rider — A form attached to an insurance contract that modifies the benefits and conditions of coverage.

Self-Employment Tax — A tax imposed in lieu of Social Security and Medicare Tax on your net earnings from a farm or personal business.

Self-Proving Will — A will requiring witnesses to sign an affidavit indicating that the testator was of sound mind, etc., at the time the will was signed and witnessed.

Simplified Employee Pension (SEP) — A plan in which a company contributes vested, tax-sheltered funds on behalf of employees who are at least 25 years old and who have worked for the company for at least three years out of the past five. The contribution amounts usually are based on company profits, so the plan becomes a pension profit-sharing plan.

Standard Deduction — For 2002, the standard deduction for non-itemizers is $7,850 for joint filers, $4,700 for single filers and $6,900 for head-of-household filers. The standard deduction is increased for individuals who are age 65 or over and for those who are legally blind.

Tax Credits — An IRS-allowed subtraction from a taxpayer's calculated tax. Income tax credits include the child tax credit and education tax credits.

Tax-Exempt Yield — The yield on a debt security that pays the holder interest that is free from federal, state and local taxes if the investor resides in the state offering the bond.

Tenancy by the Entirety — A form of joint ownership between husband and wife that includes a right of survivorship. At the death of the first spouse, his or her interest in the property will pass to the surviving spouse.

Tenancy-in-Common — A form of joint ownership between two or more individuals that does not include a survivorship element; at the death of one of the owners, his or her interest in the property may be designated to a future owner.

Term Insurance — Life insurance that doesn't feature cash accumulation and provides pure insurance protection for a specified period of time.

Testamentary — Having to do with a will. A testamentary trust is part of the will and can take effect only at death.

Testator — A person who makes a will.

Treasury Bills — Short-term debt issued by the U.S. government.

Trust — A property interest held by one person for the benefit of another.

Trustee — A person who holds money or property for the benefit of another.

Two-Share Plan — An estate plan that creates two shares: 1) the credit-shelter share, held in trust and in an amount up to the credit exemption amount; also called the "bypass trust" since it bypasses federal estate taxes at the deaths of both spouses; it typically is held for the surviving spouse's benefit and at that spouse's death is passed to the children; and 2) a marital share, held either in trust or passed outright to the surviving spouse, usually to take advantage of the unlimited marital deduction; sometimes called the "A" share.

Will — A legal document in which a person declares how his or her possessions will pass after his or her death.

Withholding — Deduction of federal and state income taxes from your paycheck for the pre-payment of your tax liability for the year.

Whole-Life Insurance — A level amount of permanent life insurance, with increasing cash values. Premiums are paid for the entire life of the insured.

Yield — The interest rate paid to investors.

Zero-Coupon Bond — A bond that is sold at a discount and doesn't pay interest. Instead, the bond's value grows over time. For example, a 20-year zero-coupon bond with a 7% effective annual yield might initially sell for $258 and pay $1,000 at maturity in 20 years. Long-term zero-coupon bonds are more volatile than long-term bonds that pay a coupon. The annual "accretions" in the bond's value are subject to income taxes (unless it's a municipal bond); so these bonds are often held in IRAs, Keoghs and SEPs.

Index

A

B

C

INDEX

F

L

M

INDEX

S

INDEX

INDEX

Notes

Notes

Notes

Ayco's *Money in Motion*® program

This unique program gives you access to The Ayco Financial Planning Center through its two main services, the toll-free (U.S. only) *Ayco AnswerLine*® and the Ayco Financial Network (aycofn.com). The *AnswerLine* connects you to an experienced and objective financial planner who can help you build a more secure future for yourself and your family by making smart decisions and avoiding key mistakes. Aycofn.com allows you to input and store financial data on a password-protected, interactive Web site, and its Online Financial Plan provides a written plan for improving your personal finances. The real strength of this very reasonably priced program, however, is that you can get personalized, one-on-one advice whenever you need it. The program's components will depend on the option you choose. See the order form on the previous page for available options. Our service components are:

The Ayco AnswerLine®

Personal financial counseling

At the core of these options is *The Ayco AnswerLine*.® Through this toll-free service (U.S. only) you can work with an experienced, professional financial planner who understands your company benefit plans and can help you integrate them into your personal plan.

The *AnswerLine* is available Monday – Friday, 9 am – 8 pm ET, to help you:

- ❖ Invest your money;
- ❖ Maximize your benefit plans;
- ❖ Plan your child's education;
- ❖ Plan for retirement;
- ❖ Protect your assets and income;
- ❖ Receive personalized reports on *Retirement Planning, Education Funding, Life-insurance Planning* and *Asset Allocation;*
  ... and much more.

The Ayco Financial Network

Interactive financial planning Web site

- ❖ A personal financial plan that can be updated anytime;
- ❖ A personal financial scorecard to assess your financial health and track progress;
- ❖ Educational materials on cash flow, debt management, investments, estate planning, insurance, education funding, tax planning and key life events;
- ❖ Helpful, easy-to-use financial calculators for financial modeling and projections;
- ❖ Answers to FAQs – frequently asked questions on financial planning issues;
- ❖ *Updates* newsletters online;
- ❖ Hot links to over 100 sites;
- ❖ *The Ayco-Approved List of Mutual Funds;* and
- ❖ Encryption technologies and password protection to help protect your data.

The Online Financial Plan

Consultation

Simplified questionnaire with straightforward questions about financial goals that takes less than 15 minutes to complete.

Assessment

Quick recap and assessment of financial goals based upon answers from questionnaire.

Interview

Interview areas include:

- ❖ Personal and household information
- ❖ Retirement
- ❖ Goals
- ❖ Income
- ❖ Social Security
- ❖ Savings
- ❖ Investments

Core Financial Plan

Comprehensive view of financial goals, with strategies and specific action items to meet those goals. Each topic includes:

- ❖ Summary and Let's Review sections
- ❖ Analysis
- ❖ Recommendations
- ❖ Explanatory text
- ❖ Links to Resources and Glossary for help.

Ayco's *Updates* Newsletter

News you can use

- ❖ Authoritative yet easy-to-read source of practical advice on planning issues specifically geared to corporate employees;
- ❖ Includes additions and deletions to *The Ayco-Approved List of Mutual Funds;*
- ❖ Published monthly except for July and December.

The Ayco-Approved List of Mutual Funds

The *Approved List* consists of approximately 60 high-quality, no-load, diversified mutual funds in each major investment category. Each fund on the *Approved List* is chosen and monitored by Ayco's Investment Planning Group. The selection process is completely objective. Ayco is not affiliated directly or indirectly with any of the recommended funds and receives no compensation from them. You are encouraged to call *The Ayco AnswerLine* for help in selecting mutual funds that are right for you.

Personal Retirement Counseling

This comprehensive service provides you with access to a qualified financial planner to help make smart financial decisions at retirement. You will discuss topics such as Investment Planning, Income Tax Planning, Estate Planning, Employee Benefits and Social Security. You will also receive the following personalized reports:

- ❖ Retirement Cash Flow Analysis
- ❖ Investment Allocation Model

You will also have a teleconference with your financial counselor to review your reports in detail and six month's follow-up access to your counselor in case of additional questions or concerns.

2002 ORDER FORM

		Cost	Qty.	Total
Option 1:	*Money in Motion* financial education system [Includes three hours of toll-free access (U.S. only) to *The Ayco AnswerLine,*® 10 *Updates* newsletters, *The Ayco-Approved List of Mutual Funds, Investing in Your Future* guidebook and the Ayco Financial Network and Online Financial Plan]	$359	_____	$ _________
Option 2:	*The Ayco AnswerLine* (up to three hours toll-free; U.S. only)	$249	_____	$ _________
Option 3:	10 *Updates* newsletters (monthly)	$40	_____	$ _________
Option 4:	*The Ayco AnswerLine* and 10 *Updates* newsletters	$279	_____	$ _________
Option 5:	*Investing in Your Future* guidebook	$30	_____	$ _________
Option 6:	*RetireRight*® — Personalized Retirement Counseling (complete with exhibits) For Retirement Planning **Option 6** please call **800/334-8963**.			

To order by phone: 800/437-6383
To order by mail, send to:
The Ayco Company, L.P. – MIM,
P.O. Box 15073, Albany, NY 12212-5073

Subtotal $ _________
Shipping and handling (*$5 per item*) $ _________
Total cost $ _________

Prices as of Jan. 2002

If you have questions about any of these options or if you would like to order with a credit card, please call our Customer Service Department at **800/437-6383** • 9 a.m. – 5 p.m. Eastern Time • Monday – Friday (except holidays). Credit card orders also can be faxed to **518/464-2121**.

To order by mail (U.S. address only), fill in the information below (please print):

Name ______________________ Social Security # ______________
(This is your identification number for the *AnswerLine*)

Street ______________________ Apt. ______________
(Please note: street address required; UPS will not deliver to a P.O. Box)

City ______________________ State ___________ Zip ___________

Phone # (daytime) (   ) ______________________

❑ Payment enclosed ❑ Please bill my credit card

Card name: ❑ MasterCard ❑ Visa

Card number: ______________________

Expiration date: ______________

____
Company (affiliation)

____
Signature (all credit-card orders must be signed)

OFFICE USE ONLY: DATE REC'D: ______________ FULFILLMENT DATE: ______________

FM-FRS-226.11/2001

Update to 2002 edition of ...

INVESTING IN YOUR FUTURE

A complete guide to financial planning ...

... for every stage of life

THE AYCO COMPANY, L.P.

Published by
The Ayco Company, L.P. • P.O. Box 15073 • Albany, NY 12212-5073

Retirement Planning

Update to page 62

Using Substantially Equal Periodic Payments

One way to avoid the 10% additional tax is to receive your distribution from an IRA — and, possibly, from a qualified plan — in "substantially equal periodic payments" (SEPPs) based on your life expectancy. To qualify for this exception, you must receive these payments at least annually over your life expectancy (or the joint life expectancies of you and a beneficiary).

Generally, once you begin withdrawing SEPPs, you must continue this distribution method for the ***longer*** of five years or until you attain age 59½. If you change the payment schedule before meeting one of these requirements, the 10% additional tax will be imposed retroactively on all early (pre-age 59½) distributions. To illustrate, if you start taking SEPPs at age 57 and modify your payment schedule before age 62, the IRS imposes the 10% penalty on all taxable withdrawals before age 59½. However, in a revenue ruling issued late in 2002 (*Rev Rul 2002-62*), the IRS indicated that, under certain circumstances, it would allow a one-time change in the payment schedule without imposing the 10% additional tax (see update to page 67). For SEPP distributions beginning after 2002, the provisions of *Revenue Ruling 2002-62* are controlling.

Calculating SEPPs — There are several ways to qualify a withdrawal as a SEPP. One is by purchasing a commercial annuity contract from an insurance company. An annuity payable for your life with a term-certain feature will also qualify under this exception. However, a form of payment consisting solely of a term certain — for example, 10 equal installments — does not qualify because it is not based on life expectancy.

You don't have to invest in an annuity to qualify under the SEPP exception. Those who have other investments in their company's qualified plan or IRA — like stocks, bonds and mutual funds — can take withdrawals (annually or more frequently) that will qualify as SEPPs. Many company savings plans offer a "life-expectancy" distribution option that qualifies as a SEPP. Or you can take SEPP withdrawals from your IRA or company's qualified plan, if there is a right to post-retirement withdrawals.

In IRS *Notice 89-25*, taxpayers were provided with three "safe-harbor" methods for calculating SEPPs. In subsequent private letter rulings, the IRS has indicated that these payment methods are intended to serve as examples and are not the only distribution methods that will satisfy its requirements. However, in *Revenue Ruling 2002-62* the IRS provided new guidance on how the three "safe-harbor" methods work. We recommend the use of one of these methods, which we've described on the following pages.

Update to pages 63 through 66

SEPP "Safe-Harbor" Methods

Required Minimum Distribution Method — Under this method, previously referred to as the "life-expectancy method," divide your account balance for that year by the appropriate life-expectancy factor for your age or the ages of you and your beneficiary. You must recalculate the payment amount each year, using your account balance for that year and your current life expectancy. If you compare the required minimum distribution method to the other two methods, it produces the lowest initial payment but provides larger amounts in later years.

Example: Account balance $50,000
Age 50
Life expectancy 34.2 years (from update to page 64)
$50,000 ÷ 34.2 = $1,462 payment for following year

In *Revenue Ruling 2002-62*, the IRS indicated that there are three life-expectancy tables that can be used for purposes of the SEPP calculation — a single-life table that we've reproduced in part at the top of the next page; a joint life table; and the Uniform Lifetime Table (see update to page 73). The same life-expectancy table that is used for the first distribution year must be used in each following year.

Additionally, the account balance that is used to determine the payment amount must be determined in a reasonable manner. Based on the revenue ruling, it would be reasonable to use the value either on December 31 of the prior year or on a date within a reasonable period before that year's distribution. For subsequent years, consider consulting a tax advisor when determining an appropriate valuation date.

Fixed Amortization Method — An alternative method is to amortize your account balance over a number of years equal to your life expectancy based on one of the three IRS-approved tables using your chosen interest rate on the date payments begin. This payment can be calculated using a financial calculator or by using the *Calculating SEPPs Using the Fixed Amortization Method* worksheet. The amount is fixed for the life of the SEPP — you shouldn't recalculate each year.

Example: Account balance $50,000
Age 50
Life expectancy 34.2 years (from update to page 64)
Interest rate 4%
$2,611 annual payment

The interest rate that may be used is any interest rate that is not more than 120% of the federal mid-term rate for either of the two months immediately preceding the month in which your payment begins. The federal mid-term rates are available through the IRS's Web site (www.irs.gov).

Calculating SEPPs Using the Fixed Amortization Method

Use the two tables on the next page to help you complete this worksheet.

		Example	You
Line 1:	Your current age	50	
Line 2:	Life expectancy (rounded)	34 years (IRS)	
Line 3:	Reasonable interest rate	4%	
Line 4:	Account balance	$50,000	
Line 5:	Factor from the following page (Look up the factor based on your interest rate and life expectancy)	19.1476	
Line 6:	Divide Line 4 by Line 5 to calculate the annual SEPP (50,000 ÷ 19.1476)	$2,611	

Note: This calculation assumes that both principal and interest are depleted gradually over your lifetime. The life expectancy in this example is based on the IRS Single Life Table.

IRS Single Life Table
Regulation 1.401(a)(9) - 9

Age	Life Expectancy in Years	Age	Life Expectancy in Years	Age	Life Expectancy in Years
25	58.2	50	34.2	75	13.4
26	57.2	51	33.3	76	12.7
27	56.2	52	32.3	77	12.1
28	55.3	53	31.4	78	11.4
29	54.3	54	30.5	79	10.8
30	53.3	55	29.6	80	10.2
31	52.4	56	28.7	81	9.7
32	51.4	57	27.9	82	9.1
33	50.4	58	27.0	83	8.6
34	49.4	59	26.1	84	8.1
35	48.5	60	25.2	85	7.6
36	47.5	61	24.4	86	7.1
37	46.5	62	23.5	87	6.7
38	45.6	63	22.7	88	6.3
39	44.6	64	21.8	89	5.9
40	43.6	65	21.0	90	5.5
41	42.7	66	20.2	91	5.2
42	41.7	67	19.4	92	4.9
43	40.7	68	18.6	93	4.6
44	39.8	69	17.8	94	4.3
45	38.8	70	17.0	95	4.1
46	37.9	71	16.3	96	3.8
47	37.0	72	15.5	97	3.6
48	36.0	73	14.8	98	3.4
49	35.1	74	14.1	99	3.1

Factors for Calculating SEPPs — Fixed Amortization Method

Remaining Life Expectancy	3%	4%	5%	6%	7%	8%	9%
10	8.7861	8.4353	8.1078	7.8017	7.5152	7.2469	6.9952
11	9.5302	9.1109	8.7217	8.3601	8.0236	7.7101	7.4177
12	10.2526	9.7605	9.3064	8.8869	8.4987	8.1390	7.8052
13	10.9540	10.3851	9.8633	9.3838	8.9427	8.5361	8.1607
14	11.6350	10.9856	10.3936	9.8527	9.3577	8.9038	8.4869
15	12.2961	11.5631	10.8986	10.2950	9.7455	9.2442	8.7862
16	12.9379	12.1184	11.3797	10.7122	10.1079	9.5595	9.0607
17	13.5611	12.6523	11.8378	11.1059	10.4466	9.8514	9.3126
18	14.1661	13.1657	12.2741	11.4773	10.7632	10.1216	9.5436
19	14.7535	13.6593	12.6896	11.8276	11.0591	10.3719	9.7556
20	15.3238	14.1339	13.0853	12.1581	11.3356	10.6036	9.9501
21	15.8775	14.5903	13.4622	12.4699	11.5940	10.8181	10.1285
22	16.4150	15.0292	13.8212	12.7641	11.8355	11.0168	10.2922
23	16.9369	15.4511	14.1630	13.0416	12.0612	11.2007	10.4424
24	17.4436	15.8568	14.4886	13.3034	12.2722	11.3711	10.5802
25	17.9355	16.2470	14.7986	13.5504	12.4693	11.5288	10.7066
26	18.4131	16.6221	15.0939	13.7834	12.6536	11.6748	10.8226
27	18.8768	16.9828	15.3752	14.0032	12.8258	11.8100	10.9290
28	19.3270	17.3296	15.6430	14.2105	12.9867	11.9352	11.0266
29	19.7641	17.6631	15.8981	14.4062	13.1371	12.0511	11.1161
30	20.1885	17.9837	16.1411	14.5907	13.2777	12.1584	11.1983
31	20.6004	18.2920	16.3725	14.7648	13.4090	12.2578	11.2737
32	21.0004	18.5885	16.5928	14.9291	13.5318	12.3498	11.3428
33	21.3888	18.8736	16.8027	15.0840	13.6466	12.4350	11.4062
34	21.7658	19.1476	17.0025	15.2302	13.7538	12.5139	11.4644
35	22.1318	19.4112	17.1929	15.3681	13.8540	12.5869	11.5178
36	22.4872	19.6646	17.3742	15.4982	13.9477	12.6546	11.5668
37	22.8323	19.9083	17.5469	15.6210	14.0352	12.7172	11.6118
38	23.1672	20.1426	17.7113	15.7368	14.1170	12.7752	11.6530
39	23.4925	20.3679	17.8679	15.8460	14.1935	12.8289	11.6908
40	23.8082	20.5845	18.0170	15.9491	14.2649	12.8786	11.7255
41	24.1148	20.7928	18.1591	16.0463	14.3317	12.9246	11.7574
42	24.4124	20.9931	18.2944	16.1380	14.3941	12.9672	11.7866
43	24.7014	21.1856	18.4232	16.2245	14.4524	13.0067	11.8134
44	24.9819	21.3708	18.5459	16.3062	14.5070	13.0432	11.8380
45	25.2543	21.5488	18.6628	16.3832	14.5579	13.0771	11.8605
46	25.5187	21.7200	18.7741	16.4558	14.6055	13.1084	11.8812
47	25.7754	21.8847	18.8801	16.5244	14.6500	13.1374	11.9002
48	26.0247	22.0429	18.9810	16.5890	14.6916	13.1643	11.9176
49	26.2667	22.1951	19.0772	16.6500	14.7305	13.1891	11.9336
50	26.5017	22.3415	19.1687	16.7076	14.7668	13.2122	11.9482

Fixed Annuitization Method — A third method is to divide your account balance by a monthly or annual annuity factor (the present value of an annuity of $1 per year beginning at your age when distributions begin and continuing for your life) based upon the mortality table published in *Revenue Ruling 2002-62*, (which is derived using an interest rate that is not more than 120% of the federal mid-term rate, determined on the date payments begin). To calculate the payment using this method, you should consult with a tax advisor or an actuary. Under this method, too, the SEPP amount remains fixed and is not recalculated. Typically, under the fixed annuitization method, the calculated SEPP is similar to, but not the same as, the payment calculated under the fixed amortization method.

Update to page 67

SEPPs: *Questions and Answers*

Until the IRS issued *Revenue Ruling 2002-62*, taxpayers had only IRS *Notice 89-25* and a series of private letter rulings (PLRs) for guidance in calculating SEPPs. It's important to note that, although PLRs are useful as a means to understand the IRS's approach to an issue, they can be relied on only by the taxpayer requesting the ruling. The answers below are based on IRS *Revenue Ruling 2002-62*, *Notice 89-25* and a series of IRS private letter rulings. Please note, however, that future IRS communications could supplement or modify these answers. Therefore, we strongly recommend that you consult your tax advisor for more information.

Q: Is it necessary to aggregate all of my IRAs when calculating SEPPs?

A: The Internal Revenue Code does not require the aggregation of IRAs for this purpose. So if you have two regular IRAs (to which you are making $3,000 annual contributions), you can take SEPPs from one and not the other (PLR 8946045). Also, according to another private letter ruling (PLR 9525062), it's possible to divide a lump sum from a company-sponsored retirement plan into numerous IRAs, and take SEPPs from only one of the IRAs.

Q: Can the method for calculating SEPPs be modified?

A: Generally, once you begin taking SEPPs, the distribution method may not be modified (other than by reason of death or disability) before the later of (1) five years after the date of the first payment; or (2) attaining age 59½. Otherwise, the 10% additional tax may be retroactively imposed. However, in *Revenue Ruling 2002-62*, the IRS indicated that, if you begin distributions using either the fixed amortization method or the fixed annuitization method, you may in a subsequent year switch to the required minimum distribution method for that year and all subsequent years and the change of method will not be treated as a modification. This ability to change calculation methods provides those choosing fixed payments with the opportunity to reduce their payments if investment experience causes their account values to decrease later. Once a change is made under this rule, the required minimum distribution method must be followed in all subsequent years.

In addition to the one-time opportunity to change from a fixed payment method to the required minimum distribution method, you may be able to influence the size of your payments under the minimum distribution method by changing your IRA investments. Since payments under this method are calculated annually, based on the account balance, investment experience has a direct impact on the size of the distribution. Further, your distribution method can account for changes in the payment amount to reflect inflation. However, the IRS has not provided clear guidance on just how to incorporate such an adjustment.

Q: Can I add to my account or make other non-SEPP distributions once I've begun SEPP distributions?

A: According to *Revenue Ruling 2002-62*, any addition to the account other than investment gains and losses, any nontaxable transfer of a portion of the account balance to another retirement plan, or a tax-free rollover of a SEPP distribution will be considered by the IRS to be a modification to the series of payments. Consequently, the 10% additional tax will be imposed retroactively on all early (pre-age 59½) distributions.

Q: What interest rate can be used for computing SEPPs?

A: In *Revenue Ruling 2002-62*, the IRS indicated that any interest rate may be used that is not more than 120% of the federal mid-term rate for either of the two months immediately preceding the month in which the distribution begins. These interest rates are published by the IRS in revenue rulings and are cumulatively available on its Web site (www.irs.gov). Note that the guidance in *Revenue Ruling 2002-62* was more direct than what had been issued previously by the IRS.

Q: What life expectancy table must I use for computing SEPPs?

A: According to *Revenue Ruling 2002-62,* the life expectancy tables that can be used are (1) the Uniform Lifetime Table in Appendix A of *Rev Rul 2002-62* (see update to page 73), (2) the single life expectancy table in §1.401(a)(9)-9, Q&A-1 of the Income Tax Regulations (see update to page 64) or (3) the joint life and last survivor table in §1.401(a)(9)-9, Q&A-3 of the regulations.

Q: My calculated SEPP distribution is $12,000, but I won't take my first withdrawal until October. Do I have to withdraw the full $12,000 in the first year, or can I take a portion for the last three months, in this case $3,000?

A: If in the first year of SEPPs you withdraw the full annual amount, then in the last year of your SEPP distribution you'll also have to withdraw the full annual amount. However, if in the first year you withdraw a *pro-rata* portion, then in the last year of SEPPs, you must also withdraw at least a *pro-rata* portion — $9,000 in this case. In either case, it is important that you stay with your schedule of payments for a full five years from the beginning date and until after you reach age 59½.

Update to page 73

Uniform Lifetime Table

Age of IRA Owner	Distribution Period	Age of IRA Owner	Distribution Period	Age of IRA Owner	Distribution Period	Age of IRA Owner	Distribution Period
25	71.3	48	48.5	71	26.5	94	9.1
26	70.3	49	47.5	72	25.6	95	8.6
27	69.3	50	46.5	73	24.7	96	8.1
28	68.3	51	45.5	74	23.8	97	7.6
29	67.3	52	44.6	75	22.9	98	7.1
30	66.3	53	43.6	76	22.0	99	6.7
31	65.3	54	42.6	77	21.2	100	6.3
32	64.3	55	41.6	78	20.3	101	5.9
33	63.3	56	40.7	79	19.5	102	5.5
34	62.3	57	39.7	80	18.7	103	5.2
35	61.4	58	38.7	81	17.9	104	4.9
36	60.4	59	37.8	82	17.1	105	4.5
37	59.4	60	36.8	83	16.3	106	4.2
38	58.4	61	35.8	84	15.5	107	3.9
39	57.4	62	34.9	85	14.8	108	3.7
40	56.4	63	33.9	86	14.1	109	3.4
41	55.4	64	33.0	87	13.4	110	3.1
42	54.4	65	32.0	88	12.7	111	2.9
43	53.4	66	31.1	89	12.0	112	2.6
44	52.4	67	30.2	90	11.4	113	2.4
45	51.5	68	29.2	91	10.8	114	2.1
46	50.5	69	28.3	92	10.2	≥ 115	1.9
47	49.5	70	27.4	93	9.6		

Income Taxes

Update to page 82

2003 Tax-Rate Schedules

Married Couples Filing Joint Returns and Qualifying Widow(er)s

TAXABLE INCOME: Over –	But not over –	TAX LIABILITY IS: Base amount	Plus	Percent	On income over
$ 0	$ 12,000	$ —	+	10.0%	$ 0
12,000	47,450	1,200.00	+	15.0%	12,000
47,450	114,650	6,517.50	+	27.0%	47,450
114,650	174,700	24,661.50	+	30.0%	114,650
174,700	311,950	42,676.50	+	35.0%	174,700
311,950	and above	90,714.00	+	38.6%	311,950

Single Taxpayers

TAXABLE INCOME: Over –	But not over –	TAX LIABILITY IS: Base amount	Plus	Percent	On income over
$ 0	$ 6,000	$ —	+	10.0%	$ 0
6,000	28,400	600.00	+	15.0%	6,000
28,400	68,800	3,960.00	+	27.0%	28,400
68,800	143,500	14,868.00	+	30.0%	68,800
143,500	311,950	37,278.00	+	35.0%	143,500
311,950	and above	96,235.50	+	38.6%	311,950

Heads of Household

TAXABLE INCOME: Over –	But not over –	TAX LIABILITY IS: Base amount	Plus	Percent	On income over
$ 0	$ 10,000	$ —	+	10.0%	$ 0
10,000	38,050	1,000.00	+	15.0%	10,000
38,050	98,250	5,207.50	+	27.0%	38,050
98,250	159,100	21,461.50	+	30.0%	98,250
159,100	311,950	39,716.50	+	35.0%	159,100
311,950	and above	93,214.00	+	38.6%	311,950

Married Individuals Filing Separate Returns

TAXABLE INCOME: Over –	But not over –	TAX LIABILITY IS: Base amount	Plus	Percent	On income over
$ 0	$ 6,000	$ —	+	10.0%	$ 0
6,000	23,725	600.00	+	15.0%	6,000
23,725	57,325	3,258.75	+	27.0%	23,725
57,325	87,350	12,330.75	+	30.0%	57,325
87,350	155,975	21,338.25	+	35.0%	87,350
155,975	and above	45,357.00	+	38.6%	155,975

Update to page 84

Special Consideration:

Phase-Out of Deductible IRA Contribution

The dollar limitations for 2003 are shown in the following table.

		Adjusted Gross Income (AGI)	
Filing status	Deductible IRA	Phase-out Range	Nondeductible IRA
Married	< $60,000	$60,000 – $70,000	≥ $70,000
Single	< $40,000	$40,000 – $50,000	≥ $50,000

Update to pages 85 through 87

Deductions: Standard or Itemized

Standard Deduction — Taxpayers who don't itemize their deductions are entitled to a standard deduction. For 2003, the basic standard deduction amounts are:

- Married/joint $7,950
- Single $4,750
- Head of household $7,000
- Married/separate $3,975

Taxpayers who are at least age 65 or are blind receive an extra standard deduction: $950 for each spouse older than 65 or blind, if married filing jointly; $1,150 single or head of household.

Itemized Deductions —

Special Consideration:

Phase-Out of Itemized Deductions

In 2003, if your AGI exceeds $139,500 ($69,750 if married filing separately), then a portion of your itemized deductions is disallowed. To estimate the amount disallowed, multiply the amount of your AGI in excess $139,500 by 3%. This phase-out does not apply to deductions for medical expenses, casualty losses or investment interest. Further, your deductions will never be reduced by more than 80% of the otherwise allowable amount. Under the 2001 Act, the limitation on itemized deductions will be repealed gradually, starting in 2006.

Personal and Dependency Exemptions

In 2003, you're entitled to a personal and dependency exemption worth $3,050 for yourself and each of your dependents. However, for high-income taxpayers the exemptions are phased out by reducing the exemption amount by 2% for each $2,500 of income over the applicable AGI threshold ($1,250 if married filing separately).

Filing Status	Full Exemptions	2003 Adjusted Gross Income (AGI) Phase-out Range	No Exemptions
Married/joint	< $209,250	$209,250 – $331,750	> $331,750
Single	< $139,500	$139,500 – $262,000	> $262,000
Head of household	< $174,400	$174,400 – $296,900	> $296,900
Married/separate	< $104,625	$104,625 – $165,875	> $165,875

Investment Planning

Update to page 115

Historical Before-Tax Returns

1-year periods

	1992	1993	1994	1995	1996	1997	1998	1999	2000	2001	YTD 9/30/02
Cash (1-Month Treasury Bills)	3.5%	2.9%	3.9%	5.6%	5.2%	5.3%	4.9%	4.7%	5.9%	3.8%	1.7
Short-/Medium-Term Gov't Bonds*	7.2	11.2	– 5.1	16.8	2.1	8.3	10.2	– 1.8	12.6	7.6	16.4
Large Co. Stock (S&P 500)	7.7	9.9	1.3	37.6	23.1	33.4	28.6	21.0	– 9.1	– 11.9	– 35.7
Small Co. Stock	23.3	20.9	3.1	34.4	17.6	22.8	– 7.3	29.8	– 4.0	22.8	– 23.8
Foreign Stock (EAFE)	–13.9	32.9	8.0	9.4	4.4	1.8	20.3	27.3	– 14.0	– 21.2	– 26.7
Inflation Rate (CPI)	2.9	2.7	2.7	2.7	3.3	1.7	1.6	2.7	3.6	1.7	3.3

5-year periods ending September 30

	1982 – 1987	1987 – 1992	1992 – 1997	1997 – 2002
Cash (1-Month Treasury Bills)	7.7%	6.4%	4.5%	4.4%
Short-/Medium-Term Gov't Bonds*	12.5	11.6	5.6	8.6
Large Co. Stock (S&P 500)	26.8	9.0	20.8	– 1.6
Small Co. Stock	22.1	3.1	24.9	1.6
Foreign Stock (EAFE)	42.4	0.2	12.7	– 5.4
Inflation Rate (CPI)	3.3	4.2	2.7	2.4

10-year periods ending September 30

	1962 – 1972	1972 – 1982	1982 – 1992	1992 – 2002
Cash (1-Month Treasury Bills)	4.6%	8.4%	7.1%	4.4%
Short-/Medium-Term Gov't Bonds*	4.5	7.4	12.1	7.1
Large Co. Stock (S&P 500)	10.5	5.7	17.6	9.0
Small Co. Stock	14.8	17.4	12.2	12.6
Foreign Stock (EAFE)	N/A	6.5	19.4	3.3
Inflation Rate (CPI)	3.3	8.8	3.7	2.5

Period from January 1, 1947 through September 30, 2002

Cash (1-Month Treasury Bills)	4.9%
Short-/Medium-Term Gov't Bonds*	6.2
Large Co. Stock (S&P 500)	11.6
Small Co. Stock**	13.0
Foreign Stock (EAFE)***	9.9
Inflation Rate (CPI)	3.9

* Five-year average maturity.

** Based on the fifth quintile of stocks on the NYSE for the period 1947 to 1981 and on the Dimensional Small Company Stock Fund from 1982 to the present.

*** Returns available from 1970.

Update to page 124

2003 Optimal Portfolio Allocations

Historical Before-Tax Return	Risk (+/–)	Risk/ Return Ratio	Cash Equivalents	Short-Term and Medium-Term Bonds	Large-Company Stock	Small-Company Stock	Foreign Stock
Stable Portfolios							
6.6%	4.9%	0.74	5%	86%	4%	2%	3%
7.0	5.1	0.73	5	79	8	5	3
7.4	5.6	0.76	5	72	13	7	3
Conservative Growth Portfolios							
7.8%	6.3%	0.81	5%	66%	16%	9%	4%
8.2	7.0	0.85	5	59	21	11	4
8.6	7.9	0.92	0	59	24	13	4
Moderate Growth Portfolios							
9.0%	8.8%	0.98	0%	52%	28%	15%	5%
9.4	9.8	1.04	0	45	32	18	5
9.8	10.7	1.09	0	38	37	20	5
Growth Portfolios							
10.2%	11.8%	1.16	0%	32%	40%	22%	6%
10.6	12.8	1.21	0	25	45	24	6
11.0	13.9	1.26	0	19	49	26	6
Aggressive Growth Portfolios							
11.3%	14.7%	1.30	0%	13%	52%	28%	7%
11.6	15.5	1.34	0	8	55	30	7
11.9	16.3	1.37	0	3	59	31	7

Projected Results for 2003 Model Portfolios

Beginning Value of $100

Stable Portfolio

- 5% Cash Equivalents
- 79% Short- and Medium-Term Bonds
- 8% Large-Company Stocks
- 5% Small-Company Stocks
- 3% Foreign Stocks

Year	"Worst Case" (5th Percentile)	Expected Value	"Best Case" (95th Percentile)
5	$116.31	$140.26	$165.21
10	148.27	196.72	245.59
15	197.20	275.90	361.22
20	261.27	386.97	525.43

7.0% Expected Return, +/– 5.1% Risk

Conservative Growth Portfolio

- 5% Cash Equivalents
- 59% Short- and Medium-Term Bonds
- 21% Large-Company Stocks
- 11% Small-Company Stocks
- 4% Foreign Stocks

Year	"Worst Case" (5th Percentile)	Expected Value	"Best Case" (95th Percentile)
5	$114.72	$148.30	$184.68
10	149.04	219.92	295.55
15	205.10	326.14	466.22
20	280.76	483.67	724.44

8.2% Expected Return, +/– 7.0% Risk

Moderate Growth Portfolio

- 0% Cash Equivalents
- 45% Short- and Medium-Term Bonds
- 32% Large-Company Stocks
- 18% Small-Company Stocks
- 5% Foreign Stocks

Year	"Worst Case" (5th Percentile)	Expected Value	"Best Case" (95th Percentile)
5	$109.26	$156.71	$ 211.10
10	141.79	245.57	365.54
15	199.25	384.82	620.46
20	277.96	603.04	1,031.42

9.4% Expected Return, +/– 9.8% Risk

Growth Portfolio

- 0% Cash Equivalents
- 25% Short- and Medium-Term Bonds
- 45% Large-Company Stocks
- 24% Small-Company Stocks
- 6% Foreign Stocks

Year	"Worst Case" (5th Percentile)	Expected Value	"Best Case" (95th Percentile)
5	$103.15	$165.49	$ 241.26
10	132.83	273.87	450.76
15	189.56	453.24	820.80
20	267.98	750.07	1,454.94

10.6% Expected Return, +/– 12.8% Risk

Aggressive Growth Portfolio

- 0% Cash Equivalents
- 8% Short- and Medium-Term Bonds
- 55% Large-Company Stocks
- 30% Small-Company Stocks
- 7% Foreign Stocks

Year	"Worst Case" (5th Percentile)	Expected Value	"Best Case" (95th Percentile)
5	$97.46	$173.11	$ 269.81
10	123.93	299.67	535.91
15	178.23	518.76	1,032.12
20	253.45	898.02	1,924.71

11.6% Expected Return, +/– 15.5% Risk

Education Funding

Update to page 228

Sample Portfolios for Education Investments

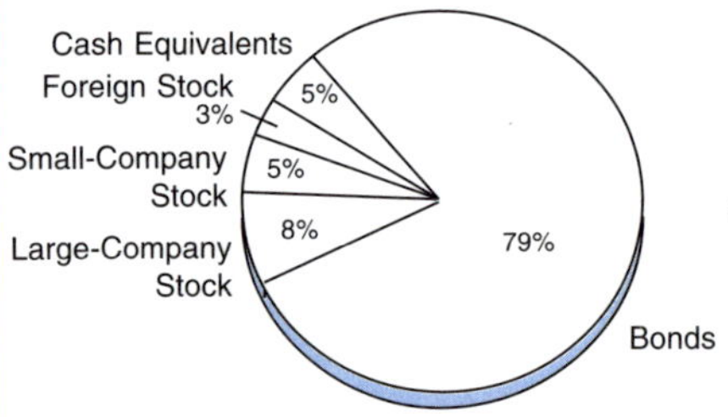

Stable: 7.0%

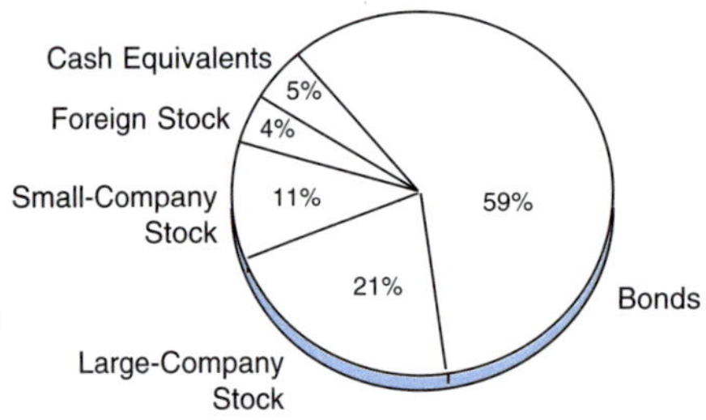

Conservative Growth: 8.2%

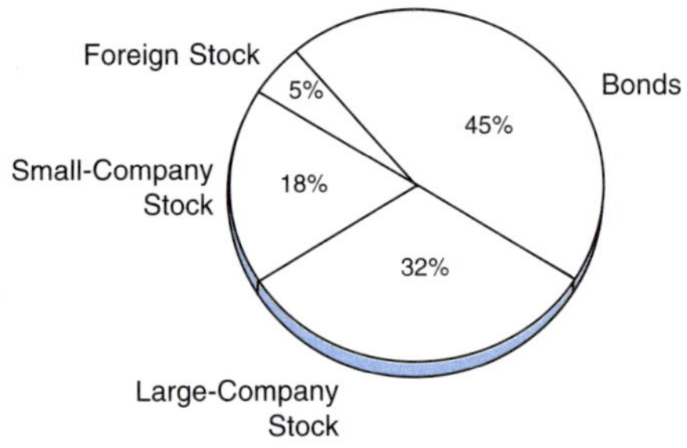

Moderate Growth: 9.4%

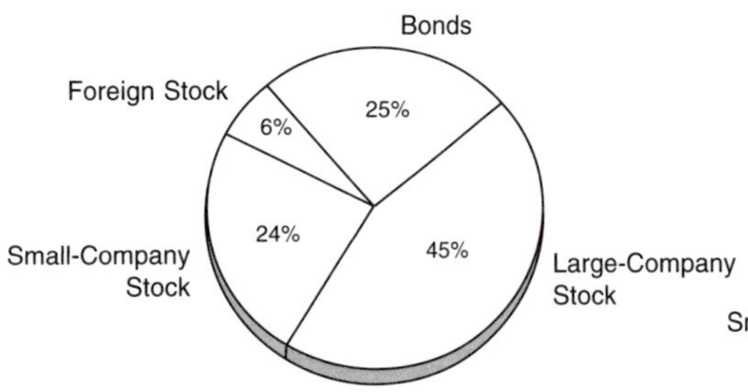

Growth: 10.6%

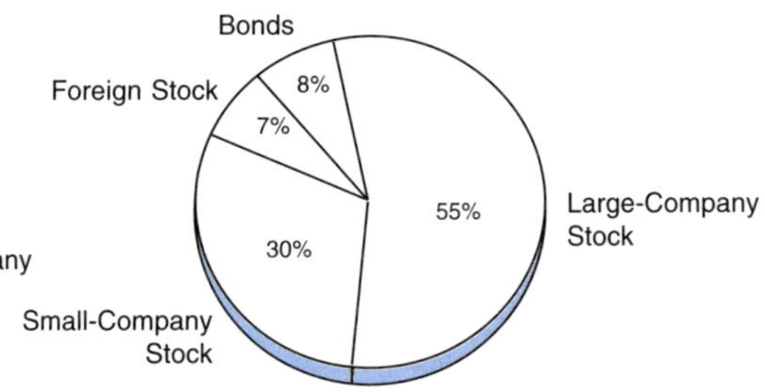

Aggressive Growth: 11.6%

Note: Allocations are based on long-term risk and return data for the various asset classes and are subject to change annually. The projected returns are not guaranteed. If you anticipate using your education fund within the next two years, consider allocating additional funds to cash equivalents in lieu of bonds in order to satisfy imminent cash-flow needs.

Social Security

Update to page 250

2003 Annual Highlights

Contributions

- A combined tax rate of 7.65% will be levied on a taxable wage base up to $87,000 in 2003.

Rate		Amount
6.20%	Social Security (OASDI)	$5,394.00
1.45%	Medicare (HI)	1,261.50
7.65%	Combined	$6,655.50

- In addition, the 1.45% rate applies to all earnings above $87,000.
- Self-employed individuals pay combined employer/employee rates up to the same wage base for Social Security and Medicare listed above. Federal income tax Schedule SE must be filed. Half of the Social Security tax is treated as an adjustment on your federal income tax return.
- No further rate increases are scheduled under current law. Maximum taxable earnings are subject to annual adjustment.

Credits

- For 2003 one work credit equals $890 of earned income. The annual maximum of four credits is given with $3,560 of earnings.

Maximum Benefits at Retirement*

- Retiree, age 65 and two months — $1,741 per month.
- Retiree and spouse, ages 65 and two months — $2,612-per-month joint benefit.
- A cost-of-living (COLA) increase of 1.4% was added in January 2003.

Earnings Limitations

- Over full retirement age — no limit.
- Year individual reaches full retirement age — $30,720 annual earnings limit; $3:$1 reduction above this limit applies only to months prior to attaining full retirement age.
- Under full retirement age — $11,520 annual earnings limit ($960/month); $2:$1 reduction above this limit.

* In 2003 the average benefit for a retiree is $895 per month.

Health-Care Coverage

Update to page 260

2003 Medicare Highlights

Part A — Hospital and Related Services

Hospital:

- Initial deductible — $840
- Coverage through day 60
- Days 61 through 90, inpatient co-insurance of $210 per day
- 60 reserve days, inpatient co-insurance of $420 per day

Skilled-nursing facility:

- Coverage through day 20
- Days 21 through 100, inpatient co-insurance of $105 per day

Part B — Medicare Services

- Monthly premium — $58.70 per person
- Annual deductible — $100 for approved charges
- After deductible, Medicare pays 80% of approved charges
- You're responsible for the remaining 20% and costs above approved amounts as well as the full amount for services not covered by Medicare.

Doctors who accept Medicare patients may not charge more than 115% of the Medicare-approved charge in your area. Some states have imposed more stringent regulations.

AYCO

The Ayco Company, L.P.
P.O. Box 15073 • Albany, NY 12212-5073
518/464-2000 • Fax: 518/464-2122